UNDERSTANDING SCHOOLS
AS INTELLIGENT SYSTEMS

ADVANCES IN RESEARCH AND THEORIES OF SCHOOL MANAGEMENT AND EDUCATIONAL POLICY

Gary M. Crow, Series Editor

Volume 1: 1990
> edited by Samuel B. Bacharach and Rodney T. Ogawa

Volume 2: 1993
> edited by Samuel B. Bacharach and Rodney T. Ogawa

Volume 3: 1995
> edited by Rodney T. Ogawa

UNDERSTANDING SCHOOLS AS INTELLIGENT SYSTEMS

Edited by KENNETH LEITHWOOD
Centre for Leadership Development
OISE/University of Toronto

JAI PRESS INC.
Stamford, Connecticut

CONTENTS

III. ORGANIZATIONAL LEARNING EFFECTS

LIST OF CONTRIBUTORS

Pamela Bishop

Faculty of Education
University of Tasmania, Australia

Janet H. Brown

Gevirtz Research Center
University of California, Santa Barbara

Jean Brown

Faculty of Education
Memorial University of Newfoundland

Salvador Castillo

Office of Institutional Research
University of California, Santa Barbara

Janet H. Chrispeels

Department of Education
University of California, Santa Barbara

James G. Cibulka

College of Education
University of Maryland

George Coffin

Creston South, Newfoundland

David P. Crandall

The NETWORK Inc.
Rowley, Massachusetts

David Dibbon

Faculty of Education
Memorial University of Newfoundland

Ross Elliott

Avalon West School District
Spaniard's Bay, Newfoundland

Philip Hallinger

Peabody College
Vanderbilt University

Bonnie Larson-Knight

Parkside Public School, The Durham
    District School Board
Ajax, Ontario

Laurie Leonard   College of Education
                                    Louisiana Tech University

Karen Seashore Louis   College of Education
                                    University of Minnesota

Helen M. Marks   School of Educational
                                        Policy and Leadership
                                    Ohio State University

Bill Mulford   Faculty of Education
                                    University of Tasmania

Susan M. Printy   School of Educational
                                        Policy and Leadership
                                    Ohio State University

Andy Scott   Trillium Lakelands District
                                        School Board
                                    Lindsay, Ontario

David Ng Foo Seong   Peabody College
                                    Vanderbilt University

Lyn Sharratt   York Region Board of Education
                                    Newmarket, Ontario

Bruce Sheppard   Faculty of Education
                                    Memorial University of Newfoundland

Halia Silins   School of Education
                                    Flinders University of South Australia

Silja Zarins   School of Education
                                    Flinders University of South Australia

PREFACE

Originally, I imagined this book would be, exclusively, a compilation of the studies on organizational learning that my doctoral students, immediate research associates (Doris Jantzi and Rosanne Steinbach), and I had undertaken in the Centre for Leadership Development (OISE/UT) over about a six-year period. The final version of the book does include this work. Chapters authored or co-authored by George Coffin, Laurie Leonard, Lyn Sharratt, Bonnie Larson-Knight, Ross Elliott, and David Dibbon are based substantially on doctoral research.

But the opportunity to develop a more comprehensive text proved irresistible. As the book was being prepared, Halia Silins and Bill Mulford were beginning to report the results of the first stage of their research in Australia, research that had been intentionally framed to allow some comparisons with our Canadian data. Bruce Sheppard and Jean Brown, close colleagues at Memorial University in Newfoundland, also were writing about the results of their recent studies, some aspects of which had been influenced by my work on transformational leadership. And long-time colleague Phil Hallinger was working on the very practical matter of designing experiences that would contribute to peoples' understandings and skills in organizational capacity development.

Of course, Karen Seashore Louis and I had recently edited together *Organizational Learning in Schools*, the book to which this is the sequel. Karen was to be a co-editor of this text, as well, until circumstances conspired against her being able to do that. Nonetheless, she and her colleagues Helen Marks and Susan

Printy were able to contribute a fine chapter describing the results of their latest research.

Janet Chrispeels and I follow one another's work on a regular basis. So I listened to her describe her most recent research, with Janet Brown and Salvador Castillo, at the annual AERA meeting and immediately knew that the book would be considerably enriched by the addition of a chapter reflecting that work. Finally, Jim Cibulka and I had occasion to share our current interests while meeting to plan the 1999 AERA program, he as Division L program chair and me as Division A chair. I learned of a review of literature he and his colleagues had been writing, subsequently reviewed it for him, and asked if he would prepare a chapter based on one section of that review.

The process for developing this manuscript, as I have described it, reflects more or less equal parts intentional planning, and what might be termed "spontaneous opportunism"—remaining open to unanticipated events and ideas, and making the most of them as they arise by adjusting one's goals and plans. I don't actually know how other academic editors work *(Note to myself: Ask a few)*. While I suspect many can relate to this process, at the very least I can confidently claim that it pretty much captures how I've gone about developing the numerous texts that I have edited during my career.

Now there is a substantive point to my ramblings here. It is this: what you will learn from this book about the characteristics of schools and the people in them, when they are behaving intelligently, doesn't differ too much from those features of the book development process I have described here. But I have described this process in very abstract terms and, as they say in the computer business, "God is in the details." So it would help if you read the rest of the book.

K. Leithwood
(September 1999)

CHAPTER 1

INTRODUCTION
UNDERSTANDING SCHOOLS
AS INTELLIGENT SYSTEMS

Kenneth Leithwood

Speeded up curricula, more attention to skills for competing in a "global economy," annual student achievement targets, explicit standards of professional knowledge and skill, site-based management, evisceration of district-level support for schools, group performance incentives, high stakes achievement testing, increased diversity of student populations, fewer resources, greater participation of parents in school decision making—these are just some of the changes facing schools at the moment. Or, to adapt the catchy title of Bill Gates' (1999) recent book "educational change @ the speed of thought."

And if only thought were enough, schools *might* be better places. On the other hand, the ancient Chinese curse "May your fondest dreams come true" is best

Advances in Research and Theories of School
Management and Educational Policy, Volume 4, pages 1-15.
Copyright © 2000 by JAI Press Inc.
All rights of reproduction in any form reserved.
ISBN: 0-7623-0024-8

appreciated these days, we suspect, by those who have had a serious romance with "strategic planning" (or thinking) and lived to tell about it, professionally speaking. Among the several features common to the changes facing schools on our list is their source. Someone outside schools has initiated all of them; governments, corporate interest groups, policy wonks (mostly from the new right), and community groups, to mention a few.

Does this mean that no one who actually works in a school has a decent thought about how it might be improved? Now you think you know our answer to this question, don't you? You think that we're going to say "Of course not." But you're wrong! For a variety reasons closely related to the nature and size of the above list, those who actually work in schools have been mostly consigned to reacting to other people's ideas. Beyond a certain threshold the blizzard of new ideas from others actually *displaces* rather than *stimulates* one's own ideas. Such displacement is especially likely when the context for one's work actively discourages experimentation, when the ideas of others form a hegemonic force buttressed by political and bureacratic power. Displacement is also more likely when relatively harsh sanctions accompany disagreement with others' ideas, and when the circumstances supporting one's commitment to the profession are seriously eroded.

What's wrong with this picture? Well, only that the knowledge, skills and insights of those "on the ground," those who actually run schools on a day-to-day basis, are being radically discounted, if not systematically ignored altogether. Does this make any sense to you? It certainly doesn't to us. Oh, if there was a history of successful school reform initiated from outside the school we might feel differently. But that's certainly not on. We hasten to add, however, that left to their own devices, in-school professionals haven't exactly turned the world of educational change on fire either.

On the surface, it may seem that we are describing the problem of finding a balance between top down and bottom up change strategies. But that is a superficial, if not dangerously deceptive, interpretation of the problem we are worried about here. The problem, more fundamentally, is how to bring together, in a way that stimulates productive change, insights about the future needs of our children rooted in broad social, economic and political analyses, with the technical skills, craft knowledge, and creative imaginations of those who spend their lives thinking about, and working toward, the growth of those children in the often tumultuous context of today's and tomorrow's schools.

"Change in complex systems," argue Klimecki and Lassleben, "is not so much the result of conscious design, but rather emerges out of the actions and interactions of the organization members. [So] ... organizational change is an evolutionary process of self-transformation" (1998, p. 407). This view of how organizations change rings true with our understanding of the evidence concerning successful school improvement processes (e.g., Louis, Toole, & Hargreaves, 1999). Additionally, "organizational transformation must aim at increasing the organization's problem solving capability, by building organizational resilience, and expanding its capacity to create, thereby widening the range of possible situations the organization will be able to cope with" (1998, p. 407).

Exploring how this might be done in schools is what this book is all about. How can schools behave smarter, especially when they so often find themselves in contexts which seem designed to make them dumber? What does it mean for individuals, groups, and whole schools to learn their way toward more productive forms of practice? Under what conditions is this most likely? Is leadership among those conditions, and, if it is, what does it look like? Are there definable stages and forms of intervention that might be used in helping schools become smarter? Together, the 12 main chapters of the book offer important insights about these questions. Some of these insights are quite novel, and most of them represent significant advances to the state-of-the art knowledge about organizational learning in schools.

THE IDEA OF SCHOOLS AS "INTELLIGENT SYSTEMS"

Our choice of title for this book was not capricious. We were not creating an oxymoron, as some of our more cynical readers will claim. Nor were we intending to suggest that, in comparison with other types of organizations, schools are especially smart, although we think that many of them are a lot smarter than they are given credit for. What we intend the title to suggest is nothing less than what for many readers will be an entirely new perspective or lens on schools. This new lens pulls into the foreground features of schools that have been little noticed through more familiar lenses. It reveals whole new "parts" of school organizations that, to date, have been largely invisible or overlooked. Furthermore, and this is the critical point, these newly visible features turn out to be a central part of the explanation for how schools change and improve.

Now just what do we mean by the term "intelligent" as in the term "intelligent systems"? A school, like any type of organization, is intelligent if it is capable of learning. So "intelligent," from this perspective, cannot be equated with what the organization already knows or is able to do. "Intelligent systems" has quite a different meaning from the term "learning organization," a term typically reserved for organizations with extensive industry-relevant knowledge, and exceptionally well developed capacities and skills. A newly born infant easily meets our definition of an intelligent system. She has a meagre knowledge base in comparison with a five year old or an adult; she is unable to walk, read, identify colors, or surf the internet. But given a bit of time, and even moderately supportive circumstances, she will learn how to do all of these things, and thousands more besides.

What about a school council? Could it be an intelligent system? This is less obviously the case than the newly born infant. Some school councils quickly become adept at setting goals for themselves and collecting information relevant to the accomplishment of those goals. Members of the council build on one anothers' capacities and create solutions to the problems with which they are grappling, solutions that are powerful and sometimes quite unique. Councils that are able to do these things clearly qualify as intelligent, not to mention learning organizations.

But what about those school councils that remain unfocused, whose members spend their time mostly squabbling among themselves over whose pet aggravation is to be given priority, and fail to see how one another's strengths can be used for the collective good. Are they intelligent? From our perspective the answer is still yes! Admittedly they are pretty dumb, a lot dumber than the newly born infant, for example. And the possibility of them becoming smarter is a lot less certain. But because they possess the potential for learning (given better leadership, or some dramatic problem that serves to bring them together around a common cause, for example) they still qualify as intelligent systems, as we use the term. So our use of the term intelligent refers to the capacity for learning, admits of more or less such capacity at any point in time, and assumes that learning capacities can change over time.

This might be a confusing use of the term "intelligent." In common parlance, "smart" and "intelligent" mean approximately the same thing. But this is a useful distinction because there are lots of smart systems whose functions are locked into place with no capacity for change. Most mechanical systems have this quality. Once built, they continue to perform the same functions for which they were designed over the duration of their "lives," often very well. This describes your washing machine and automobile, for example. These systems can be changed in form or function but it takes an intelligent system to do it. They cannot change themselves.

In comparison with many other organizations, it also should be pointed out, schools typically begin with a learning deficit. This becomes apparent when viewed through the lens of theories of distributed cognition. From this perspective, a system's capacity is distributed among, for example, individual people, the nature of the relationships among people, the tools and other artifacts available for them to work with, and the design of the physical setting in which work is carried out. Studies of work in airplane cockpits (Hutchins and Klausen,1998), and the operations room of an airline (Suchman, 1998; Goodwin & Goodwin, 1998), for example, demonstrate the extent to which learning or problem solving in these environments depends on capacities built into the system outside the heads of individual people. Such environments are saturated with tools (e.g., computers, video equipment, well rehearsed routines, operations manuals) and other artifacts that help provide sophisticated responses to the complex problems faced by those working in them. So the capacities of individual people are added to the substantial capacities built into the work setting surrounding the people.

In comparison with such smart settings, people working in schools lack sophisticated technologies with which to leverage their own expertise. The physical environments of many schools, especially those with isolated or noncollaborative cultures, is almost devoid of "outside-the-head" problem-solving tools; chalkboards, textbooks, and overhead projectors just don't cut it, in these terms. This means that individual people in such environments must be relied on for a relatively disproportionate amount of problem-solving capacity, and that relatively few safeguards against human error are built into the system.

"System" is the subject qualified in our title for the book by the term "intelligent" and at the most abstract level we mean nothing unusual or esoteric by the concept. Typical definitions refer to parts which interact to form a whole, for example, "a group of interacting bodies under the influence of related forces" (*Webster's 7th New Collegiate Dictionary*, 1971). Forms of interaction among the parts of a system may range from quite mechanical and linear to highly organic and interactive. In the case of schools, as in other organizations, the parts are often conceptualized as components of a "design," and include mission, culture, structure, and the like (e.g., Banner & Gagne, 1995). It is at this more concrete level that our meaning of the term "system" differentiates itself by its focus on learning and the processes that interact in a learning system.

FRAMEWORK FOR THE BOOK

Implicit in the table of contents of this book is the framework around which its chapters are organized. This framework assumes that a full appreciation of schools as intelligent systems requires some understanding of how learning occurs within different organizational "units"—the individual, the small group, and the whole school. Learning within these units does not just happen naturally, it is stimulated by sources that also must be better understood. Furthermore, such characteristics of the organization as its goals, culture and structure, for example, not only mediate organizational learning, they are influenced by such learning, as well. These conditions change in response to organizational learning, and these changed conditions have a direct or indirect effect, eventually, on the educational experiences of students.

Just like others who develop expertise in a complex field of practice, school professionals rely on a repertoire of knowledge and skills which they exercise in a relatively automatic fashion much of the time. Such "automaticity" is highly functional in a context which demands rapid and often spontaneous action, as is often the case in classrooms and schools. The "dark side" of automaticity, however, is the thoughtless repetition of well-rehearsed solutions even in response to problems that may require the modifications of such solutions—or different solutions altogether. Cognitively demanding environments such as these are predisposed toward the *exploitation* of exisiting practices and organizational routines, and against the *exploration* of new routines, to use March's (1996) terms.

Exploitation of existing practices is cheap; it takes minimum time and almost no cognitive effort. So what would stimulate an individual or group to modify existing practices or, even more costly, to develop or seek out altogether new practices? Our not very novel answer is the perception of some form of disequilibrium. Perceptions by those in the school of changes in their external environment would be one such source of disequilibrium, a source that could take such forms as rapidly changing student populations, new government curriculum policies, or altered parental expectations. An important point to emphasize with this source of disequilibrium, however, is that to stimulate organzational learning, at least three conditions must prevail: those inside the organization must be aware of the external environmental change; they must interpret it as creating a potential need for change; and they must judge the potential change as worth making. Much of the literature written about non-school organizational contexts assumes adaption to external environmental changes to be the major stimulus for organizational learning (e.g., Watkins & Marsick, 1993).

A second source of disequilibrium, one internal to the school organization, is the collective perception, on the part of those in the school, of a gap between what they are attempting to accomplish and what they are actually accomplishing. Student test results, expressions of dissatisfaction with their programs by students, and a new vision for school improvement, perhaps developed by a school improvement team, are examples of this form of disequilibrium. Even though internally generated, the extent to which these sources stimulate organizational learning still depends on the proportion of staff who agree that there is a gap which needs to be addressed, and the degree of consensus among staff about both the nature of the gap and best means of reducing it. Much of the contemporary literature on school improvement assumes that sources such as these can be a major stimulus for organizational learning, sometimes in combination with stimuli from outside sources.

An individual (or collective) ethic of continuous improvement is another potential source of disequilibrium which can stimulate organizational learning. Some teachers simply want to improve their practices and choose to change what they are doing from year to year based not so much on evidence of any deficiency in what they are doing as an interest in trying out new ideas. Evidence reported by Leithwood, Jantzi and Steinbach (1995) suggests that this may be a surprisingly common source of organizational learning in schools.

At least for purposes of research and analysis, it seems useful to distinguish three levels (or units) of organizational learning: whole organization learning; the learning of teams or groups; and processes used by individuals to learn in an organizational context. One of the major challenges facing organizational theorists is how best to conceptualize the process of whole organization learning. The most common solution is to use individual learning processes as a metaphor for collective learning (e.g., Simon, 1996; Cohen, 1996). From this point of view, research into organizational learning processes is guided by such questions as: How do organizations store and access knowledge? What forms of procedural knowledge are most functional for organizations? How do organizations perceive, filter, process, and store information in long term memory?

Defining learning as "self-regulated knowledge construction," Vermunt and Verloop (1999, p. 258) offer a synthesis of those individual mental activities that cognitive scientists believe permit such construction to take place. These learning activities are of three sorts: cognitive, affective, and metacognitive (or regulative). Cognitive activities include, for example, relating, analyzing, applying, memorizing, critical processing, and selecting. Affective activities include motivating, exerting effort, making attributions, appraising and dealing with one's emotions. Metacognitive or regulative activities involve planning, monitoring, adjusting, and evaluating.

Just as much contemporary learning theory fails to account for the motivational basis giving rise to individual knowledge construction (Jarvela & Niemivirta, 1999), whole organization learning processes rarely have been viewed so broadly. Most literature about these processes builds on understandings of individual learning limited to processes within Vermunt and Verloops' "cognitive" category. But this more comprehensive taxonomy of learning processes makes clear that we know more about whole organization learning than is typically thought.

With respect to organizational metacognition, for example, there is an extensive theoretical and empirical literature about each of the component processes: strategic and operational planning (e.g. Mintzberg, Ahlstrand & Lampel, 1998); monitoring, which can take such forms as indicator systems and research-based, organizational diagnostic systems (e.g., Leithwood & Aitken, 1995); and evaluating, the extensive literature on performance appraisal providing an example of this.

Similarly, those activities referred to as "affective" by Vermunt and Verloop (1999) have been the object of considerable research by social cognitive pscholgists, much of it group based and conducted in organizational settings (e.g., Bandura, 1986; Yeatts & Hyten, 1998). And most research on organizational leadership has held, as its central problem, how to motivate people and groups in organizational settings. This is the case with "new leadership paradigms" (Sims & Lorenzi, 1992) which place such personally meaningful goals as achievement and self actualization at the centre of human motivation systems. But it also is the case with earlier approaches to leadership premised on exchange theory. These approaches assume that organizational members can be motivated by extrinsic factors alone, or by appealing to such lower level goals as safety and security (Yukl, 1994).

A growing corpus of psychological theory, a body of theory not yet applied even metaphorically to whole organization learning, is quite useful in helping to understand both individual and small group learning in an organizational context. Moving away from exclusively "inside-the-head" explanations of how people learn, such theory assumes a significant role for the immediate situation in which the learner finds herself, as well as the larger cultural context in which that situation is embedded. Commonly referred to as situativity theory (e.g., Anderson, Reder & Simon, 1996), these explanations of individual learning assume that what is learned depends on the individual's interaction with features of the context, and his participation in a "community of practice" (Brown & Duguid, 1996). Because the individual's knowledge is socially constructed in this context, such features of the organization as, for example, its norms, beliefs, operating procedures, and even its physical characteristics, shape what its individual members know and are able to do.

Building on many of the same assumptions as situativity theory, theories of distributed cognition (e.g., Salomon, 1993) are especially useful in understanding small group or team learning. Each member of a well-functioning team must share some of the same understandings—the purposes for the team's work and the constraints within which the team must function, for example. But each team member also brings some unique capacities to their group's work. It is in this sense that the total capacity of the group is distributed across its members. Additionally, the organizational and/or physical setting in which the group works may add to the group's total capacity. This is the case in groups whose members develop highly interdependent sets of relationships, as in the case of London Underground line controllers described by Heath and Luff (1998). It is also the case with groups whose work is significantly enhanced by technology (see, for example, Goodwin and Goodwin's, 1998, description of the work of airport personnel).

The 12 main chapters of this book explore different aspects of this framework, sometimes making explicit use of the concepts included in the framework, and sometimes reflecting them indirectly.

OVERVIEW OF CONTENTS

Nine of the 12 main chapters in the book offer original empirical data about the intellectual capacities of schools. This is one of the ways in which the book furthers the mission we tried to serve in the previous edited text to which this is a sequel (Leithwood & Louis, 1998). The introduction to that earlier text was primarily aimed at justifying such a mission, something only touched lightly here. That text, as this one, also included several chapters devoted to reviewing and adding clarity to concepts we believe have received too little attention in previous work on organizational learning in schools. Such clarity is intended to serve as a starting point for subsequent research.

Developing the Intellectual Capacities of Individuals and Teams

Organizational contexts provide uniquely powerful sources of individual learning when they form, what Brown and Duguid (1996) term "communities of practice." And, while professional common sense and some formal evidence reinforces "on-the-job learning" as a primary source of leaders' learning, few efforts have been made to more precisely understand the nature of school leaders' communities of practice. Informed by theories of situated cognition and everyday problem solving, the study reported by Coffin and Leithwood in chapter 2 inquired about the sources of principals' learning, features of the job experience which account for such learning, and conditions in the organization which foster or inhibit such learning.

Evidence to answer these questions was provided by interviews with principals who worked in "opportunity-rich" professional communities. Each of their schools was located in one of three large districts with a demonstrated commitment to the professional growth of school leaders through, for example, the provision of ongoing inservice opportunities (but in many other ways, as well). These districts also were located in regions which included many other opportunities for professional development from such sources as local universities, professional associations and principal centres. In sum, the principals worked in contexts which offered both diverse and multiple opportunities for learning.

Chapters 3 and 4 report evidence about team development and team learning in schools. Teams have become a pervasive part of organizational life, and "high performing" systems (Yeatts & Hyten, 1998) rely extensively on the leadership provided by such teams to learn on their behalf. Teams provide a means through which those with a stake in the organization are able to express their views and help democratize the workplace. Most important from the perspective of this book, teams also create the context in which many heads have the potential of being better than one by distributing the cognitive resources required for analyzing, interpreting, applying, and the like.

In chapter 3, Chrispeels, Brown and Castillo report the results of a long term effort by the California School Leadership Academy (CSLA) to "develop the capacity of School Leadership Teams to facilitate actions within their schools that lead to powerful learning for all members of the organization." Prior research by Chrispeels and her colleagues produced a model to explain the process of team development. In this chapter, a single school is used as a case study, extended over a four year period, to further explore the dimensions and dynamics of this model. Data for the case study were acquired through surveys, interviews, observations, and documents. This is one of the few studies of how the learning capacties of teams can develop over time, and what conditions foster and inhibit that development.

Whereas Chrispeels and her associates explored the development of teacher leadership teams, Scott (chapter 4) examines the nature of learning and problem solving, and the conditions influencing such learning within secondary school administrative teams. Building on information processing constructs for understanding individual cognition, the nature of team learning was conceptualized around the processes of perception, knowledge acquistion, understanding, and knowledge distribution; these are a subset of the cognitive processes included in Vermunt and Verloop's (1999) taxonomy of learning processes. To help better understand the teams' overall approaches to learning across these cognitive processes, the teams' levels of learning were examined using March's (1996) distinction between learning which exploits existing knowledge and solutions, and learning which explores new alternatives. Conditions fostering and inhibiting team learning were examined through the lens of Senge's (1990) five disciplines: shared vision, mental models, personal mastery, team learning, and systems thinking.

Each of the three teams included in the study consisted of a principal and two vice principals, and data for the study were collected through tape recordings of team meetings, and interviews with individual team members, using the tape recordings as a stimulus. Group interviews with all team members also were conducted.

Building the Intellectual Capacities of Schools and Districts

Chapter 5 synthesizes the results of three studies aimed at identifying the conditions which foster collective learning across whole schools. Each of the three studies asked the same general questions, were guided by a common framework, and collected similar types of data. Comparing the results of the three studies, as Leithwood, Leonard and Sharratt do in this chapter, provides insights about organizational conditions which foster collective learning across contexts—a necessary but probably not sufficient set of conditions for collective learning in most schools. Results of the three studies are based on evidence collected through interviews with a total of 111 teachers in 14 schools. The stimulus for collective learning was different for the teachers in each study, as was the district and provincial context, the studies having been carried out in the Canadian provinces of British Columbia, Ontario, and Newfoundland.

Framed as a study of systemic reform, in chapter 6 Larson-Knight explores the relationship between three categories of variables each of which has been identified independently as a "key" to school improvement. These variables include organizational learning, leadership, and school culture. Research to date has had much to say about the most desirable features of each of these variables; it has, as well, explored the relationship between pairs of these variables. There is reason to believe, however, that an important part of the school improvement story lies in the interactions among all three.

Conceptualization of the three variables, for purposes of data collection and initial analysis, borrowed from a wide-ranging review of the literature, as well as theoretical orientations to each of the variables found in several earlier chapters. Organizational learning conditions were conceived of much as the authors of chapters 5 and 12 do. Leadership was initially viewed through the lens of a transformational perspective as in those two chapters, as well.

Evidence to explore the interaction among these variables was collected in three schools identified within their own district as "moving" (Stoll & Myers, 1998). These schools had reputations for innovation as well as for collaborative styles of work. Their principals were widely believed to be an important part of the explanation for the schools' successes. Within each of these schools data were collected through individual interviews with principals and teachers, as well as through focus group interviews with members of each School Growth Team (a group consisting of teachers and the principal responsible for providing leadership in relation to improvement initiatives in each school).

While chapters 5 and 6 both aimed, as a long term goal, to increase the intelligence of schools, they approached this task indirectly—by identifying organizational conditions which, if nurtured, are likely to foster collective learning. In contrast, Hallinger, Crandall, and Seong (chapter 7) propose a direct intervention for increasing a school's intelligence. The intervention is a computer-based simulation (Systems Thinking/Systems Changing™) explicitly designed to help school practitioners develop knowledge and skills needed to develop the collective learning capacities of their schools.

In chapter 8, Elliott continues the task, begun by Hallinger and Crandall in chapter 7, of outlining tools for directly influencing the collective learning of those in schools. He does this by cataloguing interventions available to districts with the potential to foster such learning. The features theoretically needed by each intervention for this potential to be realized are specified, as well. The chapter begins by clarifying the meaning of an organizational intervention: "a set of intentional activities, systematically introduced by one group of people, either inside or outside an organization, aimed at influencing productive change in the thinking and practices of another group of people inside the organization." Examples of interventions are drawn from the literature to illustrate this meaning. Elliott also reviews research evidence concerning the state-of-the-art of organizational interventions and their effects. District-level intervention research is sparse, even though there is considerable evidence suggesting that the capacity of schools is significantly related to the extent, type and quality of district intervention.

Much can be done within schools and districts to foster the collective learning of their members. But learning at both these levels of the school system is substantially influenced by the wider contexts in which they find themselves. Perhaps the most powerful of these contexts is to be found in the policies created by national and state/provincial governments, and especially in the means used to encourage policy implementation. In chapter 9, James Cibulka begins to unpack how typical approaches to such implementation fly in the face of what we know about powerful strategies for helping intended implementers learn what they need to know and be able to do before new policies can become productive sources of school improvement.

For the most part, Cibulka argues, policies are themselves the products of single-loop learning, superficial analyses of problems and the generation of policy solutions with little exploration of underlying assumptions and causes. Furthermore, strategies used for policy implementation often assume only single-loop learning on the part of implementers. In contrast, present evidence about the development of potentially helpful policies and how such policies can be well implemented strongly suggests the need for double-loop learning. Policymakers need to probe below the surface of the problems they are trying to address if truly useful policy solutions are to be developed. And implementation plans need to appreciate the role played by implementers' existing mental models and theories-of-action as they work to understand new policies and how they might wish to respond to them productively in their own settings. This chapter offers important guidance for those wishing to reform the policy context in the interest of fostering more organizational learning in schools and districts.

In chapter 10, returning to the school level, David Dibbon takes up the issue of how to develop, in a planned and systematic way, the learning capacity of a school. Based on a wide-ranging synthesis of the literature on organizational learning, the central contribution of this chapter is to describe and illustrate a plausible set of stages through which one might expect a school to pass on its way toward becoming a high performing school, or what some would refer to as a learning organization.

Organizational Learning Effects

Although the link between educators' learning and student outcomes seems self-evident, common sense associations such as this one have turned out to be wrong a shocking number of times. So systematic, empirical evidence about the relationship between organizational learning and student outcomes is quite important to accumulate; to date it has been almost entirely lacking. Chapters 11 and 12 go some distance toward filling this gap.

Chapter 11 (Marks, Louis, and Printy) reports evidence about the relationship between the capacity for organizational learning and both pedagogical quality and student achievement. The study builds on previous research from which the authors conclude that high performing schools represent unified organizational cultures built around ongoing inquiry into the quality and effectiveness of teaching and learning. Evidence for this study, as well as the previous research, was collected using a battery of data collection instruments and procedures in a carefully selected, U.S. national sample of 24 restructuring elementary, middle, and high schools.

Six dimensions defined capacity for organizational learning, the independent variable in this study. These dimensions included school structure, teacher empowerment, shared commitment and collaborative activity, knowledge and skills, leadership, and feedback and accountability. Authentic student achievement was defined and measured by students' performances in mathematics and social studies, and authentic pedagogy was a composite measure combining teachers' scores on observed classroom instruction and assessment tasks.

Summarizing the first report of results from a three year Australian study, chapter 12 by Silins, Mulford, Zarins, and Bishop also provides evidence of the link between organizational learning, leadership, and student outcomes. In this case the outcomes of interest are student engagement with school—the extent to which students participate in classroom and school activities, and their sense of identity with school. Sharing many concepts with the work reported in chapter 5, organizational learning was defined and measured as a function of environmental scanning processes, developing shared goals, establishing collaborative teaching and learning environments, encouraging initiative and risk taking, monitoring school progress, and providing opportunities for professional development. A transformational model, based on Leithwood's work (see Leithwood, Jantzi and Steinbach, 1999, for a recent synthesis) shaped the nature of data collected about school leadership.

Data were provided through responses to surveys of 2,503 teachers and principals, and 3,508 year 10 students from a stratified (by size) random sample of 96 secondary schools in South Wales and Tasmania.

By far the largest proportion of evidence concerning school improvement and organizational learning documents exemplary practices and organizational qualities, or describes processes that might be used to stimulate collective learning within school organizations. Rare indeed, are studies that trace the development of whole school organizations over time and the consequences of that development, no matter the substantive or theoretical perspective on such development. Evidence about the development of more intelligent schools—the transformation of schools into "learning organizations"—is extremely hard to find. In chapter 13, Sheppard and Brown report such rare data. Their case studies provide us with an understanding of how two Canadian secondary schools adapted to many outside pressures for change, and learned their way to significantly improved practices over about a decade. Especially interesting is the starting point for these schools. They were widely acknowledged to be very good schools, and their early responses to external pressures for change were classic examples of what Argyris (1996) refers to as "organizational defensive routines." How does a school with an image of itself as exemplary gradually modify this collective self concept in order to engage in serious school improvement intitiatives?

This was a quasi-grounded study. While many results were unanticipated, the data collection and initial analysis was informed by two sets of ideas. One set consisted of six domains of knowledge required by teachers, according to Fullan (1995), to transform schools into learning organizations. These domains closely reflect Senge's (1990) learning disciplines. The second set of ideas was about forms of effective leadership for learning and was based on a transformational approach to leadership developed by Leithwood (1994). Data for the study were extensive interviews with teachers and administrators in the two schools, as well as a content analysis of documents, and a survey of all teachers about the nature and sources of leadership in their schools.

The final chapter of the book summarizes the results of the previous chapters, and identifies a number of implications for theory and practice. Special attention is given to what has been learned about forms of leadership that are effective in fostering the intellectual capacities of schools.

REFERENCES

Anderson, J.R., Reder, L.M., & Simon, H.A. (1996). Situated learning and education. *Educational Researcher, 25*(4), 5-11.

Argyris, C. (1996). Prologue: Toward a comprehensive theory of management. In B. Moingeon & A. Edmondson (Eds.), *Organizational learning and competitive advantage* (pp. 1-6). Thousand Oaks, CA: Sage.

Bandura, A. (1986). *Social foundations of thought and action*. Englewood Cliffs, NJ: Prentice-Hall.

Banner, D.K., & Gagne, T.E. (1995). *Designing effective organizations: Traditional and transformational views*. Thousand Oaks, CA: Sage.

Brown, J.S., & Duguid, P. (1996). Organizational learning and communities-of-practice: Toward a unified view of working, learning, and innovation. In M.D. Cohen & L.S. Sproull (Eds.), *Organizational learning* (pp. 58-82). Thousand Oaks, CA: Sage.

Cobb, P., & Bowers, J. (1999). Cognitive and situated learning perspectives in theory and practice. *Educational Researcher, 28*(2), 4-15.

Cohen, M.D. (1996). Individual learning and organizational routine: Emerging connections. In M.D. Cohen & L.S. Sproull (Eds.), *Organizational learning* (pp. 188-194). Thousand Oaks, CA: Sage.

Engestrom, Y., & Middleton, D. (1998). *Cognition and communication at work*. Cambridge, UK: Cambridge University Press.

Fullan, M. (1995). The school as a learning organization: Distant dreams. *Theory into Practice, 34*(4), 230-235.

Gates, B. (1999). *Business @ the speed of thought*. New York: Warner Books.

Goodwin, C., & Goodwin, M.H. (1998). Seeing as situated activity: Formulating planes. In Y. Engestrom & D. Middleton (Eds.), *Cognition and communication at work* (pp. 61-95). Cambridge, UK: Cambridge University Press.

Hackman, J.R., & Oldham, G. (1980). *Work redesign*. Reading, MA: Addison-Wesley.

Heath, C., & Luff, P. (1998). Convergent activities: Line control and passenger information on the London Underground. In Y. Engestrom & D. Middleton (Eds.), *Cognition and communication at work* (pp. 96-129). Cambridge, UK: Cambridge University Press.

Hutchins, E., & Klausen, T. (1998). Distributed cognition in an airline cockpit. In Y. Engestrom & D. Middleton (Eds.), *Cognition and communication at work* (pp. 15-34). Cambridge, UK: Cambridge University Press.

Jarvela, S., & Niemivirta, M. (1999). The changes in learning theory and the topicality of the recent research on motivation. *Research Dialogue in Learning and Instruction, 1*(2), 57-65.

Klimecki, R., & Lassleben, H. (1998). Modes of organizational learning. *Management Learning, 29*(4), 405-430.

Leavy, B. (1998). The concept of learning in the strategy field. *Management Learning, 29*(4), 447-466.

Leithwood, K. (1994). Leadership for school restructuring. *Educational Administration Quarterly, 30*(4), 498-518.

Leithwood, K., & Aitken, R. (1995). *Making schools smarter*. Thousand Oaks, CA: Corwin Press.

Leithwood, K., Jantzi, D., & Steinbach, R. (1995). An organizational learning perspective on school responses to central policy initiatives. *School Organisation, 15*(3), 229-252.

Leithwood, K., Jantzi, D., & Steinbach, R. (1999). *Changing leadership for changing times*. Buckingham, UK: Open University Press.

Leithwood, K., & Louis, K.S. (Eds.) (1998). *Organizational learning in schools*. The Netherlands: Swets & Zeitlinger.

Louis, K.S., Toole, J., & Hargreaves, A. (1999). Rethinking school improvement. In J. Murphy & K.S. Louis (Eds.), *Handbook of research on educational administration, second edition* (pp. 251-276). San Francisco: Jossey-Bass.

March, J.G. (1996). Exploration and exploitation in organizational learning. In M.D. Cohen & L.S. Sproull (Eds.), *Organizational learning* (pp. 101-123). Thousand Oaks, CA: Sage.

Mintzberg, H., Ahlstrand, B., & Lampel, J. (1998). *Strategy safari: A guided tour through the wilds of strategic management*. New York: The Free Press.

Salomon, G. (Ed.) (1993). *Distributed cognitions: Psychological and educational considerations*. Cambridge, UK: Cambridge University Press.

Salomon, G., & Perkins, D. (1997). Individual and social aspects of learning. *Review of Research in Education, 23*, 1-24.

Senge, P.M. (1990). *The fifth discipline*. New York: Doubleday.

Simon, H.A. (1996). Bounded rationality and organizational learning. In M.D. Cohen & L.S. Sproull (Eds.), *Organizational learning* (pp. 175-187). Thousand Oaks, CA: Sage.

Sims, H.P., Jr., & Lorenzi, P. (1992). *The new leadership paradigm*. Thousand Oaks, CA: Sage.

Stoll, L., & Myers, K. (1998). *No quick fixes: Perspectives on schools in difficulty*. London: Falmer Press.

Suchman, L. (1998). Constituting shared work spaces. In Y. Engestrom & D. Middleton (Eds.), *Cognition and communication at work* (pp. 35-60). Cambridge, UK: Cambridge University Press.

Vermunt, J.D., & Verloop, N. (1999). Congruence and friction between learning and teaching. *Learning and Instruction, 9*(3), 257-280.

Watkins, K.E., & Marsick, V.J. (1993). *Sculpting the learning organization*. San Francisco: Jossey-Bass.

Webster's 7th New Collegiate Dictionary (1971). Springfield, MA: Merriam Publishers.

Yeatts, D.E., & Hyten, C. (1998). *High-performing self-managed work teams*. Thousand Oaks, CA: Sage.

Yukl, G. (1994). Leadership in organizations (3rd ed.). Englewood Cliffs, NJ: Prentice-Hall.

PART I

DEVELOPING THE INTELLECTUAL
CAPACITIES OF INDIVIDUALS AND TEAMS

CHAPTER 2

DISTRICT CONTRIBUTIONS TO PRINCIPALS' SITUATED LEARNING

George Coffin and Kenneth Leithwood

In response to fundamental criticisms of university-based programs for the pre-service preparation of school leaders (Gresso, 1993), many such programs have been extensively revised and evaluated over the past decade (e.g., Milstein et al., 1993; Murphy, 1993). Partly as a consequence of this work, the features of effective formal programs for entry-level school administration are much clearer (e.g., Basom et al., 1996; Leithwood et al., 1996). Little research to date, however, has inquired how practicing administrators continue to learn to meet the emerging challenges encountered in their schools over the course of their careers. There is only modest evidence about the qualities of demonstrably valuable formal programs aimed at this purpose (e.g., Hallinger, 1992). And there is virtually no evidence concerning the learning of principals in the everyday context of their work. This is the case even though it seems likely that the majority of their learning is situated there. If

Advances in Research and Theories of School
Management and Educational Policy, Volume 4, pages 19-38.

principals are as critical to the nature and speed of innovation in schools as much evidence suggests is the case (e.g., Hannay & Ross, 1997), then understanding better how features of their work context foster or inhibit their learning is an important contribution to knowledge about school improvement.

While professional common sense and some formal evidence reinforces "on-the-job experience" as a primary source of leaders' learning (Hamilton et al., 1996; Leithwood et al., 1992), few efforts have been made to unpack this source of learning. What features of the job experience account for such learning? What conditions in the organization foster or inhibit such learning? These are questions about one aspect of organizational learning, the learning of individuals in organizational contexts (Brown, Collins, & Duguid, 1989). Our study, in response to these questions, explicitly focused on those sources of learning identified by school leaders themselves.

ON-THE-JOB LEARNING AS SITUATED COGNITION AND PRACTICAL PROBLEM SOLVING

Theories of situated cognition and practical problem solving served two purposes in this study. The first purpose was to direct our attention, at the outset, to on-the-job learning as a promising focus for our research; the second was to provide an intellectual backdrop, and some explicit conceptual tools, for making sense of our data. These were tools we had previously used to better understand teacher learning in school contexts (Leithwood, Jantzi & Steinbach, 1996).

The work of principals can be conceptualized as practical problem solving, a type of thinking embedded in activity. A significant part of the learning required for principals to further develop their practical problem-solving expertise is usefully conceptualized as "situated." Such learning is (a) specific to the context in which it is learned (Anderson, Reder & Simon, 1996), and (b) most likely to be learned in contexts exactly the same as, or closely approximating the situations in which it is to be used, although this is a hotly debated claim (see, for example, Kirshner & Whitson, 1998; Greeno, 1997). Situated cognition requires principals to be immersed in "authentic," non-routine professional activity embedded in a supportive organizational culture. For experienced, expert practitioners, such problem solving draws on a large repertoire of previously acquired knowledge. This knowledge is applied automatically to routine problems and, through reflection, in unique patterns which appropriately acknowledge the demands of more complex, novel and/or unstructured problems (e.g., Scardamalia & Bereiter, 1990; Berliner, 1988; Kagan, 1988).

'Everyday thinking' or 'practical thinking' are terms used to portray the mental processes engaged in by expert, experienced practitioners, such as principals, as they apply their knowledge in the solving of problems. Such thinking "is embedded in the larger, purposive activities and functions to achieve the goals of those activities" (Scribner, 1986). Those goals, which may be short or long term in nature, are achieved given the actual facts of the situation as the practitioner discovers them (Wagner & Sternberg, 1986). Principals' past knowledge (which also has motivational effects) is of considerable use to them when they are engaged in practical thinking in order to solve problems in their classrooms and schools.

Scribner (1984) has identified a number of characteristics of expert practical thinking within a model consisting of five components. Expert practical thinkers, for example, demonstrate a capacity to: formulate problems within a 'situation' that can be handled using well-developed, reliable solutions; respond flexibly to similar problems, using different patterns of their existing repertoire in order to fine tune a solution to the occasion; and to exploit (positively) the social, symbolic and/or physical environment as a way of reducing the cognitive demands placed on the individual for solving the problem. Such experts also find the most economical solutions (least effortful) that are, nevertheless, effective; and make extensive use of their existing task and situation specific knowledge for problem solving.

These are characteristics similar to those associated with principal problem solving, more specifically (Leithwood & Steinbach, 1995). Expert practical problem solving by practitioners such as principals depends on ready access to an extensive repertoire of problem-relevant knowledge. Such knowledge is about what actions to take to solve the problem as well as the social and physical context in which the problem is embedded (e.g., the particular students in the teacher's class). It is also about the larger set of activities (procedures and processes) enveloping efforts to address individual problems (Mehan, 1984). As Bransford (1993) notes, this knowledge required for practical problem solving is "conditionalized." It includes information about the conditions and constraints of its use, much of which is tacit (Sternberg & Caruso, 1985) rather than self-sufficient abstract concepts only. Furthermore, such knowledge is accessed and used in ways that take advantage of the environment as solution tools (Leinhardt, 1988). So principals' situated knowledge connects leadership or administrative events with particular environmental features such as district, community, and individual people.

If the knowledge required for expert, practical problem solving is situated, what general conditions give rise to its acquisition? These conditions include participation with others in authentic, non-routine activities. The contribution of active participation in developing robust, useful knowledge is evident in Brown, Collins and Duguid's (1989) analogy of concepts as tools. Like tools, concepts can only be fully understood through experience with their use and the refined appreciations (including tacit knowledge) that occur as a result of feedback from such use.

Participation with others, especially members of the field of practice who are more expert in some areas (perhaps a more experienced district leader), substantially extends the potential for individual development. Explanations for this effect began, most notably, with Vygotsky's (1978) conception of a zone of proximal development. He argued that processes involved in social interaction are eventually taken over and internalized by a person to form their own individual cognitive processes. Hence, participation with others in addressing a problem which demonstrates processes more sophisticated than those possessed by the individual potentially stimulates growth in the individual's problem-solving capacity. This is likely when: (a) group processes are at a challenging but comfortable level of sophistication beyond the individual; (b) the group process adjusts the difficulty of tasks for individual members so that they are manageable for those members (Rogoff & Lave, 1984; Wertsch, Minick & Arns, 1984; Mehan, 1984); and (c) there are opportunities for individuals to reflect on differences between their own processes and those used by the group. So, for example, attempts by a district committee to solve a problem during a meeting that met these conditions would contribute to the problem-solving abilities of individual committee members.

For useful, robust, situated knowledge to develop most readily, participation with others must also be in activity which is 'authentic'—circumstances which involve the ordinary activities of school leadership and management. Authentic activities are situated in the social and physical context of the school, community, and district, for example, which must be accounted for in problem solving and so must be represented in the knowledge structures stored by the principal. Knowledge for problem solving will be readily accessible, as Sternberg and Caruso (1985) argue, to the extent that the cues needed at the time of access were encoded when the knowledge was originally being stored. This helps explain the contribution to principal learning of on-the-job, informal, learning as compared with more formal learning activities which may be situated outside the school, community or district.

Finally, the authentic activities in which principals participate will usually have to be non-routine, as well, if they are to contribute to further development. Non-routine activities stimulate one to examine usual practices through "fresh eyes" thereby helping to develop a capacity, as Ruddock (1988) explains, for the kind of constructive discontent with one's existing practices that will fuel the motivation for professional learning.

RESEARCH DESIGN

Sample

Twenty principals from three school districts provided data for this study. In addition to being accessible, districts from which principals were selected had to meet three other criteria. First, selected districts had to be relatively large. The reason for this criterion was the substantial evidence that as districts increase in size their contributions to student achievement decrease (Walberg & Fowler, 1987; Leithwood, 1998). Explanations for these findings point to the complexities and costs of coordination faced by large organizational units, and corresponding reductions in the proportion of resources available for student instruction. The challenges for principal learning in the context of a large district, therefore, may be quite different than they are in a small district, and we could not afford to include an adequate number of both small and large districts in our study.

As a second selection criterion, districts also had to have access to significant internal professional support resources, and such external resources as local universities or leadership centres. Districts with these characteristics at least provided opportunities for principal learning. Finally, selected districts had to be committed to site-based management. This was the case not only because site-based management creates the need for significant new learning by principals but also because the nature of that learning is at least partly about new roles and relationships with the district.

Three districts in southern Ontario were selected which met these criteria. Two were public school districts, each serving about 80,000 students, and one was a Roman Catholic separate school district serving about 40,000 students. At the time of the study, each of the districts was encouraging schools to implement several provincial and district-initiated programs (e.g., outcome-based learning, integrating technology into the curriculum, school councils).

To be included in the study, principals within these three districts had to have at least 10 years administrative experience with their district. This criterion ensured considerable distance from initial, formal training experiences, and sufficient time to fully experience the potential influence of their local district, school, and community contexts. Principals selected for the study also had to be in the process of attempting to implement in their schools some major initiative of the sort mentioned above. The total sample of principals had to be gender balanced. Of the 20 principals (10 female and 10 male) who met these criteria, and were willing to participate in the study, 17 led elementary schools and three led secondary schools.

Data Collection

Three techniques were used for collecting data. Principals were interviewed twice for approximately one hour on each occasion. Each principal was asked to describe how they learned to implement one or more of the significant initiatives they were undertaking in their schools, and also to describe the conditions which either fostered or inhibited their opportunities for such learning.

A search of school board documents was undertaken for evidence of initiatives taken by the districts explicitly aimed at influencing the learning of principals, or with the potential for such learning. These documents, describing some of the conditions which prevailed in each district and under which principals operated their schools, included mission statements, strategic plans, annual reports, organizational charts, publicized papers, and policies relating to professional development.

As a final source of data, interviews were conducted with five assistant superintendents about district initiatives and professional development policies and practices. These people provided a broad perspective on those factors which determined such district priorities as, for example, the allocation of financial resources.

Analysis

All interviews were audiotaped and transcribed. The first set of interviews were analyzed for references to learning processes principals had engaged in while implementing significant new initiatives in their schools. Two levels of coding were carried out. The first level assigned each learning process to a context (e.g., district, school) while the second level described types of activities within each context: for example, district-based learning processes have a subcategory labeled "district-sponsored inservice." Frequency of reference to learning processes within contexts were calculated. These frequencies were examined in relation to gender of respondents, employing district, level of school and district type (public versus separate).

Data from the principals' second interviews served to validate and expand on issues arising from the first interviews. The texts of these interviews were examined for evidence either supporting or contradicting claims made in the first interview. To avoid the possibility of coding references to the same sources of learning more than once, no codes were assigned to the texts of the second interviews.

Reliability of the coding process was assessed by having two independent researchers separately code a sample of 51 coded references to learning processes from the first set of interviews. After initial coding practice, and subsequent discussion of differences, the final level of agreement between coders was 98 percent.

SOURCES AND PROCESSES FOR PRINCIPALS' LEARNING

The processes or activities from which principals perceived that they learned were situated in five contexts; the district, the wider community, the school, professional associations, and self. A total of 522 statements were made about learning processes, activities or conditions within these contexts.

District

More than half of the total set of statements, statements from all 20 principals, associated some activity or process from which they learned with their school district. Each of these activities was further classified into one of nine types and the frequency of identification of each type was calculated.

Support and Direction

Superintendents (called Directors in Ontario) who held a clear sense of direction and who articulated their plans to subordinates were seen as dynamic and inspired sources of learning. One principal described the aura of influence exuded by her superintendent in this way, "You couldn't ever walk away from hearing her speak without thinking 'Wow', she was very dynamic in that sense."

Principals had much more frequent contact with other district administrative staff, mainly assistant superintendents, who articulated district and Ministry of Education policy to principals and provided information updates regularly. Access to central office administrators was essential to principals for solving a variety of problems, both large and small. Assistant superintendents and their subordinates often acted as intermediaries, intervening with displeased parents, or supporting school-initiated proposals to the district. To varying degrees, assistant superintendents helped principals develop and monitor annual plans for the school.

The quality of relationships between principals and district administrators had an important influence on the learning of principals. Respondents identified four "criteria" (our word) central to their judgements of quality on this matter. One of these criteria was interpersonal warmth. Several principals attested to a strong collaborative and supportive relationship with certain assistant superintendents, depending on the personal bond that existed between them. When the relationship was seen as a supportive, nurturing one, principals attached high value to the learning that flowed from it: "I really enjoyed those chats with [the assistant superintendent], and so he, quite often, would spur me on to look into something else." On the other hand, superintendents who were aloof and reserved discouraged the one-on-one dialogue that principals sometimes felt they needed.

A second measure of quality was the contextual knowledge and general professional expertise possessed by district administrators. Principals' learning was hampered when district administrators were not in touch with the life of the principal's school, whereas close knowledge of the school and a sensitive appreciation of the problems it was grappling with inspired principals to learn. Principals' learning was influenced, as well, by the perceived credibility of district leaders' general professional expertise, in addition to contextual knowledge. This credibility was called into question when district leaders were viewed as inadequately trained or without suitable experience. For example, those with secondary school backgrounds typically were considered to be unfamiliar with the intricacies of program implementation in elementary schools, and conversely, district administrators with elementary school training were undervalued and under-utilized as sources of learning by secondary school principals.

A third criterion of quality in relationships with district administrators was the degree of consistency evident between their actions and the espoused ideals and values of the district; a serious gap between these things diminished the strength of the collegial bond between superintendents and principals, possibly because it created doubts about the authenticity of district leaders' commitments. It was difficult for principals to believe, for example, that the board was committed to participative styles of management, and that they should develop the skills for such management when principals' input to decisions were sought and given but not heeded. As one principal said, "We talk about setting goals as a community.... It's not what I experience from the top. In fact, it's just the reverse of that."

A final criterion identified by principals as influencing the quality of their relationships with district leaders was the extent to which such leaders engaged in transformational leadership practices, especially collaborative visioning and goal setting, modelling behaviours, frequent and supportive contacts, and motivating principals to aspire to higher levels of achievement.

District support staff were helpful to principals in ways different from administrative staff. Those staff with curriculum portfolios (consultants) were brought into schools to support district initiatives, and to meet inservice needs identified by teachers and/or the principal. Facilitators, technicians, communication managers and attendance counsellors had specialized roles and, in their respective capacities, responded to particular requests from schools. Staff development departments got high praise from principals when their activities were directed toward diagnosing and responding to the professional development needs of teachers and administrators.

More generally, the culture of all three districts was perceived by principals to be supportive of their ongoing learning and work. Only a few negative aspects of that culture were identified. For example, one district had followed an unofficial "appeasement" policy with teacher unions for many years. As a consequence, almost every initiative of the district now was challenged by the teachers' federation as an infringement on collective bargaining rights. Under such conditions, principals experienced mixed loyalties: should they maintain solidarity with their teaching colleagues or their employer? The same culture of confrontation eventually found its way into schools, making it difficult for principals to motivate staff to take on new challenges. Although too little collaboration was alluded to infrequently, it was viewed as a missed opportunity for learning when it was mentioned.

Board-sponsored Inservice

Learning from formal board-sponsored inservice was the second of only two activities or processes referred to by all 20 principals in the sample. Workshop formats were preferred over lectures, particularly workshops with a clearly focused theme, the direction of an expert leader/facilitator, a practical use for what was learned, the opportunity to solve problems in small groups, and a second representative from the school to verify information and to be a partner in implementation at school. A school leadership course and study groups were rated highly by those in one district who chose to avail themselves of these services. Sixteen out of 20 principals identified planned meetings, especially special-issues meetings (as in introducing school councils), as rich sources of knowledge.

Substantial inter-district differences were evident in principal's responses about inservice. District 1 principals (the separate school district) made the greatest number of references to learning processes or activities in all contexts (mean per principal = 30.9), district 3 principals made the least (mean per principal = 19.8); district two principals fell in between. Principals from district 1 described their learning in relation to initiatives which had high district and community involvement, whereas district 3 principals focused on school-related sources. The main source of difference in the frequency of mentions of district-situated learning activities between the two sets of public school principals is district-sponsored inservice. Clearly, this was a much more important source of learning for principals in District 2 than in District 3, and principals described the forms of inservice which they found most useful. Such inservice took account of principals' already-acquired knowledge and skills, and was structured to accommodate their learning styles. Principals were motivated to learn whatever would help them deal with problems in their work in a very direct way. They also weighed the benefits they would gain from learning something on their own with the negative consequences of not learning it.

Opportunities to work in small groups, to dissect ideas, trouble-shoot, test approaches, anticipate problems, and to work through a plan for implementation in their respective schools were considered good approximations of their real-life situations. Respondents' preferences for problem oriented forms of learning was clearly articulated by one of the female principals who insisted, "We want a work session, a think session, a planning session, and then go back and use ideas that can be incorporated into our local school."

Formal Associations among Principals

Such associations gave principals opportunities to acquire knowledge and strategies concerning new initiatives, to keep informed of developments throughout the system, and perhaps most important, to engage with colleagues in meaningful discussion so that they could "take away the collective wisdom of the group."

Board Policies, Documents, and Resources

Principals' learning was influenced by the nature and quality of board policy and related documents produced by central office, and the attention given to making administrators aware of them. Policy statements were valued for the direction these gave to administrators in achieving system goals. A junior vice-principal claimed that she was coming to see policies as "tools that are useful in trying to help every child learn under the best possible circumstances and to help the school function the best that it can." When policies were well written, widely circulated to those affected, and followed consistently, the amount of time and effort principals had to put into routine problem solving was considerably reduced.

Clarity about district directions and priorities also seemed best provided to principals by those publicly available documents such as mission statements, strategic plans and annual reports, that emerged from a sequence of activities, carried out collaboratively, ranging from visioning to the actual execution of strategic and school improvement plans. Human and financial resources were allocated to accomplish the district and school goals developed through such processes.

Diminishing resources and the imminent prospect of further budget reductions reduced the motivation to learn about promising new initiatives, particularly the implementation of electronic technology for purposes of instruction. Central office staff reductions diminished the emphasis on staff development and curriculum leadership, eroding both the motivation and the opportunity, for principal learning.

District Committees

Eleven of the 20 principals made reference to serving on district committees which undertook tasks including inservicing principals on the implementation of school councils, planning for the mentoring of aspiring school administrators, studying standardized testing, and setting up a telecommunications network. Playing an accessory role or leadership role in district committees put principals at the forefront of board initiatives and therefore in a favored position for launching those ideas in their own schools.

Informal Networks

Twelve principals made 17 references to informal networks that evolved around advice seeking, problem solving, and even commiserating. The extent to which principals engaged in dialogue with each other was a function of the personal and professional relationships between individuals, resulting in some principals using this strategy more than others. Generally, networking patterns seemed to be a function of regional proximity or school level (elementary versus secondary). In one instance, however, an informal group was composed along gender lines. One member of that group valued her association highly, "It's a social event, but it's also where you air some concerns, get some advice from others, and you get to know a little more about what's happening within the board."

Modelling and Mentoring

Learning by modelling and mentoring entailed observing and emulating leadership styles, or acquiring knowledge and skills from "experts," and was noted by five principals and one vice-principal in seven references. One principal acquired expertise in special education as a result of observing special education consultants work with children in her school. Newly appointed vice-principals often became professionally and organizationally socialized through participating in decision making as part of an administrative team with the principal. Districts also used experienced principals to mentor teachers who had aspirations to administration.

Inter-school Visits

Five references were made to inter-school visitation or collaboration as a mode of learning. In one district, teams from one school visited other schools to view equipment and talk with teachers presently adapting technology to the classroom. Notwithstanding these instances, a culture of cross-school collaboration did not seem to be well developed in any of the three boards represented in the study.

Religion

References to learning activities by separate school principals (district 1) exceeded those by public school principals in all contexts. In the case of district sources, differences were quite substantial. Two explanations suggest themselves. First, the separate school district had recently mandated the setting up of school councils in all schools where none existed, and five principals in our study used that "fresh-in-the-mind" activity to describe their learning. An extraordinary number of references was made to activities involving parents. In contrast only one principal in Board 3 made reference to the setting up of a school council.

This source of learning aside, religion still emerged as a possible factor explaining both how and what was learned by principals in District 1. The symbols, the celebrations, the interpretation of curriculum, and perspectives on leadership gave a distinctive character to principals' beliefs about Catholic school leadership. Separate school principals perceived their leadership to be different from that of their public school colleagues with respect to the treatment of others and the culture of religious faith within the school.

We did not pursue the relevance of these perceived differences on leadership roles beyond noting how pervasive religious imagery was on separate school principals' thinking. Others have suggested that such thinking has little effect on practice (Kulmatycki & Montgomerie, 1993). But further research seems necessary to clarify this relationship, since leaders' thinking and action are closely linked both in theory and practice (Leithwood & Steinbach, 1995).

THE WIDER COMMUNITY

In 78 references, all 20 principals identified learning from six types of activities situated in the wider community context. Twenty-three references were made to *contacts with individual parents*, school board trustees and school councils or their precursors, parent-teachers' associations. References to school councils often related to the processes of consulting with parents, soliciting community support, and putting mechanisms in place for the creation of councils. Formal liaison with parents were regarded by principals as valuable means of communicating school goals to parents, soliciting support for initiatives, seeking advice, and reflecting the wishes of parents in the education of their children.

Conferences, workshops and research, although occurring infrequently, were significant for 11 principals who made 18 references to such activities. On occasion, districts financially supported principals who attended conferences and courses sponsored by other boards, universities, or a consortium of boards and universities. Being part of a research program with a neighbouring graduate school provided the competencies to bring about reform in the school of one secondary school principal. Two secondary principals who assisted in delivering a principal certification program valued very highly the access to current research and the opportunity to interact with other professionals that this work provided.

Legislation, regulations, curriculum and policy documents, and handbooks from the *provincial government* were cited by 11 principals as useful sources of learning. Memoranda and press releases formed the simplest and most direct means of communicating government's intentions. More sophisticated documents conveying the meaning and form of policy also came to the attention of principals, usually through formal presentations by knowledgeable people.

Five principals referred to learning from the *experiences of others,* instances where their districts sought out information and techniques from other districts as aids to schools attempting to take on new initiatives (e.g., implementation of school councils). In less formal ways, individual principals also reported seeking the advice of others outside of education where "a lot of issues are very similar, and certainly problem solving is a common thread for everybody."

While religion was identified as a factor influencing principal learning in district situations, it is a factor influencing principal learning situated in the wider community, as well. Principals in separate schools spoke of the influence of their *religious beliefs* in how they learned more about how leadership ought to be exercised in their schools. Leadership was studied from the perspective of the tenets of the faith. Provincial curriculum documents were interpreted in relation to the view of the learner as perceived by the faith community. In the words of one principal, "It's from our belief in God and his role as Creator of all of us and his love for all of us that gives credence to the way we treat one another." Including the Catholic faith in the educational system was fundamental to separate schools and adherence to that doctrine pervaded the learning of those principals.

Only four references were made to the *media*, newspapers and other forms of public announcements, as sources of learning, and then the source and what was learned was often viewed with scepticism.

School

Seventy references were made to six types of learning activities situated in the school. Slightly more than one third of these references were to activities associated with *school planning* in its various forms. Two principals in Board 1 described extensive processes by which they sought and learned from the views of community representatives, including the Church (this was the separate school district), in composing a mission statement and identifying objectives to achieve the mission. Action teams further developed "specific tactics to help implement the objectives that were set by the planning team." Similarly, a principal in Board 2 made conscious efforts to blend system plans with school-identified needs into something that "suits this community and this environment." In the most favorable of relationships, assistant superintendents and principals worked together to harmonize school-level plans with broad system goals. Typically the superintendent "comes in and goes over my management plan with me, so he knows the direction I'm taking." At the end of the year those plans are revisited and progress is assessed. The potential for learning from reflective practices is captured eloquently by a female, elementary school principal: "I think that's what's missing in a lot of schools, you don't stop and reflect on what you're doing. I believe that if you have done something for 25 years, it doesn't make it right or good. You need to stop and think, can we improve on this?" Learning from school-based planning also occurred in sessions where staff clarified values and goals, or assessed past achievements and revised goals in light of these assessments. Collaborative modes of working were evident in many of the principals' references to learning through school-based planning.

Observing the workplace was a useful strategy reported by eight principals for learning about the activities of teachers and students, for engaging in informal dialogue, and for demonstrating accessibility and openness. Learning from school-based personnel and students ranked second among principals' sources of learning in school contexts. Principals who made a special effort to stay in tune with the day-to-day operation of their schools maintained a sensitivity to staff and student needs (they also demonstrated, by their presence, an interest in the well-being of the school).

Administrative teamwork was the third most frequently mentioned category of learning activity situated in the school. Two principals valued the questions and challenges to their thinking brought forward by their vice-principals. The degree to which teamwork stimulated learning seemed to depend largely on the leadership style of the principal, the experience of the vice-principal, and the task at hand. In terms of sharing the workload, some teams worked as equals. The vice-principal was party to all major decision making and held significant responsibilities in proportion to the time available for administrative duties. In other circumstances, a junior vice-principal was mentored by the more experienced principal with the first year being a time to become oriented to the position.

Elementary school administrators tended to have more immediate daily contact than secondary school administrators. The size of the school and the corresponding number of administrators may be a factor in explaining the difference. One secondary school principal with three vice-principals assigned specific functions to each and allowed them to act independently. The principal's role was that of "facilitator." Collaboration and clarification occurred at scheduled meetings, where the events of the past week were analyzed and assessed.

Learning from experience was explicitly mentioned five times. While three references were made to learning from general experience, one principal and one vice-principal cited specific instances of transferring prior learning to similar new situations.

With only two references to *experimenting with communications technologies*, this learning activity did not appear to have much influence on principals' learning. One school received additional funding to purchase hardware and software to assist in training student teachers. The second school, under the leadership of the principal, was seeking to create a user-friendly telecommunications network for teachers, and to integrate the use of technology in all curricular areas; this principal was collaborating with private industry and the district to achieve this goal.

School level (elementary, secondary) was also related to differences in principal learning. In the three most frequently referenced contexts for learning (district, wider community school), elementary school principals identified more learning activities than their secondary school colleagues by wide margins. There was an element of autonomy, or unwillingness to be influenced, among secondary school principals that was not as evident among elementary school principals. Secondary school principals' learning tended to arise from efforts to achieve school-based goals which were being pursued without much reference to district priorities.

Elementary school principals reported more instances of collaborative interaction than secondary school principals. Perhaps the larger size of secondary schools makes it more difficult to maintain close relationships with staff. But other explanations are possible. For example, many secondary schools are traditionally organized around academic departments, which, some have argued, are resistant to change (Hannay & Ross, 1997).

Professional Associations

Intra-district principals' associations in the three districts in this study served primarily two functions—to contribute to the professional development of members, and to represent their collective interests with the district. Formal links between the association executive and the superintendent assisted with these functions. An *annual conference*, often funded by the districts, was the major professional development initiative of these associations and was generally well regarded by principals as much for its social, as its learning functions.

Principals also acknowledged learning from *teachers' federations* through inservice and professional literature. Relations between the districts and the federations sometimes enhanced learning and, in other instances, impeded it. One principal felt that the federation represented the interests of teachers more than principals, and, therefore, opportunities for learning diminished as one moved into administration.

Self

Of all the contexts in which principals situated their learning, those originating within principals themselves were the least frequently referenced (6.5 percent of the total). Those activities that were mentioned included independent reading, formal study/research, personal networks, and community leadership. Reflection, prayer, and close friends were mentioned as important sources of inspiration and learning by only a few principals.

Independent reading, apart from professional literature, and formal study (university courses) accounted for more than three-quarters of the references in this category. Principals expanded their understandings of their functions as leaders through readings of professional and general literature.

Formal study focused on themes that were common to professional development activities offered by the district, for example, outcome-based learning and computer internetting. But principals made few direct links between their academic studies and the challenges they were facing in their schools. It is possible that the academic literature encountered by these principals really did not have much value to them as many critics of traditional principal preparation programs argue (e.g., Murphy, 1992). Or, as suggested by research on knowledge utilization (Cousins & Leithwood, 1993), the primary uses of this academic knowledge may be to frame problems and to expand understandings rather than directly to inform decisions.

All secondary school respondents in our sample were male, as well, so the effects of gender and school level are difficult to disentangle. Female principals identified more instances of learning (mean = 30.0) than males (mean = 22.2). And while all principals identified learning from central office staff more frequently than from any other sources, females did so more frequently than males. Furthermore, women were more likely to describe in detail how they acquired knowledge and skills to implement an initiative. These results are in line with some evidence that males are less likely than females to adopt collaborative forms of learning (Marshall & Mitchell, 1989; Shakeshaft, 1987).

DISCUSSION AND CONCLUSION

One reason for our interest in principals' learning "on-the-job" is the preeminent contribution, according to situated cognition theorists, of the setting itself to practical problem-solving expertise. Results of our interviews with 20 principals from three large school districts may be interpreted as providing support for the power of situativity theory to explain professional learning on-the-job. With a few exceptions, principals acquired the knowledge and skills to undertake new initiatives in an overtly social situation, including the learning from policies and documents that principals cited as useful to their learning in their districts' context. Especially noteworthy was the infrequent mention of learning in the context of self alone. These results appear to add weight to the arguments of situated cognition theorists that information processing theories of cognitive functioning are not sufficient by themselves to account for learning under ecologically valid (or "real life") conditions. As Greeno explains:

> The cognitive perspective's basic concepts ... and explanatory schemata ... are about processes and structures that are assumed to function at the level of individual agents [whereas] situativity focuses primarily at the level of interactive systems that include individuals as participants, interacting with each other and with material and representational systems (1997, p. 7).

But principals' construction of their knowledge, insofar as they were able to reflect on it, took place not only in social contexts, using the broad and inclusive definition offered by Greeno. Most frequently these constructions took place in more exclusive, interpersonal, social situations where principals and others were, as Greeno says, interacting with each other quite directly. These situations usually included the relatively safe company of understanding peers and district administrators, or what Vygotsky (1978) referred to as the immediate social interactional context.

Principals' preferences for learning in interpersonal social situations may be explained by the uses to which their learning was to be applied—practical problem solving. Expertise in such problem solving requires principals' knowledge to be "proceduralized" (Van Lehn, 1990). It is not enough for principals to "know about" the obstacles to site-based management and promising strategies for overcoming them, for example; if this were the case, it seems likely that principals would have attributed more importance to their academic learning. Rather, they also must "know how to" identify such obstacles and have skill in the use of such strategies. The importance of such know how may explain the nature of the formal inservice experiences most valued from their districts by principals. Workshops, group discussion, and problem-based activity allow for the development, and some practice in the application, of procedures.

Practical problem-solving expertise requires more than just proceduralized knowledge as we have discussed it to this point, however. It also requires knowledge to be "conditionalized" (Bransford, 1993). So a workshop focused on procedures for conflict resolution may provide a principal with a useful set of propositions for dealing with conflicts arising during school council meetings. But the possession of such proceduralized knowledge may still leave that principal unable to effectively resolve those conflicts created in her own council meetings by a parent who is strongly suspicious of teachers as a result of her own unfortunate experiences as a student. To be useful to the principal, procedural knowledge about conflict resolution, knowledge that might be considered transferable across contexts, must be further enriched, modified, extended (and sometimes completely replaced) before it can be applied to settings that include the parent. Warm supportive relations with others in the district office, and networks of principals' colleagues that can be called on for advice, for example, offer resources for consultation during the process of conditionalizing one's knowledge in order to solve practical problems in their unique contexts. Knowledge on the part of district administrators about the principal's school context increases the likelihood of district administrators offering useful support for the conditionalizing of principals' procedural knowledge. Warm interpersonal relations increase principals' willingness to risk sharing the details of the dilemmas with which they are confronted, and to seek advice for their resolution.

At least two implications from our interpretation of these data merit attention. First, the district as an organizational unit and district administrators within that unit were overwhelmingly the major sources of learning for principals. This raises several important questions. From one perspective, recent world-wide efforts to implement site-based management and parallel efforts, as in Ontario, the United Kingdom, and New Zealand, to radically reduce or entirely eliminate district-level organizational structures are highly problematic. Considerable evidence points to those in formal school leader roles as keys to restructuring and school improvement initiatives (e.g., Hannay & Ross, 1997). Reducing the availability of district resources from which to learn would appear to be a formidable barrier to principals' learning how to engage in such restructuring and school improvement.

Looked at quite differently, the importance principals attached to their districts in our study could be interpreted as an excessively narrow and unproductive focus for such learning. Whether or not this is the case depends very much on the nature of the opportunities provided to principals by the district and its staff. We are persuaded by the evidence that site-based management has been oversold as a panacea for educational restructuring (Leithwood & Menzies, 1998a, 1998b; Leithwood, Jantzi, & Steinbach, 1999), and that the case is quite strong for retaining district structures that serve primarily support functions rather than largely control functions. While principals in settings with relatively long experience under site-based management structures rarely express an interest in returning to the hierarchical bureaucracies of their former districts (Bullock & Thomas, 1997), they also are of the opinion that they are substantially undersupported and sometimes overwhelmed.

If there is a strong case for the retention and development of supportive district structures, our evidence begins to identify what that support means, at least from the perspective of principals' learning. Indeed, our data suggest a quite specific purpose for senior administrators to "visit" their schools, something most such administrators feel they should do more frequently than they actually manage. This is the second implication of our data that we think merits attention. Results suggest that close collegial relations between district and school administrators are critical to such support, as are high levels of professional expertise, and close knowledge of principals' schools, on the part of senior district leaders. The study also found some evidence of the value of transformational practices by senior administrators. All these conditions for district support are more likely in smaller rather than larger district units, an implication consistent with evidence concerning the contribution of variation in district size to student achievement (e.g., Walberg & Fowler, 1987).

REFERENCES

Anderson, J.R., Reder, L.M., & Simon, H.A. (1996). Situated learning and education. *Educational Researcher, 25*(4), 5-11.

Basom, M., Yerkes, D., Norris, C., & Barnett, B. (1996). Using cohorts as a means for developing transformational leaders. *Journal of School Leadership, 6*(1), 99-112.

Berliner, D. (1988). *The development of expertise in pedagogy.* Charles W. Hunt Memorial Lecture, New Orleans.

Bransford, J.D. (1993) Who ya gonna call? Thoughts about teaching problem solving. In P. Hallinger, K. Leithwood, & J. Murphy (Eds.), *Cognitive perspectives on educational leadership* (pp. 171-191). New York: Teachers College Press.

Brown, J.S., Collins, A., & Duguid, P. (1989). Situated cognition and the culture of learning. *Educational Researcher, 18*(1).

Bullock, A., & Thomas, H. (1997). *Schools at the centre: A study of decentralization.* London: Routledge.

Cousins, B., & Leithwood, K. (1993). Enhancing knowledge utilization as a strategy for school improvement. *Knowledge: Creation, Diffusion, Utilization, 14*(3), 305-333.

Greeno, J. (1997). On claims that answer the wrong questions. *Educational Researcher, 26*(1), 5-17.

Gresso, D. (1993). Genesis of the Danforth Preparation Program for school principals. In M. Milstein et al. (Eds.), *Changing the way we prepare educational leaders: The Danforth experience* (pp. 1-16). Newbury Park, CA: Corwin Press.

Hallinger, P. (1992). School leadership development: An introduction. *Education and Urban Society, 24*(3), 300-316.

Hamilton, D.N., Ross, P.H., Steinbach, R., & Leithwood, K. (1996). Differences in the socialization experiences of promoted and aspiring school administrators. *Journal of School Leadership, 6*(4), 346-367.

Hannay, L., & Ross, J. (1997). Initiating secondary school reform: The dynamic relationship between restructuring, reculturing, and retiming. *Educational Administration Quarterly, 33*(supplement), 576-603.

Kagan, D. (1988). Teaching as clinical problem solving: A critical examination of the analogy and its implications. *Review of Educational Research, 58*(4), 482-505.

Kirshner, D., & Whitson, J. (1998). Obstacles to understanding cognition as situated. *Educational Researcher, 27*(8), 22-27.

Kulmatycki, M. B. & Montgomerie, T. C. (1993). A comparison of principals' perceptions about their leadership in Catholic and non-Catholic schools. *The Alberta Journal* of *Educational Research, 39*(3), 375 - 392.

Leinhardt, G. (1988). Situated knowledge and expertise in teaching. In J. Calderhead (Ed.), *Teachers' professional learning* (pp. 146-169). London: The Falmer Press.

Leithwood, K. (1998). Educational governance and student achievement. *Orbit, 29*(1), 34-37.

Leithwood, K., et al. (1992). Socialization experiences: Becoming a principal in Canada. In F.W. Parkay & G.E. Hall (Eds.), *Becoming a principal: The challenges of beginning leadership* (pp. 284-307). Boston: Allyn & Bacon.

Leithwood, K., Jantzi, D., & Dart, B. (1996). How the school improvement strategies of transformational leaders foster teacher development. In P. Ruohotie & P. Grimmett (Eds.), *Professional growth and development* (pp. 115-147). Tampere, Finland: Career Development Finland KY.

Leithwood, K., Jantzi, D., & Steinbach, R. (1996). Commitment-building approaches to school restructuring: Lessons from a longitudinal study. *Journal of Education Policy, 11*(3), 377-398.

Leithwood, K., Jantzi, D., & Steinbach, R. (1999). *Changing leadership for changing times*. Buckingham, UK: Open University Press.

Leithwood, K., & Menzies, T. (1998a). Forms and effects of school-based management: A review. *Educational Policy, 12*(3), 325-346.

Leithwood, K., & Menzies, T. (1998b). A review of research concerning the implementation of site-based management. *School Effectiveness and School Improvement, 9*(3), 233-285.

Leithwood, K. A. & Steinbach, R. (1995). *Expert problem solving: Evidence from school and district leaders*. Albany, NY: State University of New York Press.

Marshall, C. & Mitchell, B. (1989). *Women's careers as a critique of the administrative culture*. Paper presented at American Research Association annual meeting.

Mehan, H. (1984). Institutional decision-making. In B. Rogoff & J. Lave (Eds.), *Everyday cognition: Its development in social context*. Cambridge, MA: Harvard University Press.

Milstein, M., et al. (Eds.) (1993), *Changing the way we prepare educational leaders: The Danforth experience*. Newbury Park, CA: Corwin Press.

Murphy, J. (1992). *The landscape of leadership preparation*. Newbury Park, CA: Corwin Press Inc.

Murphy, J. (Ed.) (1993). *Preparing tomorrow's school leaders: Alternative designs*. University Park, PA: UCEA.

Rogoff, B. & Lave, J. (Eds.) (1984) *Everyday cognition: Its development in social context*. Cambridge, MA: Harvard University Press.

Ruddock, J. (1988). The ownership of change as a basis for teachers' professional learning. In J. Calderhead (Ed.), *Teachers' professional learning* (pp. 146-169). London: The Falmer Press.

Scardamalia, M., & Bereiter, C. (1990). Conceptions of teaching and approaches to core problems. In M.C. Reynolds (Ed.), *Knowledge base for the beginning teacher* (pp. 37-46). Oxford: Pergammon Press.

Scribner, S. (1984). Studying working intelligence. In B. Rogoff & J. Lave (Eds.), *Everyday cognition: Its development in social context.* Cambridge, MA: Harvard University Press.

Scribner, S. (1986). Thinking in action: Some characteristics of practical thought. In R. J. Sternberg & R. K. Wagner, (Eds.) *Practical Intelligence: Nature and Origins of Competence in the Everyday World.* Cambridge: Cambridge University Press.

Shakeshaft, C. (1987). *Women in educational administration.* Beverly Hills, CA: Sage.

Sternberg, R., & Caruso, O.R. (1985). Practical modes of knowing. In E. Eisner (Ed.), *Learning and teaching the ways of knowing.* Chicago: University of Chicago Press.

Van Lehn, K. (1990). Problem solving and cognitive skill acquisition. In M.I. Posner (Ed.), *Foundations of cognitive science* (pp. 527-579). Cambridge, MA: MIT Press.

Vygotsky, L.S. (1978). *Mind in society.* Cambridge, MA: MIT Press.

Wagner, R., & Sternberg, R. (1986). Tacit knowledge and intelligence in the everyday world. In R.K. Wagner & R. Sternberg (Eds.), *Practical intelligence: Nature and origins of competence in the everyday world.* Cambridge: Cambridge University Press.

Walberg, H., & Fowler, W. (1987). Expenditure and size efficiencies of public school districts. *Educational Researcher, October*, 5-13.

Wertsch, J.V., Minick, N., & Arns, F.J. (1984). The creation of context in joint problem solving. In B. Rogoff & J. Lave (Eds.), *Everyday cognition: Its development in social context.* Cambridge, MA: Harvard University Press.

CHAPTER 3

SCHOOL LEADERSHIP TEAMS
FACTORS THAT INFLUENCE THEIR
DEVELOPMENT AND EFFECTIVENESS

Janet H. Chrispeels, Janet H. Brown, and
Salvador Castillo

School councils or teams composed of teachers, administrators, and parents are now a common feature of the landscape of school reform (Leithwood & Menzies, 1998; Wallace & Hall, 1994). Some states have mandated school councils as a component of their school improvement programs. In other cases, districts have implemented school-based management (SBM), which delegates personnel and budgetary discretion as well as the traditional school improvement planning to a school governance committee. Other national reform models (Stringfield, Ross, & Smith, 1996) such as the *Accelerated Schools* (Hopfenberg & Levin, 1993), *School Development Model* (Comer, 1980; Comer & Haynes, 1991), *Success for*

Advances in Research and Theories of School
Management and Educational Policy, Volume 4, pages 39-73.
Copyright © 2000 by JAI Press Inc.
All rights of reproduction in any form reserved.
ISBN: 0-7623-0024-8

All and *Roots to Wings* (Slavin et al., 1990), and *Coalition of Essential Schools* (Sizer, 1992) also require a leadership team to make program and implementation decisions and to provide vehicles for empowering staff, parents, and, in secondary schools, students. Interdisciplinary teams of teachers, especially in middle schools, also have become a key strategy in school restructuring (Kruse & Louis, 1997).

The establishment of well-functioning school councils or teams, however, is a challenging process. Research indicates that these councils or teams have not always been effective (David, 1989; Malen, Ogawa, & Kranz, 1989; Stanton & Zerchykov, 1979; Weiss, Cambone & Wyeth, 1991). Some of the problems identified include: conflicts about who is selected; tensions among team members; lack of time to meet; failure to address significant issues related to student achievement; lack of clear definition of roles, responsibilities, and decision making authority; and inadequate training of members to assume these new roles. Kruse and Louis (1997) identified yet another problem with teams: interdisciplinary teams may enhance teacher enthusiasm and commitment to the profession and to the team, but may also become a divisive force, undermining a sense of total school community. Nevertheless, the involvement of teachers and community in the school improvement process and the establishment of teams or councils is regarded as essential to developing effective schools and high performing systems (Larson & LaFasto, 1989; Senge, 1990; Wohlstetter and Smyer, 1994).

Although extant research has highlighted the problems confronting teams, few studies have explored how a model of team development may help us understand how teams develop over time and how they function in bringing about school change. Therefore, the purposes of this chapter are: (1) to present the Process Model of School Leadership Teams (SLT) development as a framework to explore the work of one middle school SLT; (2) to explicate more fully the variables in the Process Model through qualitative data from this team; and (3) to examine how the team developed and changed during the four years it received SLT training.

ANALYTICAL FRAMEWORK FOR THE STUDY

Previous studies of site based management (SBM) teams have identified lists of key variables essential for team functioning (Leithwood & Menzies, 1998; Levine & Eubanks, 1992; Maeroff, 1993; Malen, Ogawa, & Kranz, 1989; Smylie, Lazarus, & Brownlee-Conyers, 1996; Weiss & Cambone, 1994). Wohlstetter, Van Kirk, Robertson, and Mohrman (1997) organize many of these variables into a framework, which they suggest provides a lens for examining school based management. Wohlstetter and colleagues (1997) argue that *Organizational Conditions* (e.g., power, knowledge and skills, information, rewards, instructional guidance mecha-

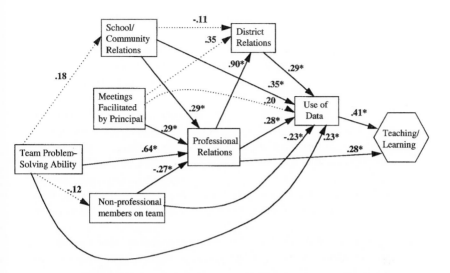

Figure 1. SLT Process Model: Secondary Schools

nism, leadership and resources) interact with *Organizational Learning and Integrating Processes* (e.g., dialogue about purpose, connectedness among participants, systemic thinking, learning from experience, connection to external environment, personal mastery, and involvement of all participants) to lead to *Innovative Practices* (e.g., teaching for understanding, use of technology, educating all students, and integrated services—the outcomes of restructured schools). Their framework begins to capture the multiplicity of factors and the processes of interaction among factors, which in turn can lead to positive outcomes for students. However, these three broad categories do not show the relationship among the many variables in a detailed model that facilitates an understanding of how they may interact to promote or constrain team development.

To explore the relationship among variables that have been identified, we collected survey data from 142 elementary and secondary teams that had completed one year of the two-year California School Leadership Team Professional Development Program (Chrispeels, Castillo, Brown, in press).[1] This data set allowed us to conduct a path analysis as a way of understanding team development and the factors that supported or constrained the team's focus on teaching and learning. For purposes of the study discussed in this chapter, we present in Figure 1 the Process Model based on data from 71 School Leadership Teams at the secondary level (45 middle and 26 high schools) surveyed either in the fall of 1995 or spring of 1996 in 10 of the 12 CSLA regions.[2]

SLT Process Model of Secondary Schools

As shown in Figure 1, seven factors proved significant in predicting the SLT Outcome: a focus on teaching and learning. These factors are:

1. Team Problem Solving—represents team members' perceptions of the team's problem-solving ability (and is the only one of eight team functioning variables—planning, meetings, problem solving, decision making, communication, understanding of self, interpersonal skills, and team dynamics—that remain in the model, see note 1);
2. Meetings facilitated by the principal—indicates whether or not the principal facilitated the work of the team at meetings and in the broader school context;
3. Non-professionals on the team—reflects whether parents and students were members of the SLT team and attended training with the teacher members;
4. Professional Relations—includes the degree of collaboration and communication among team members, the team with the rest of the staff, the team with other school groups, and with the principal;
5. School/Community Relations—reflects the team's efforts to actively solicit parent and student input and the school's initiative to involve them in a comprehensive way in school reform;
6. District Relations—encompasses the amount of support the team perceives from the district and the degree of alignment between district and school goals for improved student learning;
7. Use of Data—consists of items assessing how the team collects and uses student work, other achievement data, and research to guide its decision making.

The dependent variable in the model is labeled Teaching and Learning. It represents the outcomes of the SLT program, and includes items such as the development of a shared vision, setting standards, systems thinking, and creating a learning environment that enables all students to succeed.

As shown in Figure 1, the most powerful total effects on Teaching and Learning, the SLT outcome and dependent variable, are Use of Data, Professional Relations, District Relations, School and Community Relations, and Team Problem Solving. One variable that has the same total and direct effect is Use of Data, by virtue of it being introduced last into the regression process. Not only is Use of Data a strong predictor of the SLT Outcome, it also is responsible for a jump in the R^2 from 0.72 to 0.80, thus accounting for about 8 percent of the variance. A team's use of database decision-making was previously identified as an important element of effective teams (Chrispeels, 1992; Larson & LaFasto, 1989; Maeroff,

1993). Our finding is consistent with these earlier studies, suggests Use of Data is a distinct and significant variable, and demonstrates that it has a direct effect on achievement of the SLT program outcomes.

The variable Professional Relations is important both directly and indirectly. The Process Model confirms previous research (Larson & LaFasto, 1989; Maeroff, 1993; Weiss, et al. 1991) that well-functioning teams are important to implementation success; however, the analysis also indicates that effective teams must interact with the total school community. This finding is consistent with the findings of Kruse and Louis (1997), who identified a critical need for balance between teamwork and a schoolwide perspective. According to the model, three factors support and predict the development of positive professional relations: (1) the team's problem-solving ability, (2) meetings facilitated by the principal, and (3) the team's positive orientation toward soliciting student and parent input and providing ways for involvement. Paradoxically, based on data from this group of secondary schools, the presence of parents and students as team members was shown to have a small but significant negative effect on the team's overall professional relations.

Notable in the Process Model is the primacy of problem solving as a predictor of Professional Relations and Use of Data. We expected that more of the elements of effective teams (e.g., meetings, decision-making, team dynamics, interpersonal relations, and so on) would be significant. At the point when the teams took the Team Assessment survey, however, they already had worked together for one year, had received considerable training in group process skills and had consistently high mean scores on these variables (Chrispeels et al., in press). In other words, most teams had acquired the knowledge and skills needed for effective team functioning (Larson & LaFasto, 1989; Lawler, 1986); therefore, these factors did not have predictive power in the model.

Triangulating the Process Model with a Case Study

Through the path analysis of the Process Model we are able to offer a simplified view of a complex process of team development, which helps to highlight significant and critical elements of the development process and the relationships among them. However, we are aware it does not capture the dynamics of development. Through a case study we are able to present a more complete picture of the intricate details of the process and bring more fully to life the relationships among the variables. The Process Model provides a framework for our qualitative study. Using the Model as the analytical framework, we turn our attention to one School Leadership Team, which has been on a four-year journey to define its role within the school and lead the staff to address issues of teaching and learning.

METHOD

Context of the Study

The larger context for this study is the School Leadership Team Program (SLT), established in 1993 by the California School Leadership Academy (CSLA). The statewide program is administered through 12 regional CSLA centers, which have provided over 300 elementary, middle and high school teams with a minimum of 10 full days of professional development spread over a two-year period. The SLT seminars address both the process of team building and the content of school reform and restructuring. In some regions, and especially in the region of the case study school, the training has continued beyond the first two years to three or four years.

The goal of the SLT program is "to develop the capacity of School Leadership Teams to facilitate actions within their schools that lead to powerful learning for all members of the organization" (California School Leadership Academy, 1995). Unlike other restructuring initiatives, the SLT program does not prescribe a model, but encourages each team to engage in a process of inquiry and investigation of its own conditions and establish outcomes within its school and district context. The SLT program, however, is predicated on a social constructionist perspective of learning (Brooks & Brooks, 1993; Duffy, Lowyck, & Jonassen, 1993). Resource materials given to the teams urge the creation of classroom environments that actively engage students in the learning process (California School Leadership Academy, 1995). The structure of the professional development models uses these theories of learning by providing short sessions of direct instruction on topics such as a powerful teaching, action research, multiple assessments, needs of diverse learners, systems thinking, and team leadership. Then the teams engage in hands-on active learning around these themes, as well as plan how they will share and use what they have learned once they return to their schools.

Study Design

Throughout the three years of our study of the School Leadership Team Program we used a mixed-method design combining quantitative and qualitative data (Creswell, 1994; Morse, 1991). Such mixed-method approaches are compatible and complementary, are likely to surface overlapping and different facets of the phenomenon (Creswell, 1994), and are warranted given the complexity of the issue to be studied (Morse, 1991). Through this case study, our goal was to understand the participants' reactions and beliefs from their point of view, as is typical of studies using an ethnographic perspective. The in-depth case study supports a more fine-grained analysis of the factors that support and/or constrain the ways in which the implementation is undertaken, the ideas and practices are taken up, and the outcomes are achieved. The case study forms a telling case (Mitchell, 1984) that makes visible key factors and processes not previously identified, thus forming a basis for theory development. Through the case study we are able to explore and answer "how and why" questions about the process and consequences of the School Leadership Team Program. The case study design permits addressing organizational links that can be traced over time by drawing on a wide array of documents, focus groups and individual interviews, videos of SLT training sessions as well as survey data (Yin, 1998). These multiple data sources allow exploration of many domains and areas of interest and result in a convergence of data and a triangulation of findings.

Sample

In 1996 after collecting and analyzing the first set of survey data, we selected one middle school team whose team scores on the Team Assessment Survey and the SLT Implementation Continuum indicated that it was typical and representative of other secondary schools in the data set. In addition, we consulted with several regional directors to identify a middle school that was not an outlier in terms of implementation and interest in the SLT program. We wanted a team that would represent an "information-rich case that manifests the phenomenon of interest intensely, but not extremely" (Patton, 1990, p. 182). We contacted the school in the late spring of 1996 to ask if team members were willing to participate in the qualitative study. The principal and team agreed and arrangements were made to conduct the first interviews with the SLT team members in the late summer 1996.

Data Collection

Three sets of interviews were conducted with team members (staff and principal). No parents or students served on this SLT team. In September 1996, eight of nine teacher/staff team members were interviewed. The principal was away from the site the day the interviews were scheduled and he was interviewed at a later date. In February 1998, eight teacher/staff team members as well as the principal were re-interviewed. Seven team members, including the principal, were again interviewed in May 1999. The team members interviewed in 1999 included two who had been with the team from the beginning and four who had been on the team the previous year. The three newest members were not interviewed. Most interviews were conducted face-to-face and were tape recorded with each team member's permission. In 1996, two team members were interviewed by telephone, and in 1999, one interview was conducted by phone. In 1998 and 1999, some of the interviews with team members were conducted in groups of two or three.

In addition, to the interviews, team members also completed the Team Assessment Survey as well as the SLT Implementation Continuum Survey each year that they participated in the SLT seminars. The team was observed during training sessions twice a year from 1996 through 1999 and field notes were recorded of the sessions. We also collected the team's final action research report and test data for 1998-1999. Survey results were reported to the team each year, and in the winter of 1997 after the interview data were analyzed, a meeting was scheduled with the team to share the results.

Data Analysis

To analyze the interview data we used the computer program called Nonnumerical Unstructured Data Indexing Searching and Theory-building (NUD-IST). NUD-IST is a qualitative data analysis system that allows indexing and organization of data into a hierarchical tree structure. We used the factors from the Process Model as the initial cover terms (Spradley, 1980) for the tree structure in NUD-IST and then added new terms as they surfaced through the detailed search and analysis of the interview data. This allowed us to use the Process Model as an analytical framework and at the same time enabled us to surface new variables that were not part of the Process Model. Field notes from observations of the training sessions were also triangulated with major themes surfaced in the interviews. Simple descriptive statistics were completed on the team's surveys and matched student SAT-9 test results for 1998 and 1999 were also analyzed for gains in total reading and total math.

RESULTS

Brookside Middle School

Brookside Middle School (a pseudonym) is situated in an urban/suburban community near a large California city. It is a year-round school with an enrollment of 1,000 7th and 8th grade students—61 percent Hispanic, 21 percent Asian, 7 percent African American, and 10 percent White. In the two years prior to the school's participation in the SLT program, it experienced many changes. As one teacher summarized: "We've gone from being a traditional junior high to being a middle school, have adopted a year-round school calendar with block scheduling and interdisciplinary teaming." The school has also had four new principals in a span of seven years. The district in which the middle school is located decided in 1995 to require all of its schools to participate in the School Leadership Team professional development program. In the first two years, the team consisted of 10 members—seven teachers, a computer specialist, a counselor and the principal. According to team members and the principal, they were both volunteers and principal-selected volunteers who represented a cross-section of the school's two grade levels and various departments. After the second year of training (summer 1997), there was considerable turnover of members as some elected not to con-

Table 1. Four-year Summary of Brookside's School Leadership Team's Activities and Actions Undertaken to Bring about School Improvement

Year	Team Focus/Role	Chain of Activities	Outcomes	Constraints	Supports
1995-96 Aug.-May	Team Development Learners	1. Team of 9 selected or volunteers	1. SLT establishes itself, but concerned about leadership role and changes name to Site Liaison Team	1. Resistance and critique by FAC**	1. SLT Trn'g. helps team learns how to operate as group, lead staff development in benchmarks.
Nov-Jan	Staff Developers	2. Team attends trn'g	2. SLT led staff development	2. Union concerns about SLT	2. District provides trn'g and time, and substitutes for team to attend
Feb-June.		3. Team asked to lead staff in development of school benchmarks by principal	3. Benchmarks established	3. Uncertainty over district's long-term commitment to SLTs	3. Teachers willing to take on new roles
Jan.-June		4. Some team members work to implement technology and after-school tutoring benchmarks	4. Team stops meeting, except for trn'g.	4. Lack of role clarity	
		5. PQR* committee replaces SLT as focus of principal's attention and team stops meeting, except at trn'g.		5. Team concerned not to be seen as "leaders" dominating others	

(continued)

Table 1. (Continued)

Year	Team Focus/Role	Chain of Activities	Outcomes	Constraints	Supports
1996-97	Learners	1. Team continues with trn'g.	1. Norm of having an SLT established as trn'g continues	1. Team unclear about role	1. SLT trn'g provides team with ideas and information even though team unable to implement at this time.
Aug-May		2. Interviews conducted by Univ. research team	2. SLT begins year as dysfunctional group	2. Principal uncertain about role and responsibilities in regard to SLT	2. Research interview process
Nov.	Data analyzers of own functioning	3. Team becomes aware of own dysfunction when data shared with team	3. Interview process becomes data for team to examine itself	3. No team member willing to assume leadership role with team to call meetings and direct work of team	3. County trn'g resources to help mediate conflicts
March	Mediator of school conflicts	4. Team seeks consultant from County Office who leads school in professional culture building activity	4. Team re-energized and staff gains new insights through consultant's work	4. Deep historical divisions among some faculty; 60% of faculty hired in last five years	4. District supports to address issues and assist principal in learning new roles
April	Data collectors	5. Team collects data on student grade distribution	5. Staff works to establish new norms of behavior		
	Staff developers	6. Team revitalized and begins meeting, asked to lead last staff development day	6. Team ends year helping staff revisit Benchmarks		
May-June					

(continued)

Table 1. (Continued)

Year	Team Focus/Role	Chain of Activities	Outcomes	Constraints	Supports
1997-98 Aug/	Learners	1. Team reconstituted with new members, continues trn'g	1. Team is more comfortable with role and responsibilities	1. New members infuse team with energy, but SLT liaison member (appt. by principal) fails to take active leadership role to facilitate team work	1. Team sees district's ongoing commitment to SLTs
Nov-Mar	Data Analyzers	2. Team given training on SAT-9 Results	2. Team gain insights into student literacy needs		2. Trn'g gives team new skills in action research
		3. Team learns how to engage in action research	3. Team's work more focused as result of action research trn'g	2. Principal minimally engaged with team and frequently leaves trn'g early	3. New team members begin to take leadership
Mar-April	Staff developers	4. Team develops with the staff organization chart to clarify roles and responsibilities	4. Roles and relationships more formalized through governance chart	3. FAC/SLT tensions still under surface	4. Districtwide SLT/FAC tensions ease
April-May	Action researchers	5. Team identifies critical instructional needs and develops plan for addressing need through action research	5. Teachers gain confidence as teacher leaders		
		6. Team selects new liaison to facilitate their work			

(continued)

49

Table 1. (Continued)

Year	Team Focus/Role	Chain of Activities	Outcomes	Constraints	Supports
1998-99	Learners	1. Team continues trn'g but with new principal	1. Team/school action plan to improve literacy skills implemented	1. New principal which required team and principal to work through roles and relationships	1. Team selects its own liaison who assumes facilitator role
Sept-Dec	Action researchers and implementers	2. Team finalizes action plan and begins implementation	2. Data collection shows improvement in literacy	2. Time to accomplish all the team wants to do	2. Team liaison regularly reports to staff about work of the SLT and keeps team informed about district issues
Feb-Mar	Staff developers	3. Team leads staff in preparation for SAT-9 test, literacy strategies	4. Team energized to continue data collection and find ways to improve literacy program for 1999–2000	3. Pressure for improved student outcomes on state test and uncertainty test will measure growth	3. New principal supports work of team and encourages their leadership
April-June	Action researchers	4. Team collects data from student, parents, staff on implementation of action research	5. Team/total staff relations improved as staff understands team's work & role		4. New principal works with FAC to establish its role *vis a vis* the SLT
May	Staff developers/ communicators	5. Team helps staff SIP plan and high school's student learning expectations	6. SLT institutionalized		5. Team perceives trn'g to be focused and helpful
		6. Team presents results to staff and shares work at final SLT session attended by board members.	7. Team eager to expand its data collection from parents and students		

Notes: *PQR–Program Quality Review. All schools in California that receive State School Improvement (SIP) Funding are required to evaluate, through self-study and an external review process, their SIP Plan and Actions. At Brookside this task was given to another committee, whereas at many of the district's middle schools the task was assigned to the SLT.

**FAC–Faculty Advisory Committee, established at each school by District Contract, members are elected from each department by faculty.

tinue and others transferred to a new school that was opening in the district. Remembering previous criticism by the staff of his role in selecting the members of the first SLT, the principal invited anyone interested to volunteer to serve. Five new members joined the team. In the summer of 1998, a new principal was hired. He chose three new team members to replace a counselor and bilingual teacher who had recently left, and added his new assistant principal. In May 1999 when the last interviews were conducted, the team consisted of two members who had served from the beginning, four who had been on the team two years, and three who had served one year, and the new principal.

To understand how this team established itself within the school and the developmental path it took, we examined a cycle of activities over four years. Table 1 presents the roles the team assumed, major activities of the team, the outcomes of their activities and factors that supported or constrained their work. The findings presented in Table 1 will be discussed in relation to the framework provided by the SLT Process Model as well as themes that emerged from the case study data, but not found in the model. The following seven themes are addressed: (1) how the SLT established its role and identity; (2) the role of the principal in facilitating the work of the team; (3) professional relations of the SLT to staff; (4) SLT relations with parents and students; (5) SLT relations with the district; (6) the team's use of data; and (7) the team's focus on teaching and learning.

How the SLT Established Its Role and Identity

An important finding revealed in the interview data but not reflected in the Process Model is the variety of roles that the team assumed over the four years. These roles are summarized in the second column of Table 1 and illuminated in the third column. One of the roles the team assumed from the beginning and maintained throughout the four years was that of learners. The SLT training enabled them to learn about the content of school reform issues and the process of how to function as a team. Through videos and readings, initial training sessions introduced the team to the concepts of powerful teaching and learning, the SLT Outcome. In addition, teams engaged in activities to learn group process skills such as establishing norms for the group, brainstorming techniques, and decision-making skills (CSLA Training materials, 1995-1997). Other major topics introduced to the teams during the four years were action research, collecting and analyzing student achievement data, using multiple measures and assessment strategies, and aligning curriculum and assessment. As these topics were explored, this led the team to a second major role: staff developers.

A task assigned to each team in the first year was to guide their staff in the development of school level learning goals that would be in alignment with the district's recently adopted goals. This task pushed the Brookside team to become staff developers. The team members reported that their first introduction of benchmarks to the staff was "horrible." "Total, total resistance from people" (team interviews, 1996). However, the team reported that it regrouped for the next two staff development sessions and drew on skills they were learning in the training. "We pretty much agonized how we were going to present this stuff without getting resistance.... We worked very, very hard to present and have everyone get involved. And I think everybody did."

In the second year, three new roles emerged for this team: (1) analyzers of data presented to them; (2) mediators of conflicts; and (3) collectors of data. At the beginning of the second year, the research team spent a day in the school interviewing team members. Inadvertently, this process allowed the team to reflect on their work and to surface awareness, individually and collectively, that it had become inactive, since its intense staff development work five months earlier when the benchmarks were completed. After the interviews a report was made to the team on the findings. This prompted the team to ask a consultant to work with the staff to address issues of roles and responsibilities and professional norms for the school. Helping the school to surface and begin to address some deep-seated conflicts established a new role for the team as mediators of conflicts. Additionally, through the SLT training, the role of data collectors surfaced when the team collected data on the distribution of grades in their school, especially the distribution of students with failing grades. The team, rejuvenated sufficiently by these activities, was asked by the principal to lead the final staff development day.

In the third year, an important new role—action researchers—emerged as the team learned how to conduct action research. By the end of the year, the team identified needs, developed a plan of action to improve literacy skills, and determined the measures it would use to assess its plan. In the fourth year of SLT training, the team continued with its action research role, becoming implementers of the innovations as well as researchers of their impact. Team members expanded their staff development work by conducting sessions for the entire staff in test preparation, literacy strategies, and helping the staff align its School Improvement Plan with the nearby high school's student learning standards and expectations. The data also indicate that the team assumed the role of communicators. Now they are a regular part of faculty agendas to report on their findings or share what they currently are learning at the SLT seminars.

One role that the team members initially resisted was that of being leaders. In the first interviews, almost all team members reported that they had changed their name from School Leadership Team to Site Liaison Team. As one member expressed it, "We wanted only to be the go-between so that we could be inclusive to all staff members, so we [wouldn't] seem like big shots making decisions, because that's what everybody has trouble with." By the second time the team members were interviewed, they seemed to be more comfortable with the label "leadership team." In the third round of interviews, team members recognized that being leaders did not mean they were making all the decisions, but rather taking responsibility for key aspects of the school's work, such as collecting data or helping the staff prepare students for the state test.

Role of the Principal in Facilitating the Work of the Team

When new structures are implemented in schools (or any organization), defining roles and relationships has been identified as key to success (Larson & LaFasto, 1989; Wohlstetter, Van Kirk, Robertson, Mohrman, 1997). As the findings presented above indicate, Brookside's SLT assumed a variety of roles, which required it also to redefine relationships with others. One of the more salient relationships that emerges from the data is that of the team with the principal. The Process Model indicates that the principal's facilitation of the team's work is a significant predictor of positive professional relations. The qualitative data suggest the relationship of the principal and team is a complex one. For Brookside, principal-staff relations evolved over the course of the four years. At the end of the first year, the mean score on the Implementation Continuum Survey, the item asking about Principal/SLT relationships, was 2.78 on a 5-point scale, whereas the mean score for this item among other teams in this region was 4.25. The team indicated that the principal came to the SLT training sessions, but they did not feel that the principal and the team had a good working relationship. As one member said: "He never participated in any of the planning meetings for staff development ... [but] he does come to the training sessions with us so ... is he a member of the team or isn't he?" Another member reported that he "took over" at the training sessions and members would "just go with whatever he is saying."

According to initial interview data, the major point of contention was lack of direction. Initially the team perceived a clear mandate from the principal for the benchmark task. However, once that task was completed, the team did not know what to do and received no guidance from the principal. The principal had turned his attention to the Program Quality Review, which he had assigned to another group. One team member captured the dilemma for the team and principal this way: "I don't think (the principal) wants to be considered the prime mover of the group. I think he wants to be aware, be a participant, but I think he would be much happier if somebody would take the leadership role. But it isn't in the nature of that group to have a leader" (Interview, 1997).

After the intervention with the consultant, team-principal relationships improved. The end-of-year survey data in 1997 and 1998 indicated that the team had established a good working relationship with the principal (mean scores 3.29 and 4.25 respectively). Observations of the SLT in spring training sessions in 1998 indicated that team members were taking on leadership and directing the work of the team. They even reported that they selected the member who would be the liaison to the district, rather than leaving that decision to the principal. In the summer of 1998 a new principal was appointed. According to team members, if the previous principal had exercised a laissez-faire approach to leadership, this one was a "top down" and "hands-on" principal. As the principal himself admitted, "I pride myself in being very clear in terms of what my expec-

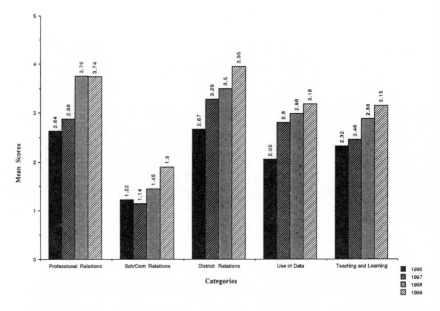

Figure 2.   Brookside Middle School's Implementation Continuum
Survey Mean Scores, by Category, from Spring 1996 to Spring 1999.

tations are and letting the staff know I am the instructional leader" (Interview, 1999). According to team members, this new leadership style led to a somewhat rocky start with a team of teachers who were now comfortable in exercising leadership. However, the team reported that the principal and the team soon developed a very positive relationship, substantiated by the Spring 1999 Continuum mean score of 4.50. Team members feel the new principal has been a "real active participant on the SLT," learning what the SLT is all about," and is "looking to the group for guidance."

Professional Relations

All schools in this district were mandated to select a School Leadership Team that would participate in the SLT training. The district's overarching goal was to improve student achievement. Within this broad directive, each team needed to negotiate its role and build relationships with the entire staff and other groups within the school. As Figure 2 illustrates, over time the SLT perceived they had made progress, with the mean score for professional relations increasing from 2.64 and 2.88 in the first two years to 3.76 and 3.74 in the third and fourth years (a significant difference at $p = .05$).

As mentioned above, the team was reluctant from the start to seem like "big shots." According to team members, this reluctance to be designated leaders in their school community was caused, in part, by personality conflicts permeating the school. As one member said, the school has "put on the brakes" and there is a lot of tension on the campus, causing some staff members to "go beyond the normal polite rules of adult behavior." The SLT, as mentioned above, initiated an intervention with an outside consultant, one of the major team activities in the second year. This action represented an attempt to break through these tensions and develop norms of collaboration. One team member described the day as a "revival." Two years later, team members still describe it as a turning point for the school. As one member reported, "We had to backup and address fundamental issues of relationships, how we would behave at a staff meeting, rules for staff behavior ... norms for the whole school, before we could begin action research" (Interview, 1999). By the 1998-99 school year, however, the team willingly assumed a leadership role and exhibited a clear identity as an action group within the school structure. As one member summarized the team's development in relation to the whole staff, "Last year we waited to be told what to do. This year, none of us waited. We just figured out what it was we were supposed to do [and] assigned tasks.... It just took off from there. I think last year we didn't feel empowered as much ... because we were still concerned somewhat about what the school felt about the SLT" (Interview, 1999).

Both survey and interview data in 1997 indicated a lack of communication also existed between the SLT and other school groups (mean score 2.22 on a 5-point scale). When asked, "How does the SLT relate to other groups at this school?" one SLT member replied, "Like Faculty Advisory Committee (FAC) or the School Site Council? Zero. None. We are just ... [in] this little box and we don't go outside that and we have not been asked." The only connections there are between groups occur when a team member is on two or more committees—and even then there seemed to be little evidence of communication between the groups. Although in the 1998 interviews it was clear that tensions still existed between the FAC and SLT, members reported a somewhat clearer understanding of the roles of the two groups. "The FAC is contractual and so they are to be consulted and involved in discussion and curricular issues and other kinds of issues.... The SLT, as I see it, is a more visionary group where we are thinking, what we would like to become, and how we can get there.... It is very rare to have the opportunity for teachers to sit down and talk and reflect" (Interview, 1998).

One SLT activity that proved pivotal to the team in both defining its role and establishing its position and relationship with other groups in the school was the development of a governance map or organizational chart. The team struggled with this activity for several months. The final chart was complex and criss-crossed with communication lines, but all the major groups were reflected on the chart and links had been identified. When the new principal arrived, he queried one of the team members saying; "This is a draft, isn't it?" She replied,

"Oh no, that took months to produce!" She quickly pressed him not to focus too much on what was on the paper, but to recognize that the discussion that produced the chart was a significant learning experience for the team and staff.

By spring 1999, roles and relationships seemed to have been clarified even more. The SLT team reported, "We have more of an identity now." As indicated in column two and three of Table 1, the team sees its role as researchers, staff developers, communicators, and mediators. The principal and team members feel the staff accepts these roles. One team member reported that the "Faculty Advisory Committee is now less of a complaint group, and is focusing on curricular issues and scheduling. I think as their focus changes they will be more open to seeing data [from the SLT]." The principal also stated, "The SLT is the focal group now and the FAC is okay with that because they are doing what they want to do." Even though tensions between groups seemed to have eased, there is little evidence of collaboration between groups (mean score on the Implementation in 1999 was 2.50 on a 5-point scale). There was overlapping membership, with SLT members reporting that they make more connections now between their work and the work of other groups, and the principal was active on all groups. As one team member reported, "We have not done any joint planning with other groups. We're not ready for that yet. But we could bring data to groups. That would be accepted."

SLT Relations with the Parent, Community and Students

The SLT at Brookside did not include parents or students on the School Leadership Team, and in the initial SLT Implementation Continuum members of the team rated themselves at the lowest level on this variable (1.22). This area of relationships has remained persistently low throughout the four years of participation in SLT. However, in 1999, there was a shift in this component. As can be seen in Table 1, in the last year under *Chain of Activities* column, the team collected data from parents and students as well as faculty. One of the tasks of the SLT in 1999 as part of the team's action research project was to identify at least three students in each category of high, medium and low reading achievement and interview them and their parents. Based on observations of the team, their action research report, and interviews, the team was very enthusiastic about what it had learned from students and parents in regard to reading. For example, the team was surprised to learn that neither students nor teachers felt that the sustained silent reading program at the end of the day was effective. Similarly, the team learned that students who were struggling readers found it helpful to be read aloud to, but the strong readers found it *boring*. As one member said, the data from students made him think about his own teaching. "Maybe I think I'm a pretty good teacher, but the kids aren't getting anything out of that strategy. Maybe I need to rethink about how I am teaching.... [The data] give you a chance to have discussions with other teachers and say, 'What do you do?... Your students seem to be doing better'" (Interview, 1999).

After a presentation at an SLT training on how to use computers to collect survey data from parents and students, the school invested in the program. They felt valuable data had been gathered from parents, students, and teachers in regard to the reading program, and they wanted ways to more easily solicit their input next year. Furthermore, the team saw students become more motivated when they were involved in the computer tracking of their own progress in reading with the Accelerated Reading Program.

From observing their feeder high school with its many student team members, the team was not convinced that adding students to the team would be beneficial. The principal agreed, but thought it could be helpful to include parents. The principal said, "We have some very dynamic parents here at the site that would flourish and help us in our endeavor to increase parent involvement." One of the teacher team members concurred, but thought it would be hard to get parents to commit to six days of training. Soliciting parent and student voices had begun and the team appeared motivated to expand their input in the coming year.

Parents and students were involved at Brookside through its recently reconstituted Parent-Teacher-Student Association, through the School Site Council and the Bilingual Advisory Council. All of these groups were placed on the SLTs organizational chart, and team members reported that SLT members were involved with each group through overlapping memberships. However, no evidence surfaced that indicated that parent and student participation on these committees influenced the SLT in its work.

Relations of the SLT to the District

As shown in Table 1, the Constraints and Supports Columns, the team perceived the district both as a constraint and a support. The team members expressed appreciation for the training that was being provided and the time to learn and reflect about issues of teaching and learning. In the interviews conducted in 1997, however, one team member stated, "There is a lot of resistance. Everybody [thinks], well, what's the point? Is there a hidden agenda from the district for this team?" The team itself became suspicious when it felt the district had taken a U-turn by requesting that the teams work on the Program Quality Review (middle and junior high schools) or the high school accreditation process. The Brookside team saw this request as district intervention and interference, especially since at their school the task was assigned to another group by the principal. These concerns are reflected in the SLT Implementation Continuum Survey with a mean score of 2.67 on the District Relations variable. However, by 1999, the mean score had risen to 3.95 (a significant difference at $p = .05$). This score means that the team perceived that "the district liaison and the SLT team work together to resolve issues that may impede the continuous improvement process," and that the "SLT's action plan and the district's goals both focus on improving student learning and they are beginning to collaborate to identify needed strategies and resources" (Response from SLT Continuum). This change in perception by the team triangulates with the process model, which indicates that strong professional relations is a predictor of positive relations with the district. In other words, as the team developed confidence in their roles and relationships within the school, it perceived its relationship with the district also more positively. By 1999, the team recognized that the district was not withdrawing its support and that they were learning useful skills in the ongoing training. The principal also perceived that there was close alignment between the SLT's work and district goals.

The Team's Use of Data to Guide Improvement

As indicated in the SLT Process Model, Use of Data is the strongest predictor that the team will be focused on teaching and learning, the SLT training outcome. In 1996, after one year of training, the team's mean score on Use of Data was 2.05. Most members felt that the team was only at the very beginning stages of working with student assessment data, assessing powerful learning, evaluating student work, or working from a research and data base. The qualitative data from interviews conducted in 1997 confirm this assessment. For example, one of the school's first goals was to reduce the number of Ds and Fs students received. But, as an SLT member stated, "without corroborating evidence of real learning, the teacher is left in the dark about the effectiveness of teaching methods and curriculum." This teacher was encouraging his department to administer pre- and post-tests and even track students after they left the school to see if real learning had taken place. Team members indicated that although Brookside Middle had developed benchmarks, it had not implemented a systematic process for collecting data to monitor achievement of the benchmarks.

Use of Data appears in the *Chain of Activities* column of Table 1 toward the end of the third year of training. At a mid-point in the 1997-1998 training, the teams were given information on how to interpret results from the new statewide testing system, and they were introduced to the concepts of action research. These activities served as the impetus for the team to identify reading as an area of need; but according to the team, their research was at a beginning level. The team reported that it spent considerable time in developing its governance chart, one of the SLT activities, which delayed the start of their action research project. However, the team felt the investment in time to clarify schoolwide communication and relationship patterns was essential to the school's ability to move forward. This assessment of the need to get buy-in from others seems warranted by the fact that the team began the fourth year with its action research plan in place. The fourth year activities illustrated that the team collected and used data to improve literacy skills. These data, including student achievement results of their intervention, were shared with the entire staff at the end of the year. Their work seemed to have engendered much enthusiasm among the team and even in the staff. Team members reported that the data had been "presented in a nonthreatening way." As one said, "The data collection focused the work of the SLT this year." Another replied, "We know where the kids are (in terms of achievement), not just our impression." And a third concluded, "We are trying to make our school a school that makes research-based decisions as often as possible." Although the team continued its staff development role in the fourth year, their role as researchers became prominent. Even their staff development work was often informed by and designed to support their literacy research project.

Powerful Learning for All

The ultimate objective of the SLT program is to improve student learning. As the Chain of Activities and Outcome Columns of Table 1 show, Brookside Middle School's SLT appeared to begin with an important activity needed to achieve this goal. They led the staff in developing the benchmarks for student learning. However, as the data presented above illustrate, the team's role and function was not yet clearly delineated and the team faltered. The second year of SLT seminars continued to expand team member skills with the team taking on a new role of mediator with the staff, but there is little attention to student learning. When team members were asked in 1997 about the role of the SLT in promoting powerful learning at the school, they reported that on an individual basis some were changing their philosophies of teaching and learning. The interview data confirm the survey data as shown in Figure 2, Teaching and Learning results. The mean score for first two years showed that discussions of teaching and learning remained only at the team level. In 1997 individual team members offered ideas for how the SLT could be involved in improving teaching and learning throughout the school, but the ideas had not yet been acted upon. For example, one team member expressed a desire for the SLT to promote better teaching strategies by providing time for teachers to "see some really good teaching going on in a non-threatening way."

Figure 2 shows there was growth in this variable over the next two years. The team survey indicated a shift from the team to schoolwide discussions in three components of the powerful teaching and learning variable (1) a shared vision for powerful teaching and learning, (2) philosophies of learning, and (3) a learning environment that supports diversity. Also by the fourth year, action research was perceived as being implemented and recognized as a tool for improving teaching and learning.

Did the work of the team make any difference for students? By the fourth year, the team reported reading gains for the students who participated in the Accelerated Reading Program: their action research intervention. The team learned that there was a direct correlation between the time spent (or number of books read) and the achievement gains of the students. For example, students who earned 10 or more points for their reading made modest gains moving from the 42nd percentile to the 45th, whereas students who earned more than a 100 points moved to the 51st percentile. Schoolwide, the 1999 SAT-9 Total Reading scores also showed overall gains of 5 percentile points when results were reported for matched scores. Although the team was happy with this growth, as they reported to their fellow staff members, "We're on the right track but we still have a way to go." They reminded the staff that 25 percent of their English as a Second Language students were reading at a 4th grade level and had reading skills too low to be successful in higher grades.

DISCUSSION

Through the triangulation of the qualitative (interviews and team documents) and quantitative data (surveys), some aspects of the Process Model (Figure 1) are confirmed, some new dimensions are identified, and some elements remain to be fully validated. In this section, we bring together the findings to highlight the areas of congruence and divergence and explore how they help to inform our understanding of team development and functioning.

The Importance of Establishing the Roles and Identity of the SLT

The literature on teams has identified that teams vary in their nature and the work that they may be asked to do (Larson & LaFasto, 1989; Mohrman, Cohen, & Mohrman, 1995). For example, Larson and LaFasto (1989) describe three broad functions teams can fulfill: (1) problem-resolution, (2) creative, and (3) tactical. The general charge to the School Leadership Teams—"to create a powerful learning community for all"—implies both a problem-resolution and creative function. The roles that SLTs might play, however, are not explicitly discussed in any of the training materials; thus each team must identify and define its role, function and responsibilities. In their studies of team-based organizations, Mohrman and colleagues (1995) found that the failure to clarify the purpose and roles of teams established within organizations is a common problem. Although roles are implicit in aspects of the Process Model, it was only through the interviews of Brookside's SLT members that the issue of team roles surfaced as a central component of team development. From Table 1 it is clear that the Brookside Leadership Team assumed a variety of roles over the four years. This study illustrates well that an active leadership team will assume several roles and that these roles will evolve over time as the team gains experience and confidence and receives training. The interview findings also suggest that roles teams are able to assume are shaped by multiple factors including training, time, designated or mandated tasks, district directives, the cultural and historical context of the team, and existing or developing expertise among team members.

In the case of the Brookside SLT, the interview data indicate that the roles assumed by the team and summarized in Table 1, increased over time and were shaped by these multiple factors. A staff development role was one of the first roles the team assumed. This in part was a result of a directive from the district, communicated through the principal, for each school to develop benchmarks in alignment with district goals. In addition, the team received training from the SLT seminars that they felt enabled them to lead their staff in this task. The SLT training influenced the team to assume two other roles, that of mediators and researchers. The group process and conflict resolution skills taught at the seminars encouraged the team to take on the role of mediator with the staff and between the staff and the principal. This role was initially envisioned neither by the SLT program nor by the team, but emerged as the team tried to address fundamental issues that the members perceived were blocking progress in their school. In the third year of training, when the concepts of action research were introduced, the team began to define a new role for itself. By the end of the fourth year, the role of researchers was becoming institutionalized and was providing an important "leadership" niche for the team in relation to other school groups. Although the ultimate goal of the SLT program (and of many programs that establish school leadership teams) is to improve student performance, student outcomes perhaps should not be the only criterion that is used to assess team effectiveness. Findings from this study suggest that teams are likely to play a variety of roles, which help the school, and that multiple measures may be needed to assess team effectiveness.

The Principal and the Team: Challenges of Shared Leadership

Similar to other studies, both the Process Model and the case study data indicate that the principal plays a pivotal role in team effectiveness. The Process Model indicates that principal facilitation of team meetings is a predictor of positive professional relations, which in turn is central to team goal accomplishment. The Brookside case study illuminates the meaning of this relationship. Brookside's principal was not initially involved in the team's staff development activities, but the team felt it had clear direction from the principal for its task. When the task was over, however, the team faltered for over a year because of lack of facilitation of its work by the principal and the uncertainty team members felt about asserting leadership themselves. Similarly, Wohlstetter, Van Kirk, Robertson and Mohrman's (1997) study of effective restructuring schools showed that principals were more likely to exhibit a facilitative leadership style. By contrast, in struggling schools principals were either "unwilling to share power... [and] suffocated the reform process" or "too laissez faire ... [and] failed to provide any meaningful direction for the school" (p. 37). Creighton (1997) also found that when a team does not accept leadership roles, it reverts to the principal.

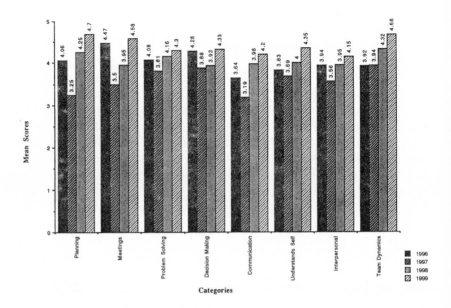

Figure 3. Brookside Middle School's Team Assessment Survey
Mean Scores, by Category, from Spring 1996 to Spring 1999

The initiation of leadership teams requires principals to shift from hierarchical to heterarchical approaches to leadership, which is not easy and demands both unlearning and new learning (Benson, 1998; Chrispeels, Strait, & Brown, 1999). Mohrman et al. (1995) also found that organizations transitioning to teams in the private sector underestimated the amount of help that "team members and managers in team settings will require to learn new behaviors. This is particularly likely in highly specialized knowledge work because of the mistaken belief that people who are highly educated have the basic skills to work effectively in team settings" (p. 337). At Brookside both principal and team needed to learn how to lead under these new conditions as well as unlearn previous patterns of behavior and interaction. The SLT training created disequilibrium for both principal and teacher team members but did not give them the tools to overcome traditional perceptions and definitions of leadership. This case study, however, shows that when the team, principal, and entire staff were given sufficient and direct outside assistance to work through relationship difficulties, the school and its team were able to move forward. Wohlstetter and colleagues (1997) also observed that successful SBM schools turned to outside resources to facilitate their efforts.

Another dimension of leadership that the case study revealed as significant was internal team leadership. The SLT training provided team members with knowledge and experience to assume a variety of team roles such as facilitator, recorder, reporter, and process observer. These roles were (1) assumed during training sessions, (2) appreciated by the team members as facilitative of its discussions and work, and (3) were reflected in the relatively high mean scores on the Team Assessment Survey (Figure 3). However, these roles did not address the need for internal team leadership, especially when the principal was not playing a facilitating role. As a result of the culture of equity among teachers in schools (Lortie, 1975), it took Brookside's team time and considerable trial and error learning before it was willing to designate one of its own as *leader*. By the end of the third year, however, the team realized it needed to select a member who would play a more active internal leadership role serving as the liaison between the district and the team, calling team meetings, and ensuring that SLT information was disseminated to the staff.

The Slow Process of Building Professional Relations

As others have shown (Lieberman, 1988; Lortie, 1975; Smylie, 1992) teachers place value on the social-emotional aspects of leadership and are reluctant to take on leadership roles that they perceive might negatively affect relationships with colleagues. Even as Brookside's team became more comfortable with taking leadership and felt empowered to do so by the principal, they continually referenced concern for ensuring support from the rest of the staff as being of paramount importance. The case study data confirmed the central role of Professional Relations in the Process Model in shaping the team's work and effectiveness. The tangled web of relationships portrayed in their organizational/governance chart, which the team created, is indicative of the challenge this team experienced in establishing productive professional relationships with the principal, with other committees and the staff as a whole. Wohlstetter and colleagues (1997) found a similar pattern in their sample of struggling schools, with one school spending "almost a year developing a policy manual that specified who had power and under what conditions" (p. 6).

The SLT at Brookside entered an organization with existing committees, such as the School Improvement Council and the Bilingual Advisory Committee established through state and federal mandates. There were 7th grade interdisciplinary teams and departments, which cut across both 7th and 8th grades, as well as a Faculty Advisory Committee, which derived its authority from the teachers' contract. As revealed in the case study, it has taken the team three years to gain confidence in the roles it has now established for itself vis-à-vis these existing structures. Fortunately by the end of the third year, the team had become sufficiently institutionalized and members self-confident enough to enable the team to quickly establish an effective working relationship with the new principal.

The challenge of integrating the work of the School Leadership Team with that of other school committees is not a problem confined to schools, but was also found in other team-based organizations (Mohrman et al., 1995). Mohrman and colleagues (1995) found that organizations used a variety of mechanisms including over-lapping members, liaison roles, management teams, cross-teams, and improvement teams as ways of insuring coordination and integration of work needed to achieve goals (p. 120). As the SLT training progressed, the SLT trainers became more aware of this need to clarify professional relations and strengthen the link among various committees. This was the impetus behind asking the teams to create the organizational charts. As the Brookside team members gained confidence in their knowledge and skills, they more productively used the over-lapping memberships as a means of sharing SLT work with others and using their knowledge to guide the efforts of these committees, but as they admit joint planning is not yet a reality.

Since the rise of the large consolidated secondary school, schools have not been reorganized or time schedules altered in ways that would significantly promote teamwork, let alone provide time for cross-team coordination (Darling-Hammond, 1997). Teachers still spend the majority of their school day isolated in their classrooms with students. Thus, a major barrier to joint planning is time. The Brookside leadership team, similar to other SLTs, invests considerable time in attending the training and then meeting at the site to carry out various tasks it sets for itself. In addition, team members also serve on other school committees that take their time and energy, but do not necessarily maximize the impact of these overlaps. Yet the release time granted for the team to receive training and to plan has engendered jealousy among non-members and complicated the building of professional relations among teams. Brookside's SLT has enhanced professional relations with other groups and the faculty by providing staff development (e.g., preparing staff and students for state testing or providing colleagues with strategies for improving student literacy skills) and collecting data needed by other committees. Without more coordinated professional efforts, however, it seems unlikely that any school such as Brookside with its high-need students can achieve substantial learning gains.

SLT's Engagement with Students and Parents in the Change Process

The Process Model surfaced a paradoxical relationship in regard to parents and students, showing both positive and negative correlations with the team. This paradoxical finding is confirmed in a study by Jenni (1993) who also found that teachers were reluctant to actively participate "by responding to ideas on the table or introducing ideas of their own" when parents were present (p. 17). Leithwood and Menzies (1998) similarly found that developing effective roles and responsibilities for parents was a common problem faced by School Based Management committees. Interview data from the Brookside team, however, substantiates the benefits to the team when it solicited parent and student input about student learning. The information gleaned from parents and students (as well as other faculty) was perceived as valuable data for the team to use in planning how to better meet student needs.

Brookside did not have parents or students on its team; therefore the negative correlation surfaced in the Process Model, which indicated that the involvement of parents and students as team members was associated with lower professional relations scores could not be explored or validated. Although team members reported that they were eager to collect more data from parents and students, they did not want students on the team and were uncertain that parents would be interested or have the time to participate. Given research findings supporting the importance of parent involvement to children's school success (Comer, 1980; Dornbusch & Ritter, 1988; Epstein, 1991; Liontos, 1992), it is important for future studies to identify ways in which parents, students and teachers can best collaborate to improve student learning. At the same time, findings from this study suggest that schools must maintain a positive sense of professionalism among teachers who are just beginning to find their voice in the school reform process.

District and SLT Relations: A Two-Way Street

The adoption of SBM by districts has frequently resulted in the delegation of authority from the central office to the site in areas such as personnel, budget, curriculum, and instruction (Wohlstetter et al., 1997). The degree of the transfer of power of course varies from district to district as does the schools' responses to this shift. The School Leadership Team program in the case study district is similar to some SBM initiatives in that all schools in the district were mandated to participate. It differs from SBM initiatives in that training for the teams was undertaken to focus the school on issues of teaching and learning. The teams were not necessarily to take on some of the management decisions typical of SBM and which other research has shown often derails the reform efforts of SBM committees (Malen, Ogawa, & Kranz, 1989; Smylie, Lazarus, & Brownlee-Conyers, 1996; Wohlstetter et al., 1997). However, from our data, it is uncertain if the district has given sufficient authority and resources to the SLT to be instructional leaders in their school. In the fourth year, the team members were drawing on their own expertise, providing their colleagues with information and strategies on how to improve students' reading skills.

The Process Model reveals an interesting relationship between the districts and the SLTs that are most focused on teaching and learning. The Model suggests that strong professional relations within the team and school are a significant predictor of positive district relations. The case study data help to illuminate how the relationship works. Initially the team was quite skeptical of the district's support for the SLT program, assuming that "this too will pass." As the program persisted a second, third and then fourth year, the SLT team members gained greater confidence in the district's commitment to the SLT. Furthermore as the team developed skills and the knowledge needed to carry out its tasks, members expressed increase confidence in its ability to address issues of teaching and learning—the district goal. As the skepticism diminished, the team members reported greater alignment between the district and school goals. Over the four years, the team also began to perceive the training being provided to the SLT as a support rather than a district mandate. The team realized how important the team's liaison to the district was in the third year, when the principal-appointed liaison neither regularly attended the district SLT meetings nor reported back to the team. By selecting its own liaison in the fourth year, the team acknowledged that it needed a regular presence at the district meetings. The team felt both pressure and support from the district as it carried out its work to improve student learning (Fullan, 1993).

The Power and Empowering Process of Using Data

The Process Model indicates that Use of Data is the most powerful predictor of the SLT teams' focus on teaching and learning. Mohrman (1994), using Lawler's (1986) High-Involvement Management model, argues that "getting people involved in the success of their organization depends upon increasing their ability to influence their jobs and work settings, to participate in identifying and solving problems in the organization" (p. 30). Larson and LaFasto (1989) describe successful teams as those that make fact-driven judgments because they have ready access to data. Collecting, analyzing and then using data about student achievement is central to the improvement process (Chrispeels, 1992). Without knowledge of current student work and performance and information about approaches that will be effective in improving student learning, the team cannot begin to impact teaching and learning. Wohlstetter, Van Kirk, Robertson, and Mohrman (1997) also found that "actively restructuring schools collected lots of information and used it to meet school priorities for improving teaching and learning" in contrast to struggling schools, which did not gather or use data systematically (p. 20).

The case study confirms the Process Model and shows how the team came to understand the power of data. The first two times the team used data it was data that had been collected by others (e.g., the interview data, which alerted the team to its inactivity; and state test data which identify reading as a need area). In the fourth year, the team collected its own data from parents, students, and other faculty in the form of interviews. Disaggregating the reading achievement data by gender and by number of points earned was a powerful experience for the team and gave them new insights about student learning. The shift from looking at data collected by others to analyzing and using data it had collected led to a shift in the team's attitude about data. The data they collected they now owned and saw it as valid and useful. In addition, they were excited to collect more data so that they could better understand how students were learning. They also recognized that students' perspectives were an untapped source of important information.

It is not clear from the case study if the team could have been introduced to data collection earlier in the development cycle and how this would have impacted their work. In interviews conducted in 1999, team members acknowledged that their improvement work had gone slowly, but they felt that engendering staff buy-in, addressing norms of collaboration, and building trust among staff members had to occur first. Paradoxically, the case data showed that collecting data can engender staff buy-in, address collaboration and build trust. The slow progress toward improvement in student learning is substantiated in other studies which indicate that significant changes often require four to five years of effort (Fullan, 1993). However, in this case study, the team's data show that the target of improved student achievement is achievable.

CONCLUSION

The vocabulary of reform for schools in the 1980s and 1990s uses phrases like *restructuring, school-based management, enhanced roles of teachers in decision-making,* and *collaborative work culture* (Fullan, 1991), but how these phrases are enacted in the day to day life of schools remains to be fully documented. This chapter, through combining both qualitative and quantitative approaches to studying the phenomena of school leadership team development and how teams impact their schools contributes to our understanding of how these constructs are translated into action by teachers and administrators. The quantitative data helps to provide the big picture of team development, whereas the case study data provides a fine-grained portrait of the process and gives meaning to the variables by providing thick descriptions of the actual work of a team. The longitudinal study provides insights into how a team develops and changes over time as it learns to assume new roles and establishes new relationships within an existing school culture. From this study, six salient and related points emerge that expand our understanding of school leadership teams.

First, the Process Model provides a useful analytical framework for understanding team development. It suggests important issues and relationships to which teams must attend in order to be effective and goal oriented. Elmore (1995) argues that to address the core technology of schools, discussion must begin with the best practices of teaching and learning and work backward from there to establish the structures needed to achieve these practices. The Process Model provides the opportunity to "work our way backwards" from the SLT goal of improved student outcomes to the processes and relationships which predict a team will achieve the goal. The Model indicates that a key role for the team, if it is to create a powerful teaching and learning environment, is to become knowledgeable and competent in the use of research and student data. Furthermore, our data indicate that schools may require several years (four in the case study) for a team and the staff to become skilled in using data and research to drive improvement. Tracing further back in the model we can see that adult/professional relationship issues may need to be addressed at the same time or before the team can fully focus its attention on Use of Data and Teaching and Learning. In fact, the Process Model and the case data indicate that strong professional relations within the team and the team with the whole school are predictors of the team's relations with the district and its use of data. Continuing to map backward, the team's problem-solving skill is a key variable that supports a team's effort to build effective professional relations. In other words, teams need to acquire skills first to help them function, then they will be able to build the professional relations needed to do their work.

A second message that emerges from this study is the importance of combining both qualitative and quantitative approaches to the study of school leadership teams. The Process Model, based on quantitative data, provides a useful analytical framework for analyzing the qualitative data; however, the qualitative data also directly contribute to our model development by surfacing the importance of team roles. Exploring the variety of roles that teams may need to assume (e.g., staff developers, mediators, problem-solvers, or researchers) in the process of moving the school toward improved student learning adds a new dimension, which previously has not been extensively investigated. Although the need for role clarity has been recognized (Larson and LaFasto, 1989; Mohrman et al., 1994), the actual roles to be assumed generally have been unexplored in the literature of site-based management teams. Understanding more fully what knowledge and skills are needed by team members to fulfill a particular role and what school context and conditions support or constrain teams in assuming particular roles can provide useful information for districts and staff developers working with school leadership teams. Our data indicate that teams may need specific training to fulfill particular roles. As Brookside's team learned problem solving and conflict resolution skills, it was able to assume a mediator role. When it learned how to conduct action research, it was able to become valuable data collectors and researchers for the school.

A third insight supported by both the Process Model and the case study data is that the relationship between the team and the principal is key to the team's eventual success. The effective schools literature frequently cites the importance of the principal as instructional leader (Blumberg & Greenfield, 1980; Bossert, Dwyer, Rowan, Lee, 1982; Edmonds, 1979; Leithwood & Montgomery, 1982; Purkey & Smith, 1982). Initially the literature portrayed a "take charge" image in which the principal defined the mission of the school, set high expectations for staff and students, and served as instructional leader by protecting learning time, marshaling instructional resources, being master of teaching and learning principles, and monitoring student progress. The case study data indicate that these functions are still important to school and student success, but they cannot be carried out in a "take charge" approach, nor can they be left entirely to the team in a laissez-faire manner. More recent conceptualizations of the principal's role portray the principal as a leader of leaders or a *leading professional* (Sammons et al., 1995, as cited in Scheerens & Bosker, 1997). The principal cannot do the job alone (Hallinger & Hausman, 1993; Scheerens & Bosker, 1997), but needs to build a professional community (Hord, 1997; Kruse & Louis, 1997) that is "characterized by shared purpose, collaborative activity, and collective responsibility among school staff" (Newmann & Wehlage, 1995, p. 37). To establish such professional communities, principals must become facilitators of teacher work teams and of the staff's professionalization (Scheerens & Bosker, 1997). This role of the principal as facilitator of the team's work is substantiated in this study of SLTs.

A fourth implication of our research, however, is that even if principals are prepared to share leadership with staff, teachers may not be fully prepared to assume roles as leaders. Part of the problem may stem from teachers' images of leadership as being power over others (Starratt, 1996). Most teachers' careers are in hierarchical organizations in which those who are leaders have power over them.

> In particular, the common image of a leader is of a powerful, larger-than-life individual, usually a male administrator, who single-handedly creates a compelling vision of the future, convinces others of his keen insight, and motivates them to invest great energy and personal sacrifice in the pursuit of the mission (Bolman, Johnson, Murphy, & Weiss, 1990, p. 5).

The teachers at Brookside did not want to assume such roles in regard to their colleagues, nor initially did they have alternate images of leadership with which they were comfortable. Rost (1993) and Burke (1997) provide definitions of leadership that are more in line with the concept of building a professional community. Rost defines leadership as an "influence relationship among leaders and followers who intend real changes that reflect their mutual purposes" (p. 102). Burke, expanding on Rost's work, addresses the hierarchical implications of leader-follower by defining leadership as a "process of cultivating vision and engaging participation through reciprocal influence between leaders and constituents in which they collectively create real changes for mutual purposes" (p. 14). Both of these definitions of leadership may reassure teachers that if they assume leadership roles they will not be regarded as "big shots." The case study data confirmed that as SLT members found effective ways of engaging with their colleagues to develop benchmarks, share teaching strategies or collect and present data, the mantel of leader became more comfortable both to the team and to their colleagues. Future research is needed to determine if alternative definitions of leadership presented early in the SLT training process would encourage greater teacher leadership from the beginning.

A fifth insight to emerge from the findings is that a team can be both struggling and successful. Too often the characterization of teams has been that they are either one or the other (Hackman, 1990; Wohlstetter et al., 1997). As we followed the Brookside team over time it was possible to see the team's development and movement from initial success, to failure and then back to a sense of accomplishment. The longitudinal data also helps to illustrate how a new group can become institutionalized within the school, surviving both turnover of team membership and changes in principals.

Finally, the case study as seen through the framework of the Process Model helps to illustrate that it is important to recognize there are two major populations who spend much of their waking hours in schools: adults and students (Fullan & Hargreaves, 1996). This study showed that the leadership team needed a multiplicity of skills to overcome obstacles and to address the needs of both groups. As Prestine and McGreal (1997) assert,

> Changes in the core technology of schools also demand a redefinition of the constructed meanings of teachers' lives. The teaching repertoires that define and give meaning to teachers' roles, relationships, and practices within the classroom will have to be seriously altered to accommodate these new kinds of changes. In essence, changes in core technology will demand a restructuring of teachers' core belief systems and the social constructions of what it means to teach (p. 397).

This study indicates that the team had to attend to many of the adult issues first. They began by developing the skills needed to function as a group, then to solve problems with colleagues. They had to learn how to craft workable forms of shared-leadership with the principal, and to learn how to collect and use data. As the team learned to work together and to establish its role vis-à-vis other adults in the school, it also began addressing student work. However, attention to student learning issues remained at a lower level of priority until the adult issues in the school were more fully resolved. This finding is significant in offering a possible explanation for why measurable reform takes considerable time and effort. Furthermore, the case study illustrated the importance of ongoing training for the team to accomplish this ambitious agenda. Schools will improve for students, especially in the long run, if attention is given to the work environment and opportunities provided for powerful learning by the adults as well as the students.

ACKNOWLEDGMENTS

Research presented in this chapter was supported by a grant from the Spencer T. and Ann W. Olin Foundation. The authors wish to thank the foundation for its generous support of our ongoing study of the California School Leadership Team program. We also thank the team members of Brookside's SLT who have graciously shared their time and their story with us.

NOTES

1. Three instruments were used to collect data from the teams. The first instrument was a Program Survey, completed by the team once. It provided demographic information about the team and school. Team members individually completed a Team Assessment Survey developed by the U.S. Department of Labor. This survey assesses eight dimensions of team functioning: planning, meetings, decision-making, communication, problem solving, understanding self, interpersonal relations, and team dynamics. The only change in the survey was the substitution of the word Team in place of Committee. The eight factors of this survey were accepted and used in the Process Model. The third instrument was an SLT Implementation Continuum developed by the research team (Chrispeels, Wiley, Jelinek, & Morgan, 1995). Following standard factor analysis procedures, including a varimax rotation, the 25 items were assigned to the factor for which they provided the largest effect size. In almost all cases (approximately > 80 percent), the factor item provided an effect size on the order of 2 or more times greater than that item provided to any other factor (Chrispeels et al., in press). The five final factors were named as follows: Professional Relations; School and Community Relations; District Relations;

Use of Data; and Teaching and Learning. The path analysis for the 71 secondary teams was determined using AMOS software. Variables that yielded negligible and statistically insignificant effects sizes and that had no appreciable effect on the coefficient of determination (R^2) were removed from consideration. We used the standard procedures embedded in the AMOS program and indices widely accepted to test the model's goodness of fit (Marsh & Balla, 1986). The Secondary Process Model had a Goodness of Fit Index of 0.84, which is slightly below the recommended 0.9, however, the Root Mean Square Residual (RMR) was 0.06, very close to the desired zero. Thus the RMR for the data indicate that very few of the variances and covariances are left unexplained by the proposed model.

2. Two regions did not participate. One was experiencing extreme financial difficulty, and the other region had a change in CSLA directors.

REFERENCES

Benson, D. (1998). *Ambushed by the principal: Parents and school councils.* Paper presented at the Annual Meeting of the American Educational Research Association. San Diego, CA. April.

Blumberg, A. and Greenfield, W. (1980). *The effective principal.* Boston: Allyn & Bacon.

Bolman, L., Johnson, S. M., Murphy, J. T., & Weiss, C. H. (1990). *Rethinking school leadership: An agenda for research and reform.* Cambridge, MA: Harvard University.

Bossert, S. T., Dwyer, D. C. Rowan, B., & Lee, G. V., (1982). The instructional management role of the principal, *Educational Administration Quarterly, 18*(3), 34-64.

Brooks, J. G., & Brooks, M. G. (1993). *In search of understanding: The case for constructivist classrooms.* Alexandria, VA: Association for Supervision and Curriculum Development.

Burke, P. H. (1997). *What does leadership look like in a fully implemented middle school model?* Unpublished manuscript.

California School Leadership Academy (1995). *School Leadership Team: An infrastructure strategy to support school change.* Hayward, CA: Author. January.

Chrispeels, J. H. (1992). *Purposeful restructuring: Creating a climate of learning and achievement in elementary schools.* London: Falmer Press.

Chrispeels, J. H., Castillo, S., & Brown, J., (in press). School leadership teams: A process model of team development, *School Effectiveness and School Improvement, 11.*

Chrispeels, J. H., Strait, C. C. & Brown, J. H. (1999). The paradoxes of collaborative leadership. *Thrust for Educational Leadership, 29*(2), 16-19.

Chrispeels, J. H., Wiley, S., Jelinek, D., & Morgan, S., (1995). *School Leadership Team (SLT) implementation continuum.* Santa Barbara, CA: Graduate School of Education, UCSB.

Comer, J. P. (1980). *School power.* New York: Free Press.

Comer, J. P., & Haynes, N. M., (1991). Parent involvement in schools: An ecological approach. *The Elementary School Journal, 91*(3) 271-277.

Creighton, T. B. (1997). *Teachers as leaders: Is the principal really needed?* Paper presented at the annual National Conference on Creating the Quality School, Oklahoma City, OK. March.

Creswell, J. W. (1994). *Research design: Qualitative & quantitative approaches.* Thousand Oaks, CA: Sage.

Darling-Hammond, L. (1995). Policy for restructuring, in A. Lieberman (Ed.), *The work of restructuring schools: Building from the ground up.* New York: Teachers College Press.

Darling-Hammond, L. (1997). *The right to learn: A blueprint for creating schools that work.* San Francisco, CA: Jossey-Bass.

David, J. L. (1989). Synthesis of research on school-based management. *Educational Leadership, 46*(8), 45-53.

Dornbusch, S. M., & Ritter, P. L. (1988). Parents of high school students: A neglected resources. *Educational Horizons, winter,* 75-77.

Duffy, T. M., Lowyck, F., & Jonassen, D. H. (Eds.). (1993). *Designing environments for constructive learning.* New York: Springer-Verlag.

Edmonds, R. R., (1979). Effective schools for the urban poor. *Educational Leadership, 37*, 15-27.

Elmore. R. F. (1995) Teaching, learning, and school organization: Principles of practice and the regularities of schooling. *Educational Administration Quarterly 31*(3), 335-374.

Epstein, J. L. (1991). Effects on student achievement of teachers' practices of parent involvement. In *Advances in reading/language research* (vol. 5, pp. 261-276). Greenwich, CT: JAI Press.

Fullan, M. (1991). *The new meaning of educational change.* New York: Teachers College.

Fullan, M. (1993). *Change forces: Probing the depths of educational reform.* London: Falmer.

Fullan, M. & Hargreaves, A. (1996). *What's worth fighting for in your school.* New York: Teachers College Press.

Hackman, J. R. (Ed.). (1990). *Groups that work and those that don't: Creating conditions for effective teamwork.* San Francisco: Jossey-Bass.

Hallinger, P. & Hausman, C. (1993). The changing role of the principal in schools of choice. In J. Murphy & P. Hallinger (Eds.). *Restructuring schooling: Learning from ongoing efforts.* Newbury Park, CA: Corwin Press.

Hopfenberg, W. S., Levin, H. M. & Associates. (1993). *The accelerated schools resource guide.* San Francisco, CA: Jossey-Bass.

Hord, S. M. (1997). *Professional learning communities: Communities of continuous inquiry and improvement.* Austin, TX: Southwest Educational Development Laboratory.

Jenni, R. W. (1993). *Observing different attitudes in school restructuring: Elementary vs. secondary.* Paper presented at the Annual meeting of the American Educational Research Association, Atlanta, GA.

Kruse, S. D. & Louis, K. S. (1997). Teacher teaming in middle schools: Dilemmas for a schoolwide community. *Educational Administration Quarterly, 33*(3), 261-289.

Larson, C. E., & LaFasto, F. M. J. (1989). *Teamwork: What must go right/what can go wrong.* Newbury Park, CA: Sage.

Lawler, E. E., III. (1986). *High-involvement management: Participative strategies for improving organizational performance.* San Francisco, CA: Jossey-Bass.

Leithwood, K. A., & Menzies, T. (1998). A review of research concerning the implementation of site-based management. *School Effectiveness and School Improvement, 9*(3), 233-285.

Leithwood, K. A., & Montgomery, D. (1982). The role of the elementary school principal in program improvement. *Review of Educational Research, 52*(3), 309-339.

Levine, D. U., & Eubanks, E. E. (1992). Site-based management: Engine for reform or pipedream? Problems, prospects, pitfalls, and prerequisites for success. In J. J. Lane & E. G. Epps (Eds.), *Restructuring the schools: Problems and prospects* (pp. 61-82). Berkeley, CA: McCutchan.

Lieberman, A. (Ed.). (1988). *Building a professional culture in schools.* New York: Teachers College.

Lieberman, A. (1995). Practices that support teacher development: Transforming conceptions of professional learning. *Phi Delta Kappan, 76*(8), 591-596.

Liontos, L. B. (1992). *At–risk families & schools: Becoming partners.* Eugene, OR: ERIC Clearinghouse on Educational Management.

Lortie, D. C. (1975). *Schoolteacher: A sociological study.* Chicago, IL: University of Chicago Press.

Maeroff, G. I. (1993). *Team building for school change: Equipping teachers for new roles.* New York: Teachers College.

Malen, B., Ogawa, R. T., & Kranz, J. (1989). *What do we know about school based management? A case study of the literature—A call for research.* Paper presented at the Conference on Choice and Control in American Education, Madison, WI. May.

Marsh, H. W. & Balla, J. R. (1986). *Goodness-of-fit indices in confirmatory factor analysis: The effect of sample size.* ERIC No: ED 267091. February.

Mitchell, C. J. (1984). Typicality and the case study. In R. F. Ellens (Ed.), *Ethnographic research: A guide to general conduct* (pp. 238-241). New York: Academic Press.

Mohrman, S. A., Cohen, S. G., & Mohrman, A. M., Jr. (1995). *Designing team-based organizations: New forms for knowledge work.* San Francisco, CA: Jossey-Bass.

Mohrman, S. A., Wohlstetter, P., & Associates (1994). *School-based management: Organizing for high performance.* San Francisco: Jossey-Bass.

Morse, J. M. (1991). Approaches to qualitative-quantitative methodological triangulation. *Nursing Research, 40*(2), 120-123.

Newmann, F. M., & Wehlage, G. G. (1995). *Successful school restructuring: A report to the public and educators.* Madison, WI: Center on Organization and Restructuring of Schools.

Patton, M. Q. (1990), *Qualitative evaluation and research methods,* Newbury Park, CA: Sage Publications.

Prestine, N. A., & McGreal, T. L. (1997). Fragile changes, sturdy lives: Implementing authentic assessment in schools. *Educational Administration Quarterly, 33*(3), 371-400.

Purkey, S. C., & Smith, M. S. (1982). Too soon to cheer? Synthesis of research on effective schools. *Educational Leadership, 40,* 64-69.

Robertson, P. J., Wohlstetter, P., & Mohrman, S. A. (1995). Generating curriculum and instructional innovations through school-based management. *Educational Administration Quarterly, 31*(3), 375-404.

Rost, J. C. (1993). *Leadership for the 21st century.* Westport, CT: Praeger.

Sammons, P., Hillman, J., & Mortimore, P. (1995). *Key characteristics of effective schools: A review of school effectiveness research.* London: OFSTED.

Scheerens, J., & Bosker, R. (1997). *The foundations of educational effectiveness.* London: Pergamon.

Scheerens, J., & Creemers, B. (1989). Towards a more comprehensive conceptualization of school effectiveness. In B. Creemers, T. Peters, & D. Reynolds (Eds.), *School effectiveness and school improvement.* Lisse: Swets and Zeitlinger.

Senge, P. M. (1990). *The fifth discipline.* New York: Doubleday.

Sizer. T. (1992). *Horace's school: Redesigning the American high school.* Boston: Houghton Mifflin.

Slavin, R. E., Madden, N. A. Karweit, N. L., Livermon, B. J. & Dolan, L. (1990). Success for all: First year outcomes of a comprehensive plan for reforming urban education. *American Educational Research Journal, 27,* 255-278.

Smylie, M. A. (1992). Teacher participation in school decision making: Assessing willingness to participate. *Educational Evaluation and Policy Analysis, 14,* 53-67.

Smylie, M. A., Lazarus, V., & Brownlee-Conyers, J. (1996). Instructional outcomes of school-based participative decision making. *Educational Evaluation and Policy Analysis, 18*(3), 181-198.

Spradley, J (1980). *Participant observation.* Fort Worth, TX: Harcourt Brace Jovanovich.

Stanton, J., & Zerchykov, R. (Eds.). (1979). *Overcoming barriers to school council effectiveness.* Boston, MA: Institute for Responsive Education.

Starratt, R. J. (1996). *Transforming educational administration: Meaning, community and excellence.* New York: McGraw Hill.

Stringfield, S., Ross, S. M., & Smith, L. (1996). *Bold plans for school restructuring: The New American Schools designs.* Mahwah, NJ: Lawrence Erlbaum Associates.

U.S. Department of Labor. (1990). *Committee effectiveness training.* Washington, DC: Author.

Wallace, M., & Hall, V. (1994). *Inside the SMT: Teamwork in secondary school management.* London: Paul Chapman Publishing.

Weiss, C. H., & Cambone, J. (1994). Principals, shared decision making and school reform. *Educational Evaluation and Policy Analysis, 16*(3), 287-301.

Weiss, C. H., Cambone, J., & Wyeth, A. (1991). *Trouble in paradise: Teacher conflicts in shared decision making.* NCEL Occasional Paper No. 8. Cambridge, MA: National Center for Educational Leadership, Harvard Graduate School of Education. ED 332 346.

Wohlstetter, P., & Smyer, R. (1994). (1994). *School-based management: Promise and process. CPRE Finance Briefs.* New Brunswick, NJ: Consortium for Policy Research in Education.

Wohlstetter, P., Van Kirk, A. N., Robertson, P. J., & Mohrman, S. A. (1997). *Organizing for successful school-based management.* Alexandria, VA: Association for Supervision and Curriculum Development.

Yin, R. K. (1998). The abridged version of case study research: Design and method. In L. Bickmand & D. J. Rog (Eds.), *Handbook of applied social research methods* (pp. 229-260). Thousand Oaks, CA: Sage.

CHAPTER 4

EXPLOITATION OR EXPLORATION?
SECONDARY SCHOOL ADMINISTRATIVE
TEAM LEARNING

Andy Scott

No one doubts that secondary schools are living in "permanent white water" (Vaill, 1989, p. 1): they are being reformed, restructured, and privatized; they are required to teach more diverse students with fewer resources; they have less support from their districts, and are being held to higher standards of performance with more transparent forms of accountability; they must implement new curricula and more authentic forms of assessment in greater partnership with others. All at the same time!

Such turbulent school environments call for especially skilled leadership by those in administrative positions. And we know a good deal about the nature of such leadership as it is exercised by individuals—principals for example (Leithwood & Duke, 1999). But in today's flatter organizations, leadership is often provided by administrative teams, about which much less is known.

Advances in Research and Theories of School
Management and Educational Policy, Volume 4, pages 75-95.
Copyright © 2000 by JAI Press Inc.
All rights of reproduction in any form reserved.
ISBN: 0-7623-0024-8

The study summarized in this chapter (see Scott, 1996, for a full report) was premised on the assumption that the quality of leadership provided by secondary school administrative teams depends crucially on the nature of their learning. For example, teams which engage exclusively in "exploiting old certainties" (March, 1996, p. 101), or "single-loop learning" (Argyris & Schon, 1978), constrain themselves to "doing things right." Exploring new possibilities, or "double-loop" learning, often will be required in turbulent contexts to "do the right things." Evidence to date about school administrative teams largely concern the nature of their decision processes and factors accounting for such processes (e.g., Brightman,1984; Grindle, 1982; Muth, 1987; Stevens & Pellicer, 1984).

What sort of learning actually takes place in secondary school administrative teams? Is there much evidence of exploratory learning? What accounts for the nature of administrative team learning? What forms of leadership appear to foster such learning? These were the questions explored in this study.

FRAMEWORK

A cognitive, information processing view of individual applied learning, as a metaphor, was used in this study to help understand the nature of collective or team learning. Senge's (1990) five "disciplines" were used to help unpack the conditions which either enhance or inhibit such learning. And a transformational perspective was adopted to better understand leadership in the context of team learning.

Individual Cognition and Collective Learning

Cognitive understandings of individual learning often have been used as metaphors for helping understand collective learning because, as Hedberg claims, while "[o]rganizations do not have brains ... they [do] have cognitive systems and memories" (1981, p. 7). This orientation is evident in the adoption of structures and functions from the cognitive sciences such as procedural memory (Cohen & Bacdayan, 1996), sense-making (Weick, 1995), and knowledge acquisition (Huber, 1991).

Metaphorical uses of individual learning bring with them the distinction between cognitive structures and the functions which they perform. This study adopted a simplified model of the mind's "architecture" (Newell, Rosenbloom & Laird, 1990), including structures labelled by some cognitive scientists as the "executive", "short term memory" and "long term memory." For purposes of this study, the processes carried out by these structures were limited to perception, knowledge acquisition, and understanding. Information distribution, a process not easily explained by this framework, but vital to an account of collective learning, was included as well.

Using the organization's goals, mission statements, beliefs, mental models, and world views, the executive serves as a perceptual screen for the organization, sorting environmental stimuli for potential relevance in helping achieve those goals and values, and allocating attention. Watkins and Marsick (1993) refer to this structure as part of a theory of action "which is a combination of its strategy and culture" (p. 148) and, more specifically, consists of the goals, strategic plans, values, beliefs, ethics, and mission statements.

Both short-term and long-term memory structures have been used to explain collective knowledge acquisition and understanding. For example, Hedberg argues that "Members come and go, and leadership changes, but organizations' memories preserve certain behaviours, mental maps, norms, and values over time" (1981, p. 6). The purpose of short-term memory is to

> search through the contents of long-term memory for previously stored knowledge capable of helping make sense of perceived information from the environment. Examples of organizational search routines that schools might use include limiting search to what staff already knows, expanding the search to include other knowledgeable stakeholders, delegating the search committee and initiating a search for relevant research (Leithwood et al., 1993, p. 59).

Long-term memory is the organization's repository of knowledge and that knowledge is acquired and stored as understanding develops. Understanding involves giving meaning to new information. Although terms have proliferated around this matter in the organizational learning literature, such understanding is often thought to occur in organizations in two quite distinct ways. Senge (1990) uses the terms "generative" and "adaptive" to make this distinction. Argyris and Schon (1978) use the terms "single-loop" and "double-loop" learning. The terms "exploitative" and "exploratory" are used by March (1996) to capture much the same distinction. One of these types of learning involves a process "that maintains the central features of an organization's theory-in-use or set of rules and restricts itself to detecting and correcting errors ... [whereas the other process] aims at adjusting overall rules and norms rather than specific activities or behaviours" (Fiol & Lyles, 1985, p. 808). As Huber explains, "the distinction between learning within a frame of reference and learning a new frame of reference seems critically important" (1991, p. 93).

The development of understanding facilitates the storage of knowledge in long-term memory in the form of declarative and procedural knowledge structures. Beliefs, ideas, concepts and theories are stored in declarative form whereas guides to action or skilled performances are stored as steps to take, routines to follow and the like, a procedural form. Retrieval and use of stored knowledge is heavily dependent on the organization of related pieces of information in knowledge structures and the richness of the associations established among knowledge structures. Documents, files, standard operating procedures and rule books constitute parts of a school or district's long-term memory (Leithwood et al., 1993).

According to one view, knowledge acquisition in organizations includes:

(1) drawing knowledge available at the organization's birth, (2) learning from experience, (3) learning by observing other organizations, (4) grafting on itself components that possess knowledge needed but not possessed by the organization, and (5) noticing and searching for information about the organization's environment and performance (Huber, 1991, p. 88).

While a model of individual cognition offers significant insights into collective learning, it does not attend to the obvious problem of how information is distributed throughout the team or larger organization, a matter also of concern in this study. Information distribution "is a determinant of both the occurrence and the breadth of organizational learning" (Huber, 1991, p. 100). This aspect of collective learning, according to Huber, brings with it a need to be attentive to how information is routed through the organization, how the status and power of individuals influence such information distribution, and ways in which communication distortions arise.

Theoretical perspectives on individual cognition described in this section, and used to frame inquiry about team learning in this study, by no means represent the latest or most sophisticated orientation to learning. Nowhere have we acknowledged connectionist theories of human cognition (Bereiter, 1991), for example. Nor has any mention been made of social constructivist or situated theories of learning (e.g., Prawat & Peterson, 1999; Lave & Wenger, 1991) which hold considerable potential for shedding light on team learning in the future. Nevertheless, the relatively simple, information processing model used in this study is both foundational to many of these other theoretical advances and capable of extending our knowledge about team learning in quite meaningful ways.

Conditions Enhancing and Inhibiting Team Learning

Organizational learning must be examined from both individual and organizational perspectives to fully understand the conditions which influence it. Senge's (1990) five disciplines provide just such a perspective. These disciplines, Senge claims, enhance learning but must operate at both the individual and organizational level. They include systems thinking, personal mastery, mental models, building shared vision and team learning. According to Senge, each discipline develops on its own, yet each influences the development of the other.

Systems Thinking

The fifth of Senge's disciplines, and the most important, systems thinking is:

a discipline for seeing the wholes. It is a framework for seeing the interrelationships rather than things, for seeing patterns of change rather than the static snapshots.... a set of specific tools and techniques.... a sensibility for the subtle interconnectedness that gives living systems their unique character (Senge, 1990, p. 69).

Watkins and Marsick (1993) suggest that individuals must not only perceive the whole, but they must develop a sense of connection (p. 265). Striving for long-term goals and improving the lives of those within and outside the organization are essential activities in the process of establishing the connection. A systems perspective is also important to an appreciation of organizational change. Hutchins (1991) states:

> Whether a change at the upper system level is considered to be the result of evolution, adaptation, or the result of design, depends on what we believe about the scope of the awareness of the subsystems. If we think that some of the subsystems have global awareness, and can represent and anticipate the consequences of possible changes, then we may view an organizational change as a result of design. If we believe that the subsystems do not form and manipulate representations of system operation, then we must view change as evolutionary. (p. 38)

Hutchins (1991) points out that organizational change often involves both evolution and design, each representing a different level of learning. Design, however, requires a global (or systems) view of the organization.

Personal Mastery

If, as Simon (1991) suggests, "all learning takes place inside the individual heads" (p. 125) then organizational learning, will not take place without individual learning. Senge (1990) applies the term personal mastery to the efforts of individuals who constantly and vigorously seek out new learning. These individuals set the spirit of the learning organization. Senge (1990) also identifies a number of principles that are necessary for the expansion of personal mastery:

- individuals must have a personal vision of a desired future state, extending beyond goals and objectives;
- the gap between current reality and the vision needs to be understood in order to serve as a source of creative energy;
- individuals need to believe that the obstacles standing between the current state and the desired state can be overcome: the sense of powerlessness, which frustrates and debilitates the individual, must be countered;
- a zealous commitment to truth is essential as individuals search for their own deceptions of reality;
- individuals need to understand the role of the subconscious; "it is through the subconscious that all of us deal with complexity. What distinguishes people with higher levels of personal mastery is a higher level of rapport between their normal awareness and their subconscious. What most of us take for granted and exploit haphazardly, they approach as a discipline" (Senge, 1990, p. 162).

- Imagery, visualization and mental rehearsals of complex tasks are examples of how the subconscious can be focused.

Mental Models

Such models are images of how things work. They affect "not only how we make sense of the world, but how we take action" (Senge, 1990, p. 175). Tacit mental models are of primary concern because "what is learned appears to be influenced less by history than the frames applied to that history" (Levitt & March, 1988, p. 324). And Morgan (1993) remarks that " [o]ur understanding of what we are seeing changes according to the frame or image that shapes our viewpoint" (p. 2).

This discipline requires the management of mental models at the personal and interpersonal level. Both reflection and inquiry skills are needed for this purpose. Skills of reflection concern slowing down our own thinking processes so that we can become aware of how we form our mental models and the ways they influence our actions. Inquiry skills concern how we operate in face-to-face interactions with others, especially in dealing with complex and conflictual issues (Senge, 1990, p. 191).

A third skill, balancing advocacy and inquiry in the process of surfacing mental models, we must, according to Ross and Roberts, lay "out our reasoning and thinking, and then encourage others to challenge us" (1994, p. 253).

Shared Vision

A shared vision, according to Senge (1990), is an integral part of a learning organization and, in fact, without it learning organizations will not be created. The term "shared" vision often refers to one held by the leader or an elite group and imposed on an organization. But for a vision to foster organizational learning it must reflect the personal visions of organizational members, one to which they are committed, wish to strive toward, and one that is "always open to the next vision" (Watkins and Marsick, 1993, p. 276). A truly shared vision

> establishes an overarching goal. The loftiness of the target compels new ways of thinking and acting. A shared vision also provides a rudder to keep the learning process on course when stresses develop. Learning can be difficult, even painful. With a shared vision, we are more likely to expose our ways of thinking, give up deeply held views, and recognize personal and organizational shortcomings. All that trouble seems trivial compared with the importance of what we are trying to create (Senge, 1990, p. 209).

The Discipline of Team Learning

Not to be confused with the earlier discussion of team learning "processes" (perception and the like), Senge's (1990) treatment of team learning is about how to foster such learning. He suggests that for learning to occur the efforts of team members must be in alignment. When this is the case "a commonality of direction emerges, and individuals' energies harmonize" (Senge, 1990, p. 234).

Team learning, as a collective discipline, requires the mastery of certain skills: fostering dialogue and discussion, dealing with conflict, and responding to defensive actions. Team learning takes place "through dialogue, in which people are willing to listen to the perspective of others, and use these new views to examine their own views" (Dechant et al., 1993, p. 8). Teams must practice these skills in controlled and structured settings in order to refine the collective skills. In addition, team learning "implies a quality of caring for other individuals" (Watkins and Marsick, 1993, p. 264). "Colleagues who know, trust, and are comfortable with each other are more likely to have the motivation and opportunity to learn together" (Leithwood et al., 1993, p. 103).

Argyris (1990), however, warns that as dialogue moves beyond the superficial level, individuals may resort to defensive patterns that inhibit dialogue:

> the first pattern ... a person who asks questions about testing hypotheses and choosing among claims of causality is accused of being "too rational" or "too scientific" ... a second pattern, in which a person believes that rationality and logic are relevant, but maintains that dialogue should not be too rational when someone is upset and feeling highly emotional ... a third pattern in which someone who questions the validity and appropriateness of a particular intervention is accused of being too evaluative, too judgmental, and punishing. The accusation that someone is too evaluative and judgmental is itself evaluative and judgmental (p. 300).

The tension between individual and team development is an important issue because team learning has a "dark side," a process of uncritical conformity to the group, unthinking acceptance of the latest solution, and suppression of individual dissent which Janis (1982) termed "groupthink." Warding off goupthink requires the team to focus on personal development and learning, and a culture which supports challenges to the the status quo.

Learning Disabilities

The absence or low level of development of the five disciplines is viewed by Senge as inhibiting collective learning. But in addition, he identifies seven variables he refers to as learning disabilities. Summarized briefly, these include:

- individuals' idiosyncratic views held about their jobs and the resulting difficulty they have understanding the contribution of their work to the overall vision for the organization;
- beliefs held by organizational members that an enemy exists outside of the organization, thus reducing the focus on improving the organizaton from within;

- misunderstandings about what constitutes proactive actions, confusing reaction with initiative taking and failing to see the gradual processes that undermine the organization;
- acceptance of the view that organizations learn from experience and a failure to recognize how difficult that actually is;
- competency traps occur when experiences with potentially superior organizational routines are minimized because of the continued transformation of an inferior, but comfortable routine and increased skill in its use;
- the myth of the management team (mistakenly viewed as a savvy group, capable of the super-human feat of managing the organization).

Leadership

Senge (1990) suggests that in learning organizations, leaders are designers, stewards, and teachers. They are responsible for building organizations where people continually expand their capacity "to understand complexity, clarify vision, and improve shared mental models" (Senge, 1990, p. 340). Leaders are responsible for the learning.

Such leadership calls on new and different skills. As a designer, the leader must have a vision of the whole and continually struggle to understand its nature. In addition, the leader must structure the organization to integrate and promote the development of the five disciplines identified by Senge (1990). As a steward, leaders need to communicate the broad picture of where the organization is headed and why. As a teacher, the leader instructs the members of the organization in the five disciplines.

These three interrelated roles foster an image of leadership referred to by some as transformational (e.g., Burns, 1978; Bass, 1985; Leithwood, Jantzi, & Steinbach, 1999). Transformational leaders assist in defining the purpose of an organization, demonstrate the ability to "communicate a lucid and compelling vision" (Louis, 1985, p. 86), and develop a widely shared vision. From a transformational perspective, the responsibility for developing the vision should rest with all members of the school, thus preventing domination by the principal (Hargreaves, 1994, p. 54).

Transformational leadership also provides individualized support, intellectual stimulation, and models practices valued by the organization. Further, this form of leadership entails the creation of collaborative cultures in which leaders acknowledge and demonstrate the need to openly probe dimensions of a situation, through constructive conflict and debate, and the willingness to question their own beliefs (Morgan, 1986, p. 92). Listening and responding positively to detractors, although requiring exceptional levels of self-confidence, humility, and objectivity, establishes a model for other members (Nystrom, 1984, p. 57). Such an environment is dependent upon the development of trust between the members of the organization (Hargreaves, 1994, p. 58).

METHODS

This was a comparative case study of administrative teams in three secondary schools, subsequently referred to by their pseudonyms: Westview Secondary School, Highlands Collegiate and Vocational Institute, and Mid-West Secondary School. These teams were randomly selected from a large, southern Ontario board of education after eliminating those which had been together less than six months. One team that was initially selected declined to participate.

Data were collected using several procedures. Each administrative team tape recorded three of their own meetings. After each meeting, one member of the team also was interviewed by the researcher. The first part of that interview entailed playing back the recording of the meeting, stopping it periodically to ask the interviewee to report everything he/she could remember, including his/her own thoughts, about the portion of the meeting just replayed. A second step in the interview was guided by a set of fixed questions aimed at exploring issues about team learning specifically related to the framework for the study (e.g., shared vision, personal mastery). Over the course of the full study, these individual interviews were conducted with all three members of each administrative team.

The final stage of data collection was a team interview intended to accomplish several purposes: to clarify information gathered during the interviews and team meetings; to probe inconsistencies in the data; to provide team members with an opportunity to reflect on what they had learned from their participation in the research project; and to allow the researcher to ask additional questions about team learning emerging from the results of prior data collection and analysis.

All interviews at each stage were tape recorded and transcribed. Protocol analysis was used with the transcripts of the individual interviews following team meetings. This technique is designed to help understand the cognitive processes and experiences of an individual from their verbal accounts (Ericsson & Simon, 1993). Discourse analysis was used to analyze all remaining interview transcripts following guidelines suggested by Potter and Wetherell (1987). This technique aims to reflect the meaning of individual ideas in the context of the full text.

Remaining sections of the chapter identify similarities and differences across the three administrative teams, summarizing evidence about the nature of their learning, the factors which either inhibited or fostered such learning, and the form that team leadership took.

THE NATURE OF ADMINISTRATIVE TEAM LEARNING

Results of the study reported in this section concern the process of perception, knowledge acquisition, understanding and knowledge distribution on the part of the teams.

Perception

Teams provided evidence about: "tools" used for noticing, screening, and allocating attention; the forms and sources of information which they encountered; and the processes they used to initially interpret that information.

Tools used by the team for noticing, screening and allocating attention to information included:

- *Values of team members.* Principals spoke of the desire to be "student focused" and to deal with individuals in a similar fashion. Conflicting values also surfaced as a "tool" and shaped the teams' discourse;
- *Plans of the administrative team, and their specific objectives.* A Highlands C.V.I. episode dealing with the central office request to consider an early school start was an example in which these tools were used;
- *Theoretical constructs.* These constructs were used to shape interpretations of information encountered by the team. One example was the "True Colours" theory of personality types which filtered the initial information received by one team and subsequently, organized the pursuit of additional information within the meeting setting;
- *Specific beliefs and assumptions.* In episodes from Westview S.S. and Highlands C.V.I. case studies, for example, references were made to a belief about a 'red-neck' group of teachers and how they would react to a given initiative. The belief that past experience provided unquestioned direction was another example of a belief that was used to screen information;
- Assumptions about the larger organization and, in particular, the teachers;
- *Sagas.* For example, the saga of Mid-West secondary school having a strong tradition of caring for the hard-to-serve, and Westview S.S.'s saga of a school that tended to be "above the rest" in terms of academic performance and experienced staff, tended to permeate each of the episodes.

There was considerable similarity across the three administrative teams in the forms and sources of information encountered by the teams. Information came to the attention of the teams in many different forms. In the cases of Mid-West S.S. and Westview S. S., this included letters, reported conversations, reports from members, and questions. Interruptions to the administrative meetings from other staff members served as stimulants for noticing issues in the Highlands C.V.I.

team. All three cases included examples of major team tasks serving to focus the attention of the teams.

The process of screening information involved talking and questioning. Evidence from all three teams illustrated how adept members were at asking questions in order to understand issues. In the case of Westview S.S., the principal completed most of the screening for the other members. In fact, he screened most information relevant to the team's work and generated the agenda. In contrast, all team members in the other schools actively engaged in the screening process, although the agenda tended to be determined by the principals.

Knowledge Acquisition

Prior experience served as the main source of knowledge for members of all three teams. Principals in all cases played a very significant role in this respect. Longer serving vice-principals relied more extensively than did younger vice-principals on past experience. Less experienced vice-principals demonstrated a greater orientation to research and other readings.

The experience of others within the school also was a major source of knowledge. The Highlands S.S. administrative team's discussion of committee size, for example, focused on experience with other committees and the impact of membership size. Experience of others outside of the school appeared to be a minor source of knowledge, except for the Mid-West S.S. team. Few references were made to what other schools had attempted, although some speculation about their actions was introduced. Meetings of the principals' associations provided a forum for exchange of information and team members identified it as a main source of knowledge. Principals' meetings with central office administrators provided another forum for the exchange of knowledge and information. Vice-principals did not attend these meetings.

Only the Mid-West S.S. team acquired knowledge extensively from other schools. For example, the experience of other schools within the district played a significant role in the response of this team to issues concerning French Immersion and the results of the provincial grade 9 reading and writing tests.

Inclusion of others from within the school in the team meetings was a strategy for acquiring knowledge used by Westview S.S. and Mid-West S.S.. In the case of Westview S.S., these outsiders to the team provided some additional knowledge, particularly if the issue being addressed fell within their area of responsibility. Overall, however, others within the school played only a minor role in directly providing knowledge for the team. In contrast, when the administrative team for Highlands C.V.I. met, members were responsible for bringing knowledge and information to the meeting, even if it required prior consultation with others in the school.

Once administrative teams were in a meeting setting, they tended to address issues with the information and knowledge at hand. In only two instances recorded by the study was an issue set aside until further information was obtained. Notwithstanding the closed nature of the information considered by the teams once their meetings began, they actively engaged in internal-to-the-team search processes through questioning one another and refining their understanding of the issue.

Four assumptions, common to team members, reduced the efforts of teams to engage systematically in knowledge search activities:

- the inclusion of other members of the school ensured a broad source of information (even in light of the minor contributions made by such people);
- team members were well informed about the issues;
- principals were a major source of knowledge—a stance not to be challenged;
- the team represented a well-informed and knowledgable unit.

Furthermore, there was little evidence of the teams using "obvious" strategies to acquire additional information. The provision of an agenda well before a meeting, for example, would have provided an opportunity for team members to actively search out information prior to the meeting. But in all three cases, the agenda evolved during the meeting and was dominated by the principal. The suspension of proceedings, until all information had been acquired, is another example of a strategy used infrequently. And finally, an orientation to the larger system and the acquisition of knowledge from the experience of other schools represented untapped potential.

Understanding

Understanding is the process of giving meaning to new information. The three teams provided evidence of single-loop, exploitative, or adaptive learning almost exclusively. In the case of the Westview team, examples of this were evident in relation to issues concerned with the allocation of supply teachers, and the Canadian flag. At Highlands C.V.I., single-loop efforts to understand were observed in relation to an episode concerning "effective schools." In all of these situations, a moment of opportunity existed for the team to enter into double-loop learning, to challenge and change their frames of reference. But the teams continued to function within their existing assumptions, declined to engage in "search and exploration of alternative routines" (Lant & Mezias, 1992, p. 46) restricting themselves, instead, to detecting and correcting errors.

The case studies shed some light on the use of dialogue and discussion to build understanding. Team members sought clarification and understanding through frequent questions. Discourse during these meetings was characterized, as well, by long breaks between statements and questions, the extension of sounds, statements of clarification, summary statements, interruptions of one another, and the placing of emphasis on key words.

The nature of the stimulus for team learning played a significant role in the level of learning engaged in by the teams. For example, a staff allocation issue arising from massive budget cuts caused the Westiew team to engage in one of the few instances of double-loop learning recorded in the study. This team examined how and why they operated in a certain manner, and adjusted "overall rules and norms rather than specific activities and behaviours" (Fiol and Lyles, 1985, p. 808). A minor budget reduction probably would not have stimulated such generative, double-loop, or exploratory learning and the cases revealed few other instances of problems striking or dissonant enough to generate such learning.

Based on this study, it seems that administrative teams rarely engage in double-loop learning, do not have processes or norms which would make it more common, and rarely encounter dissonant-enough stimuli to foster such learning.

Information Distribution

Individual team members played a significant role in the distribution of information to others within the team. Principals most often served this function because of their connections outside of the school. Talking was identified by the teams as the main medium of exchange. After meetings at the district level, for example, principals usually provided an oral report to the other team members. The extent of the report and the consistency of reporting tended to vary from one principal to another. Regardless, vice-principals relied on this information for an understanding of events at the system level. Feelings of isolation were expressed by most of the vice-principals, however, after being denied attendance at district-wide principals' meetings.

Information related to broader educational issues, not just those concerning the district, tended to be disseminated in written form. In all three cases, principals were viewed as the main sources of this information and the relative characteristics, strengths, weaknesses, or interests of the vice-principals did not influence the routing of the information; all received the material.

The speed of information transfer depended on its urgency. All members of the team engaged in making such routing decisions based on their own perceptions of urgency. The Highland C.V.I. and Mid-West S.S. teams described a constant movement from one office to another over the course of a working day.

Reactions of team members to questions about information distortion reflected their feelings about other team members. When raised as a question by the researcher, team members discarded intentional distortion as a possibility, some with considerable indignation, but failed to consider the issue of unintentional distortion. All teams, however, reported a strong orientation to pursuing "truth."

CONDITIONS FOSTERING AND INHIBITING
ADMINISTRATIVE TEAM LEARNING

Senge's (1990) five disciplines were used as a framework for classifying conditions fostering or enhancing and inhibiting administrative team learning. Both types of conditions are reported in the following sub sections.

Systems Thinking

Enhancers

According to Senge, systems thinking "is a framework for seeing the interrelationships rather than things" (1990, p. 69). It is a means of maintaining one's perception of the whole (Watkins & Marsick, 1993, p. 265). The Highlands C.V.I. team provided an exemplary case of systems thinking in practice. Dense interconnections among organizational elements were evident in every recorded episode. An episode concerning an exam request involved team members in a process of asking a series of questions to clarify the request, and in the process highlighted the connections. The principal's statement, "Okay, I guess we can't make a decision in isolation," is clear evidence of the systems thinking. In addition, an issue about a report card illustrated the complexity of the organizational elements, and how difficult it is to identify connections.

The Westview S.S. and Mid-West S.S. case studies did not provide similar examples. Evidence suggests that the prerequisites for systems thinking are an extensive knowledge of the larger organization and a team member with a systems perspective. In Highlands C.V.I., for example, one of the vice-principals attributed much of their success in systems thinking to the principal: "[name] has a tremendous ability to predict connections that may come down the road." Strong leadership from the principal appeared to be paramount.

Inhibitors

Evidence from the Westview S.S. case, in particular, demonstrated the team failing to apply systems thinking to an issue. The narrow perspective of the team inhibited it from seeing important connections in their problem solving and, as a consequence, generating superficial solutions. One of the vice-principals suggested that they were "not getting to see the big picture as much as we used to."

While systems thinking typically depends on access to information from many sources, the vice-principals in all three teams who concentrated on the day-to-day operation of the school, were excluded from many system-level meetings. They were forced to rely almost entirely on their principals for information that would help broaden their understandings. This most obviously limited their ability to engage in systems thinking. Less obviously, it precluded them challenging the views of their principals.

Personal Mastery

Enhancers

Each team provided strong evidence of members with a demonstrated commitment to individual learning. Although shared visions were articulated in vague and abstract terms in all cases, individual members were able to articulate relatively precise and concrete personal visions that affected how and to what extent they engaged in learning. The role of the principal, both in terms of role-model and facilitator, also influenced the personal mastery of individuals.

Inhibitors

The stage of an individual's career may be an important consideration in terms of personal mastery. This was the case with one of the Westview S.S. vice-principals. Approaching retirement, he expressed a sense of powerlessness in attaining his vision and overcoming obstacles. These qualities, coupled with a "day-to-day" view of his role, inhibited both his own professional learning and the team's learning, as well.

Mental Models

Enhancers

Evidence from the three teams illustrated forms of discourse associated with the collective processes of reflection and inquiry. Team members used tact in discourse with one another: "What do you think?;" "It was a good idea in theory;" "But maybe I'm out of whack;" "Do we want to invite that, though?;" and "What would you think?" In the case of Highlands C.V.I., discourse during their meetings demonstrated a high degree of respect and concern for their fellow members, and the interview data substantiated that respect and concern.

Inhibitors

The nature of the discourse that occurred during the Mid-West S.S. team's meetings offered many examples of practices that inhibited learning. Most obvious was one vice principal's habit of cutting off the principal's utterances, something one of the other vice principals said that she was guilty of, as well. Although a more open dialogue necessarily requires a flow from one member to another, team members must listen to the complete idea, modify their thoughts, and respond.

Shared Vision

Enhancers

Evidence from the administrative teams failed to shed any light on this discipline. But even though team members were unable to articulate a shared vision, other than in the vaguest terms, each team had a direction to pursue, one based on the principal's vision.

Inhibitors

In all three teams, members struggled to articulate a shared vision but were unable to do so in sufficiently precise terms for their visions to provide practical guidance to either the teams or their individual members. Team members, however, attempted to provide more concrete components of what they understood to be the shared vision for the school. In each case, according to the vice-principals, the vision of the principal dominated the "shared" vision. Teams did not engage in explicit efforts to develop a shared vision. In the opinion of their members, this accounted for their inability to articulate a shared vision.

Team Learning: The Discipline

Enhancers

The three administrative teams in this study had been together for different lengths of time, increasing the possibility of them being at different stages of development. Some evidence of this was found. In contrast to the other two teams, the Highlands C.V.I. team, with a four year history, aligned their energy, engaged in honest, open, and positive discourse, and viewed challenges as opportunities. Members of this team also treated one another as colleagues, demonstrated a sincere concern for the welfare of other members, and attempted to develop a consensus in their decision making.

Inhibitors

But even in the presence of these conditions, lack of self-disclosure and defensive routines remained serious challenges for this team. During many of the episodes captured in the data, team members refrained from surfacing their inner thoughts. Nor was socializing together, either inside or outside the school context, a common practice except for the Highland team. Indeed, many team members expressed serious reservation about socializing with fellow members outside of the school.

Inclusion of other organizational members to the administrative meetings on a regular basis, while providing additional, potential sources of information, also impaired the administrators' abilities to develop as a team. The Westview S.S. case illustrated how, under such circumstances, administrators tended to meet less frequently and have fewer opportunities to learn together.

Lack of uninterrupted time and an over-riding focus on the day-to-day operation of the school inhibited team learning, in the opinion of team members. Provision of specific meeting times addressed this concern to some extent, but other pressing demands on the vice-principals dictated expediency.

Variation in levels of respect for fellow team members accounted for significant differences in team learning. Very high levels of mutual respect among members of the Highlands C.V.I. team, especially respect for the principal, permeated every response and team action. In contrast, team members of Mid-West S.S., were openly critical of one another.

Leadership

Senge (1990) conceives of leaders in learning organizations as: designers, structuring the organization to ensure the development of the five disciplines; stewards, communicating the story of the organization and how the elements evolve and fit together; and teachers, instructing members of the organization in the five disciplines. This concept of leadership closely parallels the focus of Leithwood's (1994) "transformational" leader on people, purpose, structure, and culture. Evidence from the three cases demonstrated forms of leadership that both fostered and inhibited team learning.

The Highlands C.V.I. principal demonstrated many of the leadership qualities that fostered team learning. She empowered team members and helped them find satisfaction in their work, according to the vice-principals. As well, she pushed to uncover the "truth" and welcomed challenges to her own vision. She created a culture that fostered learning, and challenged the thinking of the team members. Her own ideas were considered by her colleagues to be clearly expressed, and she was respected by all team members. This principal, her colleagues claimed, explained the story of the organization, served as a role model for personal learning, and established clear conditions for team learning.

A precondition to leadership actively fostering learning within a team is a leader's view of team meetings as a potential forum for such learning. The Westview S.S. principal did not have this view. Rather, he used such meetings to provide information to other members of the team, and to develop support for his decisions and actions.

Team learning is also fostered when leaders grasp opportunities for questioning basic assumptions, theories, beliefs, values, and norms. Without leadership at critical moments, teams fail to become involved in more generative or exploratory forms of learning. None of the principals provided evidence of attempting such intellectual stimulation of their colleagues.

Fostering the contribution of individual members to the team-learning process is another function a leader may perform. In the case of Highlands C.V.I., the principal maintained high expectations for the vice-principal approaching retirement. In contrast, the Westview principal established lower expectations and focused the activities of the retiring team member at the school level. Consequently, the vice-principal's personal growth and development served to inhibit the collective learning.

While the leader's role was only one factor contributing to the differences in team learning evident in these cases, it was a significant one.

CONCLUSION

In comparison with ideal prescriptions for team learning, the three teams in this study were a "mixed bag." While the team which had been together for the longest time was characterized by more favorable learning conditions, time alone seems unlikely to solve the conditions inhibiting learning in the other two teams.

All of the teams were relatively adept at managing large amounts of information from many sources as they encountered it. But they did not go out of their way to systematically collect such information. And they sometimes closed themselves off to potentially useful sources of information possessed by staff in their own schools. These practices, at the collective level, are similar to routine problem-solving practices engaged in "automatically" by individuals (e.g., Norris, 1985).

The teams also relied disproportionately on information from "officially legitimate" sources: district staff in the case of principals, and principals in the case of vice-principals. This should not be surprising since these sources of information were not only undeniably authoritative, from an organizational perspective, but readily accessible as well. Indeed, these findings parallel Coffin's (see Chapter 2) discovery that principals' primary sources of professional learning are the district and the senior administrators in the district office.

Without doubt, there is much to be learned by principals from these sources, just as principals offer vice-principals readily available models of administrative practice as well as the most accessible sources of opportunity for on-the-job leadership learning. But there is a dark side to these results. When administrator learning, individually and collectively, depends to such a large extent on often verbally disseminated information from those sharing a common set of goals, and often a common set of organizational norms, the likelihood of the administrative team engaging in "routine" exploratory learning is minimal. "Routine exploratory learning" is not an oxymoron; it describes the practices of teams in which members habitually and regularly reflect on the assumptions and beliefs underlying their solutions to both well-structured and ill-structured problems, challenge the school's and district's taken-for-granted wisdom, and interpret problems from multiple perspectives (e.g., Bolman & Deal, 1991).

Left in their "natural state," nothing but single-loop, adaptive, or exploitative team learning seems likely on the part of secondary administrative teams except in response to critical or highly unusual events. The urgency of problems addressed by administrative teams, their sheer volume, and the disposition toward action characteristic of many of those in administrative roles conspires to this end. If the sample in this study reflect common practices, the most likely route to higher level learning and problem solving on the part of administrative teams will require principal intervention. Principals played pivotal roles in the learning of each team. And variation in the practices of principals seemed to account for large differences in the teams' learning.

To foster double-loop, generative, or exploitative learning on the part of administrative teams, principals must encourage and model the use of non-official sources of information. It will require them to introduce research-based knowledge and widely agreed-upon (beyond the school and district) professional wisdom as the gold standards for legitimate knowledge. They will need to develop within their teams the disposition to interpret problems through at least several lenses. To foster higher order learning and problem solving within their teams, principals need to encourage the skills of inquiry that Senge (1990) endorses.

Administrative teams supported by their principals in these ways should demonstrate, collectively, many of the same characteristics attributed to individual "experts." As compared with nonexperts, expert administrative teams will be: better able to regulate their own problem-solving processes; possess more problem-relevant knowledge; represent problems at a deeper level; develop more complex goals for problem solving; spend more time interpreting problems; and be more sensitive to the tasks, demands and social contexts within which problems are to be solved (e.g., Berliner, 1986; Leithwood & Steinbach, 1995).

REFERENCES

Argyris, C. (1990). Inappropriate defenses against the monitoring of organizational development practice. *The Journal of Applied Behavioural Science, 26*(3), 299-312.

Argyris, C. & Schon, D. (1978). *Organizational learning: A theory of action perspective.* Massachusetts: Addison-Wesley.

Bass, B.M. (1985). *Leadership and performance beyond all expectations.* New York: The Free Press.

Bereiter, C. (1991). Implications of connectionism to thinking about rules. *Educational Researcher, 20*, 10-16.

Berliner, D.C. (1986). In pursuit of the expert pedagogue. *Educational Researcher, 15*(7), 5-13.

Bolman, L.G., & Deal, T.E. (1991). *Reframing organizations.* San Francisco: Jossey-Bass.

Brightman, H. (1984). Improving principals' performance through training in the decision sciences. *Educational Leadership,* 50-56.

Burns, J. (1978). *Leadership.* New York: Harper and Row.

Cohen, M., & Bacdayan, P. (1996). Organizational routines are stored as procedural memory. In M. Cohen & L. Sproull (Eds.), *Organizational learning* (pp. 403-429). Thousand Oaks, CA: Sage.

Dechant, K., Marsick, V. & Kasl, E. (1993). Towards a model of team learning. *Studies in Continuing Education. 15*(1), 1-14.

Ericsson, K., & Simon, H. (1993). *Protocol analysis.* Cambridge: Bradford.

Fiol, C. & Lyles, M. (1985). Organizational learning. *Academy of Management Review, 10*, 803-813.

Grindle, B. (1982). Administrative team management: Four essential components. *The Clearing House, 56*(1), 29-33.

Hargreaves, A. (1994). Restructuring restructuring: Postmodernity and the prospects of educational change. *Journal of Education Policy, 9*, 47-65.

Hedberg, B. (1981). How organizations learn and unlearn. In P.C. Nystrom & W. Starbuck (Eds.), *Handbook of organizational design, 1*, 3-23.

Huber, G. (1991). Organizational learning: The contributing processes and the literatures. *Organization Science, 2*(1), 88-109.

Hutchins, E. (1991). Organizing work by adaptation. *Organization Science, 2*(1), 14-39.

Janis, I.L. (1982). *Groupthink.* Boston, MA: Houghton Mifflin.

Lant, T., & Mezias, S.J. (1992). Managing discontinuous change: A simulation study of organizational learning and entrepreneurship. *Organization Science, 3*(1), 47-71.

Lave, J., & Wenger, E. (1991). *Situated learning: Legitimate peripheral participation.* Cambridge, UK: Cambridge University Press.

Leithwood, K. (1994). Leadership for school restructuring. *Educational Administration Quarterly, 30*(4), 498-518.

Leithwood, K., Dart, B., Jantzi, D. & Steinbach, R. (1993). *Building commitment for change and fostering organizational learning.* Prepared for the British Columbia Ministry of Education.

Leithwoord, K. A., Dart, B., Jantzi, D., & Steinbach, R. (1993). *Fostering organizational learning: A study in B.C.'s intermediate developmental sites, 1990-1991.* Report to British Columbia's Ministry of Education.

Leithwood, K., & Duke, D. (1999). A century's quest to understand school leadership. In J. Murphy & K.S. Louis (Eds.), *Handbook of research on educational administration* (2nd ed.) (pp. 45-72). Washington, DC: American Educational Research Association.

Leithwood, K., Jantzi, D., & Steinbach, R. (1999). *Changing leadership for changing times.* U.K.: Open University Press.

Leithwood, K., & Steinbach, R. (1995). *Expert problem solving.* Albany, NY: SUNY Press.

Levitt, B. & March, J. (1988). Organizational learning. *Annual Review of Sociology, 14*, 319-340.

Louis, M. (1985). An investigator's guide to workplace culture. In P. Frost, L. Moore, M. Louis, C. Lundberg, & J. Martin (Eds.), *Organizational culture.* London: Sage.

March, J. (1996). Exploration and exploitation in organizational learning. In M. Cohen & L. Sproull (Eds.), *Organizational learning* (pp. 101-123). Thousand Oaks, CA: Sage.

Morgan, G. (1986). *Images of organization.* Beverly Hills, CA: Sage.

Morgan, G. (1993). *Imaginization.* California: Sage.

Muth, R. (1987). The decision seminar: A problem-solving technique for school administrators. *Planning and Changing,* 45-60.

Newell, A., Rosenbloom, P.S., & Laird, J.E. (1990). Symbolic architectures for cognition. In M.I. Posner (Ed.), *Foundations of cognitive science* (pp. 93-131). Cambridge, MA: MIT Press.

Norris, S.P. (1985). Synthesis of research on critical thinking. *Educational Leadership, 42*(8), 40-46.

Nystrom, P. (1984). To avoid organizational crises, unlearn. *Organizational Dynamics, 12*, 53-61.

Potter, M., & Wetherell, M. (1987). How to analyze discourse. In *Discourse and social psychology.* London: Sage.

Prawat, R.S., & Peterson, P.L. (1999). Social constructivist views of learning. In J. Murphy & K.S. Louis (Eds.), *Handbook of research on educational administration* (2nd ed.) (pp. 203-226). Washington, DC: American Educational Research Association.

Ross, R. and Roberts, C. (1994). Balancing inquiry and advocacy. In P. Senge, C. Roberts, R. Ross, B. Smith, & A. Kleiner (1994). *The fifth discipline fieldbook.* New York: Doubleday.

Scott, A. (1996). *Towards a theory of school administrative team learning.* Unpublished Doctoral Thesis, University of Toronto.

Senge, P. (1990). *The fifth discipline.* New York: Doubleday.

Simon, H. (1991). Bounded rationality and organizational learning. *Organization Science, 2*(1), 125-136.

Stevens, K. & Pellicer, L. (1984). Team management quick relief from the minor aches and pains of school business management. *School Business Affairs*, 53-54.

Vaill, P.B. (1989). *Managing as a performing art.* San Francisco: Jossey-Bass.

Watkins, K. & Marsick, V. (1993). *Sculpting the learning organization.* San Francisco: Jossey-Bass.

Weick, K. (1995). *Sensemaking in organizations.* Thousand Oaks, CA: Sage.

PART II

BUILDING THE INTELLECTUAL CAPACITIES OF SCHOOLS AND DISTRICTS

CHAPTER 5

CONDITIONS FOSTERING ORGANIZATIONAL LEARNING IN SCHOOLS

Kenneth Leithwood,
Laurie Leonard, and Lyn Sharratt

Synthesized in this chapter are the results of three studies (Leithwood, Jantzi, & Steinbach, 1995; Leonard, 1996; Sharratt, 1996), each of which inquired about leadership and other conditions which foster or inhibit organizational learning (OL) in schools. Each study was guided by the same theoretical framework, collected qualitative, multi-case study data, and analyzed these data in comparable ways. However, each study was conducted in quite different contexts. These contextual differences, in combination with similarities in the studies' purposes, guiding conceptual frames and methods, provide unique opportunities to explore questions about the similarity of OL conditions in different contexts. Given different

Advances in Research and Theories of School
Management and Educational Policy, Volume 4, pages 99-124.
Copyright © 2000 by JAI Press Inc.
All rights of reproduction in any form reserved.
ISBN: 0-7623-0024-8

stimuli for learning, and different organizational contexts, to what extent are there similarities and differences in the conditions which foster or inhibit such learning? Which conditions seem most robust across stimuli and contexts? Which conditions seem to vary by stimuli and context? These are the central questions explored in this chapter.

FRAMEWORK

An extensive literature on OL in nonschool organizations (reviewed, for example, in Cousins, 1996) was used to develop the framework for the three studies described in this chapter. This framework includes a perspective on the nature of organizational learning processes, the causes and consequences of such processes, and forms of school leadership likely to foster such conditions and processes. While school leadership is reasonably conceptualized among the causes and/or consequences of OL, it was of special interest to us and so is treated separately in the framework.

Organizational Learning Processes

Collective learning is not just the sum of individual learning even though individual learning is a necessary part of collective learning. Nevertheless, most accounts of collective learning assume that it is either literally or metaphorically very similar to individual learning. In these accounts, cognitive explanations of individual learning are used to represent the nature of OL processes (eg., Gioia, 1986; Hedberg, 1981; Cohen, 1996; Cohen & Bacdayan, 1996).

The metaphorical use of individual cognitive process to explain OL has added considerably to our understanding of collective learning. An obvious example of such use is Morgan's (1986) image of organizations as brains; a more subtle use is Cohen and Bacdayan's (1996) analysis of organizational routines as if they were individual procedural memories. Such evidence notwithstanding, it is important to be clear on the limitations of this approach. As Cook and Yanow (1996) inquire, why should two things so different in other ways as individuals and organizations be expected to carry out the same processes in order to learn. Additionally, cognitive conceptions of individual learning are very much under development and, in many respects, contested. While they have contributed a good deal to an appreciation of how learning occurs among individuals, they cannot be adopted uncritically, even as metaphors, for insights about OL.

"For the concept of organizational learning to be viable, it is useful to have a concept of a collective mind which is doing the learning even if such mind is not the seat of cognitive activity" (according to Wegner, cited in Weick & Roberts, 1996, p. 332). Only individuals can contribute to a collective mind and only the mind of an individual can be conceptualized as a set of internalized processes controlled by a brain. Collective mind must be an external representation, mind as activity rather than mind as entity. The collective mind, then, is to be found in patterns of behavior that range from "intelligent" to "stupid." This view of collective learning has similarities with connectionist explanations of the individual mind. From this perspective, mind can be "knowledgeable" without containing knowledge.

Collective learning develops from the actions of individuals as those individuals begin to act in ways heedful of the "imagined requirements of joint action" (Weick & Roberts, 1996, p. 338). These requirements might be implied in the organization's culture (Cook & Yanow, 1996). But they could also include more immediate and explicit demands on joint action. March (1991), Hutchins (1991), and Schoenfeld (1989) describe the type of learning in which individual members of groups engage in "mutual adaptation," an essentially connectionist view of individual learning applied to the collective.

Mutual adaptation can be of two sorts. One sort is largely unreflective. For example, in the case of Hutchin's (1991) navigation team, when individual team members confronted a change in what they believed was required of the whole team, each of the members adapted their usual contribution to the team as best they could, hoping that other members would be able to do whatever else was required. This was implicit negotiation of the division of labor. When it seemed not to be sufficient as a response to the team's new challenge, individual members then attempted to recruit others to take on part of what was assumed to be her part of the team's job, a second form of mutual adaptation.

In the case of Schoenfeld's (1989) research team, the task was to construct a coherent explanation for a set of data about a student's mathematical learning processes. Individual members or subgroups of the whole team typically constructed their own explanations of the data set first. Then they shared these explanations and engaged in some form of interaction which often produced a shared explanation significantly different than any of the individual member's or subgroup's explanations.

In both the Hutchins and Schoenfeld examples, an imagined new challenge for the team serves as the stimulus for individual team members to adapt their contributions to the team's actions. In this way, the individual is contributing to the learning of the team. As other team members adapt their contributions not only in response to their sense of the team's new challenge but also in response to the responses of other members, each team member learns about the adequacy of her initial response and perhaps the need to adapt further. This is the way in which the individual learns from the team. And, as Schoenfeld explains, "the result of the group interactions extended significantly beyond the 'natural' sum of the contributions that could have been made individually by the people involved" (1989, p. 76).

This theoretical account of OL processes is provided as important conceptual background for understanding the main focus of the chapter, the conditions influ-

encing such OL processes. Empirical evidence concerning the nature of these processes, is beyond the scope of this chapter.

Causes and Consequences of Organizational Learning Processes

Our explanation of the causes and consequences of organizational learning processes is framed by five sets of variables, and the relationships among them, identified in two extensive literature reviews described in detail elsewhere (Cousins,
1996; Leithwood & Aitken, 1995). The five sets of variables include: the stimulus
for organizational learning; out-of-school conditions influencing OL; in-school
conditions influencing OL; leadership; and the outcomes of OL. Relationships
among these variables are complex. Whereas the stimulus for OL is considered to
have a direct effect on OL processes, the nature of these processes, in response, is
mediated by leadership, out-of-school, and in-school conditions. Relationships
among these variables are themselves reciprocal. Only OL processes influence
OL outcomes.

Stimulus for Learning

OL is assumed to be prompted by some felt need (e.g., to respond to the call for
implementing a new policy), or perception of a problem, prompted from inside or
outside the school that leads to a collective search for a solution. Watkins & Marsick (1993) suggest that relatively dramatic events (a labor strike, for example)
are needed to stimulate OL. As in the case of OL processes, while this variable is
part of our framework, no empirical evidence concerning it is reported in this
paper.

Out-of-School Conditions

Included within the meaning of out-of-school conditions are initiatives taken by
those outside the school (e.g., Ministry/State personnel, district staff), or conditions which exist outside the school (e.g., economic health of the community) that
influence conditions and initiatives inside the school. Our studies focused only on
those out-of-school conditions created by the Ministry of Education, the local
school community, and the school district. We asked: What sorts of conditions
outside of schools have a bearing on OL in schools? In particular, what is it about
school districts, local school communities and the Ministry of Education that fosters or inhibits OL in schools? What would be the characteristics of such an
"external environment" which unambiguously nourished the development of
schools as learning organizations?

School Conditions

These are initiatives taken by those in the school, or conditions prevailing in the school, which either foster or inhibit organizational learning. Starting with suggestions from Fiol and Lyles (1985) and Watkins and Marsick (1993), our studies associated such conditions with the school's mission and vision, culture, decision-making structures, strategies used for change, and the nature of policies along with the availability and distribution of resources. Our studies asked: What do schools look like when they are behaving like learning organizations? Specifically, what is it about a school's vision, culture, structure, strategies, decision processes, and policies and resources which gives rise to or detracts from OL?

School Leadership

Defining our meaning of school leadership were practices of those in formal administrative roles, usually principals, that help determine the direction of improvements in the school and that influence the nature and extent of efforts by school members to learn how to bring about these improvements. Research on OL in non-school organizations suggests that leadership by those in formal leadership roles is an especially powerful influence on OL both directly and indirectly (Kofman & Senge, 1995). Mohrman and Mohrman assert that such leadership

> entails being a continual catalyst for the change process by formulating and updating a compelling change agenda, helping the organization envision the future, unleashing the energy and resources to fuel the change process and helping the organization experience change as success rather than failure (1995, p. 101).

Senge views such processes as the outcome of leaders acting as stewards, designers and teachers. Through enacting such roles, they help build organizations "where people expand their capabilities to understand complexity, clarify vision, and improve shared mental models" (Senge, 1990, p. 340).

These views resonate closely with a model of transformational school leadership developed in some of our previous work (e.g., Leithwood, 1994; Leithwood & Steinbach, 1993; Leithwood & Jantzi, 1990) and for which there was preliminary evidence of effects on OL. As a consequence, the starting point for our perspective on leadership in the three studies were the eight dimensions of leadership practice associated with this model. These dimensions include practices aimed at identifying and articulating a vision, fostering the acceptance of group goals, and providing individualized support for staff members. Transformational leadership practices also aim to stimulate organizational members to think reflectively and critically about their own practices, and to provide appropriate models of the practices and values considered central to the organization. Holding high performance expectations, building shared norms and beliefs (culture), and structuring the organization to permit broad participation in decision making also can have important consequences for OL.

With this initial view of transformational school leadership, our studies asked: What sorts of leadership practices on the part of school administrators contribute significantly to OL and to the conditions which foster OL? Are these practices consistent with our initial model of transformational leadership or should this model be revised or abandoned?

Outcomes

To be worth continuing attention, OL must result in something consequential for schools. These are likely to be individual and collective understandings, skills, commitments, and overt practices resulting from OL in schools. Such outcomes are assumed to mediate the effects of the school's learning on student growth.

RESEARCH DESIGN

A qualitative, multi-case study design was adopted for each of our three studies. For purposes of this chapter, we restrict the description of research methods to a brief summary only (see Leithwood, Leonard, & Sharratt, 1996, for a more detailed account). Each of the three studies was carried out in multiple school sites, the three studies combined having been conducted in a total of 14 schools. The bases on which these schools were chosen did not guarantee that they would be exemplary learning organizations. Nor was this important for purposes of the studies. Informed by evidence from Watkins and Marsick (1993), we assumed that organizational learning is a necessary activity within virtually all schools but the nature, direction, speed, utility, and the like, vary widely across schools.

Two issues were important in selecting the schools. First, there needed to be sufficient demand for learning in the selected schools that it would be detectable with the research methods available to us. Participation in an external reform initiative seemed to provide such a demand. Second, school conditions needed to vary significantly in order to discriminate among those which fostered, inhibited or had no effect on OL. We assumed that typically this would be the case across schools without manipulation of the selection process beyond ensuring variation in school size and level (elementary, secondary).

Study One schools were selected as promising sites of organizational learning from two sources of evidence. One of these sources was the data available about the school as a result of its participation in one or more earlier phases of our research (Leithwood, Jantzi, & Steinbach, 1995); this was the case for four schools. Another source was a school's reputation, among two or more district staff, as making substantial progress toward restructuring (two schools), something akin to Rosenholtz's (1989) "moving schools." The cases also were selected to represent the full K-12 spectrum of school levels: one primary, one elementary, a junior secondary, two secondary, and one senior secondary school. Principals in each school were asked to nominate up to 12 teachers who would be willing to be interviewed. Nominees were to be broadly representative of the staff with differences in curricular areas taught, years of experience, and gender reflecting the variety of experience and expertise within the school.

Selection of schools and teachers for studies Two and Three was constrained by the special nature of the challenges with which they were dealing. Only nine schools in total were part of the Newfoundland school council pilot study. In addition to their participation in the pilot study, the 3 schools chosen for Study Two together covered the full K-12 spectrum of grades, were not under the jurisdiction of only one school district, and were located in the same general geographic region of the province for ease of data collection. Principals were asked by the researcher to select teachers who were broadly representative of the staff; at least one of those selected had to be a member of the school council. All schools and teachers with access to the necessary computer hardware and software volunteered to participate in Study Three.

A total of 111 teachers were interviewed in the 14 schools: six schools and 72 teachers in Study One, three schools and 15 teachers in Study Two, and five schools and 24 teachers in Study Three. Interview data were collected from teachers in all schools using variations on a common, 28 item, interview guide. Results were tape recorded, transcribed and content analyzed in relation to our guiding conceptual framework.

Both geographical location and educational context were quite different across the three studies. Study One was carried out in British Columbia. At the time of the study, schools in that province were about four years into their responses to the province's comprehensive Year 2000 school restructuring policy (Ministry of Education, 1989). While these schools had their own local priorities, it would have been difficult for them not to feel acutely aware of the need to make some response to the provincial initiative and each was making such a response.

The province of Newfoundland was the location of Study Two. Schools included in this study were part of a pilot project initiated by the province in response to its new policy creating local school councils on which was strong parent and other community representation, although in an advisory capacity (Newfoundland, 1992). The aim of the pilot project was to generate knowledge which could be used by other schools in the province, beginning in 1997-98, when all were required to have such councils. An important early task facing the pilot schools was to negotiate a "protocol agreement" with their districts which set out precisely their relationship with their districts.

Schools in Study Three were located in one large school district in south-central Ontario and were part of an experiment in technology inte-

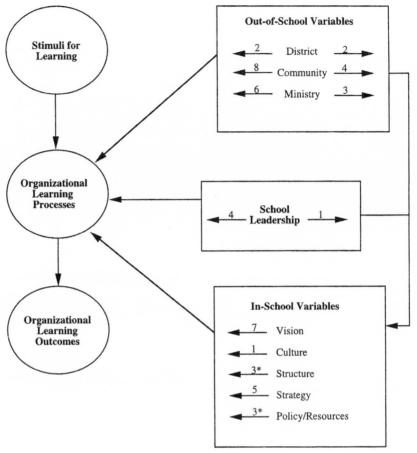

Notes: *Tied in importance
**Numbers denote relative "strength of influence" based on the frequency with which teachers associated the variable with organizational learning (OL) processes. Arrows pointing left denote direct influence on OL processes. Arrows pointing right denote indirect influence on OL processes through in-school variables.

Figure 1.   A Summary of Influences on Organizational Learning Processes**

gration. A provincial professional association had developed a set of curriculum resources for teachers of grades 7 through 9 and had made it available to teachers throughout the province in hard copy. In addition, an electronic data base including the same resources had been provided to teachers in Study Three schools along with the computer hardware and training required to access the resource in electronic form.

RESULTS

This comparison of results across studies is reported in three parts. First, relationships among the categories of variables in our framework are examined for the purpose of identifying those which exercise the greatest influence on OL processes and the extent to which their influence is context-dependent. Second, specific characteristics of each variable, identified in the first section as an especially strong influence on OL processes, are described except for leadership practices which foster OL; they are described in the third and final part.

Variables Influencing Organizational Learning Processes

This section is concerned with two questions: Which variables have the strongest overall influence on OL processes? and to what extent is the influence of these variables context dependent? Figure 1 and Tables 1, 2, and 3 provide the information available from the three studies to answer these questions. Figure 1 summarizes the framework which guided the three studies. This figure also indicates the relative influence on OL processes of nine individual variables within each of three categories of variables. Three variables are classified as "out-of-school" (district, community, and Ministry); five variables are classified as "in-school" (vision, culture, structure, strategy, and policy/resources). School leadership is treated as a single, independent variable.

The arrows in the three rectangles in Figure 1 are intended to show either direct or indirect relationships between out-of-school conditions, in-school conditions, school leadership, and OL processes. Arrows pointing to the left signify a direct association or relationship with OL processes. Arrows pointing to the right indicate a relationship with OL processes mediated by some other variable or set of variables; for example, some teachers indicated that the community influenced OL processes through its influence on such aspects of the school as its culture, structure, and the like.

The relative influence on OL processes of these variables is indicated by numbers representing a rank. Data in Tables 1, 2, and 3 are the bases for these ranks. Table 1 compares the frequency with which teachers interviewed in all three studies made explicit, direct associations in their own words between the nine variables and OL processes (e.g., expressed the opinion that frequent opportunities to collaborate with their colleagues, which we coded as a feature of their school's structure, stimulated several of them to read and discuss (an OL process) how to do authentic student assessment). For each study, the number of explicit associations made by teachers between each variable and OL processes is reported as a percentage of the total sum of all explicit associations made (see columns headed "Percentage"), including those associations made with other components of the framework. Based on these percentages, each variable is ranked in rela-

Table 1.   Direct Effects on Organizational Learning Processes[*]

	Study 1 (B.C.)		Study 2 (Nfld.)		Study 3 (Ontario)		Mean (all studies)	
	Rank	Percentage	Rank	Percentage	Rank	Percentage	Rank	Percentage
Out-of-School Conditions		(7.5)		(19.9)		(11.1)		(12.8)
• District	2	5.4	2	10.7	1	8.3	2	8.1
• Ministry	7	1.9	4	5.8	5	1.7	6	3.1
• Community	9	0.2	8	3.4	6	1.1	8	1.6
School Conditions		(18.4)		(30.1)		(20.5)		(22.9)
• Vision	8	0.7	6	4.5	7	0.6	7	1.9
• Culture	1	7.0	1	11.4	2	6.6	1	8.3
• Structure	3	3.9	7	4.1	3	6.1	3	4.7
• Strategy	4	3.8	6	4.5	5	1.7	5	3.3
• Policy & Resources	5	3.0	5	5.6	4	5.5	3	4.7
Leadership	6	2.9	3	5.9	5	1.7	4	3.5

Notes: [*]This table summarizes the relative importance of each of the nine identified variables in terms of *direct* associations teachers made with organizational learning processes in their schools. Due to the variation in the numbers of teachers interviewed in the schools and in the studies, raw frequencies were converted to percentages and, subsequently, to rankings for both the individual case studies as well as for the overall means.

Table 2.   Indirect Effects on Organizational Learning Processes[*]

	Study 1 (B.C.)		Study 2 (Nfld.)		Study 3 (Ontario)		Mean	
	Rank	Percentage	Rank	Percentage	Rank	Percentage	Rank	Percentage
Out-of-School Variables		(9.2)		(4.7)		(14.3)		(9.4)
• District	2	4.2	3	2.0	2	11.0	2	5.7
• Ministry	4	1.5	4	0.3	4	1.1	4	1.0
• Community	3	3.5	2	2.4	3	2.2	3	2.7
Leadership	1	7.1	1	4.5	1	12.2	1	7.9

Notes: [*]This table summarizes the relative importance of each of the nine identified variables in terms of *indirect* associations teachers made with organizational learning processes in their schools. Due to the variation in the numbers of teachers interviewed in the schools and in the studies, raw frequencies were converted to percentages and, subsequently, to rankings for both the individual case studies as well as for the overall means.

tion to all other variables in each study (see columns headed "Rank"). For instance, numerous associations were made between stimuli and OL processes as well as between OL processes and OL outcomes. These data,

Table 3.   Combined Direct and Indirect
Effects on Organizational Learning Processes[*]

	Study 1 (B.C.)		Study 2 (Nfld.)		Study 3 (Ontario)		Mean	
	Rank	Percentage	Rank	Percentage	Rank	Percentage	Rank	Percentage
Out-of-School Variables	—	—	—	—	—	—	—	(22.8)
• District	2	9.6	1	12.7	1	19.3	1	13.8
• Ministry	7	3.4	4	6.1	7	2.8	6	4.1
• Community	6	3.7	5	5.8	6	3.3	5	4.3
In-School Variables	—	—	—	—	—	—	—	(22.9)
• Vision	9	0.7	8	4.5	9	0.6	8	1.9
• Culture	3	7.0	2	11.4	3	6.6	3	8.3
• Structure	4	3.9	9	4.1	4	6.1	4	4.7
• Strategy	5	3.8	7	4.5	8	1.7	7	3.3
• Policy & Resources	8	3.0	6	5.6	5	5.5	5	4.7
Leadership	1	10.0	3	10.4	2	13.9	2	11.4

Notes: [*]This table summarizes the relative importance of each of the nine identified variables in terms of the combined (i.e., direct and indirect) associations teachers made with organizational learning processes in their schools. Due to the variation in numbers of teachers interviewed in the schools and in the studies, raw frequencies were converted to percentages and, subsequently, to rankings for both the individual case studies as well as for the overall means. Percentages do not total 100, as only those associations made between organizational learning processes and the nine identified variables were included for the purposes of this report.

though undoubtedly important to our further understanding of organizational learning in schools, are beyond the scope of this chapter. The two columns at the far right of Table 1 report mean percentages across the three studies for each of the 9 variables as well as the overall rank of each variable based on the mean percentage. These overall ranks appear in Figure 1 on the small arrows pointing directly (left) to OL processes.

Table 2, following the same format as Table 1, is the basis for ranking the indirect influence on OL processes of out-of-school and leadership variables. In both cases, as Figure 1 indicates, this indirect influence is exercised through in-school conditions (e.g., a teacher states that provision of substitute teachers to the school by the district allows for the school to pay for the substitutes needed to engage in the frequent meetings of colleagues which directly foster OL processes). Table 3 combines the results reported in Tables 1 and 2 reporting the combined direct and indirect effects of the three sets of variables influencing OL processes.

Variables most strongly influencing OL processes. In terms of estimating overall influence, the mean percentages across all three studies reported in Table 3 (far right column) is most useful. As the percentages of total direct and indirect associations with OL processes reported in this column indicate, the district (13.8 percent), school leadership (11.4 percent), and school culture (8.3 percent) were cited as influential much more frequently than were the remaining 6 variables.

When only overall direct associations with OL processes are considered (Table 1, far right column), both district (8.1 percent) and school culture (8.3 percent) retain their preeminent influence. In addition, school structures (4.7 percent) and policies/resources (4.7 percent) emerge as moderately influential. The direct effects of school leadership were mentioned next in frequency (3.5 percent) but not much more often than the school's strategies for change (3.3 percent), and the Ministry (3.1 percent). As Table 2 indicates (far right column), school leadership, and the district were mentioned considerably more frequently by teachers (7.9 percent and 5.7 percent respectively), as indirect influences on OL processes, than were either the community or the Ministry (2.7 percent and 1 percent).

Based on the teacher interview evidence from our three studies, in sum, the five key variables which appeared to account for teachers' individual and collective learning were (especially) the district, school leadership, school culture, and (less critical but still influential) school structure and policies/resources. The specific characteristics of these five variables are outlined in the second part of this section

Effects of context on variables influencing OL processes. Our estimate of the extent to which context affects the variables influencing OL processes is based on the degree of consistency found across the three studies in the frequency of associations made by teachers between the nine variables in our framework and OL processes. As each of Tables 1, 2, and 3 illustrate, if proportions of total associations are used to estimate consistency, context seems to make an enormous difference. In Table 1, for example, differences in the highest and lowest percentages across the three studies for each of the nine variables range from a low of 37 percent (structure) to a high of 95 percent (community) with a mean difference of approximately 60 percent. Similar ranges also are evident in Tables 2 and 3.

Using rankings rather than percentages to estimate consistency across studies in the influence of variables on OL processes tells a very different story, however. Evidence concerning direct effects on OL processes (Table 1) indicates that across the three studies there were differences of:

- only one rank position for the variables district, culture, and policy/resources;
- only two rank positions for vision and strategy;
- more than two rank positions for the remaining four variables (structure was ranked identically in two of three studies, however).

Evidence concerning combined direct and indirect effects indicates that across the three studies there were differences of:

- only one rank position for the variables district, culture, vision, and community;
- only two rank positions for the variable leadership;
- more than two rank positions for the remaining four variables although one of these (structure) was ranked identically in two of the three studies.

Table 2, concerned with indirect effects and only four variables, reported identical rankings for two variables and a difference of only one rank position for the others.

Evidence of consistency across contexts based on rankings seems quite convincing. This is especially the case for district and culture, two of the five variables most frequently associated by teachers with their OL processes. Of the remaining three variables associated most frequently with OL processes:

- leadership is the first ranked variable across all three studies in terms of indirect effects, and seemed also to be a highly ranked, combined, direct and indirect influence on OL processes with teachers in Studies One and Three, and slightly lower in Study Two;
- structure was ranked identically (3rd) as a direct influence by teachers in Studies One and Three, but quite differently (7th) by teachers in Study Two.
- policy/resources is ranked almost identically (4th and 5th) as a direct influence by teachers in all three studies.

In sum, at least the evidence concerning consistency of rankings offers reasonably compelling support for the claim that those variables most frequently cited by teachers as contributing to their individual and collective learning were similar across the different contexts of the three studies.

Specific Characteristics of Variables Strongly Influencing Organizational Learning

District

Teachers in the three studies identified five categories of district features, and a total of three dozen specific features within these categories, associated with their OL processes. Little distinction was evident in the data between district conditions which affected individual as distinct from collective learning.

The *missions and visions* of school districts were potentially fruitful sources of learning for school staffs. But to realize this potential, such visions had to be clear, well understood, and meaningful. To foster organizational learning in schools, district visions and missions also had to engender a sense of commitment on the part of school staffs. When these conditions were met, and when district visions acknowledged the need for continuous professional growth, teachers and administrators used the visions as starting points and frameworks for envisioning more specific futures for their own schools. In the process staff also were establishing the long term goals for their own professional learning. Widely shared district missions and visions, furthermore, sometimes provided filters for screening and evaluating the salience of external demands for change. Also, they served as non-prescriptive clues about which initiatives, taken by schools, would be valued and supported by district personnel. As one principal said, in the context of implementing school councils: "Most of the initiatives, for instance, on the pilot projects that we are involved in our school, they have all been district originated so for that reason I think they have a vision towards school improvement and accountability for our school."

"Collaborative and harmonious" captures much of what was considered to be important about district *cultures* when they contributed to OL. Rather than a "we-they" attitude, perceived to promote hostility and resistance toward district initiatives, learning appears to have been fostered by a shared sense of district community. This sense of community was more likely when there was interaction with other schools (e.g., feeder schools), something noticed when it did not happen. As one teacher in our studies complained:

> They don't get together here.... it wouldn't be hard for two or three schools to get together and have a little science fair and involve everybody. I don't see many of that kind of thing happening very often.

Sense of community also was more likely with clear communication, with support for district initiatives (training, professional development), and when disagreements in the district were settled in ways perceived to be "professional." District cultures fostered OL also when the need for continuous change was accepted, and when new initiatives clearly built on previous work.

District *structures* fostered OL when they provided ample opportunity for school-based staff to participate in shaping both district and school-level decisions. As one teacher in our studies explained:

> The committees get the job done because committees consist of people who are experiencing the difficulties and the questions and the problems, or the goods and the strengths of the program, and bring it back and that's what gets shared.

Participation in district decisions also taught those involved about the wider issues faced by the district and those influences not readily evident in schools that were, nevertheless, germane to district decisions. Considerable delegation of decision making to schools (possibly through site-based management) enhanced opportunities for improving the collective problem-solving capacities of staff. Such decision making also permitted staff to create solutions which were sensitive to important aspects of the school's context. Multiple forums for participation in district decision making were helpful, as was (in the case of Study Three) the electronic networking of schools.

To foster learning, it was perceived to be useful for districts to use many different *strategies* for reaching out to schools—through newsletters, workshops, informal and electronic forms of communication, and the like. Especially influential also were workshops and mentoring programs, and specific change initiatives designed to assist in achieving district goals and priorities. Strategies which buffered schools from excessive turbulence or pressure from the community were identified as helpful for learning as well.

District *policies and resources* identified as promoting learning included the provision of release time for common planning and for professional development, especially when these resources could be used in flexible ways. Access to special expertise or "technical assistance" in the form of consultants, lead teachers, and classroom visitations, for example, also was claimed to foster learning although teachers reported that such resources were, by now, quite scarce ("in the past" they had been quite useful). One means identified for creating a critical mass of expertise about a focus within the school from which others could learn was to ensure that more than one participant from a school attended the same inservice event. In districts which had professional development libraries or central resource centres, teachers cited them as significant aids to their professional learning.

Among district conditions, *policies* and *resources*, especially professional development resources, were most often cited as important by teachers in their learning. As one teacher explained approvingly: "This summer the school board offered a lot of courses—day courses, week-long courses—open and available to any teacher who chose to take advantage of them." There was, however, considerable variation among schools within the same district in the conditions which fostered their learning.

School Culture

Teachers in all three studies frequently identified specific features of their schools' *cultures* which fostered OL processes. Such cultures were described as collaborative and collegial. Norms of mutual support among teachers, respect for colleagues' ideas and a willingness to take risks in attempting new practices were also aspects of culture that teachers associated with their own learning. Some teachers indicated that receiving honest, candid feedback from their colleagues was an important factor in their learning. Teachers' commitments to their own learning appeared to be reinforced by shared celebrations of successes by staff and a strong focus on the needs and achievements of all students. Collaborative and collegial cultures resulted in informal sharing of ideas and materials among teachers which fostered OL, especially when continuous professional growth was a widely shared norm among staff. One teacher in our studies explained, for example: "I think at grade levels we keep in very close contact.... we make sure that ... we run ideas by each other. We may not be doing exactly the same thing at the same time but its more or less a team approach."

School Structure

For the most part, school structures believed to support OL were those which allowed for greater participation in decision making by teachers. Such structures included brief weekly planning meetings, frequent and often informal problem-solving sessions, flexible and creative timetabling, regularly scheduled professional development time in school, and common preparation periods for teachers who needed to work together. Other structures also associated with OL were the cross-department appointment of teachers, integrated curriculum teams, and team teaching. When decisions were made by staff through consensus, something easier to do in smaller schools, more learning was believed to occur. The physical space of schools had some bearing on teachers' learning, when it either encouraged or discouraged closer physical proximity of staff.

Policies/Resources

Teachers reported that current and sufficient resources to support essential professional development in aid of school initiatives were a decided boost to their learning. Within their own schools, teachers used colleagues as professional development resources, along with professional libraries and any professional readings that were circulated among staff. Access to relevant curriculum resources and to computer hardware and software aided teachers' learning, in their view, as did access to technical and program assistance (e.g., consultants, technology site administrators) for implementing new practices. Teachers also noted that access to some community facilities helped them to learn.

Leadership

There are good theoretical reasons, discussed earlier in the paper, to expect that transformational leadership practices foster organizational learning and empirical evidence from the three studies supported this expectation. All specific leadership practices associated by teachers in the three studies with their individual and collective learning were readily coded in relation to the dimensions of transformational leadership.

Identifies and articulates a vision: This dimension encompasses leadership practices aimed at identifying new opportunities for the school and developing (often collaboratively), articulating, and inspiring others with a vision of the future. Of the total number of associations teachers made with the principals' vision building, more than half were associated with school conditions. For example, although a relatively rare occurrence, some principals' visions were reported to have a powerful impact on the culture of the school. And a modest number of teachers described how the principal's vision directly influenced their collective learning.

Fosters the acceptance of group goals: This leadership dimension includes practices aimed at promoting cooperation among staff and assisting them to work together toward common goals. Although there was at least one teacher comment from most schools affirming their principal's role in goal development, most of the comments simply indicated that the principal initiated the process, was a member of the goal setting committee, or asked for input. For example, the principal of one school was reported to be actively involved in building a consensus about goals. That same principal was also the only one who was viewed (by three teachers) as helping staff develop individual growth plans. During goal setting, the principal in another school was perceived to foster OL by encouraging staff to systematically reflect on the activities of the past year.

Conveys high performance expectations: Included as part of this leadership dimension are practices that convey expectations for excellence, quality, and/or high performance on the part of staff. The interviews provided relatively little evidence that principals in the 14 schools, as a group, held high performance expectations for their staffs, at least that their staffs could detect. But those principals who were viewed as conveying such expectations demanded high "professionalism," and held high expectations for professional growth.

Encouraging teachers to be creative and to try new strategies were indicators of high expectations to teachers. For example, one teacher said that her principal's commitment to fulfilling provincial mandates and keeping the school on the "cutting edge" of changes in education encouraged the staff's commitment to the same vision. Another teacher in the same school said that her principal's expectation that staff will try new teaching strategies influenced her to learn about them. In another school, professional growth was a "taken-for-granted" expectation.

Provides appropriate models: This dimension of leadership encompasses practices that set examples for staff to follow and which are consistent with the values espoused by those exercising leadership. Many teachers across the 14 schools believed that their principal was a good role model and that this fostered their collective learning. These principals set an example by working hard, having lots of energy, being genuine in their beliefs, modeling openness, having good people skills, and by showing evidence of learning by growing and changing themselves. Being involved in all aspects of the school and showing respect for and interest in the students also was considered to exemplify the modeling of excellence. One principal modeled good instructional strategies in the classroom.

Provides individualized support: This dimension of leadership includes practices that indicate respect for individual members of staff and concern about their personal feelings and needs. Most teachers in all case study schools indicated that their principal provided support for their professional learning. Typically this meant providing resources to aid professional learning in the form of money, books, furniture, or materials. Teachers in several schools considered their principal to be particularly adept at procuring funds to assist with their professional development. Some teachers reported that their principals even used their own administrative professional development funds for things that teachers needed. Other kinds of tangible support for professional learning included providing release time or other scheduling help, sharing information or finding speakers, and encouraging participation in decision making by collecting and distributing information.

Providing moral support was mentioned by many teachers in almost all schools. There was the sense that these principals "are always there for us," do whatever they can to get staff what they need, and generally support what teachers do. Sometimes this support was shown by an eagerness to listen, being accessible, fair, open, and sympathetic. Sometimes support was shown by offering positive reinforcement which made staff feel appreciated and encouraged further learning. Support was also shown in the form of encouragement to take risks. And leaders' signs of appreciation were reported to build a collaborative culture.

Provides intellectual stimulation: This dimension of leadership includes practices that challenge staff to re-examine some of the assumptions about their work and to rethink how it can be performed. About a third of all teachers interviewed claimed that their principals provided such challenges. Intellectual stimulation also meant passing on information from journals or other sources, bringing new ideas into the school, and providing professional development at staff meetings. Yet other forms of intellectual stimulation included organizing and chairing professional development sessions, finding out what staff needed to learn, encouraging staff to put on workshops or to lead staff meetings, and discussing individual teacher's progress in achieving personal growth goals.

Builds a productive school culture: This category of practices encompasses behavior which encourages collaboration among staff and assists in creating a widely shared set of norms, values, and beliefs consistent with continuous improvement of services for students. Many teachers did not consider their principals to have much influence on school culture. But the majority of principals were perceived by at least some of their teaching colleagues as being fundamental to that culture. Inspiring respect, being kind, thoughtful, sincere, honest, and hard working were attributes that contributed to this perception. Demonstrating an interest in the students and clearly setting their needs as a priority was considered to be an important influence in half the schools.

A strong belief in the value of honest and open communication, collegiality and a willingness and ability to be flexible were considered to be characteristics conducive to a collaborative culture in which collective learning was fostered. Teachers also valued principals who showed them respect, treated them as professionals, and who were an integral part of the staff. Being seen as working more for the school than for the school district was mentioned by one teacher as being important. Hiring staff who share the same philosophy (eg., a commitment to the use of technology) or who can work well with existing staff was mentioned by some teachers as a way that their principals contributed to a collaborative culture. Principals also influenced culture by encouraging parental involvement in the school. Teachers in two of the B.C. schools credited their principals' philosophy with fostering their child-centered culture. One teacher said her principal set that tone by "putting student needs above timetable needs," for example. Another teacher claimed that respect among staff for students was engendered by the administrator's actions. A third teacher in the same school said the principal's actions demonstrated clearly the importance of being understanding of people from many nationalities and backgrounds. In one school, the principal's strong belief in collaborative decision making fostered a collegial culture, according to some teachers.

Helps structure the school to enhance participation in decisions: Included in this dimension of leadership are practices which create opportunities for all "stakeholder" groups to participate effectively in school decision making. More teachers talked about leadership influences on this aspect of school structure than on any other school condition. In spite of the high degree of collaboration exhibited in these schools, several teachers noted that their principals could make unilateral decisions when appropriate or for efficiency. Principals were seen to encourage participation on committees and to support the committee structure by being actively involved and by organizing or spearheading activities. Many teachers applauded the autonomy their principals gave them to make their own decisions in certain areas. About a third of the principals shared power and responsibility by asking teachers to give workshops, lead staff meetings, help manage the budget, and by delegating many duties to the vice principals.

To facilitate collaboration, some teachers said their principals altered working conditions by making changes to the physical plant (e.g., creating convenient meeting rooms), restructuring the timetable (e.g. creating large blocks of time for language arts), and by arranging for leadership positions specifically designed to foster their learning.

In sum, evidence indicates that all dimensions of transformational leadership contributed significantly to school conditions fostering OL processes as well as to OL processes directly. There were almost twice as many associations made by teachers between leadership and school conditions as between leadership and OL. This lends support to the assertion that the effects of school leadership are most often indirect (Hallinger & Heck, 1996).

DISCUSSION AND CONCLUSION

If it has not already, the term restructuring is in imminent danger of becoming simply a catch-all phrase for a host of complex and often largely untested changes hotly advocated for schools in developed countries around the world. Such changes create for schools those "postmodern" conditions of uncertainty, lack of stability, and impermanence faced by most organizations approaching the end of the millennium. These conditions severely challenge virtually all organizational designs that rely on centralized planning, control, and direction. As organizational theorists have begun to acknowledge (e.g., Morgan, 1986), productive designs in the face of such conditions must have the capacity for self organization; the complexity of this postmodern environment demands full use of the intellectual and emotional resources of organizational members. As Mitchell, Sackney, and Walker argue, "The postmodern era suggests a conception of organizations as processes and relationships rather than as structures and rules" (1997, p. 52), with conversation as the central medium for both the creation of individual meaning and organizational change. From this perspective, conceiving of schools as learning organizations seems like a promising organizational design response to the continuing demands for restructuring. And beginning to identify those specific conditions which foster organizational learning is an urgent research goal for educational researchers.

Weick and Westley (1996), however, recently have claimed that "there appear to be more reviews of organizational learning than there is substance to review. Most reviews now available are competent summaries of a common body of work" (p. 440). This is a comment on the state-of-art of empirical research on OL across all organization types. A review of empirical research on OL in schools alone would make a very quick read indeed (Leithwood & Louis, 1998). So, while there are compelling reasons to view schools from an organizational learning perspective, and some powerful theoretical tools to shape such a perspective, empirical evidence is thin, to say the least.

The three studies of organizational learning in schools described in this chapter add to this meagre knowledge base. Evidence from the studies was synthesized in order to identify conditions within and outside the school which foster the individual and collective professional learning of school staffs and to inquire about the generalizability of these conditions across organizational and reform contexts. Data for the study were provided through interviews with a total of 111 teachers in 14 elementary and secondary schools. These schools were involved in one of three significant restructuring initiatives including changes in teaching and learning processes (British Columbia), school-based management (Newfoundland), and increased use of computer technology for curriculum development (Ontario). Although many conditions were identified as influencing individual and collective learning, teachers interviewed in these studies gave greatest weight to five—the district (including its mission, culture, structure, policies and resources, and strategies for change), school culture, school structure, school policies and resources, and school leadership. The relative frequency with which teachers associated these five sets of conditions with OL was similar across the three contexts of our studies

District Conditions

Most often mentioned by teachers as directly and indirectly associated with their learning were several different sets of district conditions. Studies of district effects are relatively small in number but evidence does suggest that district-level organizations make important contributions to the work of schools. For example, the results of our three studies concerning district effects on teachers' learning have been essentially duplicated by Coffin (1997) in respect to principals' learning. In addition, for example, district culture may be important in the work lives of teachers (McLaughlin, 1990), district size (part of district structure) may explain a significant proportion of the variation in student achievement (Walberg & Fowler, 1987), and district policies intended to control curriculum and instruction may standardize the content of instruction taught by teachers (Archbald, 1997).

In general, these results appear to warrant more research energy focused on district effects and the mechanisms through which these effects are felt. From an organizational learning perspective, such research ought to inquire with greater precision than we have been able to, so far, about the nature of those district-school relationships which foster learning at the school level and those conditions which give rise to collective learning at the district level. This research ought to include the development of robust theoretical explanations for the effects of both district and school conditions fostering OL.

Evidence of potentially powerful district effects also has significant policy implications. This is especially so during a period, as now, in which district organizations seem to be every policymaker's favorite scapegoat and school-based management their restructuring instrument of choice. In New Zealand, district organizations have been eliminated, and in the United Kingdom they have been severely downsized and refocused. Canadian provincial governments are in the midst of either reducing the number of districts as in British Columbia, Ontario, and Nova Scotia, or eliminating them entirely, as in New Brunswick. Yet school personnel are being asked to learn many new practices and attitudes as schools transform their ways of doing business. So eliminating a central source of such learning seems misguided, at least until other sources of such learning are created.

From a broader perspective, it is not clear whose interests such policy directions serve? Empirical studies of school-based management effects quite clearly indicate that it is not students' interests (Leithwood & Menzies, 1998). Parents have little or no access to central provincial and state decision-making bodies, although they do have potentially greater influence in their local schools. That seems to leave politicians, who can claim to be doing something in the name of restructuring, and taxpayers, whose wins and losses through weakening or eliminating district-level organizations are by no means clear (Swanson & King, in press). In sum, rather than eroding or eliminating the functioning of district-level educational organizations, a more defensible policy goal would be to alter the nature of their relationships with schools, and to improve their capacities to support professional learning in schools.

School Conditions

Culture, structures, and policies and resources were the three school-level conditions which teachers in our studies associated most frequently with their professional learning. While these sets of conditions readily can be distinguished from one another conceptually, their effects on OL seem likely to depend on high levels of interdependence or coherence; this also is the case for district cultures, structures, and policies and resources. Shared norms, values and beliefs about, for example, professional responsibilities, the nature of teaching, and the value of colleagues' expertise influence the level of individual and collective motivation to learn. Collaborative decision-making structures have the potential to create the environment in which such learning can occur. And, policies and resources in support of professional growth, for example, may influence the extent to which teachers are able to find the time to participate in that environment. This interdependent view of what we have identified as three different sets of school conditions reflects Cook and Yanow's (1996) definition of organizational culture:

> a set of values, beliefs, and feelings, together with the artifacts of their expression and transmission ... that are created, inherited, shared, and transmitted within one group of people and that, in part, distinguish that group from others (1996, p. 440).

Two types of challenges seem especially important to address in subsequent research aimed at developing a more refined understanding of school conditions influencing OL. These are challenges suggested, for example, by Argyris' (1978) distinction between "single" and "double loop" learning and the closely related distinction by March (1996) and others between "exploration" and "exploitation" learning. While all these forms of learning are important for an organization, the conditions fostering each seem likely to be quite different. Preliminary evidence suggests that under most circumstances, however, schools engage exclusively in single loop or exploitative learning (Scott, 1996). Should such results be confirmed by further research, this means that even the modest knowledge base developed to date is only (or mostly) about the conditions influencing single loop or exploitative forms of OL. Future research about the conditions fostering OL needs to acknowledge these different forms of OL and inquire about differences in the conditions giving rise to each.

While most of what is known about conditions fostering OL may be limited to single loop or exploitative learning, this is still a little explored area. Although certainly not the only alternative, an especially promising framework for further developing knowledge in this area are the cognitive heuristics that have been found to introduce bias into learning and decision making under conditions of uncertainty (see Tenbrunsel et al., 1996, for a review). Research in non-school contexts suggests that some of the biases that shape indiviudal's learning and decision making (e.g., overconfidence, insensitivity to base rates) are also evident in the learning and decision making of groups (Sniezek & Henry, 1989). As well, groups exhibit unique biases: for example, we examined the learning of secondary school teams through Janis and Mann's (1977) conception of biases leading to "groupthink" with promising results (Leithwood, Steinbach, & Ryan, 1997). Guided by frameworks such as these, future research about conditions fostering single loop learning in schools ought to focus on such questions as: What biases are evident in the learning and decision making of school teams and the school, acting as a whole? What accounts for such biases? and, under what conditions are such biases minimized?

As already discussed, a fundamental purpose for OL is to enhance the school's capacity for "self organization" or "self design" (Morgan, 1986; Weick & Westley, 1996), processes that seem likely to depend on double loop and exploratory learning. Self organization entails organizational members working together to restructure, reculture, and otherwise reorient themselves in response to new challenges without the need for external intervention.

Several theoretical attempts have been made to identify the conditions required for self organization. For example, Morgan (1986) proposes four such conditions: minimal critical specification (providing people freedom from restrictive policies, and the like, enabling them to use their intelligence on behalf of the organization); redundancy of function (the avoidance of compartmentalized specialization adding the flexibility of organizational responses); learning to learn (getting better at problem solving), and requisite variety (many different initiatives underway at the same time as a means of expanding the alternative solutions eventually available to the organization).

As another example, Weick and Westley contend that:

in a self-designing organization, routine interaction with the task environment should generate information about ways to improve performance.... [Such] continuous updating results from a combination of continuous redesign, underspecified structures, reduced information filtering, intentional imbalance, and cultivation of doubt (1996, p. 443).

Self organization and OL seem to be optimal responses by schools to an ever-changing and uncertain organizational environment and our studies may have touched on important sources of conditions fostering self organization. But the differences between the theoretical speculations of Morgan and Weick, for example, and the empirical results of our studies suggest that a more comprehensive theory of self organizing conditions in schools, along with empirical exploration of such a theory, is an important goal for subsequent research. Until such evidence begins to accumulate, the call for self organization on the part of organizational theorists has no clear value for school practitioners.

School Leadership

Results of the three studies confirmed our initial expectations about the contribution of transformational leadership practices to OL and provided information about the specific leadership practices which teachers associated with OL. These data add to evidence that has accumulated over the past half dozen years (e.g., Hipp & Bredeson, 1995; Leithwood, 1996; Silins, 1992) in support of the general claim that transformational conceptions of leadership are well matched to the context of a school restructuring agenda, one that demands considerable new learning on the part of teachers and administrators. But such a conception of leadership, focused on building the commitments and capacities of organizational members, appears to compete with models of instructional leadership for dominance as an "ideal form," especially for those in administrative leadership positions.

Early versions of contemporary instructional leadership models had their genesis in the U.S. effective schools movement. They were highly control oriented and narrowly focused on the core technology of curriculum and instruction. But efforts to generalize the application of this model of leadership to different organizational levels (Kleine-Kracht, 1993; Murphy, Peterson, & Hallinger, 1986) have considerably broadened its focus and produced a more participative view of how it should be exercised. For example, six of the 10 dimensions of instructional leadership specified in Hallinger's model (Hallinger & Murphy, 1985), are concerned with something other than curriculum and instruction directly.

This observation gives rise to one major implication with which we conclude. There may be fewer differences than appear on the surface between current specifications of instructional and transformational leadership. An explicit comparison of the specific practices associated with each, and the identification of those practices from both models that have received empirical support could lead to a new synthesis of school leadership. For example, Sheppard (1996) reports that most of the variation in three different organizational outcomes included in his study was explained by fewer than half of the full set of practices included in Hallingers' version of instructional leadership. Similarly, a much reduced set of practices associated with Leithwood's (1994) model of transformational leadership also explains most of the variation in the handful of organizational outcomes included in his studies. This suggests the possibility of relying much less than we have to date on a priori theorizing about effective forms of school leadership and much more on model building based, first, on "what works," letting the development of a theoretical explanation for what works come second.

REFERENCES

Archbald, D. (1997). Curriculum control policies and curriculum standardization: Teachers' reports of policy effects. *International Journal of Educational Reform, 6*(2), 155-173.

Argyris, C. (1978). *Organizational learning*. Reading, MA: Addison-Wesley.

British Columbia Ministry of Education (1989). *Year 2000: A framework for learning*. Victoria, BC: Queen's Printer for British Columbia.

Coffin, G. (1997). *The impact of district conditions on principals' experientially acquired learning.* Unpublished doctoral dissertation, University of Toronto.

Cohen, M.D. (1996). Individual learning and organizational routine: Emerging connections. In M.D. Cohen & L.G. Sproull (Eds.), *Organizational learning* (pp. 188-194). Thousand Oaks, CA: Sage Publications.

Cohen, M.D., & Bacdayan, P. (1996). Organizational routines are stored as procedural memory: Evidence from a laboratory study. In M.D. Cohen & L.G. Sproull (Eds.), *Organizational learning* (pp. 403-429). Thousand Oaks, CA: Sage Publications.

Cook, S.D.N., & Yanow, D. (1996). Culture and organizational learning. In M.D. Cohen & L.G. Sproull (Eds.), *Organizational learning* (pp. 430-459). Thousand Oaks, CA: Sage Publications.

Cousins, B. (1996). Understanding organizational learning for school leadership and educational reform. In K. Leithwood et al. (Eds.), *International handbook of educational leadership and administration*. The Netherlands: Kluwer Academic Publishers.

Fiol, C.M., & Lyles, M.A. (1985). Organizational learning. *Academy of Management Review, 10*, 803-813.

Gioia, D.A. (1986). Conclusion: The state of the art in organizational social cognition. In H.P. Sims, Jr., D.A. Gioia, and associates (Eds.), *The thinking organization* (pp. 336-356)). San Francisco: Jossey-Bass.

Hallinger, P., & Murphy, J. (1985). Assessing the instructional management behavior of principals. *Elementary School Journal, 86*(2), 217-247.

Hallinger, P., & Heck, R.H. (1996). Reassessing the principal's role in school effectiveness: A review of empirical research, 1980-1995. *Educational Administration Quarterly, 32*(1), 5-44.

Hedberg, B.(1981). How organizations learn and unlearn. In P.C. Nystrom & W.H. Starbuck (Eds.), *Handbook of organizational design, vol. 1: Adapting organizations to their environments.* New York: Oxford University Press.

Hipp, K.A., & Bredeson, P.V. (1995). Exploring connections between teacher efficacy and principals' leadership behaviors. *Journal of School Leadership, 5*(2), 136-150.

Hutchins, E. (1991). Organizing work by adaptation. *Organization Science, 2*(1), 14-39.

Janis, I.L., & Mann, L. (1977). *Decision making*. New York: Free Press.

Kleine-Kracht, P. (1993). Indirect instructional leadership: An administrators' choice. *Educational Administration Quarterly, 18*(4), 1-29.

Kofman, F., & Senge, P. (1995). Communities of commitment: The heart of learning organizations. *Organizational Dynamics*, 5-22.

Leithwood, K., & Louis, K. (Eds.) (1998). *Organizational learning in schools*. The Netherlands: Swets & Zeitlinger.

Leithwood, K. (1994). Leadership for school restructuring. *Educational Administration Quarterly, 30*, 498-518.

Leithwood, K. (1996). School restructuring, transformational leadership, and the amelioration of teacher burnout. *Anxiety, Stress, and Coping, 9*, 199-215.

Leithwood, K., & Aitken, R. (1995). *Making schools smarter*. Thousand Oaks, CA: Corwin Press.

Leithwood, K., & Jantzi, D. (1990). Transformational leadership: How principals can help reform school cultures. *School Effectiveness and School Improvement, 1*(4), 249-280.

Leithwood, K., Jantzi, D., & Steinbach, R. (1995). An organizational learning perspective on school responses to central policy initiatives. *School Organization, 15*(3), 229-252.

Leithwood, K., Leonard, L., & Sharratt, L. (1998). Conditions fostering organizational learning in schools. *Educational Administration Quarterly, 34*(2), 243-276.

Leithwood, K., & Menzies, T. (1998). Forms and effects of school-based management: A review. *Educational Policy, 12*(3), 325-346.

Leithwood, K., & Steinbach, R. (1993). Total quality leadership: Expert thinking plus transformational practice. *Journal of Personnel Evaluation in Education, 7*(4), 311-338.

Leithwood, K., Steinbach, R., & Ryan, S. (1997). Leadership and team learning in secondary schools. *School Leadership and Management, 17*(3), 303-325.

Leonard, L.J. (1996). *Organizational learning and the initiation of school councils.* Unpublished doctoral dissertation, University of Toronto.

March, J.G. (1991). Exploration and exploitation in organizational learning. *Organization Science, 2*(1), 71-87.

March, J.G. (1996). Exploration and exploitation in organizational learning. In M.D. Cohen & L.S. Sproull (Eds.), *Organizational learning* (pp. 101-123). Thousand Oaks, CA: Sage.

McLaughlin, M.W. (1990). *District contexts for teachers and teaching.* Paper prepared for the annual meeting of the American Educational Research Foundation, Boston.

Mitchell, C., Sackney, L., & Walker, K. (1997). The postmodern phenomenon: Implications for school organizations and educational leadership. *Journal of Educational Administration and Foundations, 11*(1), 38-67.

Mohrman, S.A., & Mohrman, A.M. (1995). *Designing team-based organizations: New forms for knowledge work.* San Francisco: Jossey-Bass.

Morgan, G. (1986). *Images of organization.* Newbury Park, CA: Sage.

Murphy, J., Peterson, K., & Hallinger, P. (1986). The administrative control of principals in effective schools: The supervision and evaluation functions. *Urban Review, 18*(3), 149-175.

Newfoundland (1992). *Our children, our future: The report of the Royal Commission of Inquiry into Programs and Services in Primary, Elementary, and Secondary Education.* St. John's, Newfoundland: Government of Newfoundland and Labrador.

Rosenholtz, S.J. (1989). *Teachers' workplace.* New York: Longman.

Schoenfeld, A.H. (1989). Ideas in the air: Speculations on small group learning, environmental and cultural influences on cognition, and epistemology. *International Journal of Educational Research, 13*(1), 71-88.

Scott, A. (1996). *Towards a theory of school administrative team learning.* Unpublished doctoral dissertation, University of Toronto.

Senge, P.M. (1990). *The fifth discipline.* New York: Doubleday.

Sharratt, L. (1996). *The influence of electronically available information on the stimulation of knowledge use and organizational learning in schools.* Unpublished doctoral dissertation, University of Toronto.

Sheppard, B. (1996). Exploring the transformational nature of instructional leadership. *Alberta Journal of Educational Research, 42*(4), 325-344.

Silins, H. (1992). Effective leadership for school reform. *Alberta Journal of Educational Research, 38*(4), 317-334.

Sniezek, J.A., & Henry, R.A. (1989). Accuracy and confidences in group judgement. *Organizational Behavior and Human Decision Processes, 43,* 1-28.

Swanson, A. & King, R. (in press). *School finance: Its economics and politics* (2nd edition). New York: Longman.

Tenbrunsel, A.E., Galvin, T.L., Neale, M.A., & Bazerman, M.H. (1996). Cognitions in organizations. In S.R.Clegg, C. Hardy, & W.R. Nord (Eds.), *Handbook of organization studies* (pp. 313-337). Thousand Oaks, CA: Sage.

Walberg, H.J., & Fowler, W.J. (1987). Expenditure and size effectiveness of public school districts. *Educational Researcher, 16*(7), 5-13.

Watkins, K.E., & Marsick, V.J. (1993). *Sculpting the learning organization.* San Francisco: Jossey-Bass.

Weick, K.E., & Roberts, K.H. (1996). Collective mind in organizations: Heedful interrelating on flight decks. In M.D. Cohen & L.G. Sproull (Eds.), *Organizational learning* (pp. 330-358). Thousand Oaks, CA: Sage Publications.

Weick, K.E., & Westley, F. (1996). Organizational learning: Affirming an oxymoron. In S.R. Clegg, C. Hardy, & W.R. Nord (Eds.), *Handbook of organization studies* (pp. 440-458). Thousand Oaks, CA: Sage.

CHAPTER 6

LEADERSHIP, CULTURE, AND ORGANIZATIONAL LEARNING

Bonnie Larson-Knight

Until quite recently, many change theorists and strategists assumed that some features of schooling were sufficiently powerful that managing change in one of them would bring about significant school improvement. From about the 1950s, the focus of school improvement strategies has progressed, for example, from fixing the parts (e.g., curricula, teaching methods), through fixing the people (e.g., staff development), to fixing the school organization (changing the culture so people are better able to solve their own problems) (Sashkin & Egermeier, 1993). Only recently have we begun to understand the need to "fix" the system as a whole, to approach school improvement from a systemic perspective.

Advocates of systemic change (Elmore, 1993; Fuhrman, 1993; Senge, 1990) claim that approaching change by fixing the parts, people, or school does not work because these approaches tend "to be scattered, piecemeal, and, for the most

Advances in Research and Theories of School
Management and Educational Policy, Volume 4, pages 125-140.
Copyright © 2000 by JAI Press Inc.
All rights of reproduction in any form reserved.
ISBN: 0-7623-0024-8

part, weak in influencing teaching" (Elmore, 1993, p. 112). Systemic change, on the other hand, assumes that internal coherence is essential for productive change to occur. As yet, however, we have very little idea of what "systemic change" and "internal coherence" mean in practice.

The aim of the study summarized in this chapter (Larson-Knight, 1998) was to describe such meaning in the context of three elementary schools with reputations in their own district for being "moving" schools, to use a term coined by Rosen-holtz (1989). More specifically, the study inquired about the interaction among leadership, school culture, and organizational learning, variables often singled out independently as offering the "key" to school improvement. The study inquired about features of school culture that promote organizational learning, approaches to administrative leadership which influence the development of these features, and the nature of those leadership practices giving rise to the individual and collective learning of teachers.

BACKGROUND

While there have been few attempts to examine, empirically, the relationships among all three of the variables explored in this study, a corpus of theory and some empirical evidence has accumulated about the relationships among pairs of these variables. The largest portion of this work is concerned with the relationship between principal leadership and school culture in which culture is often conceptualized, more or less, as:

> a system of ordinary, taken-for-granted meanings and symbols with both explicit and implicit content that is deliberately and non-deliberately learned and shared among members of a naturally bounded social group (Erickson, 1987, p. 12).

Research on school culture (e.g., Little, 1982; Rosenholtz, 1989; Deal & Peterson, 1990; Fullan & Hargreaves, 1991; Hopkins, 1991; Scheerens, 1993) offers compelling evidence that strong, collaborative cultures contribute to school effectiveness. Little (1982) was among the first to investigate the relationship between principal leadership and school culture making the case that, because collaborative forms of school culture were most likely to have a positive influence on student learning, such forms ought to be the goal for leadership intervention.

Leithwood and Jantzi's (1990) study, conducted in 12 elementary schools, identified six categories of principal leadership practices typically identified in this corpus of research as contributing to the development of more collaborative cultures. One category of such practices includes strengthening the culture by, for example, involving staff in determining the school's goals and priorities, by blocking competing priorities, and systematically orienting new staff to the goals for school improvement. Other categories of leadership practices aimed at influencing the school's culture include: using a variety of bureaucratic mechanisms (e.g., hiring policies) to strengthen support for important school norms and values; fostering staff development; engaging in direct and frequent communication regarding norms, beliefs, and values; sharing power and responsibility; and effectively using symbols to express cultural values. These practices have a positive effect on interaction among teachers which, in turn, fosters collaboration.

There also is a body of theory and evidence exploring the relationship between culture and organizational learning. This includes not just individual learning in an organizational context (e.g., Brown & Duguid, 1996) but also the learning of small groups (e.g., Hutchins, 1991) and whole organizations (e.g., Cohen & Bacdayan, 1996). The case for this link is fairly straightforward. More opportunities for interaction among members of the staff increase the chances of learning from one another, and from building synergistically on the capacities and practices of others. Hedberg (1981, p. 6) is among those who maintain, on theoretical grounds, that culture affects all other elements of the organization, and in particular, indirectly and directly affects the organization's ability to learn, unlearn, and relearn new practices.

Evidence from Leithwood, Jantzi, and Steinbach's (1995, p. 44) study in six elementary and secondary schools offers empirical support for this position; the strongest influence on teachers' individual and collective learning was the school's culture when it was collaborative in form. This study also found that a coherent set of practices engaged in by leaders which modelled at least the leader's vision of what the school should become had a significant effect on organizational learning.

Many of the studies exploring the relationships between leadership and either school culture or organizational learning report practices on the part of leaders described in much recent writing as "transformational" in nature. With its roots in the seminal work of Burns (1978) and Bass (1985), this is a form of leadership which aims to build the commitments and capacities of staff to a set of purposes about which there is strong and widespread agreement among organizational members. A model of such leadership developed by Leithwood and his colleagues (e.g., Leithwood, Jantzi & Steinbach, 1999), in the context of school organizations, served as a framework for inquiring about leadership practices in this study (see also Bonstingl, 1992; Sergiovanni, 1990).

METHOD

The study took place in three elementary schools in one large district in southern Ontario. Four senior central office administrators with direct responsibilities, collectively, for the operation of all schools in the district were asked to identify schools meeting three criteria: the school was "on its way" to successfully implementing a major new initiative; a "school growth team" [the label for a district-required team of teachers who worked with the principal on school improvement planning] had been in place for at least three years; and the principal had been in the school for at least three years. Nineteen of the district's 93 elementary schools were identified as meeting these criteria, three of which were randomly selected for study.

Data were collected in the three schools in several stages. First, each principal was interviewed about his/her views on their own leadership, and how they perceived that leadership to influence the school's culture. These interviews, typically lasting about one and one-half hours, also asked about the individual and collective learning that had occurred among staff since the inception of the School Growth Team's (SGT's) initiative, and about both demographic and historical features of the school.

A focus group interview was conducted in each school, as well, with members of the school growth team (SGT). The same interview protocol was used to guide these interviews as was used with the principals, and the interviews lasted a comparable amount of time. Following the principal and focus group interviews, individual interviews were conducted with three members of each SGT and five non-SGT teachers in each school. These interviews focused on the same issues as the earlier interviews but probed more deeply into matters that had been raised during those earlier interviews. In total, interviews were conducted with three principals, three focus groups, and 24 individual teachers.

All interviews were transcribed and returned to interviewees for "member checks," a check on accuracy before analysis (Lincoln & Guba, 1985). Then these data were subjected to two rounds of coding. Round one consisted of a content analysis of transcripts explicitly guided by the concepts of transformational leadership, school culture, and organizational learning. Further classifications were developed within these major concept categories using quasi-grounded techniques: relevant background literature was explicitly called on for assistance in categorizing and coding data. In addition, categories were amended and augmented as needed so as not to force data into predetermined categories. These coded data were entered in a computer data base according to each of the descriptors. The frequency of coded idea units, or subcategories of the major concept categories, were totalled for each participant and entered on a master coding sheet (individual and focus group interviews were treated similarly). Frequency counts were calculated for all coded data from individual teachers, principal, and focus groups.

The second round of data analysis aimed to identify relationships among the three major concepts (leadership, school culture, and organizational learning) and sub concepts. All transcripts were re-coded to identify explicit links made by the interviewees among the concepts (see Khattri & Miles, 1993, p. 15). For example, in school 2, when Teacher 10 was asked about any individual, or collective growth that had occurred in the school, she identified "increased understanding in the use of cooperative learning" as an organizational learning outcome for the staff as a whole. She was then asked how the school's culture affected that learning. She replied:

> There are always opportunities to learn from one another. PD is encouraged. If someone on staff thinks a workshop would be good for you, or would like to take it, they will suggest, "Why don't you come with me." There is always that peer coaching going on.

In this case, the comments, "There are always opportunities to learn from one another. PD is encouraged" were coded "CCND" (Culture, Content, Norm, Professional Development) and linked to "OUTU" (Organizational Learning Outcome, Group). The statements, "If someone on staff thinks a workshop would be good for you, or would like to take it, they will suggest, 'Why don't you come with me?' There is always that peer coaching going on," were coded "CCNA" (Culture, Content, Norm, Mutual Support Among Colleagues) and linked to "OUTU" (Organizational Learning, Outcome, Group). Once links had been coded, they were recorded in the data base according to their categories (i.e., "Leadership Practices Which Influence Culture," "Leadership Practices Which Influence Organizational Learning," "Cultural Conditions Which Influence Organizational Learning"). The frequency of these links were calculated and entered on a master sheet. To give greater meaning to these data, causal maps summarizing the relationships among the main variables of interest in the study were developed for each school accompanied by a descriptive text explaining each of the maps.

RESULTS

This section of the chapter first provides a brief summary about characteristics of each school and their principals. The relative interconnectedness or coherence of the three schools is examined next, as a means of explicitly demonstrating the meaning of a "systemic" approach to change. Subsequent parts of this section report evidence concerning the relationships among, in order, school culture and organizational learning, leadership and school culture, leadership and organizational learning, and finally, all three variables.

The Schools, Principals, and Improvement Initiatives

Each of the three schools taught kindergarten to grade 8 classes. School 1, with 550 students was located in a 10 year old building and served a community characterized by the principal as having a "pickup truck kind of mentality." The area appeared to be a "traditional middle class kind of suburban neighborhood." Although there were "certainly strong elements of that," the principal pointed out that a number of houses were "split up into two and three apartments that [were] rented by single moms and recently arrived immigrant families who share[d] homes." School 2, with 400 students, was located in a 38 year old building and served a relatively stable urban and rural community with a mixed socio-economic status. In contrast, school 3 served a transient population drawn from six different areas representing a wide range of socio-economic backgrounds: it included 600 students and was housed in a building that was 35 years old.

The principals had distinct administrative experiences. Principal 1 had been in education for 24 years, four and a half years as a vice principal, and eight as a principal. This was his third year at school 1. School 2 had a relatively new administrator. She had taught for 25 years, been a vice principal for six years, and was in her third year as principal of school 2. The third principal had 30 years experience, 16 as a teacher, five as a vice principal, and nine as a principal. He had spent four years at school 3.

There were both similarities and differences in the school improvement efforts of the three schools. Each had been involved in change initiatives over the past three or four years, the impetus for change having come either from a need to keep up with technology or a need to incorporate new instructional strategies in the instructional repertoires of teachers. All three principals had implemented in their schools both organizational learning structures (e.g., P.A. days, lunch bag meetings, common preparation periods), and processes (e.g., working with grade partners, or divisions).

There was strong evidence from each of the schools that individual and collective learning had occurred. In school 1, an outcome of this learning was increased understanding in the use of Lego Dacta (manipulatives used for learning about technology): teachers also had gained new skills and practices in the area of technology. In school 2, teachers' cooperative learning skills had improved as had the application of these skills in their classrooms. The staff as a whole, it was claimed by interviewees, had become much more aware of "Multiple Intelligences" [from the work of Howard Gardner, 1993], as well: an outcome for students, for example, was that they had learned how to use the "Bridge of Conflict" in order to resolve their problems. The intermediate division of school 3 had become adept at writing integrated curriculum units which incorporated technology and modifications for special needs children. A change in practice transpired for most of the teachers as they moved from Socratic instruction to cooperative learning.

THE MEANING OF COHERENCE:
PATTERNS OF RELATIONSHIPS AMONG THE VARIABLES

The pattern of relationships among the three variables included in the study were captured using both quantitative and qualitative techniques. Quantitative descriptions of these patterns were based on calculations of the frequency with which interviewees explicitly linked two or three of the variables together with their own words. Table 1 summarizes the results of these calculations. The first column lists

Table 1. Frequency of Responses Linking Pairs of Variables
Including Leadership, School Culture, and Organizational Learning

	School 1		School 2		School 3	
	N = 135		*N = 242*		*N = 223*	
Total Comments	+	-	+	-	+	-
Culture and OL						
Total Participants	31 (23%)	4 (3%)	29 (12%)	1 (.4%)	41 (18%)	2 (1%)
Focus Group	9 (7%)		18 (7%)		13 (6%)	
Principal	2 (1%)		4 (2%)		18 (8%)	
Total	42 (31%)	4 (3%)	51 (21%)	1 (.4%)	72 (32%)	2 (1%)
Leadership & Culture						
Total Participants	27 (20%)		47 (20%)		41 (18%)	11 (5%)
Focus Groups	6 (4.5%)		28 (12%)		13 (6%)	
Principal	6 (4.5%)		10 (4%)		4 (2%)	
Total	39 (29%)		85 (36%)		58 (26%)	11 (5%)
Leadership & OL						
Total Participants	22 (16%)		48 (20%)		49 (22%)	2 (1%)
Focus Group	13 (10%)		40 (16%)		21 (9%)	2 (1%)
Principal	15 (11%)		17 (7%)		6 (3%)	
Total	50 (37%)		105 (43%)		76 (34%)	4 (2%)

the combinations of variables that might be linked together, and the three categories of interviewees serving as the sources of those links. Columns 2, 4, and 6 indicate the number of times links were made between variables that were perceived as productive in all three schools. Columns 3, 5, and 7 specify the frequency of links perceived to be unproductive.

The overall pattern of results evident in Table 1 suggests more extensive (i.e., more frequently mentioned) links of a productive sort among variables in school 2 than in either schools 1 or 3. The total number of such links for all pairs of variables is 242 in school 2 as compared with 135 and 223 respectively in schools 1 and 3. Furthermore, while only two links of an unproductive nature were mentioned for school 2, links of this nature were mentioned eight times in school 1, and 34 times in school 3. Most links were reported between culture and organizational learning in school 3; the other two pairs of variables were linked more frequently by interviewees in school 2 than in either of the other schools.

There are serious limitations to relying on these quantitative results alone for evidence concerning the pattern of relationships among variables. For example, participants in schools 2 and 3 were more "chatty" than those in school 1: on the first level of coding, the total number of comments made by participants in school 2 were 1,038 compared to 1,116 in school 3 and only 837 in school 1. Futhermore, these frequency-based results tell us nothing about the nature of the relationships.

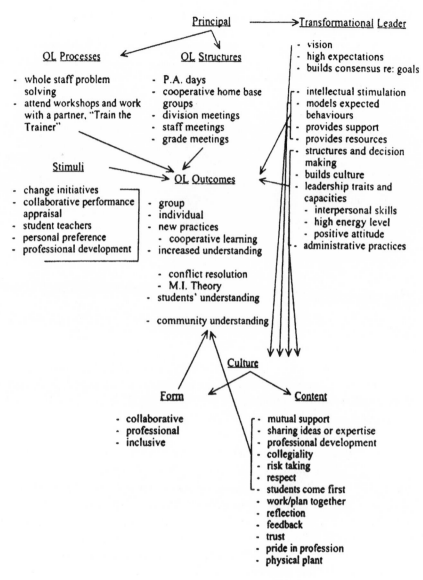

Principal ────────►Transformational Leader

- vision
- high expectations
- builds consensus re: goals

OL Processes ◄──── OL Structures

- whole staff problem solving
- attend workshops and work with a partner, "Train the Trainer"

- P.A. days
- cooperative home base groups
- division meetings
- staff meetings
- grade meetings

- intellectual stimulation
- models expected behaviours
- provides support
- provides resources
- structures and decision making
- builds culture
- leadership traits and capacities
  - interpersonal skills
  - high energy level
  - positive attitude
- administrative practices

Stimuli ────► OL Outcomes

- change initiatives
- collaborative performance appraisal
- student teachers
- personal preference
- professional development

- group
- individual
- new practices
  - cooperative learning
  - increased understanding

- conflict resolution
- M.I. Theory
- students' understanding

- community understanding

Culture

Form ◄────   ────► Content

- collaborative
- professional
- inclusive

- mutual support
- sharing ideas or expertise
- professional development
- collegiality
- risk taking
- respect
- students come first
- work/plan together
- reflection
- feedback
- trust
- pride in profession
- physical plant

Figure 1.   Causal Map for School 2

The qualitative analysis of these data culminated in a causal map for each school. Both quantitative and qualitative analyses suggested that the pattern of relationships among leadership, culture, and organizational learning was more fully developed in school 2 than either of the other schools. For this reason the causal map of these relationships in school 2 is displayed in Figure 1. This figure summarizes the more detailed results of the interviews about the specific qualities associated with each of the three variables. The arrows on this figure suggest the direction of influence of one variable on another as indicated by interviewees. For example, all transformational leadership practices appear to directly influence school culture whereas only some (e.g., intellectual stimulation, modeling expected behaviors) were directly linked by respondents to organizational learning. Principal leadership was reported to have a direct influence on organizational learning structures and processes, as well.

The pattern of relationships which exists in school 2 provides an excellent example of internal coherence. This may be as close as a real school gets to being ideal in this respect. Although schools 1 and 3 also demonstrated internal coherence, their patterns were slightly different from school 2's in particular ways, described more fully in the following sections.

Culture and Organizational Learning

Participants in all three schools talked about the relationship between features of the school culture and the learning of themselves and their colleagues. While these data were coded and frequencies calculated as in Table 1, this and the subsequent sections, are limited to a largely qualitative discussion of the five features of school culture most frequently associated with organizational learning.

"Mutual Support Among Colleagues" was viewed as a primary condition for organizational learning by participants in all schools. Four teachers in school 1, six in school 2, and five in school 3 identified this condition as contributing to their learning, as did all three focus groups, and the principals in schools 2 and 3. For example, a focus group member in school 1 asserted, "If you're supported and accepted, then you can learn." Another participant in the focus group added, "I have had major support from this staff." In school 2, one teacher said that the school's culture had affected her learning because "we are all very supportive of each other … and aware of each other's needs." A teacher in school 3 explained how mutual support affected learning. "In a supportive environment, someone who wants to excel, someone who wants to learn [can]." Another comment reiterating the profound impact of mutual support was made by a teacher in school 3. He felt that the school's culture encouraged teachers to learn, inasmuch as "teachers go out of their way to be better teachers because there's always that support there."

"Professional Development" was a condition which acquired more support from interviewees in schools 2 and 3 than school 1. Four individual teachers and the focus groups in both schools, and the principal in school 3 commented on the contribution to their learning of professional development. School 1, in contrast, had only one teacher remark on this condition. According to a teacher in school 2, "Being on this staff you are motivated. You want to be up-to-date so you need new teaching methods." One of the focus group members from the school also felt that the culture influenced the staff's capacity to learn. "You don't want to be left out ... If you are not involved [in learning], good Lord, you feel, 'Oh, geez!' They drag you along." Another focus group participant added, "That's right, and because it [learning] is such an on-going process, you could get left in the dust really quickly, but they do not let that happen in this school." The same holds true for school 3 where a teacher claimed, "I think you feel as though you should be getting out and finding out about these things.... I have felt since I have been here that I needed to find out about things [even though] it was later in my career."

"Risk Taking" was a feature of school culture linked to learning by comments from four participants in school 1, three in school 2, and one in school 3. All focus groups remarked on this feature, as did principals 1 and 3. In school 1, a focus group teacher maintained that, "We are given the chance and opportunities to go out and try new things in our classrooms, to be risk takers ... [As a result] I could just about go in and try anything new." According to another teacher in this school, "We are all open to new ideas." Yet another teacher observed, "Our culture, which is one where you feel comfortable, you can risk take, [and that] promotes learning because you're not afraid to go out and try things." Focus group teachers in school 2 made comments about this condition, as well: "We are all willing to risk take." Or, as another said, "You are willing to grow, learn, and take risks." In school 3, the principal observed, "More and more, people are ready to learn new things and see new things." One teacher in this school felt that if the school's culture did not encourage risk taking, "then you are not going to want to try. You are not going to want to learn."

"Sharing of Ideas and Resources" was a feature of school culture identified by respondents from all schools as contributing to learning. This feature received different amounts of support from the various participants, however. Another feature which was seen as important was the belief in "Students First." Five teachers in school 3 commented on this. According to an interviewee in school 3, teachers had to switch "from full rotary eight periods a day" to having their classes "for at least fifty percent of the day." They had to gain a better understanding of "more home room style teaching" because they needed to have "consistency within the classroom." They felt that spending more time with their students would provide stability for the students and improve discipline, as well as academic results. Thus, because their culture condoned doing what was best for students, the teachers were willing to move from being subject specialists to homeroom teachers.

   In sum, respondents in all three schools identified similar features of their schools' cultures as contributing to their individual and collective learning. In particular, they identified: collaborative cultures, mutual support, professional development, risk taking, sharing of ideas and resources, and the belief that students come first. Although respondents from school 3 more frequently spoke of these links, teachers, focus groups, and the principal did not necessarily assign the same importance to each feature. In school 2, however, there were more similarities in responses across sources of data suggesting greater internal coherence in this school.

Leadership and School Culture

As in the previous section, this section is limited to a largely qualitative discussion of the main results of the study as they concern the relationship between leadership and school culture. As noted earlier, data about leadership practices was coded initially in relation to dimensions of a model of transformational leadership developed by Leithwood and his colleagues (e.g., Leithwood, Jantzi, & Steinbach, 1999).

The dimension "Leader Provides Support" had the most impact on all three schools' cultures. In school 1, six teachers, the focus group, and the principal commented on this dimension. For example, one teacher remarked that principal 3 influenced the school's culture because "he supports us—helps us when we ask for help and lets us know what's going on." A third of all comments made by participants in school 2 had to do with this dimension: all eight teachers, the focus group, and the principal connected "leader provides support" to culture. Teacher 11 explained:

> She models it [culture]. She is out there and she's active and the kids know she is. She provides support by showing up on weekends for tournaments. She has one-on-one chats with you or with small groups and listens and is fair and gives feedback when it is needed. She pulls us along when we need it ... a little kick start here and there.

Four teachers in school 3, and the focus group, made positive comments about the principal's impact on culture. One teacher contended that the principal influenced the culture by spending a lot of time in the classrooms: "He's very supportive of teachers. He backs the teachers up in dealings with parents and in dealings with students. He is continually encouraging us to up-date ourselves and to go to workshops." The opposite perspective was shared by a member of the focus group, "I guess we need to see that [support] more often.... You need to feel that you are being supported." These diametrically opposed viewpoints occurred in other dimensions as well (i.e., administrative practices), thus reducing the internal coherence of school 3.

"Leadership Traits and Capacities," not part of the original set of leadership codes, emerged as an important influence on school culture. Three teachers in schools 1 and 3 and five teachers in school 2, as well as their focus groups, and principals in school 2 and 3 contended that leadership traits affected school culture. In school 2, for example, when asked what the principal did to influence culture, a teacher answered:

The whole climate has changed because of her.... she doesn't force or push, or anything like
that, but she makes it pleasant. It's just her general attitude. And she is just such a ball of fire
herself that it just gets you going too.... She listens to your ideas.

More leadership practices were linked with culture in school 2 than in the other
two schools. Indeed, school 2 participants commented on all 11 of the leadership
dimensions used for coding purposes. Participants in school 1 remarked on eight
of these dimensions and teachers in school 3 commented on ten of them (three of
the responses indicated negative and positive comments while one response was
negative only). One inference from these data is that principal 2 embodied more
of the dimensions of a transformational leader and, therefore, contributed more to
developing a collaborative culture in her school.

Leadership and Organizational Learning

Of the leadership dimensions associated with organizational learning, the most
frequently mentioned were "Leaders Provides Support," "Leader Provides
Resources," and "Leader Provides Intellectual Stimulation." In schools 1 and 2,
five teachers commented on "Leader Provides Support", as did seven teachers
from school 3, the focus groups, and the principals.

One teacher in school 1 contended that, "Any workshop that I wanted to go to,
I came and asked him [principal]. He's been really amazing that way. He doesn't
come at you personally. He sort of opens it up and lets you know about it and then
supports you if you want to go, which is great." Principal 1 maintained, "I have
always been a big fan of the notion of a plan for yourself for the year." Therefore,
he sponsored any teachers who wished to attend any staff development opportunities. A similar situation occurred in school 2. At the beginning of each year, the
principal asked, "What areas of professional growth ... we plan to pursue for the
year, and she follows up on that." Principal 3 appeared to operate in an analogous
manner; one teacher reported that the principal was always asking if teachers
wanted to attend workshops. "He doesn't shove anything down anyone's throat.
He certainly makes everybody aware of what is out there and if you would like to
go, it is not a problem.... things are presented and you are more than encouraged
to go to them." By having teachers set goals for themselves and by encouraging
people to attend professional development sessions, these three leaders fostered
learning in their schools.

"Providing resources" was another dimension of leadership which was seen as
contributing to learning. Five teachers in schools 2 and 3, four teachers in school
1, the focus groups, and the principals considered this dimension significant in
relationship to OL. In school 1, for example, the principal confessed, "I fund anything that people want to go to.... The vice principal and I cover [classes] so staff
can have time .... I find some extra time to pay off those people who give of their

own time to plan workshops for staff.... I bring people in.... [We brought] in every facilitator in the system and sprung every staff member for a day."

Principal 2 explained how she got teachers moving with technology. She provided them with "prep time, brought in the computer facilitator, and set up a schedule where they [teachers] met with the facilitator for one quarter of the day on two occasions." She felt that the stimulus for learning was there because people were excited about the changes that had occurred before and now they wanted to keep up with the technology and the Multiple Intelligences end of it. The result was they "did it"; they integrated literacy, technology, and Multiple Intelligences into their new project.

In school 3, the principal provided resources so that staff could take advantage of numerous professional development opportunities. On an individual basis, he told how the music teacher "hadn't touched anything or gone near a computer before." So he provided her with the resources to learn how to use technology in her program.

> Now we have a computer in her room and we have got a new Yamaha keyboard that has the Midi format to it and we got the Q-Base program for her so that's attached. Her focus is trying to use that software and hardware to enhance and develop her music program. So she is doing that.

All three principals also provided their teachers with intellectual stimulation. For example, principal 1 observed, "You have to be the initiator. It depends on what happens when you throw stuff out." This teacher would agree: "He just simply poses a question and allows everybody to react because he knows them [staff] well. However, when it's something he feels people are not reacting to, and they should, [Principal] starts by initiating things." Another teacher declared that "the principal is responsible for introducing staff to any new ideas and he provides lots of opportunities for us to become familiar with new policies." Yet another teacher also felt that "he has brought a lot of ideas in and sort of lets us take off with them at our own pace."

Principal 2 provided intellectual stimulation for her staff in numerous ways. According to one interviewee, "She brings in speakers." A teacher noted that, "She often hands me articles, Michael [Fullan] for instance." Principal 2 ensured that the school had professional journals (i.e., *Canadian Educator*) and she summarized articles for the staff. This principal also admitted that she used staff development officers and trainers to bring new ideas to staff.

Teachers in school 3 commented on the number of ways that their principal stimulated them intellectually. "He has brought in speakers.... He has organized workshops." One teacher remarked that the principal provided them with intellectual stimulation by "making sure we get out to the workshops and get involved in the in-services at the board." Another also pointed out, "We have a lot of contact with outside specialists.... there is a lot of contact between the administration and people of that nature who have helped the teacher in the classroom."

Organizational Learning, Leadership, and Culture

Evidence was provided in all schools of leadership, organizational learning, and school culture interacting together in both complex and synergistic ways. Twelve examples of such interaction were provided in school 1, and six in each of schools 2 and 3. In each of these cases, having both a transformational leader, and a collaborative, professional, and inclusive culture fostered the organizational learning necessary for the schools to build, year after year, on their past initiatives.

CONCLUSION

To develop a more detailed, nuanced, and explicit understanding of the meaning of systemic change, this study examined the relationships among three variables often cited independently as "keys" to successful change—leadership, culture, and organizational learning. Case study evidence from reputationally "moving" elementary schools, spoke to three questions about these relationships.

The first question was concerned with those features of school culture which teachers believed most contributed to their individual and collective learning. Features identified in this study included: mutual support among colleagues in the school, permission to take risks when attempting to improve one's practices, sharing of ideas and resources, and support for professional development; these are among the features associated by McLaughlin (1993) with professional learning communities. Also associated with organizational learning in these schools was the belief, widely held by staff and administrators, that students should come first in their deliberations and practices, a belief closely related to the "learning imperative" Beck and Murphy (1999) characterized as the central explanation for success in a case study of site-based management in one elementary school.

Administrative leadership practices influencing the development of these features of school culture was the focus of the second question addressed by this study. Results pointed to those practices recently associated with transformational leadership in schools (e.g., Leithwood, Jantzi, & Steinbach, 1999). Administrative leaders in the three schools fostered collaborative cultures by providing support to staff for their learning, explicitly speaking and acting in ways that demonstrated the importance they attached to collaboration. They also modelled expected behaviours, and worked with staff toward a vision for the school. In addition to these transformational practices, leaders' abilities to listen to the needs, concerns, and ideas of staff was also influential in building collaborative cultures.

Evidence from the study unequivocally pointed to three leadership practices fostering organizational learning, the third issue of interest in the study. These, too, were practices associated with transformational approaches to leadership, including support for the work of teachers in a variety of ways, making resources available to teachers when they were needed, and providing intellectual stimulation to teachers as they explored new ideas, or when they seemed unable to imagine alternatives to their routine practices.

The results of this study suggest the need for much greater attention to interactions between leadership and other demonstrably significant variables or features of schools and their environments. Independent effects of such variables may be not only relatively weak, but deceptive as well. This claim receives some additional support, for example, from a recent study of contextual effects on secondary school students' mathematics achievement. Wiley (1999) found evidence of an interactive relationship between transformational leadership and professional community. Specifically, her evidence suggested that transformational leadership practices "positively affects the amount of learning in mathematics in schools with below average levels of professional community, while professional community only positively affects the amount of learning in mathematics when the level of transformational leadership is above average" (p. 14).

This complex account of leadership effects conforms, more closely than is typical of leadership reseach, to the sophisticated practitioner's understanding of "how leadership works" and suggests the need for a new generation of leadership research. This research would combine variables of demonstrable relevance to student outcomes, those associated with school effects studies, for example (e.g., Mortimore, 1991), with approaches to leadership for which there is promising evidence of organizational and student impact (see Hallinger & Heck, 1999). The goal of such studies should be to build an account of how leaders contribute to student development through their interactions with teachers and other features of the school organization. As Smylie and Hart argue, from their review of the literature on social and human capital development, it "identifies interaction generally, and particular qualitative elements of interaction as crucial mechanisms of principal leadership" (1999, p. 429).

REFERENCES

Bass, B.M. (1985). *Leadership and performance beyond expectations.* New York: Free Press.

Beck, L., & Murphy, J. (1999). Site-based management and school success: Untangling the variables. *School Effectiveness and School Improvement, 9*(4), 358-385.

Bonstingl, J. (1992). The quality revolution in education. *Educational Leadership, 50*(3), 4-9.

Brown, J. S., & Duguid, P. (1996). Organizational learning and communities-of-practice: Toward a unified view of working, learning, and innovation. In M. D. Cohen & L. S. Spraull (Eds.), *Organiztional learning* (pp. 58-82). Thousand Oaks, CA: Sage Publications.

Burns, J.M. (1978). *Leadership.* New York: Harper & Row.

Cohen, M., & Bacdayan, P. (1996). Organizational routines are stored as professional memory: Evidence from a laboratory study. In M.D. Cohen & L.G. Sproull (Eds.), *Organizational learning* (pp. 403-429). Thousand Oaks, CA: Sage Publications.

Deal, T.E., & Peterson, K.D. (1990). *The principal's role in shaping school culture.* Washington: U.S. Government Printing Office.

Elmore, R. (1993). The role of local school districts in instructional improvement. In S. Fuhrman (Ed.), *Designing coherent education policy* (pp. 96-124). San Francisco: Jossey-Bass Publishers.

Erickson, F. (1987). Conceptions of school culture. *Educational Administration Quarterly, 23*(4), 11-24.

Fuhrman, S. (1993). *Designing coherent education policy: Improving the system.* San Francisco: Jossey-Bass Publishers.

Fullan, M., & Hargreaves, A. (1991). *What's worth fighting for? Working together for your school.* Toronto: Ontario Public School Teachers' Federation.

Gardner, H. (1993). *Multiple intelligences: The theory in practice.* New York: Basic Books.

Hallinger, P., & Heck, R. (1999). Next generation methods for the study of leadership and school improvement. In J. Murphy and K. S. Louis (Eds.), *Handbook of research on educational administration* (pp. 141-162). San Francisco: Jossey-Bass Publishers.

Hedberg, B. (1981). How organizations learn and unlearn. In P.C. Nystrom & W.H. Starbuck (Eds.), *Handbook of organizational design,* Vol. 1. New York: Oxford University Press.

Hopkins, D. (1991). *Improving the quality of schooling.* Lewes, Sussex: The Falmer Press.

Hutchins, E. (1991). Organizing work by adaptation. *Organization Science, 2*(1), 14-39.

Khattri, N., & Miles, M. (1993). Thinking about restructuring: The promise of cognitive mapping. In *Mapping Restructuring,* Final Report, 1991-1993. Sparkill, NY: Centre for Policy Research.

Larson-Knight, J. B. (1998). *The interdependent relationships of organizational learning and leadership practices within school cultures.* Unpublished doctoral thesis, University of Toronto.

Lincoln, Y., & Guba, E. (1985). *Naturalistic inquiry.* Beverly Hills: Sage Publications.

Leithwood, K., & Jantzi, D. (1990). Transformational leadership: How principals can help reform school cultures. *School Effectiveness and School Improvement, 1*(4), 249-280.

Leithwood, K., Jantzi, D., & Steinbach, R. (1995). An organizational learning perspective on school responses to central policy initiatives. *School Organization, 15*(3), 229-252.

Leithwood, K., Jantzi, D., & Steinbach, R. (1999). *Changing leadership for changing times.* Buckingham, UK: Open University Press.

Little, J.W. (1982). Norms of collegiality and experimentation: Workplace conditions of school success. *American Educational Research Journal, 19,* 325-340.

McLaughlin, M. (1993). What matters most in teachers' workplace context? In J. Little & M. McLaughlin (Eds.), *Teachers' work: Individuals, colleagues, and context* (pp. 79-103). New York: Teachers College Press.

Mortimore, P. (1991). The nature and findings of research on school effectiveness in the primary sector. In S. Riddell and S. Brown (Eds.), *School effectiveness research* (pp. 9-20). Edinburgh: The Scottish Office, Education Department, HMSO.

Rosenholtz, S. (1989). *Teachers' workplace.* New York: Longman.

Sashkin, M., & Egermeier, J. (1993). *School change models and processes: A review and synthesis of research and practice.* Washington, DC: U.S. Department of Education.

Scheerens, J. (1993). Basic school effectiveness research: Items for a research agenda. *School Effectiveness and School Improvement, 4*(1), 17-36.

Senge, P. (1990). *The fifth discipline: The art and practice of the learning organization.* New York: Doubleday.

Sergiovanni, T.J. (1990). Adding value to leadership gets extraordinary results. *Educational Leadership, 47*(8), 23-27.

Smylie, M., & Hart, A. (1999). School leadership for teacher learning and change: A human and social capital development perspective. In J. Murphy & K. S. Louis (Eds.), *Handbook of research on educational administration* (pp. 421-442). San Francisco: Jossey-Bass Publishers.

Wiley, S. (1999). *Contextual effects on student achievement: School leadership and professional community.* Mimeographed. Santa Barbara: University of California.

CHAPTER 7

SYSTEMS THINKING/ SYSTEMS CHANGING™
A COMPUTER SIMULATION FOR LEARNING HOW TO MAKE SCHOOLS SMARTER

Philip Hallinger, David P. Crandall, and
David Ng Foo Seong

Rapid growth is challenging the capacity of people and organizations to adapt to an onslaught of rapid, ongoing social, cultural and economic changes throughout the world (Naisbitt, 1997; Ohmae, 1995; Rohwer, 1996). The challenge to change is as great in schools as anywhere else in society—perhaps even greater. During the 1990s, the pace of change increased dramatically in schools as governments initiated a continuous stream of complex reforms (Hargreaves & Fullan, 1998).

Advances in Research and Theories of School
Management and Educational Policy, Volume 4, pages 141-162.
Copyright © 2000 by JAI Press Inc.
All rights of reproduction in any form reserved.
ISBN: 0-7623-0024-8

In this context of transformational change, learning has become the keystone to successful individual and organizational adaptation. As Barth has observed, "Any student who leaves school before or after graduation without the possibility that they will continue learning is at-risk" in today's society (1997, p. 13). It is equally true that schools and their staffs must demonstrate the capacity to learn or they are also at-risk. Unless schools can incorporate practices that foster their own continuous learning, they will be unable to keep up with the changing needs and rising expectations of the public.

Consequently, the notion of learning organizations has become highly salient to educational leaders in a relatively short time. As described by Senge (1990), a learning organization is distinguished by several capacities. A learning organization can:

- Change how it thinks and acts.
- Adapt to changing conditions.
- Do what it was never able to do before.
- Continually expand its capacity to create its future.
- Create an environment where people are continually learning how to learn together.

While the concept of a "learning organization" would seem naturally attuned to the perspective of educators, relatively few schools demonstrate these capacities. On the contrary, the traditional design of schools seems to stifle rather than foster adult learning (Barth, 1997; Fullan, 1990, 1993; Levine, Barth, & Haskins, 1987). Thus we cannot take for granted the capacity of school staffs to learn the new skills and attitudes needed for successful change (Isaacson & Bamburg, 1992; Mitchell & Sackney, 1998).

While the rationale for developing the school as a learning organization appears reasonable (Cousins, 1998; Leithwood, Jantzi, & Steinbach,1998; Voogt, Lagerweij, & Louis, 1998), only recently have researchers begun to empirically study the nature and impact of this approach (e.g., Cousins, 1996; Leithwood, Jantzi, & Steinbach, 1998). As with past reforms, it is likely that researchers will learn the most from engaging in and studying actual efforts to create learning organizations (Fullan, 1993). A crucial element will involve training staff how to think about and use the practices of a learning organization.

The challenge of designing a means for helping school staffs learn how to make schools smarter was assumed by a research and development team at The NETWORK Inc. The result of this effort was the *Systems Thinking/Systems Changing*[TM] simulation (The NETWORK Inc., 1997, 1999). In this chapter we will describe the design and use of the computer-based version of this simulation.

THE SIMULATION:
ITS ASSUMPTIONS AND INSTRUCTIONAL DESIGN

Some years ago at the close of a workshop on instructional leadership, one of the participants, a secondary school principal, voiced his feedback on the training.

> This workshop was very interesting. I'd never thought of my role in the terms described here today and would like to apply some of these ideas in my school. However, I feel like one of my juniors after they've completed their first semester of chemistry. I feel like I've learned just enough to go back and blow up my school! (personal communication, May 15, 1986).

This anecdote highlights a key challenge facing those involved in school improvement: how to take potentially useful conceptual knowledge and make it accessible and applicable for practitioners. This was what the design team tried to do with the *Systems Thinking/Systems Changing*^{TM} simulation; design a simulation that would enable practitioners both to understand the concept of a learning organization and learn how to apply it to their work in school improvement. We begin by discussing the assumptions that underlie the simulation and then proceed to describe how learners use the simulation in an instructional environment.

UNDERLYING ASSUMPTIONS OF THE SIMULATION

Several assumptions underlie the instructional design of the *Systems Thinking/ Systems Changing* simulation (Bershad, Mundry, & Hallinger, 1999). These include:

- The goal of training about the creation of learning organizations should be to *develop knowledge that practitioners can apply* (Bershad & Mundry, 1997)
- A *problem-based approach* (PBL) to learning new concepts would yield greater results given the goal of developing usable knowledge (Bridges & Hallinger, 1993, 1995; Hallinger & McCary, 1990). A key facet of PBL posits that knowledge and skill transfer will be enhanced if the content is learned in the context of a realistic problem (Bridges & Hallinger, 1995).
- An *interactive simulation* in which the learners can develop, apply and see the results of different strategies for creating a learning organization would be effective at developing capacities for higher order thinking about leading change (Bransford, 1993; Hallinger & McCary, 1990).

- Since the process of transforming schools into learning organizations would require practitioners to learn and lead in a team-based environment, *the learning process should model a team-learning format* (Bridges & Hallinger, 1995; Leithwood et al., 1998).
- Given the scarcity of time for formal staff development outside the school, *the design of the simulation should incorporate substantial cognitive scaffolding* so teachers and principals can learn at their own pace inside and outside of formal training workshops (Bershad, Mundry, & Hallinger, 1999).
- Since learning to apply any sophisticated conceptual framework takes time, it would be advantageous if the *simulation design made it convenient for learners to engage in multiple opportunities for practice* (Bershad, Mundry, & Hallinger, 1999).
- A simulation that mirrors the complexity of implementing change in the real world of schools should foster open-ended thinking about school improvement and model the assumption that *there is no one best change strategy that will work in all schools* (Hargreaves & Fullan, 1998).
- The simulation should *incorporate a mix of multidisciplinary resources drawn from theory, empirical research, and practice* (Bridges & Hallinger, 1995).

As we shall elaborate, these assumptions are woven into the instructional design of the computer-based simulation.

INSTRUCTIONAL DESIGN

The *Systems Thinking/Systems Changing* simulation was designed as a training tool for school leaders: principals, vice principals, system administrators, teachers, and school board members. Learners play in teams of two or three people per computer, even when there are sufficient computers for everyone. There are two reasons behind the use of a team-learning process.

First, the development of team-work skills represents a concurrent goal of the simulation. Teams will lead most school improvement efforts in the future, rather than individuals. Consequently, the instructional design explicitly adopts and models a team-based approach to problem solving and decision making.

Second, research as well as experience with other computer simulations shows that cooperative learning accelerates the learning of individuals in a problem-based environment (Hallinger & McCary, 1990). Working with a partner in the problem-based exercise forces each individual to surface his/her assumptions about leading school improvement. The process of discussion, resolving conflicts among ideas, and mutual reflection visibly raises the quality of thinking within the learning environment. When playing the simulation as individuals, especially the first time, there is a danger of learners short-cutting the thinking process and assuming a computer-game mentality. Thus we have incorporated a team-learning format as an essential feature in the formal initial use of the simulation.

As with all problem-based learning (Bridges & Hallinger, 1995), the simulation begins by presenting the learners with a problem rather than with the theoretical content. Immediately upon starting the simulation, the teams of learners confront their challenge: how to begin building a learning community.

YOUR TASK

You are members of a team appointed by the Superintendent of the Verifine School District (VSD) to help change the school district into a continuously improving learning community. A "learning community" is one that systematically plans, implements, and monitors its progress towards benefiting all learners and stakeholders. A learning community or learning organization is created when people work together to create the results they desire, think, and work in truly innovative ways, and are continually learning how to learn together (Senge, 1990).

In the simulation, you will work for three years to accomplish the goals of the game. Your goals are:

- To move most members of the school and community represented in the VSD through the stages of becoming a learning community—from the Awareness to Renewal stage (see Figure 1: The Gameboard).
- To produce as many learner benefits as possible through improvements in teaching and learning.

Your playing team should assume the following:

- You have the Superintendent's permission to plan but do not yet have his broader support nor the commitment of school district and community members.
- The people in the school community whom you need to influence know nothing about this effort.
- You have three years to accomplish your mission of building a continuously improving, learning organization.

The Verifine School Community includes an administrative staff and school board, a K-5 school, a 6-8 middle school, and a 9-12 secondary school. It is a community that has tried many innovations in the past with mixed success. It has a diverse student and community population. Learners will read about each

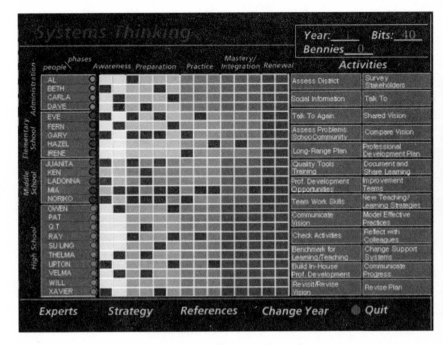

Figure 1.   The Gameboard

of the staff and community members whom they will be trying to influence in the simulation.

After reading the problem on the computer screen, the improvement team (i.e., the learners playing the simulation) begin to access other factual information concerning their situation. This information is presented via handouts and the computer screen.

The game board on the computer screen (see Figure 1), displays the school and community members on the left-hand side. Listed across the top of the board are five stages of the change process: Awareness, Preparation, Practice, Mastery, Renewal. The game pieces representing the 24 people begin "off the game board" because they have yet to begin the process of change. The goal of the school improvement team is to move these staff, parents, and students from a state of knowing nothing about learning organizations as a school improvement process to a stage of mastery and renewal (i.e., to skillful use of the concept as a guide to efforts to improve their schools).

Each of the 24 staff members has a unique personality that is conveyed through a brief description on a handout. For example, the superintendent's description reads, "Al has things running smoothly but appreciates the need for continuous improvement. He supports issues that are important to children and realizes they face a rapidly changing world." Or Irene, a primary school teacher: "Irene knows what works in her classroom; the old ways are best. She keeps students busy and has limited the time she needs for prep and correction. She will resist anything that results in more work."

The team has an budget which it may spend on activities intended to foster a learning community. The budget is represented in units called bits and is replenished each year. There are 26 activities from which the learners can choose to implement (see Figure 2). These are typical activities an improvement team might undertake: talking with staff, creating a shared vision, surveying the stakeholders, providing professional development. By spending the budget on some combination of these activities, the learners will begin to see change occur.

Each time that learners implement an activity in the simulation, they receive feedback describing what happened. For example, if the team chooses the "Talk With" activity, their budget will be reduced accordingly, the people they talk with may (or may not) move on the game board, and they will receive feedback on what happened and why. If the activity was successful the game piece(s) representing the people will move one or more spaces. If unsuccessful, they may stay put. Thus, the first time they "Talk With" Al, they receive the following feedback: "Al is very busy. He talks enthusiastically about the importance of continuous school improvement, but you wonder if he's really as supportive as he suggests." He moves one space. If they decide to "Talk With" Irene, she responds. "Why do we need more of these school improvement committees? It's simply not necessary—everything is working just fine. We've been through this before." Irene doesn't move at all. Through this process of planning, doing, getting feedback, reflecting, and acting, the improvement team, (i.e., the learners) continue to develop, implement, and see the results of their strategy for creating a learning organization.

The success of certain activities in the simulation depends upon the completion of other activities. The instruction is designed so that the learners develop the desired conceptual frameworks out of their experience in the simulation. Therefore, the simulation is designed with hidden decision rules. These require the learner to develop a strategic sequence of activities that will increase the capacity for continuous learning within the system. So, for example, before the learners are able to successfully implement the activity, Implement New Teaching and Learning Strategies, they must have successfully completed several other activities including: Assess the District, Develop a Professional Development Plan, and either Provide Professional Development or Benchmark Successful Practices. In this case, if they have not developed a sequence that builds capacity prior to trying to implement the new strategies, their effort would be unsuccessful and they would receive the following feedback: "You haven't learned enough about effective teaching and learning strategies that are being used in other schools. You risk reinventing the wheel. Do more homework about the practices in use in other schools and/or get some training in this area. No one moves."

1. Assess District Progress

Assess the district's success in meeting local, state, and national learning standards and how the community culture and climate supports and/or impedes that success.

Choose: 8 people   Cost: 4 Bits

2. Survey Stakeholders

3. Gather Social Information

4. Talk with staff, students, parents and other stakeholders

5. Talk with Again

6. Create a Shared Vision

7. Assess Problems and Processes of the Community

8. Compare Vision with Current Reality

9. Develop a Long-range Plan that Links Activities with Vision

10. Develop a System-wide Staff Development Plan

11. Conduct Quality Tools Training

12. Document Successes, Failures, Share Learnings

13. Provide Professional Development

14. Create and Maintain Improvement Teams

15. Develop Teamwork Skills

16. Implement New Learning and Teaching Strategies

17. Communicate Vision

18. Model Effective Practices

19. Check Activities Against Effectiveness of Plan and Implementation

20. Reflect with Colleagues

21. Benchmark Best Practices for Learning and Teaching

22. Change Systems to Support Vision

23. Build In-house Capacity to Provide Professional Development

24. Communicate Progress

25. Revisit and Revise Vision

26. Revise Plan Based on Current Reality

Figure 2.   Simulation Activities[1]

In addition, the success of certain activities in the simulation depends upon the readiness of people for the change. This facet of the simulation derives from the Concerns Based Adoption Model (Hall & Hord, 1987). This model assumes that people will be more successful at implementing change if the activities in which they engage address their needs or concerns. So, for example, the successful implementation of New Teaching and Learning Strategies activities also depends upon people having reached a sufficient level of knowledge, interest, and skill in the new strategies. Thus, in the prior example at least four of the eight people designated to implement the new teaching and learning strategies must have reached the Practice Stage on the game board. If not, they would receive the following feedback: "The people involved are not ready to implement new strategies. Do some more preparation with them so they have a better idea 'how to do it.' Or choose a group that is better prepared and then try again. No one moves."

The simulation also provides feedback on learning outcomes. Certain activities—generally those that involve teachers and students—also generate learner benefits. These are conveyed via the feedback and accumulate through the three years in which the simulation is played. So if Implementation of New Teaching and Learning Strategies was successful the feedback would note: "Your assessment of needs helps you make use of current research on learning and teaching. Staff begin using new strategies that—to the surprise of some—increase student interest and enhance their learning. Gain 50 Bennies for everyone in Mastery Stage and beyond. Double the number of Bennies for everyone in the Renewal stage. Every participant moves one space." Bennies are the learner benefits.

At the end of the three years the improvement team can see the results of its change strategy. Success is based on two criteria: (a) moving people through the stages of change (i.e., how many of the 24 people in the system reached the Renewal Stage?) and (b) improving learning outcomes (i.e., how many learner benefits did their team achieve?).

It is difficult in this short space to fully describe the simulation. Central to the design of the simulation, however, is the interplay among the activities learners select to create the learning organization. The players must develop strategies that take into account the interdependence of the activities. They must also select activities in order to meet the needs of people at a given point in time (i.e., in terms of where they are in the change process). It is through the iterative sequence of planning which activities to choose, implementing the activity, seeing the results (i.e., the feedback, movement of game pieces, accumulation of learner benefits), revising the strategy, implementing another activity and seeing the results, that the learners begin to see the patterns in the change process. These patterns gradually cohere into the lessons of the simulation.

As noted above, the simulation is played in three one-year cycles. When played in the context of a workshop, the instructor conducts a structured debriefing after each year. The debriefing is designed to share systematically what the various learning teams derived from their different experiences (i.e., implementation of different strategies). The debriefing is designed to model the same learning processes embedded in the simulation and that are central to the task of creating a learning community. Thus, in each of the three years, the teams proceed by planning their strategy, acting to implement it, documenting the results, reflecting and sharing their learning.

THE FIVE DISCIPLINES

SystemsThinking	Personal Mastery	Mental Models	Shared Vision	Team Learning
Assess District's Success	Talk With/Again	Survey Stakeholders	Assess District's Success	Create a Shared Vision
Survey Stakeholders	Create a Shared Vision	Gather Social Information	Survey Stakeholders	Assess Problems and Processes
Gather Social Information Plan	Professional Development Plan	Talk With/Again	Talk With/Again	Professional Development
Talk With/Again	Quality Tools Training	Create a Shared Vision	Create a Shared Vision	Quality Tools Training
Assess Problems and Processes	Document Successes and Failures	Create Improvement Terms	Assess Problems and Processes	Document Successes and Failures
Document Successes and Failures	Professional Development Training	Reflect with Colleagues	Compare Vision	Professional Development Training
Reflect with Colleagues	Implement new Learning and Teaching Strategies	Benchmark	Develop Long-range Plan	Create Improvement Terms
Benchmark	Model Effective Practices	Communicate Progress	Document Successes and Failures	Develop Team Work Skills
Change Support Systems	Reflect with Colleagues		Communicate Vision	Reflect with Colleagues
Communicate Progress	Benchmark		Check Activities Against Vision	Benchmark
Develop System-wide Professional Development Plan			Revisit/Revise Vision	Build In-house Capacity
Develop Long-range Plan Linked to Vision			Change Support Systems	
Other Features Built into Game:				
Need representative teams for most activities	Individuals' needs change over time	Learn about other team members' assumptions	Create a learning community	Play the game as a team
Biggest rewards come from changes at system-wide level	Individuals move through stages as they change	Simulation specifies clear goals for teams		Need representative teams

Figure 3.   Building the Learning Organization

THEORETICAL CONTENT OF THE SIMULATION

Although the content of the simulation draws heavily upon research, the theoretical principles underlying its operation are in no way immediately apparent to the learners. Instead, they are deeply embedded in the design of the simulation. Consistent with a problem-based format (Bridges & Hallinger, 1995), the theoretical principles that underlie the successful creation of a learning organization are revealed gradually during the simulation.

A defining characteristic of problem-based learning is its emphasis on providing access to a multi-disciplinary set of learning resources that address the problem presented to the learner (Bridges & Hallinger, 1995). Thus, although our primary goal was to develop a simulation rooted in a view of the school as a learning organization, practitioners would also need skills in a variety of related domains. Consequently, the simulation draws from knowledge concerned with learning organizations, leadership, systems thinking, total quality, continuous improvement, and change management (Bershad, Mundry, & Hallinger, 1999). Space limits discussion to but two of these domains, learning organizations and leading change (see Bershad, Mundry, & Hallinger, 1999, for discussion of the other domains).

LEARNING ORGANIZATIONS

Senge (1990) identified five inter-related "disciplines" as essential to the functioning of a learning organization: systems thinking, shared vision, mental models, team learning, personal mastery. We will briefly discuss each, illustrating how the discipline is woven into the design of the simulation.

Systems Thinking

Organizations are systems that have multiple purposes, sub-systems and processes interacting simultaneously. If you try to change one part of the system, the rest of the system works hard to bring the overall system back to its "normal" state. Although system-wide strategies provide the greatest chance for successfully changing the whole system, they are harder and take longer to implement than interventions that are more limited in scope. Moreover, they require new skills and disciplines that do not currently exist in many school communities.

Systems thinking is one of these disciplines. People using systems thinking consciously attend to the complexity of change in order to gain perspective on the whole organization. It enables them to identify patterns and interrelationships among problems and processes in various parts of the system. When you use systems thinking to foster change, you:

- involve representatives of all stakeholders and diverse perspectives in the system in making the change (i.e., mental models);
- ensure that the organization has a central purpose embraced by stakeholders in the system (i.e., shared vision);

- focus the resources and support structures on meeting the central purpose of the organization (i.e., team learning).

Systems thinking enables one to see four levels operating simultaneously in an organization: events, patterns of behavior, interrelationships within systems, and mental models (Senge, 1990). Example of events are declining test results, influx of new students, losing students to a charter school, decreases or increases in funding. Often schools view these issues as discrete events. They discuss them, often identify "who's to blame" for the problems and then jump to solutions. Many organizations never go beyond this initial level of analysis.

A second level of analysis looks for patterns of behavior that contribute to the event. Through this type of analysis, people may begin to see that test scores have been declining for some time and that they have had many families of children leaving the system over the past few years. This level of analysis begins to identify patterns in the organization, but does not lead readily to solutions.

The third level is achieved when one looks for interrelationships among trends. Each trend alone only tells part of the story. Looking for interrelationships—how trends interact with one another—helps to fill out the story of what is going on. Knowing this leads to a better understanding of what solutions might work and the realization that individuals are not usually to blame for problems. For example, in the case of unhappy parents, a principal or teacher often tries to address the concerns by increasing communication. If there is a fundamental difference between the educational approach the parents want to see and the one being used in the school, increasing communication may actually exacerbate the problem.

The fourth level of systems thinking focuses on reexamining and changing mental models. It recognizes that underlying individuals' actions in an organization are clusters of assumptions or beliefs—often untested, deeply ingrained, and implicitly sanctioned in the organizational culture. This fourth level probes these underlying assumptions that make us do things the way we do. Are these the assumptions we still wish to hold? Do these assumptions work in concert or conflict with our mission and vision?

The simulation's design encourages systems thinking among the learners through a variety of ways. First, they begin to see how certain types of activities are essential to fostering systems thinking among people in the school community (see Figure 3). For example, several activities involve data gathering. Through the feedback they receive after gathering data, the learners begin to develop a "systems perspective" on problems and issues. Other activities foster sharing of information and exploring beliefs and assumptions (e.g., Talk With, Talk With Again, Reflect with Colleagues). Certain activities provide a foundation for analyzing problems and developing a shared perspective among people in the school community (e.g., Quality Tools, Teamwork Skills).

Through these activities, the learners begin to see staff develop the capacity to uncover their mental models and identify root causes of problems. They begin to see the systemic nature of the problems and solutions in the simulation. Drivers of change (e.g., leadership and stakeholder input) as well as system-wide strategies interact to produce solutions. Through the process of assisting people in the Verifine school community, the learners start to see these interrelationships and become more effective change facilitators.

Shared Vision

A second discipline of the learning organization is shared vision among the community's stakeholders. The concept of a learning organization assumes that participants will be more effective decision-makers and learners if they understand the school's direction and feel ownership in its vision. Although the simulation includes several activities directly concerned with the system's vision of the future, the change team must work towards development of a shared vision.

Many practitioners choose "Create a Shared Vision" activity. However, if they select this activity before laying the groundwork, there are no positive results. The simulation assumes that a shared vision only emerges out of the experience of people working together. Thus, there are several prerequisites to the successful completion of the shared vision activity (e.g., Talking With key People first, Assessment of the District, involving a team comprised of the "right mix of people" in its development).

Through the simulation learners come to see several other important roles that a shared vision plays in the creation of a learning community. For example, successful development of a shared vision acts as a prerequisite to the successful completion of several planning activities (e.g., Long-range Plan). Once a vision has been developed, there must be ongoing attention to communicating its meaning to all stakeholders. Learners also come to see how a shared vision acts as a guide to the implementation of school and classroom improvement activities (e.g., Check Activities Against Vision). Finally, over the course of the three years, they see that a shared vision is not a static concept. As the system changes, so should its vision.

Mental Models

As noted above, mental models represent the often untested assumptions and beliefs held by people within the organization. These may be beliefs about anything: change, teaching, learning, the role of parents and teachers in decision making. Unexamined or conflicting mental models often represent a major obstacle to change. For example, many school improvement teams function ineffectively because the members have widely varying, often unstated, assumptions about the appropriate roles of teachers and parents in school decision making. Understanding our mental models and being able to discuss beliefs, values, and assumptions (e.g., about best practices), is a necessary skill within a learning community.

The simulation raises the issue of mental models to the fore in a variety of ways. First, feedback detailing the responses of different staff to the same issues and activities varies widely. The feedback suggests a wide range of views (i.e., assumptions, beliefs, mental models) such as would be found in most school communities. The learners confront obstacles to change in the form of existing mental models, but over the three years of the simulation they see how mental models can change under certain conditions.

Second, the learners find that they can do several things to surface mental models among school community members. They find that some training in working as a team is necessary. It is a fact that adults are only marginally more successful at using dialogue to solve problems than children.

Third, they find that data represents an important tool for testing assumptions and understanding problems. After conducting several data gathering activities in the simulation, patterns begin to appear in the true nature and possible causes of problems faced in the system.

Fourth, through their selection of activities and reflection on the results (i.e., feedback), the change team begins to understand what it takes to change the existing mental models of people in the school community. Thus, although dialogue and identification of patterns and causes in problem areas can begin to reveal mental models, activities such as benchmarking best practices that exist in communities facing similar circumstances may begin to change those models.

Finally, the interactive nature of the simulation stimulates an active consideration of the users' own mental models. That is, the simulation fosters an iterative process of thinking, discussing strategy with one's colleague, doing (i.e., implementing), viewing the results and feedback, and reconsidering causes and effects. This process supports the development of higher thinking skills and, in both subtle and not so subtle ways, encourages the learner to reexamine his/her own mental models.

Team Learning

One of Senge's (1990) central contributions was to highlight team learning as a discipline of the learning organization. In contrast to the ever-popular notion of teamwork, Senge emphasized the process of continuously improving the capacity to learn as a team. This reinforces the importance of addressing staff learning through systemic actions that enable them to learn continuously on-the-job.

Within the simulation, team learning emerges through a variety of activities (see Figures 3 and 4). Shared vision, training in team-work skills, professional development, documenting and sharing successes, benchmarking and reflecting with colleagues all contribute to an enhanced capacity for team learning. The need for developing this capacity is revealed through the obstacles that the team of learners encounters.

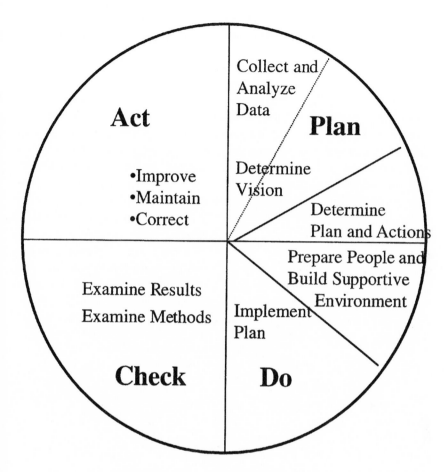

Figure 4. Plan, Do, Check, Act Cycle

For example, if the team wishes to Assess the District, they find that certain team-based skills are needed first (e.g., Develop Capacity to Use Quality Tools). Or to get the maximum benefit from the activity, Create an Improvement Team, they must also develop that team's capacity (e.g., Develop Team-work Skills). So, through selection of these activities and reflection on the feedback, learners begin to see patterns in "what works."

We would again highlight the fact that the instructional process of the simulation models the discipline of team learning. At the end of each "year" teams move through a structured set of reflection activities. Each team identifies what worked, what obstacles they faced, and what they learned. They then share these by sending a representative to "visit" the other school systems (i.e., computers) to find out what they learned from their experience of implementation. Then they reflect on the lessons gained in other settings and apply these to their next year of implementation.

Personal Mastery

In the rapidly evolving context of schooling, the skills and attitudes needed to succeed in the workplace are changing as well. Personal mastery refers to the capacity of staff to do what is needed in their work with children. There is a system responsibility and role in ensuring that staff are able to develop these changing capacities over time. Again, it is possible to view the various activities that the change team may select from in light of this discipline (see Figure 3).

This discipline also focuses specifically on the conditions for adult learning within the system. One's personal mastery is intertwined with the direction of the school system. This vision defines areas in which staff may need new skills (e.g., IT, teaching methods) in order to meet new organizational priorities. The social network of the school system influences our beliefs about why and what we should learn (e.g., our mental models). Thus, staff need opportunities to talk with other staff to make sense of why they need to learn something new. Individual learning is enhanced when there is personal commitment to the school's mission.

Certain activities are needed to foster skill development as well. It is well established that while training (e.g., professional development) is essential, other support mechanisms are equally important if real change is to occur. Thus, the change team must build other activities into their change strategy: benchmarking of best practices, modeling new practices, documenting and sharing successes, and changing support systems. Without these systemic processes that support the implementation of new learning, the learners will find that change is uneven and there will be relatively few benefits for learners.

While the above components relate directly to the development of individual capacities, systemic components come into play as well. Thus, in their attempts to change the system, the learners will confront systemic obstacles as well. They will find it more effective to adopt a systemic approach to developing individual and collective learning. In this way, identification of needs (e.g., assessment of the district) is a prerequisite to effective planning (e.g., professional development plan), some planning is a prerequisite to effective implementation (e.g., providing professional opportunities), support systems are necessary to gain the greatest benefits from implementation (e.g., changing support systems, documenting and sharing results).

LEADING CHANGE

In a recent volume, *Leading Change*, O'Toole observed that: "In all instances in modern society, change is exceptional. When it comes about, it does so primarily as a response to outside forces.... In no case does it come readily" (1995, p. 253). There is no question that with respect to schools, change is coming from the outside-in and that resistance is strong. In earlier eras, people—and organizations—had considerably more latitude to choose if, where, when, and how to change; not so today. The fact that the source of change lies outside our schools is an important feature of today's managerial landscape. School leaders increasingly find themselves leading the implementation of changes they neither chose nor initiated. The transformational context for organizational leadership also requires a change in focus for school leaders. They must focus on second order change strategies—improving the system's capacity to improve—rather than on direct administrative intervention in practice. As Engelbart has observed:

> Given the shifting nature of organizations, the increasingly complex and urgent global market forces, and the virtual bombardment of end users by vendors and consultants, organizations must keep getting faster and smarter at identifying and integrating improvements into their everyday life. Improving this improvement capability should be a key element in every organization's improvement strategy (1995, p. 30).

The notion of second order change—capacity development—is fully consistent with the concept of learning organizations and emerging beliefs about the requirements for school leadership. Second order change involves developing the "collective IQ" of the organization: making schools smarter (Engelbart, 1995; Leithwood, 1996).

The old adage, "change would be easy if it weren't for all the people" occurs to many people as they engage in the *Systems Thinking/Systems Changing*^{TM} simulation. The simulation is designed to demonstrate the importance of involving all stakeholders to create system-wide changes. Often, change efforts fail because the people who are necessary to successful implementation are not included in planning and preparing for change. There are many different forms a representative group can take. It is important for change agents to think about the many people who should be involved in a change effort and choose appropriate activities for them to become involved and committed. After all, organizational change and learning can only happen through the people in organizations.

Within the simulation the players must often select people to participate in a given activity (e.g., to attend professional development, or join a planning group). Often success in an activity depends upon selecting the "right group." Criteria built into the (hidden) decision rules of the simulation with respect to group composition include: representation across parts of the system, representation of different role groups, and level of interest as determined by personality description and progress through the change process.

It is important to remember that people approach change differently based on personal style, history, assumptions, beliefs, interests, and personality. The 24 people in *Systems Thinking/Systems Changing* reflect the range of "adopter types" described by Everett Rogers (1983) in his research on the diffusion of innovations. Rogers identified five categories of adopters ranging from innovators to resisters. The point of this, as well as other research on personality types such as the Myers-Briggs Type Indicator, is not to label people, but rather to help change agents to better plan and carry out change efforts.

Resistance to change has become a fact of life. Change agents can plan and implement flawlessly, yet they will still encounter resistance. Change agents must come to expect resistance and develop skills to diagnose and understand the basis of different forms of resistance.

In the past 20 years, change agents seeking to make changes were often told to ignore or "work around" resisters. This tactic is consistent with Rogers' work on adopter types. His research showed most resisters to have low influence in organizations. Therefore, while these people were not likely to embrace a change themselves, they did not pose a major barrier to others making the change.

In the past few years, researchers and change practitioners have suggested that we take a new look at resistance and resisters to understand the different sources of resistance and use this understanding to increase the success of a change effort. For example, O'Toole emphasizes the adaptive nature of resistance: "A world in which change is the rule would be characterized by chaos, leading to social collapse. Therefore, a society must have one foot permanently on the brake; it must have a predisposition to tradition and conservatism" (1995, p. 253).

As the paradigm for thinking about change has shifted, so must our view of resistance. In the earlier paradigm, change meant adopting a new, usually discrete practice. The job of the change agent was to persuade potential users to take on the practice and help them implement it. The most successful strategy involved a combination of pressure, in the form of a mandate or clear directive and sustained support (Crandall et al., 1982). The change agents guided a process through which users developed the ability to use the new practice. The reasons for resistance to change in this paradigm were often shifting goals, lack of a mandate, or lack of training. In these cases, change leaders viewed resistance as a problem to be remedied. The remedy was to apply more pressure on resistors and require training. Change agents developed and used mechanisms to convince and cajole and, when all else failed, said, "some people just won't change."

Hargreaves and Fullan (1998) suggest that in this postmodern era of educational change, "trying to manipulate or otherwise control the change process to minimize or eliminate resistance is not only futile, but it is exhausting" (p. 223). They suggest other reasons for resistance to change. Teachers have been reformed to death. They are constantly being asked to take on new technical skills with little or no attention to building the positive emotional energy and organizational supports needed to sustain these efforts. Leaders too often ignore the importance of building relationships among people to create hope and sustain the emotional energy needed for change. He warns: "Reformers are ill advised to work only within the balkanized cocoons of like-minded individuals. We stand more of a chance of getting somewhere if we confront differences earlier in the process, working through the discomfort of diversity than we do if we attempt to work in sealed off cultures" (p. 230).

Thus, leaders of school improvement efforts must shed the view that resisters can be overcome or ignored or that change agents can just gather up the supporters to carry the weight of the change effort. Resisters and supporters need to be involved in change initiatives, but neither can be the entire focus. Rather, change agents must promote systemic changes that will eventually reach all members in the organization.

One of the major reasons for resistance to change is that the "case for change" has not been adequately made (Kotter, 1996). People need an opportunity to explore questions such as: What are we working toward (vision)? Why are we doing what we are doing? What benefits do we expect? Does this fit with our culture? What are the positive and what are the negative aspects of the proposed change? Organizations must legitimize the surfacing of negative feelings, concerns, and issues early so they can be examined and addressed. To do this effectively, however, requires a community that can talk with and trust one another. To understand and use resistance to further education reform requires that we work on improving relationships and create time and systems for personal and group reflection (Fullan, 1997).

This paradigm of resistance to change underlies the theory that guided development of the simulation. Through their efforts to build a capacity for learning into the organization, the team begins to see the wide range of strategies needed to work with resistance and foster change. They see how it is possible to craft systemic solutions that, over the long term, can change the context in which people work and learn together.

Again we emphasize that in this problem-based learning environment, the theoretical content is revealed through an iterative process of planning, doing, observing the results, reflecting, and implementing. Learners gradually come to grasp the key principles of a learning organization through their experience of seeing what does and does not work in their simulated efforts to improve this school system.

CONCLUSIONS

The purpose of this chapter was to describe the rationale and design of the *Systems Thinking/Systems Changing*^{TM} computer simulation. This is one of several computer-based simulations we have designed to help practitioners learn how to apply the evolving knowledge base in school improvement. In this case, the simulation focuses on the concept of the school system as a learning organization. We designed the simulation so that learners would construct their own understanding of this knowledge base through an iterative process of thinking, acting, seeing the results, thinking and reconstructing.

Given the recency of the simulation's development, we are unable to provide data on its efficacy in assisting learners to meet this goal. To date the best we can say is that both American and Asian practitioners have found it to be an engaging and challenging approach to learning to think systemically about school improvement. For the future we envision the simulation playing a useful and unique role in research and development efforts centered on schools as learning organizations. Three possible areas of focus in a program of research and development stand out.

The first natural task is to assess the validity of the simulation against the practices of school systems that are functioning as learning organizations. Currently, the simulation's design is based more upon theory than empirical research (at least as regards schools as learning organizations). A program of validation would explore the extent to which the decision rules built into the simulation mirror those that characterize school systems that are high performing learning organizations. It would ask the question: are the strategies that succeed in creating a capacity for organizational learning in the simulation also successful in the real world of improving schools?

A second domain of study might focus on extending prior work on expertise in problem-solving among school leaders (Leithwood, Begley, & Cousins, 1992). The core studies comprising this domain conducted by Leithwood and colleagues used retrospective interviewing around case problems. The computer simulation offers an alternative approach with unique strengths.

With minor reprogramming the simulation could capture a variety of rich data that describe the thinking that underlies the problem-solving processes used by the learners (e.g., problem interpretation, values, strategy). Moreover, since the simulation incorporates various knowledge domains as well (e.g., change), it would be possible to study the interaction between domain specific knowledge and problem-solving processes (Bransford, 1993; Leithwood et al., 1992). This domain of research continues to hold potential for increasing our understanding of how to develop expertise among school leaders. This knowledge would allow us to improve the design of this simulation as well as training for school leaders more generally.

Finally, the computer simulation represents an interesting tool for teaching and data collection in school systems undertaking the development of their capacity for organizational learning. Improvement teams might begin by using the simulation as a training tool. After a period of implementation, they might revisit the simulation and compare their strategies in use with successful strategies in the simulation. This part of the R & D program could begin to explore the efficacy of the simulation in actual school improvement efforts.

REFERENCES

Barth, R. (1997). *The principal learner: A work in progress.* Cambridge, MA: The International NET-WORK of Principals' Centers, Harvard Graduate School of Education.

Bershad, C., & Mundry, S. (1997). *Systems thinking/systems changing: Facilitators guide.* Rowley, MA: The NETWORK Inc.

Bershad, C., Mundry, S., & Hallinger, P. (1999). *Systems thinking/systems changing: Facilitators guide for computer-based version.* Rowley, MA: The NETWORK Inc.

Bransford, J. (1993). Who ya gonna call? In P. Hallinger, K. Leithwood, & J. Murphy (Eds.), *Cognitive perspectives on educational leadership.* New York: Teachers College Press.

Bridges, E., & Hallinger, P. (1995). *Implementing problem-based learning in leadership development.* Eugene, OR: ERIC Clearinghouse.

Bridges, E., & Hallinger, P. (1993). Problem-based learning in medical and managerial education. In P. Hallinger, K. Leithwood, & J. Murphy (Eds.), *Cognitive perspectives on educational leadership.* New York: Teachers College Press.

Crandall, D., et al. (1982). *A study of dissemination efforts supporting school improvement.* Andover, MA: The NETWORK, Inc.

Crandall, D., Eiseman, J., & Louis, K.S. (1986). Strategic planning issues that bear on the success of school improvement efforts. *Educational Administration Quarterly, 22*(3), 21-53.

Cousins, B. (1998). Intellectual roots of organizational learning. In K. Leithwood & K. S. Louis (Eds.), *Organizational learning in schools* (pp. 219-236). Lisse, The Netherlands: Swets & Zeitlinger.

Cousins, B. (1996). Understanding organizational learning for school leadership and educational reform. In K. Leithwood et al., (Eds.), *International handbook of educational leadership and administration.* The Netherlands: Kluwer.

Drucker, P. (1995). *Managing in a time of great change.* New York: Talley House, Dutton.

Engelbart, D. (1995). Toward augmenting the human intellect and boosting our collective IQ. *Communications of the ACM, 38*(8), 30-33.

Fullan, M. (1990). *The new meaning of educational change.* New York: Teachers College Press.

Fullan, M. (1993). *Change forces: Probing the depths of educational reform.* London: Falmer Press.

Fullan, M. (1997). *Emotion and hope: Constructive concepts for complex times.* In ASCD 1997 Yearbook. Alexandria, VA: ASCD.

Hall, G., & Hord, S. (1987). *Change in schools.* Albany, NY: SUNY Press.

Hallinger, P., & McCary, M. (1990). Developing the strategic thinking of instructional leaders. *Elementary School Journal, 91*(2), 90-108.

Hargreaves, A., & Fullan, M. (1998). *What's worth fighting for out there.* New York: Teachers College Press.

Isaacson, N., & Bamburg, J. (1992). Can schools become learning organizations? *Educational Leadership, November,* 42-44.

Kotter, J. (1996). *Leading change.* Boston: Harvard Business School Press.

Leithwood, K. (1996). Introduction. In K. Leithwood et al. (Eds.), *International handbook of research in educational leadership and administration.* New York: Kluwer Press.

Leithwood, K., Begley, P., & Cousins, B. (1992). *Developing expert leadership for future schools.* Bristol, PA: Falmer Press.

Leithwood, K., Jantzi, D., & Steinbach, R. (1998). Leadership and other conditions which foster organizational learning schools. In K. Leithwood & K. S. Louis (Eds.), *Organizational learning in schools* (pp. 67-92). Lisse, The Netherlands: Swets & Zeitlinger.

Levine, S., Barth, R., & Haskins, K. (1987). The Harvard Principals' Center: School leaders as adult learners. In J. Murphy & P. Hallinger (Eds.), *Approaches to administrative training in education* (pp. 150- 163). Albany, NY: State University of New York Press.

Mitchell, C., & Sackney, L. (1998). Learning about organizational learning. In K. Leithwood & K. S. Louis (Eds.), *Organizational learning in schools* (pp. 177-199). Lisse, The Netherlands: Swets & Zeitlinger.

Naisbitt, J. (1997). *Megatrends Asia*. London: Nicholas Brealey.

Ohmae, K. (1995). *The end of the nation state: The rise of regional economies*. New York: Free Press.

O'Toole, J. (1995). *Leading change*. San Francisco: Jossey-Bass.

Rogers, E. (1983). *Diffusion of innovations*. New York: The Free Press.

Rohwer, J. (1996) *Asia rising*. London: Nicholas Brealey Publishing.

Senge, P. M. (1990). *The fifth discipline: The art and practice of the learning organization*. New York: Doubleday.

Senge, P., Kleiner, A., Roberts, C., Ross, R., & Smith, B. (1994). *The fifth discipline fieldbook: Strategies and tools for building a learning organization*. New York: Doubleday.

The NETWORK Inc. (1997, 1999). Systems thinking/Systems changing. Andover, MA: The NETWORK.

Voogt, J., Lagerweij, A., & Louis, K.S. (1998). School development and organizational learning: Toward an integrative theory. In K. Leithwood & K. S. Louis (Eds.), *Organizational learning in schools* (pp. 237-260). Lisse, The Netherlands: Swets & Zeitlinger.

CHAPTER 8

DISTRICT APPROACHES TO CAPACITY DEVELOPMENT IN SCHOOLS
A REVIEW OF THE POSSIBILITIES

Ross Elliott

School districts have an increasingly well-recognized influence on change in schools. This seems to be the case even when states attempt to bypass districts in their reform efforts (Fuhrman, Clune, & Elmore, 1988; Murphy, 1995). Indeed, Schlecty writes that "one of the primary reasons school reform has failed is that individual schools, no matter how vital and responsive their present programs, do not have the capacity to support and sustain change independent of the support of larger political and social units" (1997, p. 81). Teachers can create schools which are learning organizations, add Louis, Kruse, and Raywid (1996), only if they have the necessary support and resources that districts are capable of providing.

Despite this acknowledgement of districts' influence on organizational learning and change, there have been few studies of just how school districts help build the

Advances in Research and Theories of School
Management and Educational Policy, Volume 4, pages 163-183.
Copyright © 2000 by JAI Press Inc.
All rights of reproduction in any form reserved.
ISBN: 0-7623-0024-8

internal capacities of schools. This is so even though documented initiatives are under way in some districts to foster organizational learning in schools (e.g., Sheppard & Brown, 1996). According to Corbett, Wilson, and Webb-Dempsey (1996), research on school districts is out of step with the realities of district practice. A general emphasis in the research community on classrooms, schools, and school leaders, and the failure to fully appreciate the district context is a consistent pattern in educational research. Districts traditionally have provided, as Fullan notes, a "descriptive backdrop" (1993b, p. 145) to schools in education studies. Such research on districts is often characterized by "an unhelpful preponderance of negative (i.e., what not to do) findings" (Corbett et al., 1996, p. 921) with "little sense of what the new role [of districts] should be" (Fullan, 1993b, p. 145). This approach to research is increasingly at odds with the need for systems thinking (Senge, 1990) and the call for educational redesigns which affect not only individual schools but educational systems as a whole (Elmore, 1996a; Wilson & Daviss, 1994).

An important initial step in further developing a research-based understanding of how districts contribute to the capacity of schools is to catalogue the interventions typically used by districts and to clarify, at least theoretically, the features these interventions would need to possess in order to stimulate organizational learning in schools. That is the purpose of this chapter. Because other chapters in this volume have already described the range of meanings associated with "organizational learning", no further effort is made here to do that. Suffice to say that the focus of the chapter will be especially on how districts stimulate "nonroutine" learning in schools, a form of learning also referred to, for example, as "double-loop" (Argyris & Schön, 1978), generative (Senge, 1990), second order (Ciborra & Schneider, 1992), and exploratory (March, 1996).

The next section of the chapter summarizes current thinking about the concept and practice of "organizational intervention" across different types of organizations, including school districts. This is followed by the main section of the chapter describing nine categories of intervention strategies used by districts. A final section reflects on some of the more important challenges facing districts and the research community given the intervention classification system provided in the chapter.

PREVIOUS EFFORTS TO DEFINE, CLASSIFY AND ASSESS ORGANIZATIONAL INTERVENTIONS

Meaning

Intervention has been defined variously as, for example:

- "the introduction of an experimental treatment or change in one or more independent variables" (Guzzo, Jette, & Katzell, 1985, p. 277);

- "an effort which is planned, organization wide and managed from the top to increase organizational effectiveness and health through planned interventions in the organization's process" (Beckhard, 1967, p. 20);
- "[entering] into an ongoing set of relationships for the purpose of being of help ... [and of increasing] the capacity for good organizational dialectic" (Argyris & Schon, 1978, p. 159).

Borrowing from these definitions, the term intervention is used in this chapter in reference to a set of intentional activities, systematically introduced by one group of people, either inside or outside an organization, aimed at influencing productive change in the thinking and practices of another group of people inside the organization.

Examples of Intervention Category Systems

Five different category systems, only one of which was developed in an educational context, are summarized in this section as a means of clarifying the intellectual backdrop to the categories described in the following section of the chapter. The first such system, proposed by Guzzo and colleagues (1985), includes recruitment and selection, training and instruction, appraisal and feedback, goal setting, decision-making techniques, work redesign, and "socio-technological interventions," a term referring to combinations of the other categories.

A second example, initially proposed by Friedlander and Brown (1974) and subsequently adapted by Neuman, Edwards, and Raju (1989), includes broad categories of interventions labelled human-process interventions, technostructural interventions, and multi-faceted interventions, the latter combining both earlier approaches. The human-processes approach is described as one which "values human fulfillment, attempts to achieve improved organizational performance via improved human functioning and processes, and attempts to alter attitudes and perception by directly influencing people" (p. 463). Specific strategies included in this broad category are, for example, laboratory training, participation in decision making, goal setting and management by objectives, team building, and survey feedback. Technostructural interventions focus on "work content, work method, and relationships among workers" (Neuman et al., 1989, p. 464) and include job redesign, job enrichment and increased flexibility in schedules and work hours. Multi-faceted interventions use a combination of one or more human processes and/or technostructural approaches and tend to produce more substantial influences than single approaches.

Other categories of intervention are to be found in a wide range of sources, including literature on management and on technology systems. Markus (1994), for instance, describes the use of technological and computer systems for a variety of interventionist purposes: to structure work, to evaluate and motivate people, to support intellectual processes, to augment communications, and to facilitate inter-organizational transactions. While her focus is primarily on the impact of technological and computer systems, some of her assumptions are applicable to broader interventions:

> The impacts of systems are produced by the interaction of system design features with features of the organizations in which systems are used.... The ability to identify the relevant system design features and the interacting organizational features is essential to explaining, predicting or controlling system impacts (1994, p. 13).

Also part of our meaning of "interventions," and a fourth example, is what Simons refers to as "control levers" (1995, p. 7). These levers, he claims, produce either inspirational or constraining forces within the organization. Belief systems, one such lever, is used to inspire and direct the search for new opportunities. Interactive control systems, a second lever, are used to stimulate organizational learning and the emergence of new ideas and strategies. Boundary systems and diagnostic control systems are used to set limits on opportunity-seeking behavior and to monitor, motivate, and reward achievement for specified goals. The use of these countervailing forces is intended to achieve a dynamic tension: "Selecting these levers—and using them properly—is a crucial decision for managers. Their choices ... affect the probability of goal achievement, and influence the organization's long-term ability to adapt and prosper" (Simons, 1995, p. 8).

A final example of intervention categories, developed by Hall and Hord (1987), is one of the few that have emerged from a school context. This category system has a hierarchical structure with policy interventions at the highest or broadest level. These are followed by "functional" (p. 185) interventions needed to support policy, including the development of supportive organizational arrangements, training, consultation and reinforcement, monitoring and evaluation, external communication, and dissemination of knowledge about the innovation. A third, lower category in the Hall and Hord hierarchy are strategic interventions, and those tactics needed for their support. Finally, at the lowest (but not the least important) level in the hierarchy, are "incident interventions." These occur at the level of daily action and innovation implementation; Hall and Hord write that "incidents are the basic building blocks for higher level ... interventions ... [and] a change process succeeds or fails at the incident level" (1987, p. 206).

Intervention Effects

Well-run interventions, some evidence suggests, can have a significant impact on worker satisfaction and attitude (e.g., Neuman et al., 1989), productivity (e.g., Guzzo et al., 1985), teamwork, communication, and conflict resolution (Randolph & Posner, 1982). Despite this evidence, as well as the considerable emphasis on intervention approaches in the organizational development literature, Beer and Eisenstat (1996) maintain that "a research-based social technology for developing organizations does not exist" (p. 600). Rather, organizational intervention research is characterized by competing theories (Edmondson, 1996) and tentative results. Furthermore, the comparative effectiveness of different kinds of interventions remains unclear (Neuman et al., 1989).

Historically, survey feedback, laboratory training, team building and process consultation have formed the base of organizational development interventions. Tentative findings indicate that: human-process interventions have a higher impact on supervisory behavior than on the general workforce; evaluation rigor is positively linked to success of the intervention (Neuman et al., 1989); survey feedback and interpersonal process consultation show consistent and promising effects on organizational development (Fullan, Miles & Taylor, 1980); and multi-faceted interventions are superior to single interventions, possibly by satisfying a larger variety of situational demands (Neuman et al., 1989). Communication skills training, the establishment of teams, and involvement in decision making are examples of interventions which evidence suggests have some impact on organizational culture (Zamonou & Glaser, 1989).

Most organizational interventions are moderated (or mediated) by organizational context and climate (e.g., Guzzo et al., 1985). From their review of evidence, Fullan et al. (1980) concluded that in those districts which have been extensively involved in organization development interventions (e.g., professional development, use of survey data, action research, and process consultation) the extent of impact depends on such school conditions as readiness, open and skilled communication, a desire for collaboration, agreement on goals, and a supportive school administration. Moreover, districts which "define their needs in task-oriented, educationally focused terms, and consider structural changes a possibility" (1980, p. 176) are more likely to be successful in organization development interventions. This success is further enhanced by superintendents who supply strong initial support.

Results of intervention research still leave unclear the issue of which techniques work effectively together. Nor does this evidence indicate which contexts and circumstances require particular types or combinations of interventions (Neuman et al., 1989), or which provide the most leverage for effort and resources expended. While evidence specifically concerning district interventions in schools is sparse, Elmore (1996a) has argued that we do know that some interventions can improve school capacities, given enough time and personnel. What we do not know is which kinds of interventions will influence large numbers of schools at reasonable costs, a question of scale and efficiency.

The next section of this chapter describes nine categories of interventions which districts are known to use from time to time. Many of the category labels reflect those labels found in the intervention research summarized in this section. For each category, basic features of the intervention, as used in a school district context, are described. Because it is possible to implement each intervention with more or less effect, also identified are the forms of implementation most likely associated with high levels of impact on the learning capacities of schools.

A CATALOGUE OF DISTRICT INTERVENTION STRATEGIES

The nine categories of district interventions described in this section were identified from current intervention practices in school districts, and the literature on effective school districts. The literature on intervention in organizations, especially literature concerned with fostering organizational learning, was also included in the review. Each strategy described in this section is characterized by at least partially distinct underlying assumptions and features even though, in practice, districts often combine several strategies.

Educational Policy

Educational policy interventions, comparable to the highest level intervention in the Hall and Hord (1987) taxonomy, have historically been among the most frequently used category of intervention in schools. New curriculum initiatives, guidelines for new teaching practices, or new policies for special education or school councils would be examples of strategies included in this category. Increasingly, educational policy generated by states or ministries are bundles of initiatives which school districts are expected to support and implement (Kimball, 1997).

Districts themselves develop and implement their own policies about a wide range of issues (e.g., cooperative learning, whole language, reading recovery, mainstreaming). Supports behind such policies may range from the extensive research and training associated with innovations such as reading recovery (Wilson & Daviss, 1994) to less defined innovations and support systems. Most of the literature documenting failed implementation in schools (e.g., Goodlad et al., 1970; Sarason, 1971) is about failed efforts to implement educational policy. To employ distinctions used by Neuman and colleagues (1989), many of these interventions have failed because they have been regarded mainly as changes in work design and behavior rather than as complex human processes interventions.

Research generating principles of managed change (e.g., Berman & McLaughlin, 1978; Fullan, 1991) and organizational learning in schools (e.g., Louis, 1994) has also frequently been conducted in the context of implementing state or district policy. Intervention into schools through means of educational policy is likely to continue in the foreseeable future as electors express their expectations of schools through school districts or state governments. What is open to change are the means whereby educational policy is implemented, or more specifically, the ways in which intervention through educational policy is linked to other forms of intervention. Leithwood (1996), for instance, has argued for central policy initiatives that are "educative" in design, defining expected outcomes for education but helping schools develop the learning capacity to determine their own processes and methods of implementation.

Based on available evidence and further hypotheses generated from this review, organizational learning is most likely to be enhanced by this category of district intervention when:

- expected outcomes of policy are clearly established: these outcomes provide targets for learning, and have the potential to focus task activity;
- schools are encouraged to discover their own processes of policy implementation: this has the potential to encourage experimentation, dialogue, improvisation, and collective problem solving;
- structures for enabling collaboration are put in place as part of the policy implementation process: these provide opportunities for the exercise of Senge's (1990) "team learning" discipline, shared decision making, and commitment building.

Accountability and Monitoring Systems

While holding schools accountable is a standard function of districts (Bryk, Shipps, Hill & Lake, 1997; Coleman & Larocque, 1990), specific accountability initiatives also can be regarded as district interventions in school practices designed to foster organizational learning and change. Examples of such interventions include the introduction of student achievement testing, teaching standards, and personnel evaluation systems. Accountability initiatives such as these by districts have proven to be powerful sources of learning and change in schools when combined with appropriate support (Bryk et al., 1997; Coleman & Larocque, 1990).

In addition, some districts employ monitoring systems for the purpose of increasing or leveraging their demands for school accountability (Ogawa & Collom, 1999). In the context of opening school boundaries within a district to enhance school choice, for example, school-by-school monitoring and reporting of student achievement data provides parents with one basis for making their choices. The nature and design of monitoring systems, and the overall methods of accountability used by districts, have considerable impact on the success of this category of intervention (Bryk et al., 1997; Coleman & Larocque, 1990; Leithwood & Aitken, 1995). Systematic monitoring systems potentially foster organizational learning in schools by providing information for discussion and action, and focusing on tasks and outcomes. Furthermore, systematic monitoring enables schools to reduce error, increase competency and efficiency, and make data-driven decisions about refinements.

Organizational learning is likely to be stimulated in schools by this category of district strategies when there is:

- participation in, and shared expectations for, monitoring and accountability: this has the potential to engender trust, increase communication among organizational members, clarify the contributions of one's colleagues to the collective mission of the district, and arrive at better solutions by allowing for more diverse input. This feature should encourage the development of "shared vision" (Senge, 1990);
- a focus on competence or "personal mastery" (Senge, 1990), accomplishment of short and long-term goals, adherence to common procedures, and improvements in efficiency;
- mutual monitoring of both school and district processes: this potentially engenders greater trust. It also illuminates relationships between different parts of the system, and helps coordinate activities carried out by different parts of the system, all part of what Senge (1990) encompasses in his "systems thinking" discipline;
- monitoring of processes, as well as outcomes: the potential for organizational learning is enhanced in response to this feature to the extent that it encourages reflection on those means, or organizational learning processes, instrumental to the achievement of school outcomes. This collective reflection on process is another source of encouragement for building shared vision;
- coordinated centralization/decentralization of the accountability and monitoring processes: this form of coordination aims to balance order and planning with flexibility and improvisation, thereby encompassing more elements of the change process than either centralization or decentralization by itself. Because this form of coordination emphasizes relationships among different parts of the system, it also encourages systems thinking.

Information and Feedback Interventions

Overlapping the monitoring interventions described above, this form of intervention is frequently accompanied by accountability measures, although accountability interventions can exist without emphasis on information and knowledge, and vice versa. Examples of this type of intervention include: provision of student achievement data, provision of survey data on school processes (e.g., leadership, team work), or provision of qualitative data through school assessment reports and informal feedback. In a study of intervention in two schools in Scotland, Stoll and MacBeath (1997) show how "the generative power for discussion came from the ambiguities of the data [surveys of staff] and the questioning of different assumptions which lay behind the answers to questions" (p. 15).

Information-based approaches to district intervention reflect the contribution of information and knowledge use in school improvement (e.g., Louis & Dentler, 1988), and the emphasis on data driven decision making in the literature on both total quality management (Sitkin, Sutliffe, & Schroeder, 1994) and organizational learning (e.g., Leithwood & Aitken, 1995; Louis, 1994). This form of intervention helps to create the sort of information-rich environment necessary for continuous improvement (Leithwood & Aitken, 1995; Louis, 1994).

District choices within this category of intervention may influence the group processing of information and the dissemination of knowledge. Districts may provide information and let schools determine its use, or they may accompany the provision of information with interventions aimed at shaping how schools process and use the information.

The potential for this form of district intervention to foster organizational learning in schools is likely to be enhanced when:

- districts follow through with schools, providing not just information but guidance and encouragement to process the information, and to include it in their school improvement planning processes;
- the information provided is not only about student achievement, but also about processes, structures, classroom practices, student demographics, and other variables helping to explain the reasons for achievement: outcome data alone offers only meagre clues from which to learn how to improve achievement, should that be warranted;
- districts encourage school involvement in continuous information collection: this helps to establish norms around information search, sensitivity to the environment, and continuous learning.

District Improvement and Strategic Planning Interventions

Like school improvement efforts, district improvement initiatives are attempts to make the mission, vision, and goals of the district more explicit and to build support for district goals through broad involvement in the improvement process. Some districts rely mainly on broad common goals to guide action, while other districts engage in more rigorous planning to reach their objectives. At its most detailed, strategic planning is a deliberate, integrated and comprehensive planning process which clearly outlines each objective, states strategies and actions for reaching the objective, sets out expected timelines and responsibilities, and determines in advance how and when success will be evaluated.

District improvement initiatives are often pursued within a strategic planning framework which, as Mintzberg, Ahlstrand and Lampel (1998) remind us, can take a variety of forms, each based on quite different assumptions. Mintzberg and his colleagues identify ten distinct "schools" of strategic planning, for example, only one of which is preoccupied with learning. By themselves, district strategic planning interventions are attempts to influence all schools rather than to address the specific needs of single schools. Such interventions usually provide a framework for other types of interventions in schools—for example, professional development and process facilitation, the provision of specific school improvement models to schools, or accountability for schools to engage in improvement processes similar to that of the district.

Strategic planning initiatives can create significant opportunities for individual and collective learning. District leadership is usually crucial to the success of such initiatives (e.g., Coleman & Larocque, 1990; Leithwood, 1995), in addition to the cooperation of those in many other roles such as teachers, students, school leaders and parents (Louis, 1989). When strategic planning leads to significant collective learning, it often does so by aligning school goals with the direction and resources of the district, increasing a sense of district community, modeling improvement and planning processes, and building a broad base of support and understanding of district goals at the school level.

Borrowing liberally from the evidence reviewed by Mintzberg and his colleagues, organizational learning is likely to be a product of district improvement and strategic planning processes when those processes:

- are broadly participative and fluid, involving significant numbers of school-level staff, among others. Such participation is the most reliable way to develop understanding of district goals and strategies at the school level;
- are iterative and dynamic, with reflection and planning conceived as continuous and situated within action. This is in contrast to more rigid, formal, and linear planning processes which, evidence suggests, are unlikely to accomplish their desired ends in most organizations (Mintzberg, 1994; Redding & Catalanello, 1992), and certainly not in school systems (Louis, 1994);
- allow for the learning of many people in the district, in addition to the formal leaders. "There are," as Mintzberg and colleagues point out, "many potential strategists in most organizations" (1998, p. 208);
- place formal leaders in the role of managing the process of strategic learning, rather than preconceiving deliberate strategies, so that novel strategies have the opportunity to emerge;
- integrate the various elements of the organization to focus on core purposes. In schools and school districts, these core purposes should relate to instruction and student learning.

Recruitment and Professional Development

Simon argues that "an organization learns in only two ways: (a) by the learning of its members, or (b) by ingesting new members who have knowledge the organization didn't previously have" (1996, p. 176). Not surprisingly, then, recruitment and training of educators is a common form of district intervention in schools.

Viewed from Simon's perspective, recruitment is not just a means of maintaining the organization: it can be, as well, a major strategy for change when people with new ideas enter the district and are provided with opportunities to implement those ideas. Training of existing members may focus on individuals in many different roles, and on groups—training teams to lead school improvement initiatives, for example. Training may be treated as a short-term effort to build the skills required to implement a specific innovation. More rarely, it also may be considered a long-term investment in capacity development: Elmore (1996b) describes how a sustained district focus on recruitment and professional development was able "to mobilize knowledge in the service of system-wide instructional improvement" (p. 6). Changed classroom practices and increased teacher commitment can result when districts focus both planning and resources on the development of personnel through professional development (Leithwood et al., 1995). The context surrounding this category of district intervention is crucial to its success, as the considerable evidence about failed district in-service and professional development efforts attests (Fullan, 1991).

With respect to recruitment, organizational learning is stimulated when:

- recruitment criteria reflect the balance between stability and change by attending to both the ingestion of members with new ideas and socializing new members into the culture and history of practices already in place in the district;
- recruitment practices consider the "fit" between new members and the culture and needs of the school and district;
- districts regard personnel transitions, particularly administrator transitions, as opportunities to revisit organizational memory, goals, and culture.

In the case of district professional development initiatives, organizational learning is most likely when:

- professional development is explicitly related to the overall goals and mission of the district;
- formal professional development interventions reflect best instructional practices including, for example, active participation of members in the training design, use of problem-based instructional approaches, ample opportunities for the social processing of new information, and, in the case of skill development, opportunities for practice and feedback;
- the district maintains a consistent and coherent focus on professional development (Elmore, 1996b; Fullan, 1991). In Elmore's (1996b) example, professional development was successful because it was "a management strategy rather than a specialized administrative function" (p. 24). Professional development "permeate[d] the work of the organization, and the organization of the work" (p. 25).

Process and Facilitative Interventions

While this type of intervention can be viewed as a form of training and professional development (as above), its focus and methods are sufficiently different to warrant a separate category. The focus of this kind of intervention is usually on the whole school, increasing its capacity to solve its own problems by enhancing individual and collective school processes. Specific interventions in this category include working directly with school staffs or teams to facilitate problem solving, the processing of information, or the overall school improvement process.

Sange-Walters, Jennings, Sunshine, and Winitzky (1987) describe organization development interventions as focused on "clarifying communication, establishing clear goals, uncovering and resolving conflicts and problems in groups, making clear decisions that capture commitment, and self-consciously assessing the directions the work is taking" (1987, p. 3). These interventions usually assume a role for an internal or external facilitator (Fullan et al., 1980) or "critical friend" (Costa & Kallick, 1993; Stoll & Fink, 1996, p. 134), as well as the involvement of all school participants.

This category of interventions has its roots in action research and organization development processes in schools. Specific strategies included in this category also are consistent with approaches to intervention discussed in the organizational learning literature. Such approaches to district intervention assume that change cannot occur unless people, individually and collectively, learn to think and act differently. Mental models (Senge, 1990) need to be surfaced, challenged and refined, and group processes facilitating team learning need to be practised and improved.

Intervention strategies of this sort have been proposed by, among others, Schein, Senge, and Argyris. In her comparison of these strategies, Edmondson claims that all are based on some common assumptions: "tacit sources of ineffectiveness must be made explicit in order to be changed" (1996, p. 590); intervention is essentially at the cognitive level; and "blindnesses are unlikely to correct themselves without an outside interventionist" (1996, p. 590). Differences in such approaches may be in the methods and directness of intervention, and the degree to which they focus on systems thinking, mental models, or other cognitive processes.

These types of interventions can be combined with other types such as strategic planning, and the provision of information and feedback. Indeed, the availability of information about current processes in the school can serve as a stimulus for examining and improving collective processes (Leithwood & Aitken, 1995).

From an organizational learning perspective, the aim of this category of district interventions is to enhance the long-term capacity of the school by overcoming barriers to learning and establishing more productive ways of interrelating within the school. These outcomes are increasingly likely to the extent that:

- mental models, conflicting norms, and ineffective structures are surfaced and confronted, thereby improving the quality of dialogue among members of the school, as well as changing dysfunctional beliefs and structures;
- training in systems thinking is provided so that individuals and groups are better able to see relationships of one part of the system to another, of action to outcome, and of surface detail to underlying structure;
- assistance in team learning processes is provided as a means of increasing reflection on group interaction, and experimentation with new ways of relating;
- the facilitator is able to engender greater trust among members of the school as a means of increasing their willingness to experiment, to surface mental models, and to change unproductive ways of relating;
- there are explicit discussions with participants and facilitator about the degree of continued assistance by the facilitator. This helps ensure continued support as long as needed while also encouraging ownership of the intervention process, and allowing participants to assess their progress and further needs for support.

Provision of Models and Information for School Improvement

Usually included in this category of interventions are elements of other approaches such as professional development and provision of information about the school. In this form of intervention, the district provides the school with information about educational innovations and/or with one or several models for school improvement or problem solving. Such information may or may not be accompanied by clear expectations for the school to implement innovations, to adopt one of these models, or to undergo a development process. As a method of professional development, this category of intervention usually targets the whole school rather than its individual members. Robinson (1996) argues that the provision of change models is a means of "reducing problem novelty through the provision of a solution-rich educational environment." (p. 30).

Rather than providing data about the school and environment, however, this intervention provides information about approaches to change that either have been tried in other contexts with some success, or that are theorized to be useful. Evidence suggests that this is an important role for districts. For example, Louis (1989) found that most new information that might affect improvement efforts appears to reach local school systems through the district office. In effect, school districts influence the knowledge base on which schools act (also see Coffin & Leithwood, chapter 2, this volume). In addition, Anderson (1996) suggests that dissemination of information by districts must be accompanied by advocacy in order to have much influence, and that it is essential for schools to further develop the capacity to find information and create knowledge.

Organizational learning is more likely to result from this type of district intervention when:

- the provision of models and information is accompanied by other forms of intervention: this provides a choice of alternative solutions as well as linkages to other interventions to help determine the choice of solutions. It also assists in transferring known strategies and enhancing technical success;
- assistance, assessment, and expectation relating to the use of models and information for school improvement are part of the intervention: this engenders feelings of support among school members. It also helps to clarify goals for improvement and provides feedback useful in adjusting plans and actions;
- expectations for the use of school improvement models include local adaptation of the models in recognition of unique aspects of school contexts and needs: this protects local autonomy and stimulates local problem solving without unrealistically assuming complete knowledge on the part of those in the school;
- the intervention includes activities aimed at developing school capacity to find more information, and to create and integrate knowledge: this encourages communication with other organizations and collective interaction around issues of information and knowledge; it also helps to develop norms of efficient search and continuous learning.

Structural Intervention

Changing school structures, or the structures of other parts of the system with which the school interacts, in order to facilitate some desired result takes such forms as creating opportunities for more teacher collaboration and shared decision making, and the introduction of site-based management. This category of intervention may include, as well, mandating school improvement teams, strengthening formal leadership roles, and changing the organization of time and space for students or teachers by, for example, semestering secondary schools. As previously noted, Neuman and colleagues (1989) classify such interventions as "technostructural" in nature.

Many current structural interventions involve some form of decentralization. Such initiatives are based on the assumptions that decentralization empowers (usually) teachers and parents and this, in turn, unleashes the capacities and creativity prerequisite to school improvement. But even though decentralized structures are generally viewed as important to the improvement of schools and to organizational learning (e.g., Fullan, 1991), decentralization has made, at best, uncertain contributions to the improvement of teaching and learning. This has fostered the search for paradigms of change and intervention that are more precisely targeted (Robinson, 1995) and that place reculturing before restructuring (Fullan,

1993a). According to the best evidence presently available, structural changes, in the absence of cultural change and a shared understanding of purpose, stand little chance of improving schools.

Notwithstanding these weak effects by themselves, structures which allow for communication, empowerment, and the maximizing of human and physical resources are generally regarded as a crucial contribution to more comprehensive strategies for improving teaching and learning, and for building the long-term capacity of the school (e.g., Watkins & Marsick, 1993). Failure to change organizational structures in support of other initiatives is a well documented cause of failed implementation and failed reform (Fullan, 1991).

It seems likely that there is no one "best" structure, and that most structures need to be viewed as temporary and according to purposes and context (Mintzberg, 1989; Stringfield, 1995). Specific structural interventions, while meaningful in the short run, will be less important in the long run than the development of structural flexibility. This is a challenge for the collective learning of school staffs: learning how to know when a change in structure is called for, what form the new structure ought to take, and how to make the structural change that is needed. Such learning seems more likely when:

- reculturing precedes restructuring, and restructuring is understood to be in service of the norms, values, beliefs, and practices endorsed by the culture, the goals for change in the school, and the tasks required to pursue those goals;
- structure is viewed flexibly according to task and context, and the focus is on learning to adjust structures as necessary.

Cultural/Organizational Learning Intervention

This type of intervention, combining elements of some of the other interventions already described, may exist more as a theoretical ideal than as a practice actually observable in districts. While the exact nature of this kind of intervention has yet to be codified, it grows out of several premises that are quite clear:

- changes in culture should precede changes in structures (Fullan, 1993a);
- appropriate structure is determined by task and circumstance (Stringfield, 1995);
- decentralization and teacher collaboration by themselves rarely improve teaching and learning;
- a focus on "culture, climate and interpersonal relationships" (Louis et al., 1996, p. 786) holds more promise for improvement than a focus on structure.

What emerges from these premises is the need for interventions that are intended to influence the culture of schools and also to ensure target-oriented behavior (Robinson, 1995) or "heedful minding" (Weick & Roberts, 1996), in concert with the capacity for structural flexibility as required by task and context. This category of intervention is aimed at building the internal capacity of the school to change continuously in pursuit of its goals.

The defining feature of schools with these capacities is a culture of ongoing collective learning about the most appropriate goals to aim for, the practices likely to achieve the goals, and the structures most likely to be helpful in implementing and sustaining those practices. In such a culture, there is productive interaction between the cognitive capacities of people and task demands of the organization. According to Robinson (1995), "there is considerable payoff in identifying those features of task-related logic whose accuracy is crucial to task success, and those features where greater ambiguities and uncertainties can be lived with" (p. 13).

What features should be part of cultural/organizational learning interventions by districts is an active area of research at present. Dibbon (see chapter 10, this volume), for example, has tentatively identified a number of "levers" which could be important in enhancing organizational learning in schools. The large-scale research program by Louis and her colleagues (e.g., Louis & Kruse, 1999) about the nature of professional learning communities is a rich source of insight into these features. This kind of intervention needs to be aligned with (or subsume) strategies for helping to develop team learning and for encouraging the adjustment of mental models.

CONCLUSION: NEXT STEPS

The nine categories of district intervention strategies examined in this chapter do not exhaust all possible types. Different combinations of these nine, for example, may provide many other possibilities. Nevertheless, this category system provides a point of departure for addressing some issues quite crucial to the contribution districts are able to make to capacity building in schools. One of these challenges, perhaps for qualitative research, is to describe more fully how each of these interventions looks in practice. A related question is whether the forms of implementation most conducive to organizational learning, presented theoretically in this chapter, can be further substantiated and extended through empirical research. Additionally, four other complex issues have yet to be taken up in a substantial way by the research community although, of course, district leaders must grapple with them every day.

The Context Issue

One of these issues is which category of intervention is best suited to the situation or context being faced at the moment. This issue is especially complex because "context" has many dimensions that may be relevant to the choice of intervention. Randolph and Posner (1982), for instance, show that the impact of inter-group development interventions is different depending on the stage in the life cycle of the organization. While schools might not experience life cycles in the same sense as business organizations, schools are certainly at different stages in their school improvement and development processes. Dalin (1993) identifies three cycles of school improvement which he calls the fragmented school, the project school, and the organic school. In the organic school, "the drive for change comes from within rather than being driven by external forces or a critical friend ... [and] the school becomes a genuine self-sustaining learning organization" (Stoll & MacBeath, 1997). Similarly, Dibbon (this volume) has distinguished among schools which are coping, emerging, and high performing on an organizational learning continuum, and has theorized that desired changes in the learning levers and the dimensions of learning will be contingent upon the stage of growth of the school. Central to the question of context is how to best help "stuck" schools (Rosenholtz, 1989), or schools which have not improved despite apparent efforts from within and from outside (Stoll & Macbeath, 1997).

The Cost Issue

A second issue facing districts in the choice of interventions is cost, broadly conceived. While one category of approach (e.g., process facilitation) may be valuable in many situations, it also may be so labor intensive or time intensive that its large scale use is beyond the resource capacity of a district. Many districts, for example, could not find the resources that superintendent Tony Alvarado devoted to his teacher and leaders' training intervention (Elmore, 1996b) in New York City. Presumably, most districts face the problem of finding an intervention that produces "acceptable enough" results at a cost they can afford. One research challenge is to identify low cost interventions which provide considerable leverage and to determine the contexts in which these interventions might best succeed.

The Mix and Match Issue

Also poorly understood at this time is what happens when different intervention categories are combined. Theoretically, some combinations are likely to work well together. Information and feedback are frequently associated with accountability interventions, for example. But it is more difficult even to theorize about other combinations. At first glance, for instance, process facilitation might appear incompatible with accountability interventions because the trust and openness required for process facilitation seems unlikely to develop in a context of sanctions for failure and little tolerance for experimentation. On the other hand, the urgency and expectations of accountability interventions may provide a focus and framework for process facilitation, and heighten the need for a "critical friend" (Stoll & Fink, 1996, p. 134). How these two categories of interventions, and others, might interact under various conditions are intriguing and as yet unanswered questions.

What remains to be seen is whether systematic research about such combinations can shed further light on the collective learning of schools. Evidence that does exist on this matter suggests that the answers are complex. For example, multi-faceted interventions, it is claimed (e.g., Guzzo et al., 1985; Neuman et al., 1989), are more effective than single interventions. Yet Guzzo and colleagues (1985) also point out that the total effects of combined interventions are generally less than the sum of single effects: "the effect of intervention programs in combination are neither additive nor synergistic" (p. 286). This may simply mean that deeper and complex changes are more difficult so that even combined interventions fail to address the most difficult dimensions. However, it is also possible that some interventions conflict and the effects of one are cancelled by the effects of the others. Further evidence in educational settings may help us to resolve these issues.

The Scale Issue

The size and scale of the problem which the intervention is designed to solve is another potentially important issue facing those choosing district intervention strategies. Such problems can be of concern to all schools in the district or to only one school. Problems may range from a relatively superficial matter requiring routine adjustments to issues such as student achievement which strike at the heart of the educational enterprise. Some types, or combinations, of interventions, for example, may be better suited than others to addressing large-scale complex problems for which nonroutine learning would appear to be necessary.

The failure of research up to this point to grapple with the four issues discussed here, each one of vital importance to schools and districts, highlights the current gap between what districts do and research on what they do (Corbett et al., 1996). Considerable research is needed before the nature and effects of district interventions are well enough understood to help guide practice. Such research should focus not on schools or districts separately, but on the interactions between district initiatives and school processes as these "helping relationships" (Sarason, 1971) evolve. If research is to inform district practice, the challenge is not only to determine the impact of district action, but also to learn and describe *how* these interactions with school processes occur. In so doing, educational research itself may come to refine its mental models regarding the nature, importance, and dynamics of district interactions with schools.

REFERENCES

Anderson, S.E. (1996). Dissemination techniques in education. In T. Plomp & D.P. Ely (Eds.), *International encyclopedia of educational technology* (2nd ed.) (pp. 282-289). Oxford, U.K.: Elsevier Science Ltd.

Argyris, C., & Schön, D. (1978). *Organizational learning: A theory of action perspective.* Reading, MA: Addison-Wesley.

Beckhard, R. (1967). *Organizational development: Strategies and models.* Reading, MA: Addison-Wesley.

Beer, M., & Eisenstat, R.A. (1996). Developing an organizational capable of implementing strategy and learning. *Human Relations, 49*(5), 597-619.

Berman, P., & McLaughlin, M.W. (1978). *Federal programs supporting educational change. Vol. VIII: Implementing and sustaining innovations.* Santa Monica, CA: The Rand Corporation. (ERIC Document Reproduction Service No. ED 159 289).

Bryk, A., Shipps, D., Hill, P., & Lake, R. (1997). *Decentralization in practice: Toward a system of schools.* Paper presented at the annual meeting of the American Educational Research Association, Chicago.

Ciborra, C. V. & Schneider, L. S. (1992). Transforming the routines and contexts of management, work and technology. In P.S. Adler (Ed.), *Technology and the future of work* (pp. 269-291). Cambridge, MA: MIT Press.

Coleman, P., & Larocque, L. (1990). *Struggling to be "Good Enough": Administrative practices and school district ethos.* London: Falmer Press.

Corbett, D., Wilson, B., & Webb-Dempsey, J. (1996). Decentralization, collaboration, and normative leadership: Implications for central office practice and research. In K. Leithwood et al. (Eds.), *International handbook of educational leadership and administration*, Vol. 2 (pp. 921-922). The Netherlands: Kluwer Academic Publishers.

Costa, A.L., & Kallick, B. (1993). Through the lens of a critical friend. *Educational Leadership*, 51(2), 49-51.

Dalin, P. (1993). *Changing the school culture.* London: Cassell.

Edmondson, A.C. (1996). Three faces of Eden: The persistence of competing theories and multiple diagnoses in organizational intervention research. *Human Relations, 49*(5), 571-619.

Elmore, R.F. (1996a). Getting to scale with good educational practice. *Harvard Educational Review, 66*(1), 1-26.

Elmore, R.F. (1996b). *Staff development and instructional improvement, Community District 2, New York City.* Unpublished paper prepared for the National Commission on Teaching and America's Future, March.

Friedlander, R., & Brown, D. (1974). Organizational development. *Annual Review of Psychology, 25,* 313-341.

Fuhrman, S., Clune, W.H., & Elmore, R.F. (1988). Research on education reform: Lessons on implementation of policy. *Teachers College Record, 90*(2), 237-257.

Fullan, M. (1991). *The new meaning of educational change.* New York: Teachers College Press.

Fullan, M. (1993a). *Change forces: Probing the depths of educational reform.* London: The Falmer Press.

Fullan, M. (1993b). Coordinating school and district development in restructuring. In J. Murphy & P. Hallinger (eds.), *Restructuring schooling: Learning from ongoing efforts.* Newbury Park, CA: Corwin.

Fullan, M., Miles, M., & Taylor, G. (1980). Organization development in schools: The state of the art. *Review of Educational Research, 50*(1), 121-128.

Goodlad, J.I., & Associates. (1970). *Behind the classroom door.* Belmont, CA: Wadsworth.

Guzzo, R.A., Jette, R.D., & Katzell, R.A. (1985). The effects of psychologically based intervention programs on worker productivity. A meta-analysis. *Personnel Psychology, 38,* 275-291.

Hall, G.E., & Hord, S.M. (1987). *Change in schools*. New York: State University of New York.

Kimball, K. (1997). *District responses to educational reform: When enough is too much*. Paper presented at the American Education Research Association, Chicago.

Leithwood, K. (1995). Toward a more comprehensive appreciation of effective school district leadership. In K. Leithwood (Ed.), *Effective school district leadership* (pp. 315-340). Albany, NY: SUNY Press.

Leithwood, K. (1996). Commitment-building approaches to school restructuring: Lessons from a longitudinal study. *Journal of Educational Policy, 2*(3), 377-398.

Leithwood, K., & Aitken, R. (1995). *Making schools smarter*. Thousand Oaks, CA: Corwin Press.

Leithwood, K., Jantzi, D., & Steinbach, R. (1995). An organizational learning perspective on school responses to central policy initiatives. *School Organization, 15*(3), 229-252.

Louis, K.S. (1989). The role of the school district in school improvement. In M. Holmes, K. Leithwood, & D. Musella (Eds.), *Educational policy for effective schools* (pp. 145-167). Toronto: OISE Press.

Louis, K.S. (1994). Beyond managed change: Rethinking how schools change. *School Effectiveness and School Improvement, 5*, 2-24.

Louis, K.S., & Dentler, R.A. (1988). Knowledge use and school improvement. *Curriculum Inquiry, 18*(1), 33-62.

Louis, K.S., & Kruse, S. (1999). Creating community in reform: Images of organizational learning in schools. In K. Leithwood & K. Louis (Eds.), *Organizational learning in schools*. The Netherlands: Swets & Zeitlinger.

Louis, K.S., Kruse, S., & Raywid, M.A. (1996). Putting teachers at the centre of reform: Learning schools and professional communities. *Teachers for the 21st Century*, Bulletin/May.

March, J.G. (1996). Exploration and exploitation in organizational learning. In M.D. Cohen & L.S. Sproull (Eds.), *Organizational learning* (pp. 101-123). Thousand Oaks, CA: Sage.

Markus, M.L. (1994). *Systems in organizations*. Marshfield, MA: Pitman Publishing.

Mintzberg, H. (1989). *Mintzberg on management: Inside our strange world of organizations*. New York: The Free Press.

Mintzberg, H. (1994). *The rise and fall of strategic planning*. New York: The Free Press.

Mintzberg, H., Ahlstrand, B., & Lampel, J. (1998). *Strategy safari: A guided tour through the wilds of strategic management*. New York: The Free Press.

Murphy, J. (1995). Restructuring in Kentucky: The changing role of the superintendent and district office. In K. Leithwood (Ed.), *Effective school district leadership* (pp. 117-134). Albany, NY: State University of New York Press.

Neuman, G.A., Edwards, J.E., & Raju, N.S. (1989). Organizational development interventions: A meta-analysis of their effects on satisfaction and other attitudes. *Personnel Psychology, 42*, 461-489.

Ogawa, R.T., & Collom, E. (1999). *Educational indicators: Instruments for bounding rationality or grounding legitimacy?* Paper presented at the annual meeting of the American Educational Research Association, Montreal. April.

Randolph, W.A., & Posner, B.Z. (1982). The effects of an intergroup development OD intervention as conditioned by the life cycle state of organizations: A laboratory experiment. *Group and Organization Studies, 7*(3), 335-352.

Redding, J., & Catalanello, R.F. (1992). The fourth iteration: The learning organization as a model of strategic change. *Thresholds in Education*, May/August, 47-53.

Robinson, V.M. (1995). Organizational learning as organizational problem-solving. *Journal of the Australian Council for Educational Administration, 1*(1), 3-18.

Robinson, V.M. (1996). *Organizational learning: A conceptual framework and empirical study*. Paper presented at the annual meeting of the American Educational Research Association, New York.

Rosenholtz, S.J. (1989). *Teachers' workplace*. White Plains, NY: Longman.

Sange-Walters, P., Jennings, J., Sunshine, P., & Winitzky, N. (1987). *Total school intervention programs: A state initiative to improve staff development through organization development.* Paper presented at the annual conference of The American Association of Colleges for Teachers Education, Washington, DC, ED279089.

Sarason, S.B. (1971). *The culture of the school and the problem of change.* Boston: Allyn and Bacon.

Schlechty, P.C. (1997). *Inventing better schools.* San Francisco, CA: Jossey-Bass.

Senge, P.M. (1990). *The fifth discipline.* New York: Doubleday.

Sheppard, B., & Brown, J. (1996). Taylor High: An emerging learning organization. *The Canadian Administrator, 36*(3).

Simon, H.A. (1996). Bounded rationality and organizational learning. In M.D. Cohen & L.G. Sproull (Eds.), *Organizational learning* (pp. 175-187). Thousand Oaks, CA: Sage.

Simons, R. (1995). *Levers of control: How managers use innovative control systems to drive strategic renewal.* Boston, MA: Harvard Business School Press.

Sitkin, S.B., Sutliffe, K.M., & Schroeder, R.G. (1994). Distinguishing control from learning in total quality management: A contingency perspective. *Academy of Management Review, 19*(3), 537-564.

Stoll, L., & Fink, D. (1996). *Changing our schools.* Buckingham, UK: Open University Press.

Stoll, L., & MacBeath, J. (1997). *Changing perspectives on changing schools.* Paper presented at the annual meeting of the American Educational Research Association, Chicago.

Stringfield, S. (1995). Attempting to enhance students' learning through innovative programs: The case for schools evolving into high reliability organizations. *School Effectiveness and School Improvement, 6*(1), 1-30.

Watkins, K.E., & Marsick, V.J. (1993). *Sculpting the learning organization.* San Francisco: Jossey-Bass.

Weick, K.E., & Roberts, K.H. (1996). Collective mind in organizations: Heedful interrelating on flight decks. In M.D. Cohen & L.G. Sproull (Eds.), *Organizational learning* (pp. 330-358). Thousand Oaks, CA: Sage Publications.

Wilson, K.G., & Daviss, B. (1994). *Redesigning education.* New York: Henry Holt and Company.

Zamonou, S., & Glaser, R. (1989). *Communication intervention in an organization: Measuring the results through a triangulation approach.* A paper submitted to the Applied Communication Section of the 1989 Speech Communication Association Conference. ED314808.

CHAPTER 9

ORGANIZATIONAL LEARNING IN EDUCATIONAL POLICY SYSTEMS

James G. Cibulka

INTRODUCTION

One of the main interests in the academic field of policy analysis has been to describe how policymakers go about making decisions and to use the theories and models generated by these inquiries to improve policymaking. This same interest in how to improve organizational decision making has preoccupied organizational learning (hereafter OL) theorists. Nonetheless, despite the similar problems they have tackled, there has been almost no cross-fertilization between these two relatively young fields of study. Why? First, OL theorists have employed an *organizational* frame rather than a *policy* frame. Consequently, students of policy generally have not looked to the literature on OL for insights about how to improve policy adoption and implementation. A second reason for this gap between the

Advances in Research and Theories of School
Management and Educational Policy, Volume 4, pages 185-210.
ISBN: 0-7623-0024-8

two fields of inquiry may reflect the fact that OL theories draw heavily on the discipline of psychology for their concepts. By contrast, the study of policy analysis, which also has matured as a "discipline" during roughly the same time period as OL has been informed primarily by the disciplines of economics and political science rather than psychology.[1] One branch of policy analysis, for example, has relied heavily on positive political economy to understand both "economic" behavior in the political process and "political" behavior in the marketplace. The root of this perspective is the depiction of individuals as utility-maximizing, self-interested agents. Institutions help these individuals deal with essential problems of exchange, collective choice, and collective action. This perspective has generated the "new political economy" of public policy from macroeconomics, game theory, and social choice theory (Alt & Alesina, 1996). Insofar as "learning" is addressed at all in this policy literature, it tends to be framed within the a priori assumptions political economists bring concerning what motivates policy actors, including voters, and the choices available to them working within an arena where collective (indivisible) goods must be produced (Ostrom, 1990).

One of the few attempts to bridge the divide between the study of policy and the interest in learning is found in the work of Sabatier and Jenkins-Smith (1993). Mawhinney (1993) applied their model to Canadian education. They refer to *policy learning*, which occurs primarily within and across advocacy coalitions which seek to translate their beliefs into public policies. While this chapter does not employ their model explicitly, it draws on some hypotheses contained in the theory.

In this chapter I examine what potential there is for the application of OL ideas to the study of education policy systems, particularly at the K-12 level. Only in recent years have students of education become interested in OL (for reviews see Cousins, 1996; Huber, 1991; Rait, 1995). Consequently, there may be opportunities to integrate a policy emphasis in this line of work on education which has not been characteristic of the mainline work on OL. I will argue that this frame of reference is likely to capture increasing interest because of policy developments already underway within education.

My approach here will be somewhat different from Cohen and Barnes (1993), who offer one of the few attempts to apply the idea of learning to education policy. They argue that major policy reforms in recent decades, such as Head Start, Title I of the 1965 ESEA, and the back-to-basics movement of the 1970s, require learning on the part of teachers, the principal enactors of those policies. Each policy can be seen as carrying a pedagogy, namely, the educational approaches policymakers have employed to get teachers to teach differently. Pursuing this line of analysis, Cohen and Barnes argue that the pedagogy of these policies has been largely didactic, replicating the traditional approaches to pedagogy familiar to teachers. Little effort is given to trying to understand how teachers perceive the policies, or to engage them in conversations from which policymakers might learn how to improve the policy. As the authors point out, this lapse seems especially serious as new policies press schools to teach "higher-order thinking" (and more recently, to assure that students master rigorous standards). Their indictment extends to a broad range of actors who have shaped several generations of these ambitious policies directed at reform of teaching—professors, elected legislators, cabinet officers, program managers, and citizen advocates, among others.

While Cohen and Barnes cite various reasons for this apparent failure to employ a better "pedagogy of policy," some of them rooted in factors that shall be discussed below, in the end the authors attribute to teachers the responsibility, as well as the remedy, for the injustices visited upon them. "If teachers typically behave in these ways, why should policymakers act differently?" they ask, pointing out that policymakers, like the rest of us, learn about teaching and learning as students.

My approach in this chapter, in contrast to Cohen and Barnes, is not to attribute responsibility for our policy shortcomings to teachers, or for that matter, to any one set of actors. Rather, in this analysis I will take "the policy system" itself as a point of departure. I ask if the policy system could function more effectively, not only by helping teachers change their teaching, but in a host of other ways. I will argue that the literature on OL offers a helpful frame of reference for examining this question.

Essential Features of Organizational Learning

Since the readers of this volume undoubtedly are familiar with much of the literature on OL, there is no need to summarize it here. Instead, I will concentrate on one salient concept in this literature which has great potential for application to the field of policy—double-loop learning.

Double-loop Learning

Argyris and Schon (1996) describe single-loop learning as instrumental organizational inquiry that identifies causal relationships between organizational strategies and actions and desired organizational outcomes. This type of organizational inquiry occurs without challenging the underlying assumptions and values on which the organization's actions and goals are based. Single-loop learning, and the concomitant first-order error detection, frequently results in short term goal attainment but fails to explore underlying causes, expectations and relationships that may inhibit long term goal attainment or the redefining of organizational goals.

Typically organizational reforms are characterized by single-loop learning processes (also known as "Model 1") which undermine the potential for long term remedies. Argyris and Schon (1996, pp. 281-284) identify the typical pattern that these reforms efforts take. First, problems are described in "discussable domains" regardless of individuals' deeper understanding of the underlying issues. In addition the "undiscussables" are ignored or not acknowledged. Second, the reform efforts and policy solutions attend only to the "discussable" aspects of the problem. Third, the reform initially appears to be successful but as time passes the effort falls short of its identified goal. Fourth, in order to have greater success with the reform, policymakers must acknowledge the "undiscussables" or choose not to make changes that will result in the desired effects, knowingly allowing the reform to fail. Finally, reformers deny personal responsibility by attributing reform failure to external causes.

In contrast, double-loop learning, as described by Argyris and Schon (1996), occurs when organizations not only make changes in their strategies and actions to promote goal attainment, but they also question the underlying values and theories in use. This "Model 2" double-loop learning requires collective problem solving of underlying and tacit problems, not just surface technical issues. As a result, second-order error detection, those errors that result from tacit values and beliefs, are identified and related to organizational action and goal attainment. When double-loop learning processes are invoked, the potential for reform success improves.

Argyris and Schon (1996, p. 20) identify three types of productive organizational learning that are dependent on double-loop learning. They are "(1) instrumental learning that leads to improvement in the performance of organizational tasks; (2) inquiry through which an organization explores and restructures the values and criteria through which it defines what it means by improved performance; and (3) inquiry through which an organization enhances its capability for learning of types (1) or (2)." Double-loop organizational learning requires the exploration of not only the objective facts related to inefficiency but also the reasons and motives behind those facts and requires a continual questioning of the status quo.

The Argyris and Schon framework, then, underscores that learning is a pervasive feature of organizational life, and by implication here, for the world of policy as well. What is critical is how to transform the learning which occurs "naturally" in the current system into new and different forms of learning. The theory therefore moves from description of the organizational (and policy) world as we actually find it to a prescription for its improvement. Learning, in this approach, entails not only the identification of problems, but also the will and capacity to alter behavior to address those problems more effectively.

LIMITS ON OPPORTUNITIES
FOR LEARNING IN POLICY SYSTEMS

Since Argyris and Schon portray double-loop learning as an ideal toward which we need to restructure organizations (and by extension, policy systems), it is not surprising that as they presently exist, policy systems operate in ways which impede Model II double loop learning. In order to understand how these constraints shape the potential for reform, I will begin with a brief discussion of the most significant of these impediments.

Bounded Rationality and Garbage Can Decision Making

If organizations fall victim to the cognitive limitations on rational comprehensive decision making, by extension the same must apply in policy settings. Simon (1957) initially examined why decision making in organizations fails to obey the assumptions of comprehensive rationality. Some of these limitations inhere within the capacity of individuals to process complex information and to account for multiple factors simultaneously (March & Simon, 1958). Also, organizational decision making resembles a "garbage can" (Cohen, March, & Olsen, 1972) because decisions are a product of independent streams of events in organizations—problems, solutions, participants, and choices opportunities. The result is an organized anarchy. Organizational structures also help to routinize the way problems are addressed and limit the frames of reference actors use. In the fashion of disjointed incrementalism (Lindblom, 1959), solutions often chase problems, rather than the reverse. Indeed, the very meaning attached to events in organizational settings is problematic (Weick, 1976). As a result, many organizational theorists view organizations as natural systems oriented toward survival rather than goals (Gouldner, 1959; Scott, 1987). Indeed, utilizing the new political economy perspective on institutions mentioned above, institutions are efforts to reduce the transaction costs incurred when a principal, for example, the public, wishes to hold an agent, for example, an elected official or a bureaucrat, accountable for achieving some desired outcome. Due to imperfect information, problems in observing quality, difficulties in enforcing agreements, the need to delegate, and so on, the transaction costs of organizing and bargaining can lead to inefficiency and even goal displacement in institutions. The problem is to organize institutions so as to minimize the incidence of these costs, but this is not easily accomplished (Williamson, 1993).

At the level of policy, the limitations on comprehensive rationality as a method of decision making could hardly be expected to be any less. Policymakers, like organizational decision makers, are confronted with a myriad of problems to address. They cannot possibly give all of them equal attention in drafting legislation, any more than the solutions they entertain framing the policy will be based on a comprehensive survey of policy options. On the contrary, as Kingdon (1984) explains, policy emerges only in the rare circumstances where a "policy window" opens and permits the normally separate streams of problems, solutions, and politics to converge.

It is not only the policy-setting stage which faces these limits on rational decision making. As over two decades of research have established, what happens after policy is created is crucial. Policy implementation often is associated with deviation from, if not breakdowns in, the original intentions of the policy framers.

Initially, this was blamed on the different goals or incompetence of the imple-menters (e.g., Pressman & Wildavsky, 1973). This perspective on implementation as a "problem" grows out of the same body of work on organizational bureaucra-cies cited above, in which organizational conditions often reify the cognitive lim-its decision makers bring to their work. Later work on implementation viewed it as problematic for the implementers, who were required to engage in "backward mapping" as they sought to implement legislation/policy with fidelity (Elmore, 1982). More recent work in implementation recognizes that it is a venue for work-ing out flaws in policy designs and unresolved goals of the policy framers (e.g., Goggin, 1990; Marin & Mayntz, 1992), and thus is less a source of breakdown than it is an extension of policy setting itself. Thus, the bounded rationality of the policy process contributes to, and is reinforced by, the behavior of the bureaucrats who implement and enforce those policies.

Institutionalized Behavior

The work of the "new institutionalists" (Crowson, Boyd, & Mawhinney, 1996; March & Olsen 1989; Meyer & Rowan, 1977; Rowan & Miskel, 1999) has helped to explain why schools have been so slow to change their perfor-mance and have been so resistant to change despite decades of efforts at planned change. One of the salient characteristics of schools is that they operate within institutions whose orientation is to their own survival and legitimacy, often at the expense of concern for goal achievement. (For a more complete exposition of this approach to institutionalism, see Cibulka, 1995.) Institutions are affected by the larger *societal environment*, which is characterized by such diverse phe-nomena as demographic shifts, flows of capital, residential patterns, shifts in values, changes in political regimes, and international influences. The institution consists also of an *organizational structure* (formal and informal), attendant pol-icies, practices, norms, and legitimating myths affecting goal achievement and survival. Feedback loops link the societal environment, institutional environ-ment, and organizational structure. Thus, organizations are embedded in a large, complex set of interrelationships extending beyond the organization itself and cannot be reformed without attention to the institution within which they are sit-uated. This is why changing a single school into a learning organization is diffi-cult unless it enjoys the support of its sponsoring school system. School officials are dependent on resources, support, and legitimacy from institutional sources, which if they are not also supportive of this shift, will undermine the efforts of a single deviant unit within the organization.

Schools adapt to demands from their environment with symbolic and ritualized responses. Compliance with state standards becomes an end in and of itself rather than a means for new learning and improved performance. Thus, DiMaggio and Powell (1983) refer to the "iron cage" of "institutional isomorphism" in which the culture of schools is oriented toward conformity and conservatism, and resistant to the risk-taking and inquiry upon which OL rests.

Fragmentation of Intergovernmental Authority

The fact that education policy is implemented within a policy system which is fragmented makes it difficult for policymakers to communicate and to learn from one another. In the United States, and in other federal political systems, power is divided between the central government and subordinate units. While the American system locates primary constitutional responsibility with the states, both the federal government and local units of government have considerable authority and influence. Many urban school systems, for example, are heavily dependent on federal aid programs targeted at addressing their special needs, and any school system accepting even small amounts of federal aid is subject to a wide range of federal laws and regulations. Federal court decisions cover virtually every aspect of public schooling, narrowing the discretion of state and local officials. Local units of government determine a significant share of funding and shape the curriculum, student grouping, staffing, and a host of factors which determine educational quality and student opportunities to learn. They jealously guard their prerogatives against state and federal power, just as state officials seek to protect their autonomy from federal "control." Amid such multilayered authority, and resulting diversity, it is hard for any one level of the policy system—such as an individual school—to set its own course. Of course, this interdependence is not so much an accidental feature of federalism as it is an intended effect. Divided power, as James Madison reminded his readers in *The Federalist Papers*, is an antidote to the mischief of factions. Thus, while the concept of checks and balances has proven to be a remarkably effective doctrine in preventing abuses of centralized political power, it has inhibited the capacity of actors in such a divided polity to work together toward common goals, which is a *sine qua non* of OL. For example, insofar as implementation processes require mutual learning by all actors, the federal system creates formidable roadblocks (Kettl, 1983).

Partisan Competition

Inherent in the system of divided powers is political party competition, both in presidential and parliamentary systems. This system evolved into what Lowi (1969) called "interest-group liberalism." The public interest came to be viewed as the product of a process of partisan bargaining. This procedural view of the purpose of democracy is a substitute for substantive views of the public interest, which begin from particular ideologies about individual rights, the nature of civil society and social purposes, the role of the state, and other fundamental questions.

As it relates to OL, political partisanship imposes sharp limits on coherent policy action. Rival political leaders and political parties have a vested interest in not cooperating with one another. In its most egregious manifestations, the partisan model champions strategies and tactics designed to gain political advantage over one's opponents in order to maintain a favorable public image. In the U.S. Congress, for example, legislators pass bills which they know the president will veto, but which provide them with ammunition in the forthcoming election campaign, where they hope to curry favor with voters. In short, under the rules of political partisanship, the collaborative search for "truth" and common ground in policy-making and implementation can become subordinate to the means for gaining and maintaining power.

The degree to which this occurs, however, can vary within quite a wide spectrum, depending on other factors in the political system. Bipartisan cooperation is a norm which mitigates political partisanship. However, bipartisanship has declined. The weakened role of the political leadership in the U.S. Congress and decline of the seniority system often are cited as reasons.

Fragmentation and Partisanship Within School Systems

I have argued that the educational policy system, like the larger political system, is characterized by fragmentation and competition, and that these conditions make OL difficult. The same impediments to OL work within individual school systems, which operate as subsystems within the larger political system. Rather than being characterized as unitary decision-making structures, they have plural authority structures and pluralistic power relationships. How to overcome fragmentation in the pursuit of organizational goals is a primary problem for organizational leaders, including the superintendent, school principals, and even teachers. The existence of partisan competition within the organization, often extending from the school board at the top, down through the organization, makes this leadership challenge more complex. The ability to command allegiance and build loyalty cannot be easily separated from the pursuit of particular organizational goals and policies. It is difficult to build collaborative policy systems if the leaders of individual school systems, or its subunits, are constantly struggling to maintain the authority and influence to act effectively. Rebuilding the system from the top down to encourage OL must also include rebuilding structures from the bottom up. Hence, both fragmentation and partisanship tend to create a bias toward what Argyris and Schon call "Model 1" decision making with inordinate attention to protective, defensive, decision-making routines.

FACTORS STRENGTHENING
ORGANIZATIONAL LEARNING IN POLICY SYSTEMS

If the above impediments to OL were the only factors at work in policy systems, there would be little likelihood that OL might take on a greater role in the future.

However, this is not the case. The root of this optimism centers on the fact that educational policy systems are not merely arenas for the exercise of power. They are created to address societal needs and hence rooted in instrumental action directed toward resolving pressing problems. Thus, despite the fragmentation of authority just discussed, a cluster of important trends are at work which are strengthening the role which ideas play in shaping public policy, in contrast to policy being largely determined by interests and power. Of course, the reassertion of ideas as the foundation of public policy making will not in and of itself lead to the emergence of OL, a point to which I will return later, but it provides an important precondition.

The first of these influences is the growing interest in *efficiency* (Majone, 1996), and its closely related cousins, *effectiveness*, and *productivity* as values which should drive policies in education. Redistributive policies in which equality and equitable treatment are the primary goals of policymakers are no longer as dominant as they were from the 1960s to 1980s. Those policies seek to win advantage for subordinate or unorganized groups. By definition, redistributive policies must be obtained at the expense of others, typically those with power. By contrast, efficient policies, by definition, seek to improve the well-being of everyone in society, or nearly so. This shift from redistributive to distributive politics has been especially true in education policy. Efforts to improve the quality of schooling replaced an earlier concern about equal access to education by a variety of groups, defined in terms of race, gender, disability, and other traits.[2]

A number of factors have contributed to this rediscovery of efficiency. Some argue that the growing strength of economic and social conservatives has played a role, although whether this mobilization is the fundamental cause or merely reflects a basic disenchantment with the liberal welfare state is debatable. Clearly the intellectual foundations of political pluralism were severely eroded by the 1980s, when conservative governments captured power in many nations. According to Majone (1996, p. 613), "a keener awareness of the economic and political costs of group politics gave new plausibility to the idea that there is a public interest or a right public policy quite apart from the sum of group interests." In place of group struggle, rational decision making could be held out as the appropriate model for policymaking. Efforts by economic conservatives to introduce market principles as a way of approaching a variety of public problems was merely one thrust within a larger search for the right ideas as having an important place in policymaking.

The key significance of this shift is *not* that efficiency generates better ideas than redistributive policies. Commitment to either one can be pursued with a narrow, partisan allegiance. Rather, because policies oriented toward efficiency raise concerns for the entire polity, at least as a general principle, they provide the foundation for cooperation across ideologies. Socially redistributive policies directed at increasing inclusiveness and fairness are framed within a dialogue which now addresses improvement of the entire system. If such policies are to work effectively, they require both efficiency advocates and advocates of socially redistributive programs to "learn" how to talk with one another to achieve "win-win" policy solutions. Policies which ignore the special needs of students of poverty are unlikely to succeed over the long run. In short, the shift to efficiency in policy dialogue provides only a precondition for improved learning by policy makers.[3]

Another factor already in play which has elevated the role of ideas as an independent factor in framing public policy (and one which helps to offset the dangers just discussed) is the growing *complexity of public policy.* Here again, public education provides a good example. A generation ago it was considered acceptable to tolerate large variations in student achievement and outcomes and wide disparities in performance among schools and school districts. These performance differences often were blamed on the characteristics of the pupils, such as their reputed lack of ability, motivation, preparedness, or other deficiencies. The politics of education policy in the 1990s has drastically altered this tolerance for education failure as either inevitable or socially acceptable. A variety of policies now seek to make students, teachers, and administrators accountable for their performance. Underlying these accountability policies is a greatly heightened set of expectations for what schools as institutions should be able to accomplish, despite the societal constraints under which they operate.

In other policy areas as well, a similar trend toward "results" prevails, despite efforts to curtail expansion of government programs. International developments undergird this concern with outcomes. National economies now rely to a much greater degree on services, and they are tied together by global economic integration and competition. These forces have led policymakers at all levels to elevate their expectations for the outcomes which public policies can be expected to achieve.[4] Concomitantly, these new policies represent a different approach to economic and social regulation from those of the past, because not only do they deal with technologically complex problems but they seek to modify attitudes, expectations, consumption habits, and production patterns of large numbers of individuals, firms, and government units (Majone, 1996, p. 616; Schultze, 1977, p. 12).

The role of experts, whose forte is their command of ideas, may well be strengthened under this set of contemporary forces. It is not altogether clear how this is playing out at present. The delegation to independent commissions and to special purpose governments has a particularly long tradition in the United States, and these governance regimes gave experts considerable influence as managers and policy advisors. Many of these traditional solutions are now being questioned, such as the idea that public schools should be operated autonomously from mayors. Still, in many contexts, policymakers are looking to experts for ideas on how to shape effective policies. In the United States, a number of major pieces of federal education legislation reflect this attempt to rely heavily on experts to create credible comprehensive school reform models and to build sound policies on reading. In addition, of course, there is the role which evaluation experts play in judging the effectiveness of policies, to be discussed more below.

A number of trends have occurred in thinking about public administration which also create possibilities for OL. Two are worthy of brief mention. First, the decline of the old command and control approach to public administration has been replaced by greater emphasis on collaboration and networks rather than self-sufficiency (Peters & Wright, 1996). Effective public administrators must coordinate their organizations with the private sector and with other public organizations at multiple levels. This collaborative approach will generate superior ideas compared to what a solitary approach to administration is capable of, and it will increase commitments to institutional success. Arguably, the advantages for such collaboration are especially strong in public education, where the nurturing of intellectual and social development requires commitments from virtually the entire society. The challenge for educators is to mobilize those commitments and human resources across different institutions.

Second, the new public administration has been influenced by the managerial revolution begun in the private sector which seeks to "empower" employees and shift accountability for results downward. Similarly, it is argued that clients of public organizations should be given a greater role. In education, this has fueled proposals for charter schools, public choice programs, and vouchers. While much controversy attends the appropriateness of these efforts at empowerment of employees and clients, these proposals open up a new conception of the roles which these actors should play. Employees, it is argued, have far more ability and expertise than they have been allowed to exercise and develop, and consumers likewise are capable of exercising judgment based on sound information to improve the quality of education. In other words, both groups are expected to bring new ideas and fresh insights into educational governance. If these fresh ideas are to prove efficacious in improving overall performance of the educational system, significant learning will be required.

Both of the developments in public administration are, it should be pointed out, only one piece of a larger policy system. Administrators can change their approaches in ways which increase the potential for OL to take root. Yet just as quickly these influences can be counteracted or diluted by legislators or elected executives which operate on different premises. As noted below, however, pockets exist throughout the entire policy system which favor the possibilities for OL. These provide the foundation for a more systemic shift in the operation of educational policy systems. In the following section these influences are discussed.

EXISTING STRUCTURES FOR
ORGANIZATIONAL LEARNING IN POLICY SYSTEMS

Happily, there are within policy systems some norms, processes, and structures which encourage cooperative pursuit of common goals in a manner which makes Model II learning possible, even if they are not *systemic* in their reach. Many of these elements are longstanding, preceding the recent drive toward efficiency in educational policy which arguably has increased the role of ideas in policy setting; although some are of recent origin. In this section I will examine some major examples of these devices and discuss whether they have the potential to take on greater importance in educational policy systems.

Commissions

Commissions take on a number of forms, from short-term structures to address a policy problem to free-standing structures which perform basic government functions, such as the regulation of interstate commerce, or which encourage collaboration, such as the Education Commission of the States. In this paper, I will refer to the former and describe them as "study commissions." When study commissions are working at their best, they perform two functions. First, they render advice from experts on how to resolve thorny and complex political problems, such as the future of Social Security. The legislature and the executive can then rely on the recommendations of this commission to frame its agenda. Second, commissions can mobilize public support to address a problem, such as the commission which produced *A Nation at Risk*. Deal (1985), argues that commissions should be viewed as ceremony. "Ceremonies are symbolic events that reinforce, dramatize, and transform fundamental issues and beliefs." (p. 155) They mobilize energy and refocus attention on institutional needs. They offer hope that a problem may be resolved and provide the possibility that diverse constituents can unite in support of public education. They are, in other words, a call to action.

There are, of course, limitations to study commissions. Deal acknowledges that commissions document certain kinds of needs more effectively than others. They deal most effectively with the needs of individuals and give attention to structural improvements while at the same time giving short shrift to reshaping of political and cultural requirements for reform. A sharper criticism comes from Peterson (1983). He points to the fact that the work of commissions does not meet the test of policy analysis standards, which require focused statements of the problems to be analyzed, methodological evaluation of existing research, reasoned consideration of options, presentation of supporting evidence, and arguments for well-specified proposals. Because commissions tend to be broadly representative and lack power and authority, he argues, they are not accountable. Therefore, their reports tend to exaggerate the problem they address through selective use of evidence, deal in generalities, make unrealistic recommendations, provide no details of the proposed innovations, avoid calling for fundamental reorganization of institutions, and fail to document the value of the solutions they propose. To be sure, these faults reflect the fact that commissions are asked to address broad problems which are not susceptible to easy solutions. Also, typically they are under intense pressures to produce a report quickly and one dramatic enough to capture media and public attention. In the end, according to Peterson's analysis, commission reports serve to reassure the public that an issue is being addressed. Such reports also tend to follow public opinion rather than shape it.

The two roles of commissions tend not to occur simultaneously. Study commissions are more likely to rely heavily on experts and provide an in-depth report which is not "sexy" and therefore does not grab media attention. Conversely, commissions which have a political membership tend to frame problems and policy solutions in simpler terms and be more sensitive to how to gain widespread attention and acceptance of its recommendations. Both approaches foster "Model II" learning, the first by carefully dissecting problems and distinguishing symptoms, causes, and solutions, the second by creating a shared awareness of the significance of a problem and the need to address it.

The ability to place an item on the public agenda is a significant achievement. Normally this function is reserved to politicians rather than to policy advocates (Kingdon, 1984). Commissions, because they typically consist of distinguished citizens with stature independent of politicians (some of whom may sit on commissions as well), are one of the few devices for opening a "policy window" independently.

One cannot always cite short-term effects from commissions. But insofar as they contribute to reshaping policy directions, they can have long-term effects. Wimpelberg and Ginsburg (1985) could find few short-term effects from the publication of *A Nation at Risk* in the state of Louisiana, yet no one today, a decade and a half later, would deny that it has profoundly reshaped education policy in that state and across the nation.

Sometimes commissions serve as a public conscience and may even be cynical devices by politicians to "stall" for time hoping that the energies of proponents of change will dissipate and lose their capacity to threaten the status-quo. The racial protests of the 1960s led to myriad commissions, perhaps the best known being the Kerner Commission report on the causes of racial unrest in the 1960s. While not leading to substantive changes at the time, they often have long "shelf-life" and are cited decades later in policy debates or lawsuits.

It is difficult, and perhaps erroneous to make sweeping generalizations about commissions. Certainly one can cite commissions which do have a profound impact on reshaping policy for decades. This was true of the Sondheim Commission convened in Maryland in 1989 by then-Governor William Shaefer and chaired by a distinguished business leader (who still remains active on the state board of education as its president). The commission, in a report remarkably prescient of national policy developments to follow, cited the inability to determine how well the state's public school system was performing, and recommended standards-based student assessments, as well as rewards and sanctions for schools. This commission report has remained the foundation for major state education policies. The report certainly was ahead of its time and cannot be dismissed as a platitudinous regurgitation of the obvious. While lacking some of the substantive evidence Peterson argues should characterize policy analysis, the report did galvanize the state board and state policymakers around a common agenda, despite many specific debates over the last decade on particular policies which grew out of the report. The report created the "policy space" for stakeholders to refocus their attention.

In the end, the largest limitation of commissions may be that they operate as an adjunct to the basic political processes for passing laws and administering them. They become necessary because the normal processes for addressing political problems through laws and regulation have failed. They function as a safety-valve to help introduce new ideas or to generate consensus around their pursuit.

Legislative Committees

Like commissions, legislative committees are arenas within which information about a problem or about a policy can be examined in depth. All members of a legislature stand to benefit from more and better information, and legislative committees perform this role, since not every legislator has the time or interest to acquire such expertise. Thus, delegation is a rational strategy for taking advantage of specialization. Not only do legislators hear from experts, frequently individual legislators *become* experts as they acquire mastery of a policy arena. Thus committee members acquire both the power to set agendas (legitimate power), and deference based on what they are deemed to know (expert power.) Although it has not been established empirically, it has been hypothesized that legislatures with strong committee systems, including strong, majoritarian conference committees, are able to institutionalize this information dissemination function more effectively than those legislatures which are free to ignore the expertise developed by committees (Alt & Alesina, 1996, p. 654).[5] Thus, legislative committees can contribute to the conception of the policy process as the pursuit of best information for optimal outcomes rather than as an arena principally designed to distribute benefits to partisan interests.

Program Evaluation and Nonpartisan Structures for Conducting Evaluation

Weiss (1982, p. 619) describes evaluation as the use of the methods and techniques of social science in the service of rational allocation of resources and the improvement of welfare policy. It is a rational tool conducted in the context of policy decision making, which departs from a rational model of decision making in dramatic ways. Not surprisingly then, it is difficult to cite examples of how a particular evaluation of a policy or program actually alters the choices which policymakers select. Policymakers have limited access to research and often quote research selectively. Sometimes their preconceived biases cause them to seek out research that supports their perspectives, while ignoring or dismissing research which contradicts their preconceptions. Those who sponsor research, from petroleum institutes to think tanks, often expect those whom they hire to conduct a policy-relevant study to reach certain conclusions consistent with their interests. Similarly, legal firms often retain academics who serve as expert witnesses in court litigation. Cynics describe them as "hired guns" because they argue that almost any expert can be found to articulate a desired perspective. While there is some truth to the assertion that "academics for hire" is the dark side of evaluation research, it is also true that there rarely is unanimity about any issue, even in the so-called "hard" sciences. Thus, evaluation research can become part of a war of ideas used to legitimate or undercut existing policies. This is a far cry from the rationalist view of the policy process, in which evaluations contribute to improvement of promising or successful programs and the elimination of poor ones.

Despite its limitations evaluation has at least three salutary effects on the policy process. First, it opens "policy space" for the discussion of new goals and their effects. Even if such research does not provide unequivocal answers to complex policy questions, it serves to focus policymakers' attention on a policy's effects. Legislatively mandated policy studies, such as the numerous studies of Chapter 1 of the Elementary and Secondary Education Act, also serve to focus attention on certain key issues or problems, particularly when legislation is being reauthorized. The executive branch often has considerable influence over the specific mandates of such studies, who is selected as the contractor, and even the findings and recommendations, so it would be wrong to view this brand of policy research as totally free of bias or political influence.

Second, as Weiss points out, policy research creates "knowledge creep" over the long term, because it influences the language and concepts policymakers employ when they discuss policy. It is even the case that some legislation, such as the Comprehensive School Reform Demonstration Program (Public Law 105-78, the so-called Obey-Porter legislation), purports to be based on the latest research findings. Thus, there may be a drift towards increasing use of social science evidence in creating education policy.[6]

A third benefit of evaluation is that it has generated specific agencies whose explicit mission is to conduct nonpartisan research. At the federal level, the Congressional Budget Office has a reputation for competence and impeccable neutrality in its projections of federal budget surpluses and deficits. Some states have created agencies which act as appendages to the legislature to conduct program audits and evaluations at its request, or to gather information on the effectiveness of laws in other states which bear upon intended legislation. These agencies are staffed by evaluation experts whose reputations depend on impartial judgement.

Such agencies create another "policy space" for policymakers to utilize research and evaluation in their deliberations. The way the information is used, like the case of externally funded evaluation reports, is not within the control of the evaluators who prepare the reports. Thus, the information itself is but the foundation for OL, rather than learning itself.

One of the limitations of the evaluation paradigm has been that it has focused on individual performance or that of operating units rather than the operation of the entire policy system (Guthrie, 1990). In the 1990s the National Science Foundation began to invest heavily in evaluating its local and state systemic reform efforts through new evaluation models. The techniques appropriate to evaluating pieces of a policy system are not the same as those appropriate when the entire system is being remodeled simultaneously. It is also the case that new advances in evaluation apply meta-analyses to policy issues and other statistical techniques for measuring change in complex social systems. As evaluation specialists give more attention to evaluation of policies themselves, rather than programs within a policy framework, we can expect increasingly sophisticated methodologies to influence the study of policy.

Evaluation experts distinguish between *summative* evaluation for purposes of assuring external accountability and the use of *formative* evaluation for program improvement. Since many new programs and policies have unclear goals and/or unclear implementation plans, the evaluator can assist local decision makers in clarifying their purposes and developing workable implementation strategies, for example, Rossi and Freeman (1993) and Patton (1990). Depending on the evaluation approach, this can be an iterative process which undergoes continual revision. Thus, helping teachers and administrators (and other stakeholders) to employ a systematic learning process is the substance of the evaluation. The evaluator is an external resource to the organizational unit. This conception of evaluation complements the conception of schools as learning communities of teachers focused on data-based decision making and self-improvement. Yet evaluation remains a largely foreign idea for decision makers at the school level. Indeed, those proposing to introduce OL concepts into schools all but ignore the evaluation literature. Unfortunately, the dominant conception of evaluation is that of a technology which serves institutional decision makers whose aims are largely external to those of school officials.

Accountability Reporting

In the 1980s many states began to produce reports providing performance information on the state educational system, including student test scores, graduate rates, financial information, qualifications of staff, and a variety of other factors. The first generation of these reports was largely ignored by educational decision makers, although often they were published in newspapers once each year when the performance information was released. The information also was eagerly sought by real estate agents wishing to advise their customers about the quality of local schools.

However, as these performance reports have undergone revisions in the last decade, they have become more potent tools for external accountability. There are a number of factors driving this greater visibility. First, the development of content and performance standards caused student assessments to move away from exclusive reliance on norm-based, paper and pencil, multiple-choice tests. The move to newer, more rigorous assessments meant that high performance on the assessments was no longer guaranteed for schools in socially advantaged communities and thus captured their attention and effort. Second, in many states the performance information is reported at state, district, and school levels, making it easier to access relevant information about performance than it was a decade ago. In some cases the information is available on-line and can easily be downloaded or even manipulated to produce comparisons. Third, in an increasing number of jurisdictions the performance reporting now is tied to consequences—rewards for schools with high or improved performance and sanctions for those with poor performance. Some jurisdictions have closed low performing schools, while others have linked teacher or administrator compensation and job security to having their students do well on the assessments.

This new paradigm of reporting performance information, like evaluation, remains largely external to the daily life of most schools. To be sure, low-performing schools placed on a watch list or designated as "reconstitution eligible" (the language employed in the state of Maryland) are forced to comply with state or local requirements designed to elicit their improvement. Yet the information provided in the performance report, the way it is formatted, the timetable for its release, and other critical variables normally are not determined with school personnel as the primary "learners" in mind. Teachers and administrators may be "targets" but they are not co-producers of the knowledge or co-strategists in how it shall be utilized. On the contrary, the design of such reporting policies tends to reflect almost exclusively the priorities of state or district policymakers operating external to teachers and school-based administrators. Therefore, while performance information reporting has introduced new more sophisticated information in the policy arena, its use for OL certainly has not reached its full potential.

Development of Academic Standards for Students

Standards for student learning and performance are a policy development which parallels performance reporting, and which accelerates its impact. Reforms of this genre aim to align the curriculum, instructional standards, and student assessments. By the late 1990s most states had some form of standards, a majority have moved to link curricula and student assessments (sometimes locally developed) to these standards, and a handful of states have linked all of the above to rewards and sanctions for students, teachers, or administrators, or schools.

The standards movement has changed the nature of education policy discussions in some states such as Colorado and Maryland, where it has been a framework for pulling together the diverse interests in the education policy arena around a common set of goals (Cibulka & Derlin, 1998). However, the focus on student outcomes can be a source of division among those with different values, for example, religious conservatives, and politicians and groups who have different kinds of expectations for schools. In other states such as California and Wisconsin arguments over standards became highly politicized and led to major disputes involving the electorate or public officials. The focus on results, in other words, does not in and of itself promote double-loop learning. However, by focusing policy issues on critical outcomes for students, standards-based reform generates a new dialogue and reframes old disputes such as what constitutes an adequate education for all pupils regardless of ability or whether improved funding should be provided for schools serving the urban and rural poor. Standards-based reforms are an example of the shift from redistribution to efficiency in educational politics. Yet the constituency for efficiency is often, as is the nature of the politics of efficiency, diffuse and ill-organized and must overcome particularistic and well-organized interests. For these efficiency politics to succeed, they must satisfy redistributive constraints in order to be politically acceptable (Majone, 1996, p. 618). Standards introduce the possibility of new policy outcomes, but these depend on new learning by political actors who are accustomed to the old politics in which redistributive policies gave mainly lip-service to efficiency.

Managerial Approaches to OL in Schools

In the literature on OL developed by Argyris and others, responsibility for creating a "double-loop" learning environment rests primarily with managers. Similarly, within education there have been a number of developments which, if not always closely linked to the attempts to apply OL ideas, are nonetheless potentially compatible with its precepts.

Efforts to devolve greater discretion to the school site, mentioned earlier as an example of the new managerialism in public administration, represent one such thrust. This reform nostrum is described by a number of closely related ideas, such as site-based management (SBM), school-based planning, and data-based decision making. The rationale for these reforms can vary, as Weiler (1993) points out in his analysis of the philosophical bases for decentralization. Perhaps the most common perception is that SBM, planning, and use of data by school-based actors will increase their motivation and capacity to raise student achievement. Yet after a spate of interest a decade ago, SBM is now perceived as having yielded disappointing results. Among the most common criticisms is that too little authority is given to the school, that site-based councils often dwell on the trivial, and that they are not particularly democratic in the way discourse is managed and decisions are made (Malen & Ogawa, 1988). The advocacy of data-based decision making is a more recent idea, often associated with the trend toward use of performance information discussed above. While there have been few attempts, as yet, to formally evaluate data-based decision making, a number of impediments are surfacing. Teachers and administrators often are unskilled in the use of data and feel overwhelmed or threatened by it. Also, schools have not been structured to permit sufficient time for planning and reflection by teachers, particularly collaboratively. Which data to focus upon also proves to be a troublesome issue. The recent trend toward assessment-driven decision making certainly provides one approach to the use of student achievement data by teachers to inform their own teaching, and by administrators in their efforts to improve instruction.

In recent years school-based strategies for reforming K-12 education have become popular. These approaches begin with the school site and emphasize school wide renewal processes. Advocates of school-based reforms believe that student learning can be improved through new designs which either are locally developed or which bring the school into interaction with national reform networks such as Success-for-All, Accelerated Schools, or others. These approaches frame school renewal as a design problem and therefore are at their root managerial. To be sure, institutional actors can support funding for new school designs or authorize their enactment, but they are not part of the designs themselves. And while teachers are necessarily involved in the implementation of these new school designs, the degree to which teachers are viewed as central drivers of the new school design varies widely. Many designs, such as Success-for-All, are very prescriptive with respect to what they expect of teachers and leave relatively little room for their own autonomous action. Thus, to examine whether comprehensive school reform models promote OL requires a close examination of the particular design and its commitment to teacher learning. Perhaps the biggest gap in this approach to OL, from a policy system perspective, is that it treats most of the policy system as a "black box" whose role is unspecified. Devolving the action to the school site level still requires district and state support and engagement of the resources of the broader community. While this point is recognized by the proponents of comprehensive school reform, the conception of the entire policy system as a group of learners is not well developed.

Another set of conceptual developments potentially serves to move educational administration in the direction of OL. Newer conceptions of principal leadership by Leithwood, Begley, and Cousins (1994), Murphy (1992), and others focus upon the principal's facilitative, transformational role, as distinct from that of manager or instructional leader. Principals must empower teachers to share the instructional leadership role by cultivating the development of collaborative decision-making processes and promoting professional development to improve the curriculum, instructional practices, and assessment. Speck (1999) advocates that the principal's role is to create a learning community, which requires a concern for cultivating opportunities for teachers to be learners. As a part of the effort to create an LC in a school, Speck (1999, p. 56) advocates a reflective practice model for a principal, which serves as a model of learning and growth for the entire LC. From this perspective, the principal is responsible for creating strong professional communities (Louis & Kruse, 1995) in which teachers have high levels of autonomy and flexibility to respond to specific needs they see.[7]

While this literature on the changing role of the principal begins to look more fully at teachers and their needs than it did in the past, the cluster of ideas which we have just discussed tends to be quite vague about how the principal mediates pressures coming from the institutional level with concerns coming from teachers and others at the school level. The conception of a principal as political mediator among competing visions and interests, both external to the organization and internal to it, has not been well explored. For the most part, the recent attempts to conceptualize schools as LCs draw more heavily on ideas concerning professional community than they do notions of political community or neighborhood community. The word policy is almost never mentioned in this literature, and discussions of power are typically confined to *empowerment* of teachers rather than power as mobilization of consent, management of demands, or exchange of benefits—conceptions which are likely to be the most prevalent when institutional actors are engaged. At the other extreme, the concerns which often preoccupy teachers when they think about a learning community are not, at least yet, a central part of these managerial ideas which appear to promote LC. I turn to this last problem next.

Teacher Learning

There is a robust literature—or more properly, *groups* of literatures—which concern themselves directly with the needs of teachers. As was discussed at the outset, much educational policy has altogether ignored teachers or treated them as objects of change rather than viewing them as learners. Insofar as teachers were believed to be required to learn anything new to improve their content mastery or pedagogy, a behavioral approach to learning dominated this conception. Teachers were to be introduced to new ideas through short-term, structured professional development opportunities planned "for" them. Moreover, they were assumed to learn individually, in a manner which mirrored the social isolation of their classrooms. Adult learning theory had almost no impact on professional development for teachers (Guskey, 1995). Not surprisingly, research suggests that individual workshops aimed at transmitting technical knowledge to individual teachers are ineffective (Hamilton & Richardson 1995; Lieberman & Miller, 1991). In recent years the conception of teachers as learners has been influenced by the social aspects of teacher learning. In this view, an individual participates in constructing knowledge with others in a socially and culturally shared context (Saloman & Perkins, 1998).

This new, expanded conception of teachers as learners has a number of important implications for the way schools need to function in order to improve professional practice. First, effective professional development opportunities must be shaped by teachers themselves, guided by an exploration of their own experiences as learners and by an examination of their own deeply-held beliefs that emerge from their experiences (Ball, 1988; Zeichner & Liston, 1987). Second, the practice of teaching needs to be deprivatized, and opportunities for collaboration need to be created through a focus on student learning, shared values and norms, and reflective dialogue. All these can lead to a professional community (Louis & Kruse, 1995).

Clearly, for such teacher learning opportunities to occur, and for them to lead to professional communities in schools, would require dramatic shifts in the culture of schools. How to achieve such dramatic reform on a large scale is just now being examined. One approach is to develop a district-wide approach in which professional development is the top priority of the superintendent and other administrators (Elmore, 1997). Another approach discussed earlier is to adopt "proven" school reform models on a school-by-school basis, seeking to engage teachers in the decision process on which reform to adopt and, depending on the model selected, in guiding aspects of the implementation.

However, both of these approaches confine OL's space within the overall policy system. As a reform strategy, these approaches, which center on teacher learning, focus primarily on the technical level (the comprehensive school reform approach) or on its interface with management (the district approach to professional development as a top priority). Neither addresses the institutional level as part of the learning system. This example symbolizes the overall dilemma with the examples of learning in policy systems which have been reviewed here. They are for the most part discrete, disconnected programs, structures, and practices. Unless a way is found to tie them together more effectively, even the forces which have accelerated the role of ideas in the policy process are unlikely to have any transformative impact.

CONCLUSION: TOWARD POLICY SYSTEMS WHICH VALUE LEARNING

There can be no grand strategy for converting policy systems into arenas where double-loop learning (becoming better at avoiding mistakes) is a dominant trait. This is because policy systems are necessarily fragmented, with somewhat different problems and needs operating at national, state, and local levels and cutting across those levels, at institutional, managerial, and technical levels. At the institutional level politicians often operate using majoritarian rules, often proceeding on the assumption that unanimity is impossible where a policy improves the condition of one group at the expense of another group's loss, because no losing group will freely vote against its best interest. This is the essence of redistributive policymaking, where the public interest is a zero-sum game and conflict is inevitable. Thus, policymakers often give short shrift to consultation with those who must implement the policies because the assumption is that the costs of searching for unanimity would be too high, perhaps futile. The presence of high levels of conflict usually impedes opportunities for new learning (Sabatier & Jenkins-Smith, 1993, pp. 49-50), although under certain conditions of moderate conflict where, among other things, the protagonists have the technical resources to engage in informed debate, new knowledge can emerge from political conflict. They argue that policy-oriented learning is most likely where there exists a forum prestigious enough to bring together different coalitions in dialogue and one which is dominated by professional norms.

By contrast, most managerial decisions and operations at the technical level proceed on the assumption that there is one best solution to each problem, and that use of a unanimity rule will assure that everyone gains from a solution which increases aggregate welfare. Unanimous agreement, freely reached, guarantees that the solution is Pareto-efficient (Majone, 1996, p. 619). Under such conditions, collective choice decisions should involve discussion, compromise, and building of consensus. Of course, the unanimity rule is an idealized model of collective decision making, and is rarely fully implemented in educational organizations. Many administrators find it easier to achieve unanimity by fiat rather than consensus-building, and in any event the costs of building consensus on every decision would be inordinately high, perhaps unrealistic. Despite failure to implement the unanimity principle fully, it is important to recognize that it is in fact rooted in a different style of policymaking than is customary among institutional decision makers. Thus, all policy systems must straddle two different traditions of collective decision making.

If OL is to take root throughout policy systems to a greater degree than at present, ways must be found to bridge these different worlds. One of the most important bridging mechanisms is direct communication. Policymakers rarely understand the "micro-realities" within which teachers and administrators work, except as these are reported to them by interest groups purporting to represent the latter. Conducting regular hearings, making visitations to local sites, and commissioning process evaluations of a policy are simple ways to increase the flow of information "upward" from the field to policymakers. At the same time, teachers and administrators often operate in isolated environments sheltered from the political realities of institutional decision makers. Reaching out to hear what school board members, state legislators, and chief executives have to say is a way to advance OL. For teachers, attending professional conferences is still too rare an occurrence.

Because each operates under different traditions and constraints, the means for incorporating OL will differ. At the school level, one of the main impediments to OL has been the attitude of administrators who resist creating a school culture in which teacher learning can flourish. The command and control approach to the principalship is incompatible with OL. Site-based management has proven to be a limited avenue for achieving OL, in part because creation of structures for decision making is formalistic without attempts to alter the culture of the school to encourage teacher learning. OL also implies a sufficiently open-system approach to school governance so that parents and other community resources are part of the decision apparatus, although there are many ways to achieve this more inclusive culture (Pounder, 1998).

Policymakers cannot mandate these changes lower in the policy system, although they can bring about change in two ways. First, they can promulgate new policies which support the restructuring of schools where professional learning is taken seriously. For example, they can provide financial support for new approaches to professional development which are built on a commitment to teacher learning which has as its explicit aim improved learning outcomes for all students. Second, policymakers can proceed on the assumption that the policymaking system requires more arenas for information sharing before new policy learning can occur. This includes a willingness to learn from teachers and administrators in order to fulfill their policymaking role effectively. This would require normative changes in the way educational policy systems now operate. The goal of such communication should not be viewed as the achievement of consensus, although under certain conditions that may emerge. Rather, it proceeds on the assumption that the benefits of increased multilateral communication will in the end improve the quality of policies which are established by policymakers and the commitment of teachers and administrators to carrying them out effectively. I have described many individual elements of the current educational policy system which favors an expanded role for OL—a new interest in improving the entire educational system, emphasis on standards, new conceptions of leadership, and so on. However, these are disjointed threads. To come together as a systemic change, the two above preconditions must occur: new policies which explicitly support schools' professional learning cultures and new collaborative norms in the policy system which expand opportunities for communication.

ACKNOWLEDGMENTS

Support for this work has been provided by the Office of Educational Research and Improvement, U.S. Department of Education, Contract No. RFP-97-010. However, the views I express here are my own and are not intended to represent the views of the U. S. Department of Education. I wish to acknowledge the research assistance of Michelle Nakumura in preparing this chapter.

NOTES

1.   The influence of psychology on policy studies is not entirely absent, reflected in the work of Harold Lasswell and Herbert Simon.

2.   This assumption fits some new educational initiatives better than others. Policies directed at ending racial isolation do reduce the advantages whites enjoy in segregated school environments. By contrast, the creation of special education programs serving children previously underserved or excluded from school may have the net effect of expanding opportunities for a new group without reducing benefits enjoyed by those served by traditional education programs. Accordingly, applying the term "redistributive" indiscriminately to all new educational initiatives directed at special needs populations deserves a note of caution.

3.   The burden of my argument is that one kind of policy tends to dominate in a particular period, but not to the total exclusion of other policy values. For example, during the 1930s the Roosevelt administration launched a wide series of initiatives which reflected both efficiency and social redistribution, even though today the redistributive aspects of Roosevelt's policies are remembered first. Also, I do not mean to imply that efficiency and equality are the only operative values or forms of public policy.

4.   Sabatier and Jenkins-Smith (1993, p. 22) argue that such exogenous forces can facilitate policy learning.

5.   Of course, such delegation by the majority to committees can involve "agency costs" if the experts abdicate their responsibility to become experts and instead rely on partial or wrong information provided by lobbyists, members of the executive branch, or others. Thus, the challenge for legislators who rely on committee recommendations is to avoid abdicating control over policy (Lupia & McCubbins, 1994).

6.   One should not be surprised if this trend has its limitations, however, not only for the aforementioned reasons but also because policy often leaps ahead of sound research. When President Clinton proposed in his 1999 State of the Union address to attach sanctions to low-performing schools, he did not rely on sound research because very little was available. Reconstitution of failing schools is a "hot" policy idea spreading across the country, and the President attached his name to it. In such circumstances, when public pressure for "action" is intense, policy developments will not wait on the slow, laborious time frames of education researchers.

7.   At the same time, Louis and Kruse (1995) point out that it is not clear what approach to professional leadership is most efficacious in creating strong professional communities which promote high levels of student achievement.

REFERENCES

Alt, J. E., & Alesina, A. (1996). Political economy: An overview. In R. E. Goodwin & H. Klingemann (Eds.), *A new handbook of political science* (pp. 645-674). New York: Oxford University Press.

Argyris, C., & Schon, D. A. (1996). *Organizational learning II: Theory, method, and practice*. Reading, MA: Addison-Wesley Publishing Co.

Ball, D. L. (1988). I haven't done these things since high school: Prospective teachers' understanding of mathematics. In M. Behr, C. Lacampagne, & M. Wheeler (Eds.), *Proceedings of the tenth annual meeting of the North American chapter of the International Group for the Psychology of Mathematics Education* (pp. 268-274). DeKalb, IL: Northern Illinois University.

Cibulka, J. G. (1995). The institutionalization of public schools: The decline of legitimizing myths and the politics of organizational instability. In R. T. Ogawa (Ed.), *Advances in research and theories of school management and educational policy* (Vol. 3, pp. 123-158). Greenwich, CT: JAI Press.

Cibulka, J. G., & Derlin, R. L. (1998). Authentic education accountability policies: Implementation of state initiatives in Colorado and Maryland. *Educational Policy, 12*(1&2), 84-97.

Cohen, D. K., & Barnes, C. A. (1993). Pedagogy and policy. In D. K. Cohen, M. W. McLaughlin, & J. E. Talbert (Eds.), *Teaching for understanding* (pp. 207-239). San Francisco: Jossey-Bass.

Cohen, D. K., March, J. G., & Olsen, J. P. (1972). A garbage can model of organizational choice. *Administrative Science Quarterly, 17,* 1-25.

Cousins, J. B. (1996). Understanding organizational learning for educational leadership and school reform. In K. Leithwood, J. Chapman, D. Corson, P. Hallinger, & A. Hart (Eds.), *International handbook of educational leadership and administration.* Dordrecht, The Netherlands: Kluwer Academic Publishers.

Crowson, R. L., Boyd, W. L., & Mawhinney, H. B.(Eds.). (1996). *The politics of education and the new institutionalism.* New York: Falmer.

Deal, T. (1985). National commissions: Blueprints for remodeling or ceremonies for revitalizing public schools. *Education and Urban Society, 17*(2), 145-156.

Dimaggio, P., & Powell, W. W. (1983). The iron cage revisited: Institutional isomorphism and collective rationality in organizational fields. *American Sociological Review, 48,* 147-160.

Elmore, R. F. (1982). Backward mapping: Implementation and policy decisions. In W. Williams (Ed.), *Studying implementation: Methodological and administrative issues,* (pp. 18-35). Chatham, NJ: Chatham House Publishing.

Elmore. R. F. (1997). *Investing in teacher learning: Staff development and instructional improvement in Community School District #2: New York City.* Washington, DC: National Commission on Teaching and America's Future, Consortium for Policy Research in Education.

Goggin, M. L. (1990). *Implementation theory and practice.* New York: HarperCollins.

Gouldner, A. (1959). Organizational analysis. In R. K. Merton, L. Broom, & L. S. Cottrell, Jr. (Eds.), *Sociology today* (pp. 400-428). New York: Basic Books.

Guskey, T. R. (1995). Professional development in education. In T. R. Guskey & M. Huberman (Eds.), *Professional development in education* (pp 114-134). New York: Teachers College Press.

Guthrie, J. (1990). The evolving political economy of education and the implications for educational evaluation. *Educational Review, 42*(2), 109-131.

Hamilton, M. L., and Richardson, V. (1995). Effects of the culture of two schools on the process and outcomes of staff development. *Elementary School Journal, 95*(4), 376-385.

Huber, G. P. (1991). Organizational learning: The contributing processes and the literatures. *Organizational Science, 2*(1) 88-115.

Kettl, D. F. (1983). *The regulation of American federalism.* Baton Rouge, LA: University of Louisiana Press.

Kingdon J. (1984). *Agendas, alternatives, and public policies.* New York: HarperCollins.

Leithwood, K., Begley, P. T., & Cousins, J. B. (1994). *Developing expert leadership for future schools.* New York: Falmer.

Lieberman, A., & Miller, L. (1991). Revisiting the social realities of teaching. In A. Lieberman & L. Miller (Eds.), *Staff development for education in the 90s* (2nd ed.) (pp. 92-109). New York: Teachers College Press.

Lindblom, C. E. (1959). The science of muddling through. *Public Administration Review, 19,* 79-59.

Lupia, A., & McCubbins, M. (1994). Designing bureaucratic accountability. *Law and Contemporary Problems, 57,* 91-126.

Louis, K. S., & Kruse, S. D. (1995). *Professionalism and community: Perspectives on reforming urban schools.* Thousand Oaks, CA: Corwin Press.

Lowi, T. J. (1969). *The end of liberalism: Ideology, policy, and the crisis of public authority.* New York: Norton.

Majone, G. (1996). Public policy and administration: Ideas, interests, and institutions. In R. E. Goodwin & H. Klingemann (Eds.), *A new handbook of political science* (pp. 610-627). New York: Oxford University Press.

Malen, B., & Ogawa, R. T. (1988). Professional-patron influence on site-based governance councils: A confounding case study. *Educational Evaluation and Policy Analysis, 10,* 251-279.

March, J. G., & Olsen, J. P. (1989). *Rediscovering institutions: The organizational basis of politics.* New York: Free Press.

March, J. G., & Simon, H. A. (1958). *Organizations.* New York: Wiley.

Marin, B., & Mayntz, R. (1992). *Policy networks.* Boulder, CO: Westview.

Mawhinney, H. B. (1993). An advocacy coalition approach to change in Canadian education. In P.A. Sabatier & H.C. Jenkins-Smith (Eds.). (1993). *Policy change and learning: An advocacy coalition approach* (pp. 59-82). Boulder, CO: Westview.

Meyer, J. W., & Rowan, B. (1977). Institutionalized organizations: Formal structure as myth and ceremony. *American Journal of Sociology, 83,* 340-363.

Murphy, J. (1992). *The landscape of leadership preparation: Reframing the education of school administrators.* Newbury Park, CA: Corwin Press.

Ostrom, E. (1990). *Governing the commons.* New York: Cambridge University Press.

Patton, M. (1990). *Qualitative evaluation and research* methods. Newbury Park, CA: Sage.

Peters, B. G., & Wright, V. (1996). Public policy and administration, old and new. In R. E. Goodwin & H. Klingemann (Eds.), *A new handbook of political science* (pp. 628-641). New York: Oxford University Press.

Peterson, P. E. (1983). Did the Education Commission say anything? *Education and Urban Society, 17*(2), 126-144.

Pounder, D. G. (1998). *Restructuring schools for collaboration: Promises and pitfalls.* Albany, NY: State University of New York Press.

Pressman, J., & Wildavsky, A. (1973). *Implementation.* Berkeley: University of California Press.

Rait, E. (1995). Against the current: Organizational learning in schools: In S. B. Bacharach & B. Mundell (Eds.), *Images of schools: Structures and roles in organizational behavior.* Thousand Oaks, CA: Corwin.

Rossi, P., & Freeman, H. (1993). *Evaluation.* Newbury Park, CA: Sage.

Rowan B., & Miskel, C. G. (1999). Institutional theory and the study of school organizations. In J. Murphy & K. S. Louis (Eds.), *Handbook of research on educational administration* (2nd ed.). San Francisco: Jossey-Bass.

Sabatier, P. A., & Jenkins-Smith, H. C. (Eds.). (1993). *Policy change and learning: An advocacy coalition approach.* Boulder, CO: Westview.

Salomon, G., & Perkins, D. N. (1998). Individual and social aspects of learning. In P. D. Pearson & A. Iran-Nejad (Eds.), *Review of research in education 23* (pp. 353-389). Washington, DC: American Educational Research Association.

Scott, W. R. (1987). *Organizations: Rational, natural, and open systems* (2nd ed.). Englewood Cliffs, NJ: Prentice-Hall.

Schultze, C. L. (1977). *The public use of private interest.* Washington, DC: Brookings.

Simon, H. A. (1957). *Administrative behavior* (2nd ed.). New York: Macmillan.

Speck, M. (1999). *The principalship: Building a learning community.* Upper Saddle Hill, NJ: Merrill.

Weick, K. E. (1976). Educational organizations as loosely coupled systems. *Administrative Science Quarterly 21,* 1-19.

Weiler, H. N. (1993). Control versus legitimation: The politics of ambivalence. In J. Hannaway & M. Carnoy (Eds.), *Decentralization and school improvement: Can we fulfill the promise?* (pp. 55-83). San Francisco: Jossey-Bass.

Weiss, C. (1982). Policy research in the context of diffuse decision making. *Journal of Higher Education, 53*(6), 619-639.

Williamson, O. (1993). The emerging science of organization. *Journal of Institutional and Theoretical Economics, 149,* 36-43.

Wimpelberg, R., & Ginsburg, R. (1985). Are school districts responding to *A Nation at Risk? Education and Urban Society, 17*(2), 186-203.

Zeichner, K. M., & Liston, D. (1987). Teaching students to reflect. *Harvard Educational Review, 57,* 23-48.

CHAPTER 10

DIAGNOSING THE EXTENT OF ORGANIZATIONAL LEARNING CAPACITY IN SCHOOLS

David Dibbon

When an evolving and enhanced understanding is translated into action, organizational learning is like the fountain of youth.... Unfortunately, understanding organizational learning has been almost as elusive as locating the fountain of youth.
—Inkpen & Crossan, 1995, p. 597

Organizational learning in schools has received very little attention until quite recently, and, as a consequence, remains poorly understood. Even less understood are the processes by which schools become better at it. Based on a more extensive study reported elsewhere (Dibbon, 1999), this chapter describes a multi-dimensional conception of growth in a school's organizational learning capacity. Although empirical data are used to illustrate this conception, it remains a theory,

Advances in Research and Theories of School
Management and Educational Policy, Volume 4, pages 211-236.

at this point, in need of careful validation in schools. One central purpose for developing the conception of growth was to transform a potentially useful, but eclectic and unsynthesized literature, into a form readily useable by practitioners engaged in school improvement intiatives. It may have uses for research, as well.

The term "learning organization" is often used as a metaphor to describe the fully developed, ideal organization (e.g., Senge, 1991). Learning organizations are exceptionally good at "organizational learning." They possess powerful individual, small group, and whole organization learning capacities for potentially or actually changing patterns of organizational practice. Such change can be cognitive or behavioral, or both. Cognitive change includes, for example, changes in organizational beliefs, attitudes, opinions, values, understanding, and know how. Behavioral change includes changes in organizational patterns of action.

Inkpen and Crossan (1995) claim that the strongest organizational learning entails a combination of cognitive and behavioral changes. Changes in behavior without a corresponding change in cognition, and vice versa, are transitional states that will impact on learning by resulting eventually in powerful learning or no learning at all. An example of a change in behavior without a change in cognition occurs, for example, when a district or department of education legislates a change in teaching practice (e.g., whole language). While individuals may feel forced to change their behaviors to comply with the new regulation—their beliefs that the old way is better, does not change. An example of a change in cognition without a change in behavior is when individuals discover new approaches to teaching (i.e., computer-mediated distance education) but cannot implement them due to the nature of school policies or inadequate resources. Using this example, integrated learning would require teachers to be both enabled and empowered to use their new knowledge. While individual and collective learning occurs in all schools, some are much better at it than others.

DESIGN

The study summarized in this chapter was conducted in two phases. Phase one consisted of an extensive review of the organizational learning literature and the development, from that review, of an initial, quite sketchy framework for describing growth in the organizational learning capacity of schools. Because of space limitations, this chapter provides a brief synopsis of the framework resulting from that review only. Those interested in the details are referred to the larger study on which this chapter is based (Dibbon, 1999).

Phase two consisted of interviews with a total of three principals and 22 teachers in four secondary schools (five to seven interviews in each school). Focused on respondents' perceptions of organizational learning in their schools, the purposes of this phase, based on "grounded theory" methods (e.g., Strauss & Corbin, 1990) were both elaboration and illustration of the initial framework. After a pilot testing and revision process, the 25 interviews were conducted, tape-recorded, transcribed, and coded using the constant comparative method (Strauss & Corbin, 1990). As with the first phase of the study, this chapter is limited to a summary of results rather than a complete reporting of data.

Both phases of the study helped to generate a set of questions for collecting information to profile the current status of a school's organizational learning capacity. While these questions were further developed into a survey instrument which was subject to a preliminary field test in the larger study, further work is needed before the survey can be published. The diagnostic questions themselves are included in this chapter, however.

PHASE ONE:
RESULTS OF THE LITERATURE REVIEW

The initial framework resulting from the literature review, summarized in this section, conceptualizes growth in a school's organizational learning capacity as a four-stage process occuring within three "units" of the organization (individual, team, and whole school). No assumptions are made in this conception about parallel growth across units; while whole organization learning depends critically on individual (and likely team) learning, for example, individual learning can develop to a fairly sophisticated level without any necessary learning "payoff" at the whole organization level. So growth in learning capacity may be quite uneven, and certainly not lockstep.

The first part of this section will describe growth in whole school learning capacity. It does so in enough detail to illustrate four plausible stages of capacity development that the literature seems to warrant. Then, in the second part of this section, a much briefer description is provided of the nature of growth in both individual and team organizational learning capacity.

A Four-Staged Conception of Capacity Development
Using Whole School Learning for Illustrative Purposes

Stage theories have proven useful in helping to understand many different kinds of changes; moral development (Kohlberg, 1970), ego development (Loevinger, 1966), teacher development (Fuller, 1969), and increasing fidelity of innovation implementation (Hall, Wallace, & Dossett, 1973) for example. Even when stages are considered to be no more than a heuristic marker or snapshot of a phenomenon at one point in time (the weak version of stage theory), they offer some promise as tools for diagnosing, and beginning to manage, the hitherto slippery concept of organizational learning capacity development.

Descriptions of stages in organizational learning have been reported by Huber (1991), Dibella, Nevis and Gould (1996), and Dixon (1994). Common to these efforts is the characterization of this process as non-linear, and iterative but one that can be described as a number of stages, nevertheless. For example, Huber (1991) identified the stages as knowledge acquisition, distribution, interpretation and organizational memory. DiBella, Nevis and Gould (1996) suggested the stages of knowledge acquisition, sharing and utilization, and Dixon (1994) outlined a four-step organizational learning cycle including knowledge generation, integration, interpretation and action.

Together, these views suggest that organizational learning follows a cycle including: (1) a stimulus that makes new learning necessary, (2) acquisition of new knowledge coupled with an initial interpretation of that knowledge, (3) transferring and sharing the new knowledge throughout the organization, (4) collectively interpreting and utilizing the new knowledge in an organizational context (new learning), and (5) documentation or codification of the new knowledge.

This cycle may capture, fairly well, essential features of the organizational learning process. But it tells us almost nothing about changes in the extent of a school's capacity for organizational learning, or how to manage the process for improvement purposes. For these purposes, we need answers to such questions as "How can the rate at which a school moves through this cycle be increased?" and "How can we help ensure that the knowledge acquired adds value to the school's improvement capacities?" What is required to answer questions such as these is a better understanding of the organizational conditions that account for variation in the speed, efficiency, and effectiveness with which an organization learns, and how the state of each of these conditions changes as organizational learning capacity increases.

Summarized below is a four-stage description of growth in a school's organizational learning capacity inferred from the review of literature.

Stage 1: The Coping Organization

Schools in the coping stage are maintaining their traditional approaches to education even though changes in their environments may warrant significant change. These schools "exploit" (March, 1991) their existing repertoires of knowledge and routines engaging almost entirely in single loop learning (Argyris, 1976), and resist innovation through, among other things, widespread use of "organizational defensive routines" (Argyris, 1990). Since organizational members are committed to retaining the status quo, there is very little stimulus for "exploratory" (March, 1991) or "double loop" (Argyris, 1976) learning. These schools do not see the need for change and generally feel that they are doing a good job. There is no evidence of a learning plan (Sheppard and Brown's chapter in this text describes two such schools at the beginning of their journey to become learning organizations). These schools are primitive learning systems, at best, often engaging in "superstitious learning" (Levitt & March, 1988)—drawing flawed, or just plain incorrect, lessons from their experiences.

Stage 2: The Emerging Organization

Schools that are in the emerging stage have become active, if incomplete and immature, learning systems. There is usually a consensus beginning to form in the school that large-scale change is necessary and some understanding that "systems thinking" (Senge, 1991) will be required to successfully bring about such change. There is at least one, and usually a group of people, in the school prepared to champion this change, and to engage in the new learning this will entail. Indeed some people in the school are prepared to engage in double loop or exploratory thinking for this purpose. There is, as well, signs of the development of conditions and strategies (or levers) for intentionally fostering collective learning (creation of more collaborative cultures, for example). But these schools are only beginning to emerge from their protective shell; they still engage in organizational defensive routines occasionally. These schools need to design improvement plans for altering how they go about their collective learning (for example, how they can more systematically collect relevant knowledge from outside sources), as well as how they can actively intervene to improve the rate and efficiency of their learning.

Stage 3: The Developing Organization

Schools at this stage are relatively mature learning systems but have to work explicitly and quite self consciously at their learning, occasionally slipping back into old, more defensive patterns. From time to time, they can be seen engaging in both single loop and double loop approaches to learning but sometimes they choose the wrong approach for the problem or situation at hand. These schools have developed an impressive repertoire of knowledge, skills and related practices but have few procedures or structures in place to ensure the reliable delivery of these practices. At this stage, schools are very open to promising ideas and practices from elsewhere. Occasionally, however, they are faddish in their approach to such ideas, adopting them with insufficient assessment, and implementing them with too little attention to the modifications warranted by their context.

Stage 4: The Learning Organization

Schools at this stage are sophisticated learning systems. An ethic of continuous learning creates a culture in which both exploratory/double loop learning strategies are balanced, as the occasion warrants, with exploitative/single loop approaches to learning. At this stage, schools recognize what it is they do very well and are vigilant about engaging in those practices, or delivering those services, in a highly reliable way (Stringfield, 1995). They also are quick to recognize good ideas from outside the organization that hold promise of substantially improving their own effectiveness. These ideas are carefully examined and the implications for changes in the school determined in a deliberate fashion. There is a widely shared, but adaptable plan for continuous improvement which serves as a guide for such deliberation. Schools at this stage share many of the features that Leithwood associates with his "high reliability, learning community" (Leithwood, Jantzi & Steinbach, 1999, chap. 13).

Individual and Team Learning Capacity Development

A comprehensive appreciation of growth in a school's organizational learning capacity requires a description of growth, at the individual and team levels, like the one outlined above for the whole school level. This section offers a briefer synopsis (i.e., not four stages) of what the literature suggests such growth is like.

Individual Learning

Organizations are critical contexts for individual learning, as theories of situated and distributed cognition (Cole & Engestrom, 1993; Salomon, 1993) help to explain. In Brown and Duguid's terms (1996), organizations serve as "communities of practice" for their members, creating unique learning environments, and shaping the nature of the knowledge considered functional for individuals in those environments to acquire.

In some organizations there is very little evidence of individual learning while others are dynamic learning communities. In its least well developed state, individual learning in organizations is exclusively tacit and largely unintentional, a function of daily work routines alone. In a more fully developed state, such learning occurs intentionally as well as unintentionally, aided by personal reflection at least some of the time. The most fully developed state of individual learning in organizations adds planned and formal educational experiences.

Team Learning

Teams increasingly are being called on to learn on behalf of their organizations (e.g., see chapters by Chrispeels et al. and Scott in this text for the rationale). But teams and groups are complex organizations in their own right, and it is possible for team learning to be highly valued yet poorly practiced. Janis (1982) has described a dysfunctional form of team learning which he labelled "groupthink." Teams in this immature state often follow courses of action with which their individual members disagree and know to be dysfunctional. The reasons for this, well documented by Janis (1982) and many others, include for example, unwillingness to challenge other members ideas, overestimation of the groups knowledge, and unclear goals. Neck and Manz (1994) use the term "teamthink" to describe a highly sophisticated set of processes engaged in by groups. Such processes, described by Leithwood, Steinbach, and Ryan (1997) as "expert problem solving," allow the group to be smarter than any of its individual members acting alone. Expert groups cherish the uniqueness of their individual members, encourage dissenting views, and seek out knowledge from all available sources, for example.

A fully adequate description of growth in a school's organizational learning capacity will encompass the conditions accounting for variation in learning capacity across all three units within which organizatioal learning occurs. The second phase of this study, to which we now turn, addressed this requirement directly.

PHASE TWO:
RESULTS OF DATA COLLECTION IN FOUR SCHOOLS

This second phase of the study, informed but not constrained by the results of the literature review, inquired about organizational learning processes in four secondary schools. Its purpose was to offer an initial, empirical account of changes in schools' organizational learning capacity, and to compare that account with the account summarized in Phase One based on the literature review.

The schools in which the interviews were conducted were expected to be at different stages of capacity development, although the selection process could not guarantee this. Results of the analysis suggested, however, that this was the case: using pseudonyms for the school names, organizational learning capacity varied from least to most in Janjonner, CAL, Nicom, and Floridav. This variation was not uniform for all aspects of learning, but it was a reasonably consistent pattern.

The 25 interview transcriptions were analyzed using the constant comparative method (Strauss & Corbin, 1990), imposing on the analysis, in advance, only a four stage structure, and a requirement that changes across the four stages be described for each of the three units of organizational learning (individual, team, whole organization). Results are reported in this section for each unit of learning considered separately.

Stages of Growth in Individual Learning Capacity

Analysis of the interview data suggested that individual learning occurs along a continuum that ranges from very little interest in individual professional learning, in schools that are at Stage 1 (The Coping Stage) to a very sophisticated level of individual learning in organizations that are at Stage Four (The Learning Organization Stage). Table 1 provides an outline of the basic features of growth across the stages.

Table 1. Stages of Growth in Individual Professional Learning Capacity

Factors	Stage 1: The Coping Stage	Stage 2: The Emerging Stage	Stage 3: The Developing Stage	Stage 4: The Learning Organization Stage
Attitudes about Individual Professional Learning	Reluctance and skepticism: given low priority	Some skepticism but a recognition that it is important; responsibility given to school committees	Viewed as critical for growth; but responsibility of entire organization	Critical for growth; people enthusiastic and committed to learning; responsibility shared by organization and individual
Support for Individual Professional Learning	Very little internal support even though there may be strong external support	Strong internal support but weak external support	Strong internal support but weak external support	Strong internal and external support
Administrator Involvement in Individual Professional Learning	Very little support—nothing more than paying lip service	Viewed as a high priority; little personal involvement	Viewed as a high priority; administrators get personally involved	Viewed as a high priority; high expectations for all teachers; administrators get personally involved
Planning for Individual Professional Learning	Focus on one-shot deals; no follow-up; no long term planning	Focus on one-shot deals; organizational goals are considered; no evidence school-wide planning	Still some focus on one-shot deals, but some evidence that learning is integrated into daily work; little evidence of school-wide planning; learning needs based on perceived needs of the future	Focus on learning as a continuous process; teachers are involved and learning is integrated into work life; individual and oranizational goals are considered; there is a long-term plan
Nature of Opportunities for Individual Professional Learning	External sources available but rarely used	On-site, one day sessions for entire staff; periodic off-site sessions for individuals; some planned follow-up on key items	On-site, one day sessions for entire staff; periodic off-site sessions for individuals; some evidence of learning integrated into daily work	Wide variety of choices customized to meet needs of the learner; on and off site sessions; focus on continuous learning; evidence of integration into daily work life

In the first stage of development (The Coping Stage) there is very little evidence of individual professional learning and organizational members give it a fairly low priority. Also, training and professional development are often viewed with skepticism and the little learning that does occur results from attending district planned in-service or outside training sessions that are viewed as mandatory. While discussing professional learning, one of the English teachers at Janjonner claimed "without being cynical, I find an awful lot of my colleagues are reluctant to get involved." The science teacher felt professional learning wasn't a big issue in the school, stating "notices get read out in staff meetings but that's about all." At this stage, there is external support for professional learning, however, at the school level it is viewed as a one-shot deal and not as a continuous process. The English department head at Janjonner clarified this when he said:

> This board has a lot of opportunities that you can take advantage of.... they occur outside of school time and you can sign-up if you are interested, but the onus is on the individual teacher to be interested enough to want to sign-up.... Within the school there is a PD committee and they plan our school-wide PD days but that's only going to be twice a year.

Another characteristic of schools in the first stage of development is that administrators do not openly support professional learning—their own or others. In most instances, there is little formal follow-up to ensure that what is learned is used on the job. One of the science teachers at Janjonner who had taken a summer course on Kegan Structures claimed she was using it in her teaching but there was no direct follow-up with the board or the school.

At this stage, there is no evidence to support long term planning for professional learning of any sort. When asked if there was a professional learning plan for the school, all five of the teachers at Janjonner answered a definitive "No." When asked if anyone took responsibility for working out an individual professional learning plan, once again all answered "No." The French teacher said "anyone can go to the PD committee and ask for money to go somewhere, and you'll probably get it but in my opinion there is really no push or encouragement." It was her feeling that professional learning was entirely the responsibility of the individual teacher.

In Stage Two, individual learning is still not widespread. There are pockets of individual learning but there are also many teachers who resist the notion. As one of the more experienced English teachers at CAL stated: "There's a small group of us who have a genuine interest in learning but the vast majority—unless they're being paid every minute for everything they do—they just won't do it." Administrators see continuous professional learning and professional development for all teachers as a high priority and but they do not become actively involved in coaching and mentoring teachers and there is no evidence of planning for individual professional development. As the principal at Nicom articulated:

I try to take a personal interest in every member of the staff in terms of how they are, what their
well-being is, if there's anything I can do for them, or whatever the issue. I try to identify what
the trends are and to provide direction for the school and I try to encourage people by saying,
now listen you might as well be ready for this change when it comes. However, I do not have
an individual professional plan on every staff member, I just don't have the time.

This principal and the principal of CAL also supported the views of their teachers in that there was strong internal support (from the school administration) for
professional learning but very little external support from the district and the ministry. As the learning resources teacher at Nicom so forcefully pointed out "You
know, there are a number of us who were prepared to do training at our own
expense but we couldn't get the leave time—I think teachers are willing to get
involved but we need some support."

In schools at Stage Two, learning opportunities are still scarce. Most are the
result of one-day district or ministry-mandated in-services, or one-day workshops
planned by the school. In these schools there is little evidence of school-wide
planning for learning and there is little planned follow-up to ensure that new
learning gets integrated into administrators' and teachers' daily activities. When
asked about follow-up after inservice and professional days the English teacher at
CAL stated: "There's not much really, but lately there is an emphasis on technology and we are constantly being asked how it's going and we are encourage to use
it as much as possible."

In schools that are in the third stage of development, individual professional
learning is seen as critical for school growth. The teachers at Nicom recognized
the need for professional learning opportunities but were frustrated by the lack of
resources and external support to make it happen but, as the science department
head said: "we have to learn as we go. Things are changing so fast you can't wait
for the board—we have to do it ourselves." This staff had taken responsibility for
their own learning and was developing new curriculum, experimenting with technology and one person was engaged in an action-learning research project.

In schools at this stage, there is an understanding that professional learning
helps teachers and administrators do their jobs better and helps prepare them for
new challenges. The teachers at Nicom felt that despite the number of new initiatives there was not a clearly articulated school-wide plan for learning but they did
acknowledge that the new learning initiatives did focus on the perceived future
needs of students. All of the teachers mentioned the increased dependence on
technology and the Future Pathways program as clear examples of new initiatives.
The principal at Nicom claimed the new learning initiatives were all about keeping pace with changes in the local community and society in general in an attempt
to improve educational opportunities for students. With reference to the Future
Pathways program he said "we're looking out to the community and inward
towards the child, because we believe strongly that this is so relevant for any kid
who walks out of school these days." In addition, teachers at Nicom viewed individual professional learning as essential to the school's ability to change (even

though they felt it was an organizational rather than a personal responsibility) and to prepare organizational members (administrators, teachers and students) for an uncertain future.

Also, in the third stage, learning opportunities may involve district planned in-service, school-based workshops or outside training sessions. While there is a focus on providing opportunities for learning, there is still little follow-up to ensure that what gets learned gets integrated into administrators' and teachers' daily activities. At Nicom, administrators did become involved as co-learners (with the new technology initiatives and the Future Pathways program) but there was no evidence that they were engaged in coaching or mentorship activities.

At stage four, individuals are enthusiastic and committed to lifelong learning and professional learning is viewed as critical for school and personal growth. At this level there is tremendous internal support (from administrators and other teachers) and external support (from school district and community) for learning, and teachers and administrators have high expectations of each other. The staff development teacher at Floridav described just how strong a commitment was required in her school:

> In order to come here you had to have a certain level of professional development, you had to be a lifelong learner, you had to be a risk-taker, you had to be a change agent, you had to be a lot of things because at this school we do things quite differently. It involves a lot of work but there are a lot of rewards and I think generally speaking, you have to be a very energetic, forward thinking person to be here.

Administrator and teacher learning is addressed through a wide variety of choices designed to meet the needs of the organization, along with the learner. This includes learning from other staff members, cross-training, accepting new teaching assignments and from formally planned training sessions. Also, at this stage most of the learning occurs on-site, through training, professional development sessions and action learning projects that are customized to meet the needs of the learners. A major focus at this stage is that new learning is integrated into teachers' classrooms and becomes a part of their daily work routines. For example, at Floridav, teams of teachers meet regularly, on a weekly basis, to reflect on their work and to develop new approaches to teaching. Also, some teachers were able to develop new teaching units as a component of their performance appraisal.

QUESTIONS FOR DIAGNOSING THE LEVEL OF INDIVIDUAL LEARNING IN A SCHOOL

Diagnosing the level of individual learning in a school requires questions to help determine: whether attitudes about individual professional learning are positive or negative in nature; the level of support that exists within and outside the school; whether or not school administrators become actively involved in the learning of

Table 2. Stages of Growth in Team Learning Capacity

Factors	Stage 1: The Coping Stage	Stage 2: The Emerging Stage	Stage 3: The Developing Stage	Stage 4: The Learning Stage
Evidence of Teams	Little evidence of teams but there are some ad-hoc committees	Little evidence of teams but committees with a low degree of responsibility are common	Evidence of some teams and team learning but focus is still on committee work	Teams are a part of normal operations; team learning occurs as a natural part of work; there are some committees
Stimulus for Team Learning	Improvement initiatives usually externally initiated	Implementation of new curriculum; usually externally initiated	School leadership promotes learning for improvement; new curriculum implementation	School leadership supports learning for improvement; new curriculum implementation; as a part of performance appraisal
Team Learning Processes	Scarce evidence to suggest teams are used	Scarce evidence to suggest teams are used	Some evidence that teams are formed to generate new knowledge; analyze complex issues; take innovative action and collectively solve problems	Extensive evidence that teams are formed to generate new knowledge; analyze complex issues; take innovative action and collectively solve problems
Leadership Support	Administrators not familiar with teams or team processes; teachers skeptical about teams; team decisions not respected	Teachers not comfortable with teams; do not want responsibility of decision making; no quality time provided; no team training	Leadership promoting teams as a way to work; no quality time provided; no team training	Administrators possess team building and teamwork skills; respect decisions of teams; provide quality time for teams; ensure teachers are knowledge able about teams
Team Structure	Principal led management committee	Principal led leadership committee	School leadership team led by the principal; some task forces and curriculum teams	School-wide involvement; teams are organized for leadership and management functions; task forces; curriculum planning

(continued)

Table 2. (Continued)

Factors	Stage 1: The Coping Stage	Stage 2: The Emerging Stage	Stage 3: The Developing Stage	Stage 4: The Learning Stage
Team Operating Principles	No evidence of operating principles	Groupthink	Teams dominated by powerful personalities; some evidence of dialogue	Open and honest communication (dialogue); a collaborative work culture
Team Learning Outcomes	No evidence of team learning	No evidence of team learning	Team learning gets transferred to entire organization	Team learning gets transferred to entire organization

their teachers; and whether this learning occurs purely by chance or whether there are carefully designed plans for individual learning.

Analysis of the interview data suggests, as well, the need for questions about: what stimulates individuals to learn in an organizational context; what are the sources of individual learning; and what do individuals do with the new learning once they have acquired it.

Stages of Growth in Team Learning Capacity

Team learning is a complicated skill and schools in the early stages of developing their organizational learning capacities are unlikely to be very productive at it. Analysis of the interview data indicated that fairly sophisticated learning occurred within teams at the third and fourth levels of development but there was little evidence of such learning in schools at the coping and emerging stages. Table 2 provides an overview of the basic features of team learning across the four stages of development.

In Stage One, individuals do not formally work in groups or teams. When organizational members come together it is primarily as members of ad hoc committees that are established by the administration. In these schools administrators are not familiar with the use of teams or team learning processes, and teachers are often skeptical about working as a part of a group because they feel that these committees are primarily a means for them to provide input before administrators make the final decision. As one of the more experienced English teachers at Janjonner claimed:

> Well, with the former principal and the particular administrative group that was here, there were a lot of committees, and I would say that there were a lot of decisions that would be made, or recommendations that were made by a committee which then got nixed by the administration. I think a lot of people felt there was a lot of wasted time.... you know, you attend this meeting and everybody puts forth their ideas and you come to some consensus and then it goes to the front office and they say, no. Well, why bother?

At this stage, in an effort to improve teaching and services to students, groups may form along subject department lines. At Janjonner, all teachers claimed there were no formally organized teams but that they did get together as a department to analyze issues and to help solve problems (e.g., student performance). They also indicated that they were very busy and that there was no time to share with people outside their department. The senior science teachers said, "I've often felt we should talk about our work a little more but there really isn't a forum. Staff meetings are too busy and most people just want to get it over with anyway and our PD days are usually on more general topics." There was no evidence to suggest that groups operated as teams or that there was any team learning.

In schools that are in Stage Two, formal teams are virtually nonexistent, as well, many organizational members prefer to "go it alone" as opposed to working with others to accomplish a goal or solve a problem. The principal at CAL described this phenomenon as he expressed some of his frustration in trying to organize work-teams.

> I started a senior leadership team earlier this year and I cancelled it.... department heads weren't very strong here ... and to be quite honest with you, after the third meeting, I got tired of speaking, because they were used to being spoken to and not used to having a real role and they couldn't get over it. So I put it on the back burner until such a time I can get the staff more empowered.

In this stage administrators are beginning to see the benefits of organizing in teams but they still provide little in the way of support to help members function as a part of an effective team. Many teachers are still skeptical about participating in decision making activities. There is no evidence of any formal training in team learning skills and processes for either administrators or teachers, and there is no time provided for groups or teams to work collaboratively. For the most part, when people come together, the group comprises a committee with a low level of responsibility and little decision-making authority. These groups often do things routinely and do not question modes of operation (single loop learning).

In Developing Schools (stage 3), groups of people come together in a variety of forms (task forces, management teams, and curriculum teams) to analyze complex issues and tackle organizational problems. At Nicom, groups came together to develop new curriculum, experiment with and implement technology, and to work on improving school operations and sometimes groups formed automatically along departmental lines, usually for the purpose of improving departmental effectiveness while at the same time improving services to stakeholders. The principal of Nicom explained how teams formed in his school:

> Some of them form out of common interest and a lot of them out of common training like Nicom Growing Naturally, for example, a group of teaches with a common interest came together and look at what happened. It's the same for technology, a lot of people with an

interest in technology came together to form that team.... another group would be the Future Pathways group, they have a bit more expertise in curriculum development.

There is some evidence of new learning at the team level getting transferred throughout the organization, but it was a fairly slow process. The science department head, who was one of the leaders on the technology team described the process:

> As members of the technology group, we had experimented with web pages and saw the benefits of other teachers using them in their teaching. We started with a workshop that focused mainly on getting them [teachers] up and running.... we made sure there was a computer in the staffroom and the rest was done through osmosis. We learned from each other. The science department adopted a project for all science courses that was a web-page design. For some of the science teachers who would not have done this ordinarily it was a stretch, and some of them didn't go willingly but it caught on and other people picked up the idea. We were lucky in that we had a person in every department that was pretty keen and that person attempted to take somebody else with them. We had a follow-up workshop a couple of weeks ago and we concentrated on curricular uses and it was well received by everyone.

Leaders are supportive of teams at this stage, and are beginning to see the benefits of organizing into cross-functional work teams. But they have a limited knowledge of teams and how teams work. There is no formal teamwork, or team learning, training for teachers or administrators, and teachers are not provided quality time to work collaboratively. At this stage, team learning is valued but still poorly practiced.

At stage 4, teamwork is highly valued and effectively practiced. Teams are a part of normal operations and team learning occurs as a natural part of work. The guidance counselor at Floridav explained how the school growth team was functioning and learning as a group:

> The group has evolved and become more diverse ... as the staff has grown. This year there are probably more, not conflicts, but disagreements in terms of how to go about doing things and making decisions.... but essentially the issue gets talked through... and through discussion and consensus building we have been able to make good decisions.

Schools at this stage employ a wide variety of teams in order to explore complex issues, generate new knowledge, solve problems and take innovative action. Floridav, for example, used task forces, a leadership team, a management team, and curriculum teams.

Teachers at this stage are organized into cross-functional work units that are designed to help solve organization-wide and departmental problems, while at the same time working to continuously improve services to stakeholders. And, they are provided with quality time to work and explore collaboratively. These teams create opportunities for professional staff to learn from one another and to share new learning experiences with each other and the rest of the organization. The science teacher at Floridav, for example, explained how her team was helpful to her and her colleagues: "So, that's the time when we meet as a department, we meet as a subject area, we meet as colleagues with problems, we reflect. We build that time in. So we come in at 8:30 and the kids don't get here until 10:15."

One of the teachers on the school growth team described how a collaborative culture resulted in open and honest dialogue:

> There are 13 School Growth Team Members and each one facilitates a small liaison group and that's how we run our staff meetings. So every staff member is involved in a liaison group. The school plan was developed through these groups and it was really interesting to watch these groups work. The dialogue was intense and when people came to these meetings they had their homework done. It was really a synergistic process as teachers and administrators came together to arrive at a set of goals that were beneficial to the school.

Also at this most mature stage of team learning, administrators are supportive of teams and team learning processes, and they provide quality time for members to work and plan collaboratively. They encourage team members to arrive at decisions based on critical analysis and they respect the decisions of the teams, making themselves available for input and to provide information and advice when it is requested, without trying to lead the debate. Leaders in schools at this stage possess team building and teamwork skills, and they ensure that team members receive special training on how to function as a member of a team. The principal at Floridav explained her role in working with teams: "In terms of all of the things that happen, I am just a voice. On the committees and in the places where it's so important to have staff take ownership, be part of the decision, and make the decision, I'm just one of the people."

Questions for Diagnosing the Level of Team Learning in a School

Diagnosing the level of team learning in a school will require that questions be asked about the existence and structure of workgroups and teams. Questions are needed to solicit information on how team learning occurs, who participates on teams and why, as well as how, teachers are prepared to work as a part of a team, and the role that administrators play in team learning. Questions that help determine the stimulus for, as well as the outcomes of, team learning will also have to be posed.

Additional questions that will help diagnose the stage of team learning in a school include: What are the principles that govern team learning? How do team members transfer new learning to other members in the organization once they have acquired it? What are the sources of new knowledge for team learning? and How do team members document their learning so it is available to current and new organizational members?

Table 3. Stages of Growth in Whole School Learning Capacity

Factors	Stage 1: The Coping Stage	Stage 2: The Emerging Stage	Stage 3: The Developing Stage	Stage 4: The Learning Stage
Stimulus to Learning	Externally imposed demands	Change in leadership; externally imposed demands	Organizational survival; a response to changes in society	A response to changes in society
Knowledge Acquisition	Primarily through workshops and conferences	Primarily through workshops and conferences; scanning the environment	Through conferences in and out of province; bringing in external consultants; benchmarking and monitoring progress; partnering with external agencies; environmental scanning	Through conferences in and out of province; bringing in external consultants; benchmarking and monitoring progress; partnering with external agencies; environmental scanning
Knowledge Generation	No evidence of new knowledge generation	No evidence of new knowledge generation	Experimentation and risk-taking are promoted; teachers are encouraged to develop new curriculum; some evidence of action learning	Experimentation and risk-taking are promoted; teachers are encouraged to expand current curriculum and develop new curriculum; many action learning projects are ongoing; teacher mentorships

(continued)

Table 3.   (Continued)

Factors	Stage 1: The Coping Stage	Stage 2: The Emerging Stage	Stage 3: The Developing Stage	Stage 4: The Learning Stage
Knowledge Transfer	Information transfer through memos, reports, letters, bulletin boards, etc.; departmental meetings; informal networks	Information transfer through memos, reports, letters, bulletin boards, etc.; departmental meetings; informal networks	Knowledge and information transfer is planned; through distribution of memos, reports, letters, bulletin boards, etc.; departmental meetings; informal networks; face-to-face communications; electronic communications	Knowledge and information transfer is part of a sophisticated plan; through distribution of memos, reports, letters, bulletin boards, etc.; departmental meetings; informal networks; face-to-face communications; electronic communications
Collective Interpretation of Knowledge	Information and knowledge gets disseminated but not collectively utilized	Information and knowledge gets disseminated but not collectively utilized	Some knowledge moves beyond the team or the individual to become the collective property of all members	Knowledge moves beyond the team or the individual through a sophisticated process, to become the collective property of all
Knowledge Documentation and Storage	No formal plan but policy manuals exist; informal knowledge resides in organizational routines	No formal plan but there are promotional brochures; a webpage; minutes of meetings; informal knowledge resides in organizational routines; no plan for sharing	Formally in promotional brochures; a webpage; minutes of meetings; on video recordings; informal knowledge resides in organizational routines; teachers share across departments	There is a formal plan for document ation; a school succession plan is in place; there are policy manuals, teacher and school webpages; promotional brochures; videos; teacher journals; and organizational structures designed to facilitate storage and easy retrieval of knowledge

Stages of Growth in Whole School Learning Capacity

While individual, team, and whole organizational learning are interrelated, whole organization learning is more than the sum of individual and team learning. Notwithstanding that individuals and groups are the agents through which whole organizational learning must take place, the process of learning is influenced by a much broader set of social, political and structural variables. Whole organization learning involves accessing new knowledge, sharing this knowledge with organizational members and ensuring that the knowledge is stored and made easily accessible for organizational members.

Results of the data analysis indicated that whole school learning is unlikely to occur in a productive manner left entirely to chance. In schools where new knowledge is accessed and shared with organizational members, processes are in place to ensure that it happens. This is much more likely to occur in the later stages of growth in organizational learning than in the early stages. Table 3 outlines the stages of growth in whole school learning capacity based on interview evidence in the four schools.

In Stage One there are few organization-wide changes or innovations and no growth or improvement plans. There is no sign of a knowledge management plan and there is no evidence of new knowledge creation. Most organizational members don't pay much attention to what happens outside their school. Nor are there any internal efforts to be innovative. This type of school keeps up-to-date with societal trends by reacting when something major happens, or when they are forced to react by an external agency like the school board or the Ministry of Education.

When asked if there were any school-wide initiatives that the school was involved in, the English department head at Janjonner stated:

> I wouldn't say there is one ongoing project at this time. A few years ago when the Transitions Years [a government curriculum-related innovation] initiatives were coming in, there was a large number of staff who were involved in the planning and the implementation, and I would expect a similar sort of thing will take place once the Secondary Reform package [a new government innovation] comes out.

In schools at this stage, new knowledge is acquired through workshops and conferences, but any sharing of knowledge happens through formal memos, letters and bulletin boards, or by chance on an informal basis. This knowledge rarely receives widespread collective use. A Janjonner social studies teacher summed up how teachers kept up-to-date this way:

> It can be difficult, because it's such a large school physically as well as in the number of students, I think we tend to become departmentalized and so we operate mostly within our own departments. There's an opportunity to share within the department but on a school wide basis, besides the staff meeting, it really doesn't happen.

There is no formal plan, at this stage, to document knowledge. And the tacit knowledge that develops resides in organizational routines and with individual department members; it is available to others only if they know where to look, who to ask, and what the right questions are. The science teacher at Janjonner described what happens when new teachers come to her department: "they're always working with someone on a course…. So, we don't have a formal buddy system sort of thing, it's more the people that you would be teaching particular courses with who would be the ones to learn the ropes from."

In Stage Two schools, plans for organization-wide growth and improvement are still in the formative stages. There is little evidence of new knowledge generation, but new knowledge does enter the school as school administrators and other key individuals try to keep in touch with what is happening in the outside environment. At CAL, a school that was largely content with the status quo, the new principal was trying to address the problem:

> I try to get out as much as possible, I'm on a number of committees and I've urged every single teacher on this staff that if they want to do anything professional this summer … I would pay the full tuition for them, no questions asked. I've passed on information … and made funds available. So, I'm encouraging all of my people to get away. And that will happen over the next year.

There is little evidence at this stage of cross-functional sharing as administrators assume responsibility for transferring most knowledge throughout the organization. Information and knowledge does get disseminated but it is not collectively utilized. The principal of CAL raises this matter as follows:

> Well, this year it's been very, not an excellent system I suppose … like something comes from the board office, it comes through the office obviously and I make sure it gets to the right department. And we hope the department gets it to the teachers. That's the established pattern. I suspect it's not working as well as it should. If something's important and I want all teachers to see, I make sure it gets posted on the bulletin board. It's very much general office oriented.

There is no formal plan to document knowledge in schools at this stage, but tacit knowledge is stored and made available to teachers on a need to know basis. It also can be accessible to others if they know where to look, who to ask, and what the right questions are. While knowledge management skills are poorly developed at this stage, these schools have documented prior learning in the form of minutes, brochures, and a school web page. But much of the documentation is in the form of retained past learning experiences that are imprinted on organizational actions. One of the teachers indicated that he relies on other, more experienced, teachers to keep him informed on school policy: "I generally go to my department head if I need to know something. If he doesn't know the answer then it probably isn't a critical issue." The science department head at CAL explained how he was responsible for researching prior knowledge about the school improvement process:

> My task at the time was to go through the six or seven years of our school improvement process and compile the agendas from all the meetings and as many notes as possible from those meetings and to put it together in a folder in such a way that an external evaluation team would be able to see almost step-by-step what our school improvement has been to this point.

At Stage Three, major organizational changes and innovations are part of a formal plan that is developed by administrators and department heads, then communicated to other stakeholders. Long term growth and improvement plans focus on the school and its perceived future needs. At Nicom, the family studies teacher, who was new to the staff, explained her interpretation of how the school vision was crafted:

> I think the driving force is the administration. There is an administrative council where I believe a lot of these innovative ideas get hashed out. I haven't been part of it so I don't know exactly what happens.... I only know there is a group of people who review whatever initiative or new thing that comes along—I think it goes through that group first before it comes to the rest of us for our approval. I sense that a lot of these initiatives are coming from the principal.

Schools at this stage are skilled in both knowledge acquisition and generation. They develop their own knowledge internally, and constantly scan the environment for new ideas from other organizations. When asked how he and his staff kept up-to-date on things that were happening in the community, the principal of Nicom replied: "Through conferences!... it's really where a lot of the action is these days. If you're not getting out there and you're not listening and being attentive to what's going on, then you're slipping behind." The family studies teacher, who was also working on developing the Future Pathways program, credited the principal with coming up with the idea, citing his vision as the driving force behind that and other new initiatives.

> We have a lot of people who can do administrative work but unless you have someone out in front who sends the right instructions to the right people and holds the vision together you will fail because then everybody starts to work independently and nothing unites. And that applies to the Future pathways, the technology and all of the other initiatives—if he supports us in our work we can make things happen.

Some of these ideas do move beyond the individual and the team level to be collectively interpreted at the organizational level. For example, at the beginning of the school year most staff members were not technology users but toward the end of the year almost all were using technology, in some way, in their teaching. However, these schools are still not skilled at knowledge transfer, collective integration, utilization and documentation, as new knowledge tends to move slowly. All of the teachers at Nicom and CAL claimed a lack of time for reflection and new learning as a barrier to knowledge movement. At Nicom, old knowledge is documented in the form of videos, brochures, handbooks, web pages, and organizational routines. But there is no formal documentation process to ensure that new knowledge is retained.

In schools at Stage 3, experimentation and risk-taking are encouraged as teachers combine their talents to develop new curriculum and create new learning opportunities for students. For example, the family studies teacher working on the Future Pathways project at Nicom claimed that the administration were very supportive and encouraged the project team to be creative when designing the new curriculum. "They are pretty good, they told us to be creative, to create something other schools would envy, and they gave us the freedom to make most of the decisions—we still report back to them but it feels like it's our decision." The learning resources teacher said, "I've become more relaxed with the aspect of taking a risk ... and I think that's good, that's healthy."

In the fourth stage of developing whole school learning capacity major organizational changes and innovations are part of a formal plan that is developed by administrators and department heads in consultation with the other stakeholders. Long term growth and improvement plans recognize that the future cannot be predicted and that schools must prepare students for an uncertain future. Once the growth or improvement plans have been developed they are reviewed frequently and modified as needed. In this type of school, knowledge is often generated internally at the grass roots level; in fact, administrators encourage innovation and facilitate the movement of successful innovations throughout the school. The guidance counselor at Floridav, for example, described how an innovative idea that originated with student assistants got utilized by all staff members:

> So, this is an idea that started with the student assistants, was shared with the classroom teachers, got brought to the school growth team and then passed on to staff. And, as I said the staff were involved in developing the school plan ... so they bought into that as a goal, as ensuring student success was one of the goals identified in the school plan. As a result of that we had professional development sessions and more are planned.

At this stage there is also a high level of awareness of external trends and forces and how they might impact the organization. Teachers are quick to identify and adopt the "best practices" of other schools. For example, the principal of Floridav explained how she had visited a school in Calgary that offered what she felt was a very innovative educational program. She went on to say that she had been successful in getting her school board to agree to incorporate portions of that model for the plan they were developing for Floridav.

At this stage, sharing among staff is quite common and staff members have established a collaborative culture in which learning evolves through both formal and informal means. It can happen formally as a result of carefully planned events and processes (e.g., memos, reports letters, bulletin boards, staff meetings, briefings, cross-functional work teams, and electronic communication networks). This sharing and transfer of knowledge also happens informally as a result of networks that develop within and between departments and through peer-to-peer communication. As is illustrated in the case of Floridav High, schools at this stage use cross-functional teams, weekly planning meetings, a flattened organizational structure, and egalitarian principles to facilitate the transfer and collective integration of knowledge beyond the individual and team level to that of the entire organization.

At this stage, knowledge is actively managed and there is a formal plan for documenting knowledge and ensuring that knowledge from prior learning experiences is stored and easily accessible for organizational members to utilize when needed. Floridav provides a good example of how knowledge documentation is viewed from both an individual personal perspective (through the use of journals, and homepages on the web) and as a publicly documented body of knowledge (through policy manuals, promotional brochures, videos, and a homepage on the web). Teachers and administrators are aware of the need to retain important knowledge and to share this knowledge with others in the school and the school system. For example, the Floridav principal mentioned the need for a succession plan to ensure that knowledge was retained at the school level:

> With this being a new and innovative school I am sure we will have a high turnover rate, in the coming years; as teachers get experience I suspect they will want to move into leadership positions in other schools. It is important that when this happens we do not experience learning gaps.

Questions for Diagnosing Stages of Whole School Learning Capacity

For purposes of diagnosing a school's stage of whole school learning capacity, questions are needed to determine: the stimulus for whole organization learning; the sources of new knowledge (e.g., is new knowledge acquired from outside, generated internally or a little of both?); and how that knowledge is shared and transferred around the organization (through formal or informal plans and networks). Questions also need to be asked about: how individuals and groups interpret new knowledge once it is transferred; how that new knowledge is used; how new knowledge is stored for future use; and how it is made accessible to other and new organizational members.

CONCLUSION

As the larger text in which this chapter is located argues, the intellectual or organizational learning capacity of schools increasingly is being viewed as a major source of variation in the productivity of schools' responses to change. If this is the case, an important practical task for school leaders and others managing change is to diagnose the extent of that capacity, locate areas of strength and weakness in capacity, and take steps to further develop it. The main purpose of this chapter was to begin to codify, synthesize, and extend knowledge useful for carrying out this practical task.

This purpose was accomplished using a two-phased research design. The first phase identified, from an extensive review of literature, the main dimensions along which the development of organizational learning capacity could be described. These were dimensions of individual professional learning in a school context, as well as dimensions of team, and whole school, learning. The second phase, informed by such dimensions, collected data in four secondary schools which varied substantially in their organizational learning capacity. Informed by the literature review in the first phase of the research, these data were used to create a four-staged profile of growth in individual, team, and whole school learning capacity, and to develop questions useful in locating a school within one or more of these stages.

Stage theories are always controversial, provoking questions about validity which take a variety of forms. For example, stage theories raise the ire of those who are offended by "reductionism," the inevitable simplification of the phenonmena which stage theories atttempt to describe. And then there is the popular post-modern view that just the concept of stages implies the basically wrong-headed notion of orderly progression and the possibility of managing that progression when the "truth" of the matter is that most social phenomena are almost entirely iterative and inherently unmanageable.

But these and other objections to stage theories are typically invoked by theorists, at the same time as those who must act in worlds of practice embrace the leverage that stage theories provide for making their jobs a bit easier and quite a lot more effective. It would be surprising if theorists and practitioners reacted differently to the stages of growth in organizational learning capacity outlined in this chapter.

This is not to say, however, that no more work is needed. Far from it. This description needs to be tested with larger samples of secondary schools; it needs to be tested against data from elementary schools as well.

Much more work is needed to assess the reliability and validity of the diagnostic questions, especially in survey form. And carefully documented efforts to use these diagnostic tools in the context of significant school improvement initiatives will be helpful in learning how best to implement these tools. Should educational practitioners wait until this work is completed before using the results of this chapter? Hardly. Practice can never be based on perfect knowledge, only the best knowledge available at the time.

REFERENCES

Argyris, C. (1976). Single-loop and double-loop models in research on decision making. *Administrative Science Quarterly, 21*(3), 363-375.

Argyris, C. (1990). Inappropriate defenses against the monitoring of organization development practice. *Journal of Applied Behavioral Science, 26*(3), 299-312.

Brown, J.S., & Duguid, P. (1996). Organizational learning and communities of practice: Toward a unified view of working, learning, and innovation. In M.D. Cohen & L.S. Sproull (Eds.), *Organizational learning* (pp. 58-82). Thousand Oaks, CA: Sage Publications.

Cole, M., & Engestrom, Y. (1993). A cultural-theoretical approach to distributed cognition. In G. Salomon (Ed.), *Distributed cognitions: Psychological and educational considerations*. Cambridge, UK: Cambridge University Press.

Dibbon, D. (1999). *Assessing the organizational learning capacity of schools*. Unpublished doctoral dissertation, OISE/University of Toronto.

DiBella, A., Nevis, E., & Gould, J. (1996). Understanding organizational learning capacity. *Journal of Management Studies, May*, 361-379.

Dixon, N. (1994). *The organizational learning cycle*. New York: McGraw-Hill.

Fuller, F. (1969). Concerns of teachers: A developmental conceptualization. *American Educational Research Journal, 6*(2), 207-226.

Hall, G., Wallace, R., & Dossett, W.F. (1973). *A developmental conceptualization of the adoption process within educational institutions*. Austin, TX: University of Texas at Austin.

Huber, G.P. (1991). Organizational learning, the contributing processes and the literatures. *Organization Science, 2*(1), 88-115.

Inkpen, C., & Crossan, M. (1995). Believing is seeing: Joint ventures and organizational learning. *Journal of Management Studies, 32*(5), 595-618.

Janis, I. (1982). *Groupthink* (2nd ed.). Boston, MA: Houghton Mifflin.

Kohlberg, L. (1970). *Moral development*. New York: Holt, Rinehart and Winston.

Leithwood, K., Jantzi, D., & Steinbach, R. (1999). *Changing leadership for changing times*. Buckingham, UK: Open University Press.

Leithwood, K., Steinbach, R., & Ryan, S. (1997). Leadership and team learning in secondary schools. *School Leadership and Management, 17*(3), 303-325.

Levitt, B., & March, J. (1988). Organizational learning. *Annual Review of Sociology, 14*, 319-340.

Loevinger, J. (1966). The meaning and measurement of ego development. *American Psychologist, 21*, 195-206.

March, J. (1991). Exploration and exploitation in organizational learning. *Organization Science, 2*(1), 71-87.

Neck, C.P., & Manz, C.C. (1994). From groupthink to teamthink: Toward the creation of constructive thought patterns in self-managing work teams. *Human Relations, 47*(8), 929-952.

Salomon, G. (1993). No distribution without individual's cognition: A dynamic interactional view. In
    G. Salomon (Ed.), *Distributed cognitions: Psychological and educational considerations.*
    Cambridge, UK: Cambridge University Press.
Senge, P. (1991). The learning organization made plain. *Training and Development, 45*(10), 37-44.
Strauss, A., & Corbin, J. (1990). *Basics of qualitative research: Grounded theory, procedures and
    techniques.* Newbury Park, CA: Sage Publications.
Stringfield, S. (1995). Attempting to enhance students' learning through innovative programs: The
    case for schools evolving into high reliability organizations. *School Effectiveness and School
    Improvement, 6*(1), 67-96.

PART III

ORGANIZATIONAL LEARNING EFFECTS

CHAPTER 11

THE CAPACITY FOR ORGANIZATIONAL LEARNING
IMPLICATIONS FOR PEDAGOGICAL QUALITY AND STUDENT ACHIEVEMENT

Helen M. Marks, Karen Seashore Louis, and Susan M. Printy

Does the capacity for organizational learning increase the ability of schools to deliver high quality instruction and strong student performance? Although empirical evidence addressing the question is limited, the link is logical. Improved academic achievement, according to researchers who synthesized the literature on the organization of effective secondary schools, depends on schools' reforming the technical core of instruction (Lee, Bryk & Smith, 1993). If reform of the technical core—the means of producing student achievement—results from the purposeful

Advances in Research and Theories of School
Management and Educational Policy, Volume 4, pages 239-265.
Copyright © 2000 by JAI Press Inc.
All rights of reproduction in any form reserved.
ISBN: 0-7623-0024-8

and collaborative efforts of the school community, the school has probably engaged in organizational learning (Rait, 1995).

Our own research leads us to agree. Where strong school performance distinguishes schools, we have found teachers involved in mid-level decisions that affect the technical core of teaching and learning (Marks & Louis, 1999). Teachers take collective responsibility for making the school a good work environment for both themselves and their students. Site-based management permits shared decision making, and teachers step beyond their roles in classrooms to design work settings on the school level. These schools demonstrate common organizational properties—participative decision making, professional community, and collective responsibility for student learning.[1] Ongoing inquiry into the quality and effectiveness of teaching and learning unifies their organizational cultures. Taken together, these elements suggest that the high performing schools engage in organizational learning.

Twenty-five years ago organizational learning was a novel idea; today, organizations of all types are under a learning imperative. Organizations succeed if they learn to see things in new ways, gain fresh understandings, and innovate throughout on a continuing basis (Argyris & Schön, 1996). As critics question the effectiveness of public education, support for organizational learning in schools has emerged as a strategy to meet challenging and ever-changing environments. Flatter organizational designs facilitate innovation and high performance; local school professionals, rather than outside consultants or change models, develop ideas and weave together the action and reflection instrumental to school improvement.[2] Organizational learning enhances the school's ability for self-organization, enabling organization members to work together "to restructure, reculture, and otherwise reorient themselves to new challenges" (Leithwood, Leonard, & Sharratt, 1998, p. 271).

Recent empirical studies have identified characteristics of healthy schools that position them to engage in the continuous and often arduous self-inquiry which organizational learning demands (Louis & Kruse, 1995; Leithwood, Leonard, & Sharratt, 1998; Marks & Louis, 1999). If building the capacity for organizational learning is to become a valid strategy for school improvement, teachers and administrators must be able to assess the strength of their schools on these characteristics and determine whether they are tied to improving school performance. To help inform those efforts, we develop a conception of the capacity for organizational learning and examine its relationship to pedagogical quality and student achievement on both authentic and standardized measures.

RESEARCH FRAMEWORK

The literature on organizational learning has accumulated over the last 30 years in a more or less unbounded way resulting in lack of consistency among authors, but allowing the field to expand in vitality and innovation.[3] Its central concepts include (1) identifying and correcting problems, (2) learning from past experience, (3) acquiring new knowledge, (4) processing issues on an organizational level, and (5) changing the organization. An organization that learns, works efficiently, readily adapts to change, detects and corrects errors, and continually improves (Argyris & Schön, 1974).

Emphasizing its sociocultural aspects, we view organizational learning as transcending the aggregated learning of individual members. Individuals engaged in a common activity in a way that is uniquely theirs process knowledge as members of a collective possessing a distinctive culture. The social processing of knowledge, or the sharing of individually held information in ways that construct a clear, commonly held set of ideas, constitutes organizational learning. Learning takes place within collaborative groups as the members mutually confront problems and develop solutions. Basic assumptions acquired through solving problems of adaptation and integration become the cultural values, beliefs, and norms that the group passes on to new members.[4]

Organizational learning seeks to improve competitiveness, productivity, and the ability to innovate in uncertain circumstances. At their most effective, organizational learning strategies are used discriminantly and intentionally, as means to improve performance and increase expertise—not as ends in themselves.[5] Organizational learning emerges from the efforts of the organization and depends on at least three favorable conditions (Probst and Büchel, 1997). Knowledge, the first of these conditions, is supported by a number of learning instruments, such as a vision statement and means to stimulate discussion and self-analysis. Ability, the second condition, includes structures and processes to facilitate the sharing of information. Intention, the third, is the willingness on the part of organization members to learn collectively as measured by their shared ethical and professional values.

Teachers, as the primary service providers in schools, play a key role in establishing organizational learning as a normal, but essential, orientation. Teacher development directed at organizational learning demands a professional rather than bureaucratic definition of teachers' work. When professional inquiry is an integral element of teachers' practice, organizational learning will be systematically reinforced.[6]

Organizational Learning and School Reform

Superficial change, fads, and hodge-podge innovations are inadequate to improve schools. Unlike these mistaken and shallow approaches to school reform, organizational learning sets in motion a process of deep and ongoing change that involves the staff in continually monitoring, evaluating, and modifying innovation through organizational inquiry, offering the promise of ongoing school improvement.

Prescriptive reforms (for example, Total Quality Management or TQM) are inadequate approaches to school improvement. Such reforms follow a predictable life cycle (Argyris & Schön, 1996). When first proposed, a prescription for organizational reform is accompanied by "plausible-sounding theory" and stories of successful practice.

> Often at the core of the reform there lies a significant insight, for example, managers *should* be freed up to take on greater responsibility and make greater use of local knowledge, or organizational processes *should* be rethought in the light of the possibilities opened up by advanced information technology. Usually, however, the prescription is converted by its advocates and the consultants who undertake its dissemination into a readily understandable package of procedures (p. 249).

Wanting quick solutions to their own complex predicaments, organization managers adopt the convenient package and then pass the idea onto other managers, who also adopt the package so as not to miss out. Over time, the good intentions of the reform are subverted by organizational defensive routines, and soon, a "literature of disillusionment" begins to appear.[7] As a result of normal cynicism, managers at all levels point at others and blame them for the failure of the reform initiative. But before long, the "readiness for the next reform package begins to take shape" (Argyris & Schön, 1996, p. 250). This life-cycle of reform is familiar to most educators. Time after time, schools refuse to learn from their experience, and they fail to tap their internal resources in seeking solutions for their difficulties. The short-lived success of packaged reform explains the call for organizational learning as a needed approach to continuous school improvement.

Dimensions of School Capacity for Organizational Learning

High-performing schools, where both teachers and students are involved in work of intellectual quality, have integrated their reform efforts into a coherent and effective program that we believe reflects the capacity for organizational learning. Based on our study of these high-performing schools, we have identified six dimensions of this capacity—school structure, participative decision making grounded in teacher empowerment, shared commitment and collaborative activity, knowledge and skills, leadership, and feedback and accountability. The following sections contain brief descriptions of each dimension.

Structure

Building the capacity for organizational learning requires altering traditional structural arrangements in schools. Removing structural impediments may be more critical to the success of programs to improve performance than adding new resources (Sarason, 1996). School features inherent to the work of teachers present obstacles to organizational learning and compound the challenge of the social processing of information. Isolation from colleagues, time constraints, and expanding societal expectations are difficulties exacerbated by shrinking resources. Limited and fragmented structures to coordinate activities within the school and between school and community, low interdependence in teaching roles, and formal decision-making processes that are viewed as unfair or arbitrary by many participants impede healthy exchange.

Hierarchical controls may also present hindrances, in that organizational learning requires boundary spanning activities and coordination through social norms rather than a chain of command. The size and complex organization of schools that enroll large numbers of students are also obstacles to the capacity for organizational learning, since such environments restrict the development of professional community. Learning takes place as staffs decide school matters through consensus, something easier to do in smaller schools.[8]

Teacher Empowerment

Teacher empowerment generally refers to policies intended to guarantee teachers a voice in school operations through shared decision making. The exercise of empowerment may vary, ranging from representation on school-based governance councils to increased professional autonomy in the choice of curriculum and instructional practices. As a separate strategy for enhancing instructional practice and student outcomes, empowerment has shown uneven results.[9] Empowerment works to the academic advantage of students, according to our research, when it supports teachers' collective efforts to improve the quality of their instruction and assessments and aims at involving and challenging students intellectually (Marks & Louis, 1997). Student achievement is enhanced when teachers help to set mid-level school policies related to the improvement of teaching and learning—policies with a range broader than a single classroom yet narrower than the management of school operations.

A recent study identifying school conditions that foster organizational learning highlighted the opportunity for school-based staff to participate in shaping both district and school-level decisions (Leithwood, Leonard, & Sharratt, 1998; this volume, chapter 5). Though this study did not examine the effects of empowerment on student achievement, the findings indicate that participation in district decisions enhanced opportunities for improving the collective problem-solving capacities of the staff, and permitted staff to create solutions that were sensitive to the particular needs of the school. School professionals who engage in processes of reflection and exploration to examine practice on the schoolwide level may find such inquiry legitimate, applying the same process of inquiry at the classroom level to examine and improve teaching and learning (Rait, 1995).

Shared Commitment and Collaborative Activity

Organizations that learn recognize the value of individuals and the contributions each member can make to the group's collective knowledge. The goal of "social processing" or team learning leads members to forge consensus about what counts for quality in organizational performance and how they might achieve it. Social processing in schools, if it occurs at all, tends to happen within small, fragmented groups, grade levels, or departments. By contrast, schoolwide social processing is critical to the capacity for organizational learning, since learning by a social system extends beyond the sum of the learning experienced by individuals.[10]

Learning in the workplace is best understood in terms of community. In community personal identities are changed, employees become practitioners, and innovation occurs (Brown & Duguid, 1996). Because strong professional community is a vehicle for schoolwide knowledge processing, creating professional community enhances the capacity for organizational learning. Teachers no longer work in isolation but collaborate within a professional culture. Reflective dialogue, open sharing of classroom practices, developing a common knowledge base for improvement, collaborating on the design of new materials and curricula, and establishing norms for pedagogical practice and student performance are hallmarks of a professional culture and demonstrably related to student achievement.[11]

Knowledge and Skills

Learning depends upon an existing knowledge base and openness to new ideas—conditions that may come from three sources: (1) individual knowledge that is "inherent," that is, already held by professionals, parents, students, and community members; (2) knowledge that is "imported" from experts and the experiences of other schools; and (3) knowledge that is created by members of the school community to address specific questions or problems (Kruse, 1995; Huber, 1996).

Organizational learning requires permeable boundaries—internally, to allow the flow of information to reach all areas of the organization and, externally, to connect community-based knowledge resources in multiple ways with personnel in schools. Many high schools, like universities, are discipline based. While disciplines facilitate knowledge transmission and the creation of supportive networks, they may also result in balkanization within the school and fragmented communication with constituencies outside the school. Organizational learning is dependent on active inquiry that promotes the acquisition of needed information. When they function most effectively, "knowledge intensive firms" also organize themselves to promote sharing of expertise and to spark entrepreneurship and open discussion among decentralized groups throughout the organization.[12]

Leadership

Building the capacity for organizational learning demands forms of leadership differing from conventional models.[13] Effective school leaders not only manage the organization, they also stimulate serious intellectual interaction around issues of school reform. In an organization that learns, the leader extends across boundaries the lessons learned from experience and experiments. A learning leader assesses the adequacy of the organization's culture, detects its dysfunctionality, and promotes its transformation (Schein, 1992). Such a leader fosters learning assumptions in the culture of the organization. Among the most important of these assumptions are the beliefs that people want to contribute and can be trusted to do so; that the role of the leader is to model a process of learning; and that the process of learning is a central part of the culture.

Paradoxically, effective organizational leadership must sometimes be directive in order to promote such transformations. Both supportive and authoritative methods, used alternately or at times together, determine effective organizational leadership in developing professional community.[14] Similarly, the cycle of "pressure and support" from the district office is often critical to maintaining implementation of programs over time (Miles & Huberman, 1984).

Feedback and Accountability

Organizational learning requires continual development of new understandings, models, and practices. This process of active inquiry is dependent on valid and regular feedback, from agents both inside and outside the organization (Senge, 1990) and may result either in single-loop or double-loop learning. Single loop learning results in changes in strategies and assumptions while leaving the core values of the organization unchanged, while double-loop learning changes core values in addition to altering strategies and assumptions (Argyris & Schön, 1996).

Increasing organizational learning requires that schools be made more autonomous—and more accountable—for their work.[15] Performance standards and incentives for learning that result from collective decision making enhance the capacity for organizational learning. Colleagues examining the relationship of accountability to organizational capacity have used a capacity index tapping teachers' participation in school decision making, knowledge and skills, shared commitment, and collaborative activity (Newmann, King, & Rigdon, 1997). These researchers documented a positive relationship between internal accountability (to peers and others in the school) and organizational capacity, but they found a negative relationship for external accountability (to the public) and organizational capacity.

Research Objective

The point of this study is to investigate the relationship of the capacity for organizational learning to the central intellectual activities of schools—teaching and learning. We expect that schools where the capacity for organizational learning is strong will be high-performing in these core endeavors. To show how the capacity for organizational learning supports high performance, we will then compare two schools that differ on this characteristic and illustrate how and why the capacity for organizational learning affected the quality of teaching and learning.

METHOD

Sample and Data

To study the effectiveness of school restructuring, the Center on Organization and Restructuring of Schools searched nationally for public schools that had made extensive change in their practice in the areas of students' experiences, teachers' worklives, school governance, and the coordination of school and community resources.[16] The search identified more than 300 such schools. From this pool, the center selected a sample of 24 elementary, middle, and high schools where restructuring had been most thorough (see Berends and King, 1994; Newmann and Associates, 1996, for a discussion of sample selection procedures). Most of the schools are urban and enroll substantial proportions of economically disadvantaged and minority students.[17] Data for the study were collected using a battery of quantitative and qualitative instruments.

Teachers responded to a *survey* querying them about their instructional practices and professional activities, the school culture, and their personal and professional backgrounds. Response rates were high: 910 teachers, more than 82 percent of the teachers in the sampled schools, turned in surveys, completing 95 percent of the items. Teams of three researchers spent two weeks at each school during the fall and spring of its study year. During their site visits, the researchers interviewed 25-30 staff members, most of them twice. They collected data on teachers' instructional practice and worklife, the nature of social and professional interaction, issues related to governance and decision making, and involvement in the school's reform efforts. The researchers questioned school and district administrators about the relationship between the broader organizational objectives and the realities of change at the school site. Researchers also *observed the governance and professional meetings* that occurred during the site visits, and they collected and analyzed written *documentation* pertaining to the school's restructuring efforts.

The instruction and assessment practices of 144 core-class teachers (three mathematics and three social studies teachers from each school) received extensive scrutiny. Center researchers, trained to evaluate instruction according to standards of intellectual quality, rated the instruction in each core class at least four times. Half the classes were observed by two researchers, whose inter-rater reliability was .78. All 144 teachers were asked to provide two written assessment tasks that they assigned students in the fall and the spring and that were typical of how they assessed learning. Subject matter specialists from the center staff in collaboration with teacher practitioners were trained to rate the tasks on standards of intellectual quality. A two-person team scored the tasks independently. If they did not agree on their ratings, they discussed their differences and arrived at a mutually agreeable consensus score.

The teachers also provided the center with the work students submitted in response to the assessment tasks. Applying standards for authentic achievement, trained researchers and practitioners rated over 5,000 pieces of student work. More than one-third of these papers received evaluations by two raters. The inter-rater reliabilties were .77 for social studies, .70 for mathematics. (For more information about the instruments and procedures for observing teachers, collecting and rating assessment tasks and student work, see Newmann, Secada, & Wehlage (1995), Newmann, Marks, & Gamoran (1996), and Newmann & Associates (1996).

Each research team prepared a case study portraying the school the team visited. The teams produced 24 *case studies*, about 150 single-spaced pages in length and following an identical topic outline. The cases summarized and synthesized the interview, observation, and documentation data. Other center staff members reviewed and critiqued the drafts of the case studies. In response to this rigorous peer review, each team revised the initial draft. Using a preset list of categories developed by the full team of researchers, two members of each team independently *coded the respective case study* If they disagreed on a coding, they discussed the matter until they arrived at a consensus.

Measures

Authentic Academic Achievement

The authentic achievement measure sums student scores in mathematics and social studies on three standards for performance—analysis, disciplinary concepts, and elaborated written communication.[18] *Analysis* refers to students' ability to demonstrate and explain their thinking by such means as organizing, synthesizing, interpreting, hypothesizing, evaluating. *Disciplinary concepts* refers to students' demonstrating understanding and ability to work with and manipulate the ideas, concepts, and theories of the discipline. *Elaborated written communication* refers to work which is clear, coherent, well-articulated, and richly argued.

NAEP Achievement

At the beginning of the study year, all students in the target (i.e., observed classes) were asked to complete a test of basic knowledge and skills in mathematics and reading/writing. Students in mathematics classes were given a test appropriate to their grade level constructed from selected items in the National Assessment of Educational Progress (NAEP) mathematics test. Students in the social studies classes were given a test made up of selected items from the NAEP reading tests and a test of writing scored by the center staff using NAEP criteria.

Authentic Pedagogy

Authentic pedagogy is a composite measure combining teachers' scores on observed classroom instruction and assessment tasks. The standards applied to classroom instruction are four—higher order thinking, substantive conversation, depth of knowledge, and connections to the world beyond the classroom.[19] *Higher order thinking* involves students in manipulating information and ideas, rather than merely reproducing them. *Substantive conversation* entails sustained interchanges among students and teacher and/or among students themselves in ways that build improved understanding of concepts and ideas. *Deep knowledge* calls for students to focus on ideas or concepts central to the discipline with sufficient thoroughness to produce an understanding of complex relationships. *Connections to the world beyond the classroom* represents the linkage between knowledge and students' own lives or public issues.

Assessment tasks comprised seven standards—organization of information, consideration of alternatives, disciplinary content, disciplinary process, elaborated written communication, problem connected to the real world, and an audience beyond school. *Organization of information* asks students to organize, synthesize, interpret, explain, or evaluate complex information. *Consideration of alternatives* asks students to consider alternative solutions, strategies, perspectives, or points of view. *Disciplinary content* asks students to show an understanding of disciplinary ideas, theories, or perspectives. *Disciplinary process* asks students to use the methodological approach of the discipline. *Elaborated written communication* asks students to express their understanding, explanations, or conclusions through extended writing. *Problem connected to the real world* asks students to address an issue, problem, or concept external to the school. *Audience beyond the school* asks students to communicate with an audience beyond their teacher and class or schoolmates.

The Capacity for Organizational Learning

The major independent variable, an index of the capacity for organizational learning, taps the six constituent dimensions discussed above—school structural conditions, teacher empowerment, shared commitment and collaborative activity, knowledge and skills, supportive leadership, and feedback and accountability.

(1) *School structure* includes three components constructed, respectively, from school profile, coding, and teacher survey data: (a) school size (reversed); (b) extent of decentralized governance; and (c) the amount of time teachers spend meeting with colleagues.

(2) *Teacher empowerment* combines two constructs. The first, an empowerment index developed from survey reports, sums measures of teacher influence in four domains: teachers influence over school policy, their work lives, their classrooms, and aspects of their students' school experience.

The second construct, taken from the coding data, is a scale measuring teachers' actual influence over curriculum, instruction, student assessment, discretionary budget, and staff development.

(3) *Shared commitment and collaborative activity*, constructed from teacher survey and coding data, represents the extent to which a common direction of effort unites the faculty. Its five components include: (a) an index of professional community constructed from teachers' self reports; (b) a composite score on professional community from the coding data; (c) a measure of goal consensus from the teachers' survey data; (d) responsibility for student learning from the teachers' survey data; and (e) the extent to which the staff is regarded as competent to analyze problems and to solve them.

(4) The index of *knowledge and skills* comprises three measures: (a) an index of school-oriented staff development taken from the coding; (b) a construct from teachers' survey data tapping the openness of the school and its staff to innovation; and (c) pedagogical content knowledge and ongoing opportunities for curricular and instructional improvement.

(5) The *leadership* construct is broad-based, comprising cognitive, affective, and behavioral elements. Its three components derive from survey and coding data: (a) intellectual leadership taps the extent to which new information reaches the school from either outside sources—for example, a structural arrangement with a college or university, or the significant input of a district office or external professional network—or internal sources, for example, significant input from the principal, another administrator, a teacher or a group of teachers; (b) supportive leadership reflects how much the principal or administrator supports and encourages teachers, welcomes their ideas, and has positively influenced restructuring; and (c) facilitative leadership measures an administrative style enabling shared power relations among faculty and administration.

(6) The *feedback and accountability* construct includes (a) information on performance provided to groups outside the school; (b) rewards or reprimands from

constituent groups based on students' performance; (c) the influence of students' parents on school restructuring; and (d) the extent to which teachers feel respected by stakeholders both internal and external to the school.

Control Variables

To take into account background characteristics of students that prior research has shown to be associated with achievement, we incorporate several control variables: gender; race; ethnicity; and socioeconomic status, a composite measure of parents education and household possessions. To control for ability, we use the student's self-reported GPA.[20]

Analytic Approach

Because schools and the students they enroll can vary considerably, we compare the variables we have described across grade levels to identify any significant differences in the elementary, middle, and high schools.[21] To evaluate the relationship of the capacity for organizational learning to pedagogical quality and student achievement, we use a multilevel analytic technique appropriate for analyses of nested data, such as teachers or students nested within schools.[22] After estimating the amount of variation in pedagogical quality and student achievement present among the 24 restructuring schools in the sample, we examine how much of that variation can be explained by the capacity for organizational learning. For the pedagogical quality analysis, we take into account classroom compositional features that could influence pedagogy, incorporating statistical adjustments for the proportion of students who are female, African-American, Hispanic, the average socioeconomic status of the students, and the students' NAEP achievement. Similarly, in the student achievement analyses, we adjust for female gender, race, ethnicity, the student's socioeconomic status, and ability (measured by GPA).

RESULTS

Observed Differences According to Grade Level

Because the measures of the teaching and learning outcomes were standardized for the analysis, means are expressed as standard deviation units (Table 1). Accordingly, grade level differences can be interpreted in standard deviation metric. Although the means for pedagogical quality vary by grade level, the differences are not statistically significant. Students differ by grade level on the achievement measures. Middle school students average the highest score on authentic achievement, but the grade level differences are not significant. Elementary school students

Table 1. Observed Differences on Major Variables by School Grade Level

	Elementary	Middle	High
Teaching and Learning Outcomes			
Pedagogical Quality[a]	.31	−.07	−.24
Authentic Achievement[a]	−.40	.45	−.05
NAEP Achievement[a]	.68*	.01	−.69
Organizational Learning			
Capacity for Organizational Learning Index	.60*	.04	−.64*
Student Background			
%Female	50.6	52.3	51.7
%African American	14.9	10.1	31.7***
%Hispanic	36.8***	11.8	15.7
Socioeconomic Status[a]	−.01	.16***	−.15
Grade Point Average[a]	.12	.16***	−.31

Notes: [a]Standardized variable, M=0; SD=1.
*P ≤ .05; ***P ≤ .001

score highest on NAEP achievement—.68 SD above the mean, with high school students scoring more than 1.3 SD units below at −.69, $P \leq .05$.[23] The capacity for organizational learning is greatest, on average, in elementary schools at .6 SD above the mean; high schools are more than 1.2 SD below elementary schools in their capacity for organizational learning ($P \leq .05$).

Although student gender differences among the grade levels are not significant, most other student background characteristics do vary significantly. About 32 percent of the high school students are African American, a higher proportion than in elementary (15 percent) and middle (10 percent) schools ($P \leq .001$). About 37 percent of the elementary school students are Hispanic, a significantly greater proportion than in middle schools (12 percent) and high schools (16 percent) ($P \leq .001$). Middle school students average the highest on the socioeconomic status measure, .16 SD above the mean and high school students the lowest, .15 SD below the mean, while elementary students are at the mean, −.01 ($P \leq .001$). Middle school students' GPAs are highest, .16 SD above the mean, followed by elementary school students at .12SD and high school students at −.31 SD below the mean.

Psychometric Properties of the Dependent Variables

The HLM analyses attempt to account for variance in the dependent variables—pedagogical quality, authentic achievement, and NAEP achievement—by estimating the effect of the capacity for organizational learning on these outcomes. For pedagogical quality, the proportion of variance

Table 2. Psychometric Properties of the Dependent Variables

	Pedagogical Quality	Authentic Achievement	NAEP Achievement
Intraclass Correlation	26.0%	21.0%	17.5%
HLM Reliability	.93	.94	.66

Table 3. Capacity for Organizational Learning and Pedagogical Quality

	Dependent Variable
Fixed Effect	Pedagogical Quality
Intercept[a]	−.23
% Female	.01
% African American	.23
% Hispanic	.19
Socioeconomic Status[b]	.06
GPA[b]	.49***
School Capacity for Organizational Learning[b]	.58*
% Variance Among-Schools Explained	25.7

Notes: [a]Coefficients expressed in effect size (ES) metric. See note 24 for details.
 [b]Variable standardized, M=0; SD=1; grand mean entered for HLM computation.
 *$P \leq .05$; **$P \leq .01$; ***$P \leq .001$

among schools is 26 percent; thus, the remaining 74 percent is attributable to differences among the teachers *within* schools (Table 2). For authentic achievement, 21 percent of the variance is among schools; for NAEP achievement, 17.5 percent. The HLM reliabilities are highest for pedagogical quality, .93, and for authentic achievement, .94. The HLM reliability for NAEP achievement is .66.

The Capacity for Organizational Learning and Pedagogical Quality

In estimating the effect for the capacity of organizational learning on pedagogical quality, we adjust statistically for the compositional characteristics of classrooms. Table 3 displays the results of this analysis. As a benchmark to measure the magnitude of the relationships displayed in Table 3, we use the effect size metric, an indicator of relative size. An effect size (ES) is small, if less than .1; moderate, if between .2 and .5; and large, if .5 or over (Cohen, 1977; Rosenthal & Rosnow, 1984).[24]

The social background of students in a class is not influential in predicting the quality of the pedaogy they experience, but ability is. Higher ability classes have a greater the likelihood of receiving high quality pedagogy, a large effect (ES=.49, $P \leq .001$). School capacity for organiza-

Table 4. Capacity for Organizational Learning and
Student Achievement: Authentic and NAEP

	Dependent Variables	
Fixed Effect	Authentic Achievement	NAEP Achievement
Intercept	−.14	.06
Female	.36***	.25*
African American	−.52***	−1.05***
Hispanic	−.31*	−.61**
Socioeconomic Status[a]	.19**	.44***
GPA[a]	.48***	.60***
School Capacity for Organizational Learning[a]	.46*	.46*
% Variance Among-Schools Explained	29.2	51.2

Notes: [a]Coefficients expressed in effect size (ES) metric. See note 24 for details.
[b]Variable standardized, M=0; SD=1; grand mean entered for HLM computation.
$*P \leq .05; **P \leq .01; ***P \leq .001$

tional learning, the predictor of interest in our study, exerts a large effect on pedagogical quality (ES=.58, $P \leq .05$). The model explains 26 percent of the variance among schools in pedagogical quality.

The Capacity for Organizational Learning and Authentic Achievement

Girls score higher than boys on the authentic assessment measure, ES=.36, $P \leq .001$ (Table 4). Minority students score lower than their white peers, a large negative effect for African Americans, ES=-.52, $P \leq .001$; a moderate negative effect for Hispanics, ES=-.31, $P \leq .05$. Students with advantaged socioeconomic backgrounds tend to score higher on the authentic assessments than their less privileged peers, ES=.19, $P \leq .01$. GPA is a strong predictor of success on the authentic measures, ES=.48, $P < .001$. The capacity for organizational learning bears quite strongly on the school average level of authentic achievement. To the extent it is high, student achievement on authentic measures will be high. ES=.46, $P \leq .05$. The model accounts for 29 percent of the variance among schools in authentic achievement.

The Capacity for Organizational Learning and NAEP Achievement

Except in the case of gender, social background has a greater effect on students' success on standardized measures of achievement than on authentic. Girls are an exception, in that the effect of female gender on NAEP achievement is lower than on authentic measures, ES=.25, $P \leq .05$ (Table 4). African American students fare far less well on the standardized test, ES=-1.05, $P \leq .001$. Hispanic students are also less successful on the NAEP assessment, ES=-.61, $P \leq .01$. Students' socioeconomic status influences their achievement on the NAEP assessment, ES=.44, $P \leq .001$. GPA is a strong predictor of success on standardized assessments, ES=.60, $P \leq .001$. The capacity for organizational learning influences school average scores on standardized assessments at the same level as authentic assessments, ES=.46, $P \leq .05$. Interestingly, the proportion of variance in the standardized assessment model is large, 51 percent, and considerably greater than for the authentic achievement model, 29 percent.

Organizational Learning in Two Restructuring Schools

The quantitative findings document the relationship of the capacity for organizational learning to school performance for the entire sample. To provide a picture of this relationship in practice, we draw on the qualitative data and focus in some depth on two representative schools. Typical of the elementary schools is Lamar, one of the highest scoring schools in the capacity for organizational learning and in the measured outcomes—pedagogical quality, authentic achievement and standardized achievement. South Glen, like most of the other high schools, scores well below the mean on all of the dimensions in the study (middle schools tend to be in the middle ranges on all measured dimensions).

Though one is an elementary school and one is a high school, Lamar and South Glen have important features in common including consistent, positive leadership over a long period of time, and high levels of external support. Both schools have operated for 10 or more years in district contexts that promote site-based management. Neither school is extremely large or small. About 40 percent of each school's students are Hispanic and/or African American. Despite their similarities, the schools differ on many salient dimensions of the capacity for organizational learning and their relationships to pedagogical quality and student achievement.

School Improvement Initiatives

Lamar Elementary began operation in 1977 as a teacher- and parent-initiated alternative to the district's mastery learning policy. The features basic to Lamar's identity have remained largely unchanged since its inception—a commitment to parent involvement, non-graded cluster organization, a thematic curriculum, and an emphasis on higher order thinking skills. Lamar was granted charter status in the late 1990s, although teachers remain part of the district's bargaining unit. Charter status has increased Lamar's financial flexibility both in fund raising and spending, over and above the discretion allowed by district site-based management policies.

A teacher-parent council (on which the principal sits ex-officio, without a vote) governs Lamar. The council is representative of the parent populations due to an early decision to hold elections by geographic residence areas. A cohesive group, the council has operated "with a siege mentality against the district" and an adamant commitment to maintaining the structure and philosophy of the school.

Teachers work in teams, having joint curriculum responsibility for multi-grade clusters. The school provides a considerable amount of time for the cluster teams to meet and plan jointly. Lamar allocates many of its eight pupil-free days and six additional half-days per year to team coordination. Governance meetings involving teachers are held in the evenings. From the teacher's perspective, the primary problem with the democratic organization is its intensity; several teachers commented on the overload, noting the need to choose constantly between professional and personal interests. Departing from union contractual guidelines, most teachers work hours far in excess of the district norm.

South Glen High School, by contrast, is located in a state that is highly centralized. Schools have little budgetary discretion, the State Board of Education determines teacher salaries, and the school must meet state curriculum standards, including student assessments at the end of most core courses in English, math, science, and social studies. South Glen has adopted a variety of structural innovations that were, according to the principal who initiated them, designed to improve the professional environment for teachers and to provide more opportunities for students. While increasing graduation requirements and making more academic courses available to students—changes South Glen initiated in 1986, the school also eliminated traditional departments and adopted a block schedule with 90-minute class periods. Lead teachers replaced department chairs and held additional administrative responsibilities, but in return they received an extra planning period and additional secretarial help for routine tasks. The school adopted a shared governance structure in the form of a representative school-wide governance council. A faculty council was empowered to consider and act on issues of curriculum and instruction, and the district adopted a school-based management policy that permitted discretion to schools in hiring and policy development.

Subsequently, however, the impact of much of this innovation has diminished. The purpose for the teams and the coordination between them has eroded to the point that they function just like the previous departments. The new principal dissolved the ineffective faculty council. Initiatives for school change or improvement come either from the district (for example, moves to develop quality management and authentic assessment/mastery learning) or from the principal (for example, an emphasis on implementing Steven Covey's *Seven Habits*). Teachers rarely collaborate and they demonstrate little efficacy. While school administrators set an ambitious agenda for continued reform, teachers do not buy into it.

Contrasting Cultures

At Lamar Elementary, in contrast, the sense of shared purpose is almost tangible. The staff maintains this shared purpose by hiring teachers who share their philosophy of progressive education and project-based learning. Speaking of teachers' embrace of the school's mission, the principal said, "We say it over and over again.... We say it 12,000 different ways." The school does not enforce conformity to a particular pedagogical model, however, but allows flexibility within the frame. One teacher emphasized the teaching teams' freedom to interpret the mission and the concept of the "open classroom" within their clusters. "Everybody has the same picture," another teacher reported. "It's sort of how they paint that's different."

Teacher commitment to collaboration is particularly evident in the clusters, where teams spend considerable time planning. "That's what makes it work, " a teacher noted, "the give and take and sharing, and having a stake in this place." Most teachers report discussing problems of practice with team members and look to them for professional support. To develop positions on school-wide issues to be placed on the agenda of the governing board meetings, teachers have lunch together on Tuesdays. Teachers spend one full day per year developing the year's curriculum theme, and they "touch base" around the theme several times during the year. The governing board, comprising parents and teachers, is also active on many curriculum issues through its committee structure.

Staff at Lamar view the district norm-referenced tests and the state proficiency tests as obstacles. Although compared to other schools in the district, Lamar does well on the tests, teachers remain distrustful, fully aware that state-developed standards and syllabi will change their curriculum.

At South Glen High School, teachers do not take advantage of the structures for collaboration. Lead teacher meetings, rather than serving as forums for substantive discussion, have degenerated into "gripe sessions." Teachers rarely use their daily 90-minute prep period for common planning. Because of the focus on the state's end-of-course examinations, the staff sees no reason to work on curriculum or locally generated student achievement objectives. All South Glen teachers report that the state end-of-course tests drive their instruction and allow little opportunity for local curriculum development. The state tests are high stakes for the school and teachers—reported to the public and used to determine financial rewards—but are lower stakes for students, who may graduate as long as they pass their courses.

South Glen's faculty devotes little energy to meetings, a decided change from the early days of restructuring when faculty discussed and argued their views on issues. When asked whether his colleagues talk about teaching in team meetings, one South Glen teacher responded, "We tell each other why we want to teach what we want to teach." Teachers frequently commented about the lack of focus on the part of the teaching staff. Not all of the teachers even believe in their ability to affect student learning. Not surprisingly, teachers are unable to forge consensus on implementing mastery learning and alternative assessment. Though the policies are part of the district's agenda, South Glen teachers do not collaborate around the meaning of the policies. While teachers do emphasize the state's end-of-course tests, the school's state assessment scores have been falling. Yet, teachers do not report any substantive discussion about the problem. Unlike the teachers at Lamar, teachers at South Glen do not regard the problems they encounter as opportunities for change and improvement.

Professional Development

Lamar teachers see themselves as professionals who teach adults as well as students. Parents receive gentle attention from teachers, who conduct off-site meetings with parents to explain the school's philosophy and who socialize with the parents through committee meetings and potluck suppers. Teachers are generally enthusiastic about the level of parent participation among both minority and majority parents. About half the families volunteer to help in the school, and almost all parents attend the special events. When disagreements arise over issues—for example, the desire on the part of some parents to pay more attention to the statewide testing results, and a committee recommendation for a new report card structure—all relevant parties negotiate them. When the school struggled with assessment, in part because of their distaste for standardized tests; they sought assistance from assessment experts at a local university to develop a model alternative program.

Although Lamar allocates staff development days generously, most teachers view formal staff development as less valuable than collaborative and committee work. Many teachers take advanced course work at one of the nearby universities or participate in local teacher networks. One math teacher, for example, had met for about 15 hours during the past year with an informal group of professional friends from around the city to work on an integrated math and science curriculum.

At South Glen, little consensus has emerged around the goals articulated by school and district administrators—specifically, more professionalism and more challenge for students. Most teachers either resist or are slow to change. When South Glen adopted block scheduling, most teachers continued to do what they had always done, but in different time frames: "Those that were lecturing before are still doing it." The same "no change" attitude has affected the new initiative for authentic assessment/mastery learning: "Most people don't know what [it] would look like and wouldn't know how to implement it.... People here are not risk-takers."

The low level of skill in pedagogical methods is, in part, a consequence of limited professional development opportunities. Most teachers complain that they had only a cursory introduction to block scheduling. The district has focused most of its professional development resources on the introduction of authentic assessment/mastery learning and promoting the principles of quality management, but the training has taken the form of one-way informational sessions, according to the current superintendent, to create "a shared sense of urgency for change."

Overall, the problem-solving capacity at South Glen is low: Many teachers do not like the current class size configurations (large classes for lower ability students), the block schedule, the rigid state assessment system, and the new top-down innovations, but they feel unable to mitigate their concerns. Relationships between parents and the school are typically remote or, in the case of minority parents who are suspicious about the segregating effects of mastery learning, prone to conflict. Only the minority of parents whose children are likely to go to college have much influence in the school, and they focus on maintaining the status quo.

The Leadership Equation

The founding principal at Lamar Elementary provides strong intellectual leadership, although she takes a back seat in formal decision making. She has taken the lead on resolving the concerns among parents and teachers around assessment, and initiated contact with a local university to provide assistance. She works slowly and through consensus. When Lamar decided to request charter status, the principal recommended 100 percent buy-in on the part of teachers and the governing board. One of her most important roles has been to protect the school from district policies that would negatively affect the school's operations. Respect and trust between staff and the principal are high; but to encourage free discussion, teachers also meet weekly without her to discuss school-wide issues.

When the founding principal announced her retirement, the Lamar staff voluntarily paid for an overnight retreat to discuss what they wanted in a new principal. One teacher captured the necessity for a common vision. "The new person must understand learning and curriculum so thoroughly.... as we trust the kids to create, the principal must trust us."

South Glen has had five principals in less than 10 years, but all have been supportive of change and have been active in networking to obtain resources for the school, including financial and public relations support from the state and local business. Further, support for school-based management and teacher involvement in decision making has been consistent, and a close relationship between school and district administration persists. Nevertheless, the development of internal school leadership through the faculty council and the lead teachers has not fulfilled administrators' hopes of creating a more supportive intellectual environment for change.

Learning Orientation

Lamar Elementary, although not a perfect school, is engaged with continuous improvement and learning. Both teachers and parents are dedicated to making the school a better place for urban children to learn. All factors that we have identified as potential predictors of organizational learning are present to a significant degree, and the anticipated retirement of the principal has mobilized rather than discouraged participants. The focus on what is best for students is palpable in all observations and interviews. While committed to their philosophy of open learning, teachers appear to be searching constantly for new approaches to increase student achievement according to the criteria that they set, rather than the district's standardized tests. Lamar is successful in involving parents in substantive discussions around issues of curriculum and learning; they have been rewarded by enthusiastic parent support in fund-raising and advocacy.

South Glen is clearly not an effective learning organization. The absence of many of the conditions that we identify as related to learning is conspicuous. Teachers prefer solo practice and traditional teaching methods, and have not coalesced around the demonstrable problem of student achievement. Despite more than ten years of experience with faculty governance and district support for change, no consensus has emerged around common strategies to identify and solve student problems. Staff do not believe in the value of data that are available to them through state tests, and have not sought assistance in obtaining any additional information that might help them improve.

CONCLUSION

A school's ability to identify and deal with issues and problems gives some indication of its capacity for organizational learning in the school. Lamar teachers locate issues and problems to address them—improving parent involvement, developing more effective assessment strategies, and coordinating curriculum across grades and disciplines. South Glen teachers, on the other hand, narrow their focus to the content state tests cover, and see their problems—state mandates, large class sizes (smaller than those at Lamar), and ineffective faculty governance—as largely insoluble. The school rarely calls upon available outside expertise—the district, the Business Forum, or parents—for help in understanding or mediating issues that surface. Their failure to seek outside resources may be due to a lack of discussion around problems or an unwillingness to invest in finding solutions.

Professional knowledge and skills that permit problem solving vary between the two schools. Lamar hires teachers because they are already committed to alternative approaches to curriculum and instruction; South Glen also recruits teachers because they "fit in," but the context is traditional. Teachers interested in experimenting with pedagogy are in the minority and feel out of place with the other teachers who present themselves as co-workers not colleagues. Lamar teachers—viewing learning as both a collective and an individual responsibility—work hard at learning from each other, especially through teams, and they actively seek professional contacts and expertise outside the school. South Glen teachers, although they are within easy driving distance of several universities, do not turn to them for professional development.

Both Lamar and South Glen enjoy supportive leadership and structural innovation aligned with achievement, yet only Lamar Elementary operates as a learning organization. Why has Lamar succeeded and South Glen failed in organizing effectively to improve pedagogical quality and student achievement? A look at their differing school cultures is informative. The culture at South Glen is deeply and firmly established in the reciprocal links between a conservative community and an equally risk-averse staff. While administrators and business leaders voice a sense of urgency for change, the teachers and the residents of the school district prefer to "let well enough alone." Individualism and solo practice remain largely intact despite ten years of retreats and leadership training for teachers. Although they are vaguely dissatisfied, South Glen teachers expect to find little personal fulfillment in their work or iteractions with their peers.

Lamar's culture of growth and change, on the other hand, drives teachers to experiment, to analyze their own performance, and to see themselves as collectively responsible for the school's success, independent of administrative support. Change, a core value of Lamar's founding parents, persists. Lamar teachers continue to engage parents, whenever possible, as active partners in education. The staff's consistent emphasis on the collaborative and consensual nature of all activities, and their willingness to confront and resolve differences, stand in dramatic contrast to South Glen's preference for letting each individual student and staff member rise or fall to their own level of competence.

Lamar Elementary enjoys a culture that revolves around the core technology of the school, while South Glen High School does not. Both schools have the structures and processes to facilitate the sharing of information. Lamar has the necessary knowledge and support in the form of a mission and the means for self-analysis in its structures and work routines; South Glen has some of these but they are fewer and far less developed. What Lamar has in abundance and South Glen lacks, is the intention to learn on the part of members involved in a professional community. While leadership for change at Lamar is widely shared, leadership for change at South Glen has been a series of top down, largely ineffective efforts.

The capacity for organizational learning supports high performance on the central intellectual activities of the school—teaching and learning. The presence of only some of the dimensions of this capacity is not sufficient to activate organizational learning. Democratic structures and supportive leadership, for example, are not effective by themselves. Only in concert with the other dimensions of the capacity for organizational learning do they positively impact pedagogical quality and student achievement. Thus, these findings advance an understanding of both the importance of all six dimensions of the capacity for organizational learning—structure, empowerment, shared commitment and collaborative activity, knowledge and skills, leadership, and feedback and accountability—and the subtle interactions between them.

ACKNOWLEDGMENTS

The project from which this study draws its data was conducted under the auspices of the Wisconsin Center for Education Research and the Center on Organization of Schools and supported by the U.S. Department of Education, Office of Educational Research and Improvement (Grant No. R117Q000005-95). An earlier version of this chapter was presented at the annual meeting of the American Educational Research Association, Montreal, Canada. The opinions expressed are those of the authors and do not necessarily reflect those of the supporting agencies.

NOTES

1. Studies linking high performance of schools to the common properties follow: teacher empowerment (Marks & Louis, 1997), professional community and collective responsibility for student learning (Louis, Marks, & Kruse, 1996), high quality pedagogy (Newmann, Marks, & Gamoran, 1996; Marks & Louis, 1997), and strong intellectural performance among students (Newmann, Marks, & Gamoran, 1996; Louis & Marks, 1998).

2. Support for organizational learning as a strategy for meeting the changing demands for schools is offered by Darling-Hammond (1996). Rait (1995) discusses the impact of organizational learning on school improvement.

3. Cohen and Sproull (1996) advise against drawing lines around the field of organizational learning as it is still new, vital and innovative.

4. The social and cultural aspects of organizational learning are developed in Cook and Yanow (1996). Schein (1985, 1992) describes the process by which individuals learn as groups develop solutions to problems; those solutions lead to changes in values, beliefs and norms.

5. Mai (1996) emphasizes the connection between organizational learning, competition and success, while Dodgson (1993) emphasizes the importance of organizational learning during times of uncertainty. Both Kuchinke (1995) and Dodgson (1993) caution that organizational learning should be thought of as a strategy for improved performance, not as an end in itself.

6. Teachers who are involved in inquiry and social processing of information guarantee organizational learning in schools (Rait, 1995; Shedd & Bacharach, 1991).

7. Defensive routines are actions or policies intended to protect individuals within an organization from experiencing embarrassment or threat while protecting the organization from having to identify the source of that threat in order to correct problems. Defensive routines are based on logic which is embedded deep within the organization and which follows these rules: (1) send messages that contain inconsistencies; (2) act as if the messages do not contain inconsistencies; (3) make the inconsistency in the messages undiscussable; and (4) make the undiscussability of the undiscussable also undiscussable (Argyris & Schön, 1996).

8. Several studies have focused on the need for structural changes in schools, particularly Kruse, Louis, & Bryk (1995) and Bryk, Camburn, & Louis (1996). Impediments to organizational learning include isolation and shrinking resources (Rait, 1995), lack of coordination and interdependence (Louis & Kruse, 1998), hierarchical control (Starbuck,1996), and size and complexity of schools (Lee & Smith, 1997; Leithwood, Leonard, & Sharratt, 1998).

9. Both Conley (1991) and Smylie (1994) have shown that empowerment alone does not consistently improve student performance.

10. Organizational learning in schools entails "social processing" of information to set strategies for improvement (Marks & Louis, 1999) which goes well beyond any one person's knowledge (Probst & Büchel, 1997).

11. See Louis and Marks (1998) and Louis, Marks, and Kruse (1996) for a discussion of the effectiveness of professional community in improving both pedagogy and student achievement.

12. McDonald (1996) discusses the flow of information from outside to inside the school. Siskin (1994) and Kruse (1995) detail the results of departmentalization in schools. Starbuck (1996) emphasizes the importance of sharing expertise and open discussion.

13. Leadership in learning organizations must take on a different character (Murphy & Louis, 1994; Leithwood, Jantzi, & Fernandez, 1994). Essential are an abililty to provide intellectual leadership (Newmann & Associates, 1996) and an ability to encourage the transfer of learning (Ulrich, Jick, and Von Glinow, 1993). Particularly important is the leader's modeling of the learning process and the learning orientation (Schein, 1992).

14. Leaders in organizations that learn must at times be authoritative rather than supportive (Marks & Louis, 1999; Bryk, Camburn & Louis, 1996).

15. Schools must be responsible for their effectiveness and must have the ability to make changes for improvement if organizational learning is to be enhanced (National Academy of Education Panel on Standards-Based Education Reform, 1995; Rothman, 1995).

16. The center, located at the University of Wisconsin-Madison and funded by a grant from the Office of Educational Research and Improvement (OERI) of the U.S. Department of Education, was co-directed by Fred M. Newmann and Gary G. Wehlage.

17. Compared with public schools nationally, schools in this sample are larger (enrolling, on average, 777 students compared with a national average of 522 students) and they enroll more minority students. In the sample elementary and middle schools, NAEP achievement levels in reading and mathematics are at or above the national average. In the high schools, NAEP achievement is below the national average (a result that may be attributable to a high school sample of mostly 9th and 10th grade students taking a NAEP test normed for 12th grade students. For additional comparative information about characteristics of the sampled schools, see Marks and Louis, 1997.

18. Student work was scored on each standard, using a scale of 1-4. The overall performance score is the sum of the scores on the three rubrics. The possible range of the performance scale is 3-12.

19. The score for authentic pedagogy is the sum of a teacher's instruction score on each standard (on a scale of 1-5 and averaged over four observations) and assessment task score (on a 1-3 or 1-4 scale and averaged over two tasks). The range of possible authentic pedagogy scores is 11-43. Appendix A contains a more detailed description of all the variables used in these analyses. See also Newmann et al., 1995.

20. In other studies based on these data in which we and our colleagues investigated effects on achievement, the outcome variable has been "authentic achievement" and the ability control, "NAEP achievement." In this instance, because we are interested in effects on both authentic and standardized measures of performance, we use students' self-reported "GPA" as a control for ability. All three of these measures are correlated to a comparable degree, that is, for GPA and NAEP achievement, .31, $P \leq .001$; for GPA and authentic achievement, .25, $P \leq .001$; and for NAEP achievement and authentic achievement, .34, $P \leq .001$.

21. Means were computed using oneway analysis of variance (ANOVA).

22. The multilevel statistical technique is hierarchical linear modeling—HLM (Bryk & Raudenbush, 1992; Bryk, Raudenbush & Congdon, 1994).

23. Elementary students' scores were at the national average in mathematics and slightly above in reading. Middle school students scored above the mean in both mathematics and social studies. High school students scored below the mean in both subjects, a consequence, perhaps,

of the high school NAEP norms being based on twelfth grade students, while most of the high school students who completed the tests were in tenth grade or below.

24. The effect size (ES) metric is in standard deviation units, computed by dividing the HLM gamma coefficient (standardized for continuous variables [M=0, SD=1], other wise dummy-coded [0,1], by the HLM-estimated standard deviation for the appropriate outcome variable.

REFERENCES

Argyris, C., & Schön, D. A. (1974). *Theory in practice: Increasing professional effectiveness.* San Francisco: Jossey-Bass Publishers.

Argyris, C., & Schön, D. A. (1996). *Organizational learning II: Theory, method, and practice.* Reading, MA: Addison-Wesley Publishing Company.

Berends, M., & King, M. B. (1994). A description of restructuring in nationally nominated schools: Legacy of the iron cage? *Educational Policy, 8*(1), 28-50.

Brown, J. S., & Duguid, P. (1996). Organizational learning and communities-of-practice: Toward a unified view of working, learning, and innovation. In M. D. Cohen & L. S. Sproull (Eds.), *Organizational learning* (pp. 58-82). Thousand Oaks: CA: Sage Publications.

Bryk, A.S., Camburn, E., & Louis, K. S. (1996). *Promoting school improvement through professional communities: An analysis of Chicago elementary schools.* Paper presented at the annual meeting of the American Educational Research Association, New York City.

Bryk, A.S., & Raudenbush, S. W. (1992). *Hierarchical linear models: Applications and data analysis methods.* Newbury Park, CA: Sage.

Bryk, A.S., Raudenbush, S. W. & Congdon, R. T. (1994). *Hierarchical linear modeling with the HLM/ 2L and HLM/3L programs.* Newbury Park, CA: Sage.

Cohen, J. (1977). *Statistical power for the behavioral sciences.* New York: Academic Press.

Cohen, M. D., & Sproull, L. S. (Eds.). (1996). *Organizational learning.* Thousand Oaks, CA: Sage Publications.

Conley, S. (1991). Review of research on teacher participation in school decision-making. In G. Grant (Ed.), *Review of research in education* (Vol. 17, pp. 225-265). Washington, DC: American Educational Research Association.

Cook, S.D.N., & Yanow, D. (1996). Culture and organizational learning. In M. D. Cohen & L. S. Sproull (Eds.), *Organizational learning* (pp. 430-459). Thousand Oaks: CA: Sage Publications.

Darling-Hammond, L. (1996). What matters most: A competent teacher for every child. *Phi Delta Kappan, 78*(3), 193-200.

Dodgson, M. (1993). Organizational learning: A review of some literatures. *Organization Studies, 14*(3), 375-394.

Huber, G. P. (1996). Organizational learning: The contributing processes and the literatures. In M. D. Cohen & L. S. Sproull (Eds.), *Organizational learning* (pp. 124-162). Thousand Oaks: CA: Sage Publications.

Kruse, S. D. (1995). *Community as a foundation for professionalism: Case studies of middle school teachers.* Unpublished doctoral dissertation, University of Minnesota.

Kuchinke, K. P. (1995). Managing learning for performance. *Human Resource Development Quarterly 6*(3), 307-316.

Lee, V. E., & Smith, J. B. (1997). High school size: Which works best and for whom? *Educational Evaluation and Policy Analysis, 19*(3), 205-227.

Lee, V. E., Bryk, A. S., & Smith, J. B. (1993). The organization of effective secondary schools. In L. Darling-Hammond, L. (Ed.), *Review of Research in Education* (Vol. 19, pp. 171-267), Washington, DC: American Educational Research Association.

Leithwood, K.A., Jantzi, D., & Fernandez, A. (1994). Transformational leadership and teachers' commitment to change. In J. Murphy & K. S. Louis (Eds.), *Reshaping the principalship: Insights from transformational reform efforts* (pp. 77-98). Thousand Oaks, CA: Corwin Press Inc.

Leithwood, K., Leonard, L., & Sharratt, L. (1998). Conditions fostering organizational learning in schools. *Educational Administration Quarterly, 34*(2), 243-276.

Louis, K. S., & Kruse, S. D. (1995). *Professionalism and community: Perspectives on reforming urban schools.* Newbury Park, CA: Corwin.

Louis, K. S., & Marks, H. (1998). Does professional community affect the classroom? Teachers' work and student experiences in restructuring schools. *American Journal of Education 106*(4).

Louis, K. S., Marks, H. M., & Kruse, S. D. (1996) Teachers' professional community in restructuring schools. *American Journal of Education, 33*(4), 757-798.

McDonald, J. (1996). *Redesigning school.* San Francisco: Jossey-Bass Publishers.

Mai, R. P. (1996). *Learning partnerships: How leading American companies implement organizational learning.* Chicago: Irwin Professional Publishing.

Marks, H. M., & Louis, K. S. (1997) Does teacher empowerment affect the classroom: The implications of teacher empowerment for instructional practice and student academic performance. *Educational Evaluation and Policy Analysis, 19*(2), 245-275.

Marks, H. M., & Louis, K. S. (1999). Teacher empowerment and the capacity for organizational learning. *Educational Administration Quarterly, 35*(5) .

Miles, M. B. & Huberman, M. (1984). *Qualitative data analysis: A sourcebook of methods.* Beverly Hills: Sage Publications.

Murphy, J., & Louis, K. S. (Eds.). (1994). *Reshaping the principalship: Insights from transformational reform efforts.* Thousand Oaks, CA: Corwin Press, Inc.

Newmann, F. M., & Associates. (1996). *Authentic achievement: Restructuring schools for intellectual quality.* San Francisco: Jossey-Bass Publishers.

Newmann, F. M., King, M. B., & Rigdon, M. (1997). Accountability and school performance: Implications from restructuring schools. *Harvard Educational Review, 67*(1), 41-74.

Newmann, F. M., Marks, H. M., & Gamoran, A. (1996). Authentic pedagogy and student performance. *American Journal of Education, 104*(4), 280-312.

Newmann, F. M., Secada, W.G., & Wehlage, G. G. (1995). *A guide to authentic instruction and assessment: Vision, standards, and scoring.* Madison, WI: Center on Organization and Restructuring of Schools, Wisconsin Center for Education Research, University of Wisconsin.

Probst, G.J.B., & Büchel, B.S.T. (1997). *Organizational learning: The competitive advantage of the future.* London: Prentice Hall.

Rait, E. (1995). Against the current: Organizational learning in schools. In S. B. Bacharach & B. Mundell (Eds.) *Images of schools: Structures and roles in organizational behavior* (pp. 71-107). Thousand Oaks, CA: Corwin Press, Inc.

Rosenthal, R., & Rosnow, R. (1984). *Essentials of behavioral analysis: Methods and data analysis.* New York: McGraw-Hill.

Rothman, R. (1995). *Measuring up: Standards, assessment, and school reform.* San Francisco: Jossey-Bass Publishers.

Sarason, S. (1996). *Revisiting "The culture of the school and the problem of change."* New York: Teachers College Press.

Schein, E. (1985, 1992). *Organizational culture and leadership.* San Francisco: Jossey-Bass Publishers.

Senge, P. M. (1990). *The fifth discipline: The art and practice of the learning organization.* New York: Doubleday/Currency.

Shedd, J. B., & Bacharach, S. B. (1991). *Tangled hierarchies: Teachers as professionals and the management of schools.* San Francisco: Jossey-Bass Publishers.

Siskin, L. (1994). *Realms of knowledge: Academic departments in secondary schools.* Washington, DC: Falmer Press.

Smylie, M. (1994). Redesigning teachers' work: Connections to the classroom. In L. Darling-Hammond, (Ed.), *Review of research in education* (Vol. 20, pp. 129-177). Washington, DC: American Educational Research Association.

Starbuck, W. H. (1996). Learning by knowledge-intensive firms. In M. D. Cohen and L. S. Sproull (Eds.). *Organizational learning* (pp. 484-515). Thousand Oaks, CA: Sage Publications.

Ulrich, D., Jick, T., & Von Glinow, M. A. (1993). High-impact learning: Building and diffusing learning capability. *Organizational Dynamics, Autumn*, 52-66.

CHAPTER 12

LEADERSHIP FOR ORGANIZATIONAL LEARNING IN AUSTRALIAN SECONDARY SCHOOLS

Halia Silins, Bill Mulford, Silja Zarins and
Pamela Bishop

INTRODUCTION

Too often educational reforms have been thwarted by the robust nature of established school practices (McLaughlin, 1998; Bishop & Mulford, 1999, Sarason, 1998). Some forms of school restructuring, however, are proving to be more beneficial than others. Schools moving from competitive, top-down forms of power to more collective and facilitative forms (Mulford, 1994) are finding greater success, as are those attempting to make not only first-order

Advances in Research and Theories of School
Management and Educational Policy, Volume 4, pages 267-291.
Copyright © 2000 by JAI Press Inc.
All rights of reproduction in any form reserved.
ISBN: 0-7623-0024-8

changes (i.e., in curriculum and instruction) but also those second-order changes (i.e., culture and structure) which support efforts to implement first-order changes. Louden and Wallace's (1994) research on the Australian National Schools Network concludes that reforms, no matter how well conceptualized or powerfully sponsored, are likely to fail in the face of cultural resistance from teachers.

Resistance to change is likely given that certain forms of restructuring challenge some existing teacher paradigms. Smylie, Lazarus, and Brownlee-Conyers (1996) have shown, for example, that the greater the participative nature of decision making, the greater the increase in perceived accountability, the more organizational learning opportunities for teachers. The greater the increases in accountability and the more learning opportunities available, the greater are the reports of instructional improvement. The greater the reports of instructional improvement, the more positive are the teacher-reported student outcomes, and the more likely are improvements in reading and mathematics achievement test scores. However, at each stage of this sequence, teachers also reported a decline in perceived individual autonomy. The change in paradigm seems to be away from the individual teacher in his or her own classroom to the development of learning communities which value differences, support critical reflection and encourage members to question, challenge and debate teaching and learning issues (Peters, Dobbins, & Johnson, 1996). How to promote this change is far from clear, but we believe the area of organizational learning (OL) offers valuable clues.

The indications are that the successful restructuring agenda depends on teams of leaders, whole staffs and school personnel, working together in collaboration with community members. The challenges these groups face require significant development of their collective, as well as their individual, capacities. While such OL has long been the object of study in non-school organizations (e.g., Watkins & Marsick, 1993), until recent times little attention has been given to its nature or the conditions which foster it, including leadership practices, in schools (Mulford, 1998).

This chapter seeks to redress this situation by first examining some of the research on leadership and OL in school reform and then reporting in detail on the first phase of a major Australian research project, the Leadership for Organizational Learning and Student Outcomes (LOLSO) Project. This project is focussing on the nature of leadership contributions to the stimulation of OL in secondary schools and the effects of both leadership and OL on desired student outcomes.

LEADERSHIP AND ORGANIZATIONAL LEARNING RESEARCH

Leadership

The contributions of school leadership to past and current reform efforts have been found to be undeniably significant. Extensive research by Leithwood and his collaborators has identified those leadership practices that facilitate school restructuring in general (Leithwood, 1992, 1993, 1994; Silins, 1992, 1994a, 1994b). Most of the practices identified by this research are encompassed by a transformational model of leadership (Leithwood, Jantzi, & Steinbach, 1999). Research describing productive forms of leadership has referred to aspects of this transformational model of leadership, for example, leadership which is empowering (Reitzug, 1994); sensitive to local community aspirations (Limerick & Nielsen, 1995); supportive of followers (Blase, 1993); builds collaborative school cultures (Deal & Peterson, 1994); and emphasises the importance of developing a shared vision (Mulford, 1994). The transformational conception of leadership includes: developing a vision for the school and maintaining its relevance for all concerned; developing and maintaining a school culture supportive of the school's vision and the work required to achieve that vision; and nurturing the capacity and commitment of staff (Duke & Leithwood, 1994). This view of leadership also includes: structuring the school to facilitate the achievement of its vision and goals; ensuring the continuous improvement of programs and instruction; building and maintaining high levels of support for the school among parents and the wider community; and providing administrative support for the achievement of the school's vision and goals (Leithwood & Duke, 1999).

Leithwood, Jantzi & Steinbach's (1998) study of six Canadian schools that were considered promising sites of organizational learning, including four secondary schools, sought to link leadership and other conditions which fostered organizational learning. They found that school leadership practices had among the strongest direct and indirect influences on OL. Those practices included identifying and articulating a vision, fostering the acceptance of group goals, structuring the school to enhance participation in decisions, providing intellectual stimulation, and conveying high expectations. In other words, practices associated with the transformational conception of leadership made uniformly positive contributions to OL.

Organizational Learning

While the literature on OL in non-school situations continues to expand, unconstrained by criticism, such as the charge of a lack of a common language (Gheradi, 1999), there is also growing support for the importance of OL in schools (Chapman, 1997; Leithwood, Leonard, & Sharratt, 1998; Louis, 1994; Mulford, Hogan, & Lamb, 1997; Leithwood & Louis, 1998). However, as Leithwood and Louis (1998, p. 7) point out, while the logical case for OL is compelling, "empirical support for the claim that increases in such learning will contribute to organizational effectiveness or productivity is embarrassingly slim." These authors conclude that a "review of empirical research on organizational learning in schools alone would make a very quick read indeed."

A review of the empirical work that is available from countries as wide apart as the Netherlands, Canada, Britain, the United States, and Australia (Berends et al., 1998; Bishop & Mulford, 1999; Bodilly, 1998; Brown et al., 1999; Glennan, 1998; Hannay & Ross, 1999; Louis & Marks, 1998; Sheppard & Brown, 1999; Van Den Berg & Sleegers, 1996), while not always specifically addressing OL, does suggest that common themes are emerging about secondary schools which are successfully restructuring for change. These themes include a school's commitment to, and ownership of, transparent, inclusive, collaborative efforts that include greater use of distributed leadership, taking the initiative rather than always reacting, focusing on the learning needs of all students, and recognizing and acting on the need for all staff to be continuously learning.

Five studies are illustrative of these themes. Van Den Berg and Sleegers (1996), for example, selected Dutch secondary schools as highly innovative or lowly innovative on the basis of how early they began with the preparation for a core curriculum initiated by the government as well as their tradition of quickly and frequently implementing innovations. Schools of high, as opposed to low, innovative capacity were found to have greater team involvement, more people working for a harmonious atmosphere, fewer barriers to discussing professional matters including alternative opinions about an innovation, more delegation and distributive leadership, and more teachers feeling the need to continually develop themselves. Those findings have recently been confirmed by the authors in Dutch primary schools (Geijsel et al., 1999).

Case studies of two Canadian high schools recognized as outstanding in dealing with multiple changes resulted in Sheppard and Brown (1999) identifying key factors in a successful change process. Those factors included taking ownership of and formalizing their collaborative efforts, focusing directly on the learning of all students, recognizing the need for all staff to be continuous learners and taking action through professional development activities, and establishing partnerships with outside groups. Also in Canada, Hannay and Ross (1999) explored the reform efforts of nine secondary schools over a three-year period. The reform efforts were triggered when an Ontario school district empowered their secondary schools to develop site-specific organizational structures which deviated from the traditional subject departmental structure. While the mandated mantra that "the status quo was not acceptable" began the process, it was only when participants examined the contextual needs of their students that deeper cultural beliefs were challenged. In order to identify and act on these needs, members of each school staff had to engage in dialogue about what was important for their schools. Collaboration was found to be the first reculturing outcome to emerge followed by an acceptance of change and a whole school focus. Staff collectively developed a common direction and functioned in an interactive and reflective manner. Continual stress was placed by participants in the study on the importance of transparency of process, that is, of openness, communication, and dialogue. The leadership role in the school was also found to be broadened beyond line authority positions.

A study of 21 secondary schools in northwest England and Wales (Brown et al., 1999) examined interview evidence of alternative models of management of decision making as perceived by principals and heads of departments. Vast differences were found between what they categorized as "type A" and "type C" schools. Type A schools were completely committed to, and put formal structures in place for, team management and sharing of expertise. As well, staff felt actively involved and consulted in whole school policy and decision making, and good communication and systems of information-sharing were in place. Words such as dialogue, collaboration, problem solving, enabling, valued, open, empowered, respect, and trust were commonly used in type A schools. In contrast, type C schools had little collaboration, sharing, or consultation. Static, hierarchal management structures that focused on being reactive to external pressures were common. The result of those differences was evident, for example, when heads of departments in type A schools expressed a real sense of job enjoyment, satisfaction, and motivation whereas those in type C schools did not.

Finally, Louis and Marks (1998) examined teachers' work and student experiences in U.S. public schools which had made substantial progress in organizational restructuring. The sample included eight primary, eight middle, and eight secondary schools. It was found that the organization of teachers' work in ways that promoted professional community had a positive relationship with the organization of classrooms for learning and the academic performance of students. While middle and secondary schools were more organizationally complex, had less respect from the community, less participation in decision making, and were less open to innovation than primary schools, on other factors that contributed to professional community, there was no significant difference by level of school. Those factors included a supportive principal, feedback from parents and colleagues, and focused professional development. The authors argued that the significance of professional community for what happens in classrooms demands attention to school work-place relationships that promote openness, trust, genuine reflection, and collaboration focused on student learning.

Partnerships with other groups, especially the central office, are also an emerging theme in secondary schools that are successfully restructuring for change. For example, in a recent in-depth case study of a secondary school in Australia, Bishop and Mulford (1999) reported that teachers employed strategies of resistance in response to externally imposed edicts. Teacher resistance emerged when principals required staff to implement an externally imposed curriculum. Teachers' perceptions of this curriculum change as being unnecessary and of the principal being co-opted by the central authority (and thus changing from an educational leader who was "one of them" to being "the doer of the center's bidding") contributed to feelings of personal alienation and disempowerment, which underpinned teachers' strategies of resistance. Of particular concern, were the negative effects on the trust relationship between teachers and their principal. For example, critical comment, which may have benefited the school, was often a casualty when teachers perceived they could not be sure of the consequences of frank dialogue with their principal.

In 1991, in the United States, a multi-million dollar New American Schools initiative was begun to fund the development of designs aimed at transforming entire schools for improved student performance and then scaling up the designs to form a critical mass of schools within partnering districts. RAND Education's (e.g., Berends et al., 1998; Bodilly, 1998; Glennan, 1998) large-scale monitoring of this initiative indicated that schools were likely to make more implementation progress if, among other factors, they did not have leadership turnover and were involved with design teams that emphasized curriculum and instruction and supported implementation with whole school training. As well, implementation progress was greater where schools had districts with stable, supportive leadership, a culture of trust between the central office and schools that provided some school-level autonomy, and resources for professional development and planning. Leithwood, Jantzi, and Steinbach's (1999) research also pointed to the important role played by the central, or in their case, district office. The crucial elements in this relationship were district professional development policies and resources that facilitated the social processing of new ideas.

As we have pointed out previously (Mulford, 1998), and despite the continuing paucity of educational OL research, what is available suggests some consistency of definition and similar lists of identifying characteristics are emerging. In addition, some of the interrelationships among these characteristics are becoming clearer. For example, the identifying characteristics tend to describe OL as a journey rather than a destination, and to group themselves sequentially and developmentally. The first stage of OL largely focuses on developing common understandings, honesty, and trust through dialogue, sharing and distributive leadership, plus managing the inevitable risk and conflict involved. These learning processes are then employed to make links to the outside, to examine current practice critically, to develop shared values as well as a vision for the school. The processes, the content (or identified changes), and shared values are employed in actually making the changes that have been identified and include a commitment and ability to repeat the stages, that is, to continuously learn and improve. These organizational and leadership characteristics are set within more or less powerful external parameters such as central office policies, especially toward professional development.

However, while the promise of the OL vision for restructured schools would appear to be significant, insufficient empirical evidence remains concerning the specific characteristics of schools able to operate as learning organisations and the contribution leadership makes to these characteristics. One of the aims of the Australian LOLSO Project is to provide such evidence.

THE LOLSO PROJECT

LOLSO is a collaborative research project funded for three years (1997-1999) by the Australian Research Council. The partners in this project are Flinders University of South Australia, the University of Tasmania, the South Australian Department of Education, Training and Employment, the Tasmanian Department of Education, and the Centre for Leadership Development, University of Toronto. The LOLSO Project addresses the need to extend present understandings of school restructuring initiatives that aim to change school practices with the intention of supporting enhanced student learning and development of students. The LOLSO Project is unique in Australia in a number of ways including its: large sample; longitudinal nature; attempt to operationalise the concept of organizational learning; examination of the relationships among leadership processes, organizational learning and student outcomes; use of a measure of student outcomes that is wider than standardized testing; international comparisons; and use of findings to develop professional development for educational leaders.

In brief, the LOLSO Project aims to extend present understandings of the nature of effective leadership in the context of school restructuring in Australian public schools. It focuses on investigating the nature of leadership contributions to the stimulation of OL and inquires about the effects of both leadership and OL on desired secondary school student outcomes. This chapter focuses on the first of these relationships. What school and leadership characteristics and processes are associated with secondary schools identified as learning organizations?

Research Design

The research design of the LOLSO Project required three phases of data collection conducted over three years. In Phase 1, surveys of Year 10 students, their teachers and principals were conducted during 1997 in 96 secondary schools from two Australian states, South Australia and Tasmania. South Australian Year 12 students, teachers, and principals in those schools were resurveyed in 1999. In the second phase of the study (1998), cross-sectional and longitudinal case study data were collected from schools selected from the sample to triangulate and enrich the information generated by the survey data. The third phase in 1999 also saw the results from the quantitative and qualitative data gathering used to develop and try out professional development interventions for school leaders. Thus the project design allowed for iterative cycles of theory development and testing, using multiple forms of evidence.

Toward the end of the project, comparisons will be made with similar data collected from three Canadian provinces by Professor Kenneth Leithwood, Centre for Leadership Development, University of Toronto, Canada.

The LOLSO Project is addressing the following specific research questions:

1. How is the concept of organizational learning defined in Australian secondary schools?
2. What conditions inside and outside Australian high schools account for variations in organizational learning? That is, why are some schools seen as learning organizations and others are not?
3. Does the level of organizational learning in secondary schools contribute to the extent of students' participation in and engagement with school?
4. What proportion of organizational learning is accounted for by school leadership?
5. What leadership practices promote organizational learning in schools?
6. What leadership training experiences can develop such practices and capacities in leaders?

The results reported in this chapter of the analysis of data obtained from the first phase of the data collection provide the findings that address aspects of research questions 1, 2, 4, and 5.

Teacher and Principal Questionnaire

From an extensive review of the mainly nonschool literature, we defined learning organizations as schools that: employed processes of environmental scanning; developed shared goals; established collaborative teaching and learning environments; encouraged initiatives and risk taking; regularly reviewed all aspects related to and influencing the work of the school; recognized and reinforced good work; and, provided opportunities for continuing professional development. This definition provided the constructs representing organizational learning items incorporated in the questionnaire. Subsequently, the questionnaire was piloted, revised and then administered to teachers and principals in our study.

School management variables were also included in the questionnaire. These were drawn from items developed by Leithwood and Jantzi, Centre for Leadership Development, University of Toronto. Examples of the variables used were: processes employed for effective staffing; instructional support available for teachers; proximity of administrators to the core work of the school (i.e., teaching); the level of community focus in the school; and teachers' perceptions of the degree of school autonomy secured by the administrators.

The sources of leadership in the school and the principal's leadership practices were identified. The questionnaire items were informed by the transformational model of leadership (Duke & Leithwood, 1994). In relation to the principal, the following categories of items were included: setting the tone of the school; the nature of the decision-making struc-

Table 1. Conceptual and Operational
Definitions of the Six Factor Model for Leader

Construct	Description
Vision and Goals	Works toward whole staff consensus in establishing school priorities and communicates these priorities and goals to students and staff giving a sense of overall purpose. Ex. The principal helps clarify the specific meaning of the school's mission in terms of its practical implications for programs and instruction.
Culture	Promotes an atmosphere of caring and trust among staff, sets a respectful tone for interaction with students and demonstrates a willingness to change his or her practices in the light of new understandings. Ex. The principal shows respect for staff by treating us as professionals.
Structure	Supports a school structure that promotes participative decision making, delegating and distributing leadership to encourage teacher autonomy for making decisions. Ex. The principal distributes leadership broadly among the staff representing various viewpoints in leadership positions.
Intellectual Stimulation	Encourages staff to reflect on what they are trying to achieve with students and how they are doing it; facilitates opportunities for staff to learn from each other and models continual learning in his or her own practice. Ex. The principal is a source of new ideas for my professional learning.
Individual Support	Provides moral support, shows appreciation for the work of individual staff and takes their opinion into account when making decisions. Ex. The principal provides moral support by making me feel appreciated for my contribution to the school.
Performance Expectation	Has high expectations for teachers and for students and expects staff to be effective and innovative. Ex.The principal has high expectations for us as professionals.

tures; the level of individualized support and intellectual stimulation provided; and, establishment of school direction, goals, and performance expectations.

Sample

The teacher and principal survey yielded a total of 2,503 responses. A random sample, stratified by size, of 50 schools was drawn in South Australia. This represented just over half of the public secondary schools in South Australia. The Tasmanian sample consisted of 46 schools repre-

Table 2*.   Conceptual and Operational Definitions of
the Four Factor Model for Organizational Learning

Construct	Description
Collaborative Climate	Schools where collaboration is the norm and discussions amongst colleagues are open and candid; staff seek information to improve their work and use colleagues as resources. Ex. There is ongoing professional dialogue among teachers.
Taking Initiatives and Risks	Schools where staff are empowered to make decisions and school structures support staff initiatives; school administrators are open to change and reward staff for taking the initiative. Ex. People feel free to experiment and take risks.
Improving School Practices	School staff participate in school-level policy decisions and have a shared sense of direction; current practices are reviewed and problems are solved by teachers and administrators working together; information is shared with parents and the community; the climate promotes cooperative learning. Ex. Effectiveness of the teaching program is regularly monitored.
Professional Development	Staff are encouraged to develop professionally; other schools, external advisers and professional reading are sources of learning; developing skills of working in teams and sharing knowledge is seen as important. Ex. Adequate time is provided for professional development.

Notes: *The Organizational Learning and Leadership questionnaire has been developed to provide information on the school as a learning organization, the nature and source of the leadership in the school and the principal's leadership practices. The full questionnaire is available from the first author, email halia.silins@flinders.edu.au

senting the full population of secondary schools. The analysis of the data from a total of 96 schools has proceeded in three stages.

Stages of Analysis

Stage 1 involved the exploration and identification of the nature of the teacher, principal and student information for South Australia and Tasmania. Version 6.0.3 SPSS statistical software package was used to develop working files containing the data from teacher and student questionnaires for each state. Several data reduction procedures were employed including: rating scale analysis from the Quest program (Adams & Khoo, 1993) to reduce the number of questionnaire items to be analyzed to those that fitted the Rasch scale and to establish unidimensionality for each section of the two questionnaires; exploratory factor analysis with principal component extraction and varimax rotation to help develop scales underlying the constructs to be used in further analysis; and principal component extraction to confirm scales. Reliability estimates for each scale were calculated using Cronbach alpha. All scales indicated a high reliability in the range of alpha = 0.74 – 0.92.

Stage 2 involved an empirical investigation of the dimensions of the hypothesised variables. The structure of the Leader construct was confirmed and defined in terms of a six factor nested model. The six factors are operationally defined and presented in Table 1. Also, the development of the OL construct was confirmed as a four factor nested model. The four factors are operationally defined and presented in Table 2. Empirical investigations of the dimensions of these two hypothesised variables were carried out using confirmatory factor analyses and analysis of covariance structures employing the maximum likelihood estimation process with the LISREL 8 program (Jöreskog & Sörbom, 1989). The procedures and results of this process have been reported elsewhere (Silins, Zarins, & Mulford, 1998; Mulford & Silins, 1998).

Stage 3 involved the development of a Path Model. This development included the formulation of hypothesised models to test the nature and strength of the relationships between the variables included in the study and to understand the interactive nature of leadership and OL. A hypothesized model, Model 1, was developed using path analysis with latent variables to investigate the nature and strength of all the relationships in the model and to address aspects of the research questions of the project. In summary, the main aims of developing a path model were:

- To test the construction of the latent variables from the observed or manifest variables (provided by the strength of the estimated loadings of the observed measures on the constructed variables),
- To examine causal relationships between the constructs or latent variables of the model (provided by the strength of the path coefficients between the variables in the model),
- To estimate the magnitudes of the hypothesized relationships (provided by the estimates of variance explained for each variable).

In Model 1, 11 latent variables (described in Table 3) were constructed from the manifest variables, based on questionnaire items, and used to examine the influence of school, leader, and teacher variables on OL as an outcome measure. The selection of variables for the study was made taking into account the review of the leadership and educational restructuring literature and the preliminary correlation analysis. OL was defined by four factors (Collaborative Climate, Taking Initiatives and Risks, Improving School Practices and Professional Development).

A combination of contextual external and internal influences on the organization and functioning of schools as learning organizations were selected from the teacher data base. External predictors were school profile (size in 1997, area [metropolitan or country], and principal's gender) and teacher profile (years in education, years at their school, age and gender). The internal organization predictors were based on teacher responses and included: resources (perceived availability of resources to improve staff effectiveness); leader (principal's transformational practices); community focus (the extent that the school is working with the community); distributed leadership (a profile of the identified sources of leadership in the school); staffing policies (the extent to which staff are placed in areas of competence and consulted); active involvement (evidence of administrators' interest in student progress and extent of positive presence in the school); staff valued (the extent to which new staff are welcomed and all staff contributions valued equally); and school autonomy (extent of teacher satisfaction with leadership and the level of autonomy secured for the school by the principal).

Path Analysis

The path model was tested using a latent variables partial least squares path analysis (PLSPATH) procedure at the school level of analysis with 96 schools (Sellin & Keeves, 1997). The initial design of the model was fully recursive wherein each variable was positioned as it was predicted to influence the succeeding variables in the model. Along with the contextual factors in Model 1 (School Profile and Teacher Profile), resources, leader factors, and the internal school organization factors depicted as community focus, distributed leadership, staffing policies, active involvement, staff valued and school autonomy were hypothesised to influence organizational learning. Resources, leader, community focus, distributed leadership, staffing policies, active involvement, staff valued and school autonomy were depicted as mediating variables by their placement between the antecedent external variables and the criterion variable, OL.

Analysis proceeded in two stages. First, the outer model was refined by successively deleting the manifest (direct measure) variables that did not contribute to explaining the latent variable (construct). All measures that had a loading (in the same sense as a principal components analysis) of at least twice their standard error were retained. Once the outer model was stable, the inner model was refined. Again, all paths were deleted where the path coefficient (similar to regression coefficient) was less than twice its standard error.

The final model, Figure 1, illustrates the variables that exerted an effect on both the outcome variable and the other latent variables. Table 4 reports the direct, indirect and total effects along with the jackknife standard errors and correlations.

The School as the Unit of Analysis

The LOLSO Project's research focus is on school level factors associated with leadership, OL and student outcomes. School characteristics such as size of school, school area (metropolitan or country) and gender of the principal as well as teacher profiles consisting of years of educational experience, years at their school, age and gender were included in this

Table 3. Description of Variables in the Model of
Factors Influencing Organizational Learning—Model 1

Variables description and coding	Mean	S D	*PLS Estimation Loading
SCHOOL PROFILE [outward mode]			
Area (country or metropolitan)	.56	.50	.86
Size in 1997	632	283	.90
Principal's Gender (deleted)			
TEACHER PROFILE [outward mode]			
Years in Education	4.6	.65	.98
Years at their School (deleted)			
Age	3.04	.49	.97
Teacher's Gender (deleted)			
RESOURCES [unity mode]			
Resource to improve staff effectiveness	3.26	.36	1.0
LEADER [outward mode]			
Teacher level of agreement on six aspects of principal's leadership practices in the school.			
1=strongly disagree; 2=mostly disagree; 3=in between; 4=mostly agree; 5=strongly agree.			
Goal	3.57	.44	.98
Culture	3.63	.54	.96
Structure	3.68	.40	.95
Intellectual Stimulation	3.34	.43	.95
Individualised Support	3.50	.50	.94
Performance Expectation	3.89	.36	.88
COMMUNITY FOCUS [outward mode]			
Teacher level of agreement on four aspects of working with the school community.			
1=strongly disagree; 2=mostly disagree; 3=in between; 4=mostly agree; 5=strongly agree			
Administrators sensitive to community (Ld5)	3.73	.37	.95
Administrators work with community reps. (Ld8)	3.67	.40	.95
Administrators incorporate community values (Ld18)	3.44	.41	.95
Productive working relations with community (Ld20)	3.47	.44	.95
DISTRIBUTED LEADERSHIP [outward mode]			
Teacher identification of the leadership sources in the school and their strength of influence.			
1=minimal; 2=moderate; 3=considerable; 4=very strong.			
Principal	3.30	.46	.31
Deputy principal	3.04	.44	.46
Department heads/coordinators	2.84	.27	.52
Individual teachers	2.68	.26	.61
Teacher committees/teams	2.57	.28	.76
Whole staff working together	2.64	.41	.79
School counsellors	2.17	.46	.52
Students	2.08	.27	.65
School Council	2.20	.34	.59
Union representative(s)	2.03	.43	.34
Parents/other community members	2.08	.30	.69

(continued)

Table 3.   (Continued)

Variables description and coding	Mean	S D	*PLS Estimation Loading
STAFFING POLICIES [outward mode] Teacher level of agreement on three aspects of staffing. 1=strongly disagree; 2=mostly disagree; 3=in between; 4=mostly agree; 5=strongly agree			
Staff placed in areas of competence (Ld6)	3.40	.46	.91
Staffing is fair and equitable (Ld10)	3.20	.46	.87
Staff consulted on staffing requirements (Ld13)	3.05	.56	.87
ACTIVE INVOLVEMENT [outward mode] Teacher level of agreement on eight aspects of administrative involvement in the school's activities. 1=strongly disagree; 2=mostly disagree; 3=in between; 4=mostly agree; 5=strongly agree			
Administrators have positive presence (Ld2)	3.64	.58	.94
Administrators visible (Ld7)	3.75	.57	.93
Administrators easily accessible (Ld12)	3.92	.47	.93
Administrators interested (Ld16)	3.50	.50	.96
Administrators observe or inquire (Ld14)	2.71	.52	.89
Administrators work with teachers (Ld17)	3.00	.44	.93
Administrators discuss educational issues (Ld22)	3.86	.33	.89
Administrators review student progress (Ld21)	3.54	.42	.86
STAFF VALUED [outward mode] Teacher level of agreement on three aspects of staff being valued. 1=strongly disagree; 2=mostly disagree; 3=in between; 4=mostly agree; 5=strongly agree			
Induction process for new staff (Ld3)	3.28	.68	.54
New staff valued and welcomed (Ld15)	3.78	.39	.91
Staff contributions valued (Ld19)	3.23	.46	.91
SCHOOL AUTONOMY [outward mode] Teacher level of agreement on perceived school autonomy and satisfaction with school leadership. 1=strongly disagree; 2=mostly disagree; 3=in between; 4=mostly agree; 5=strongly agree			
Secured high degree autonomy	3.50	.40	.94
Teacher satisfaction with leadership	2.56	.39	.96
ORGANIZATIONAL LEARNING [outward mode] Teacher level of agreement on four outcomes related to organizational learning. 1=strongly disagree; 2=mostly disagree; 3=in between; 4=mostly agree; 5=strongly agree			
Collaborative climate	3.62	.32	.88
Taking initiatives and risks	3.20	.33	.94
Improving school practices	3.41	.35	.95
Professional development	3.22	.22	.90

Note: *PLS Path Estimation reported as factor loadings

study. The SES and Home Background variables were taken from the student data that were then aggregated to the school level. The school is a well-defined and logical unit of analysis for addressing the research questions in this study.

Research in the field is often associated with constraints, which have to be accommodated if the research is to proceed. At the time of this study, teachers in South Australia were involved in industrial action and they were particularly reluctant to be identified on the questionnaires. Schools were more likely to participate if students and teachers remained anonymous. Analysis of the data was restricted at the outset to the school level since information that would allow complete nesting of the student data within teachers, and teachers within schools, was not obtainable.

School level models have been presented to indicate the way in which teachers, students and principals work and think in the school. Aggregation to the school level has an inherent meaning in this study since the teachers and leader are providing information about the same leader and his or her operation in the school. Aggregation bias will inflate the intensity of the same level relationships in the model although the relative strengths of the variables included in the model will probably be preserved.

In order to counteract the effects of aggregation bias that are present, a parallel individual-level teacher model was developed and compared with the school level teacher model. An examination of the nature and strength of the relationships in this teacher level data model indicated a picture not inconsistent with the relationships in the school level model. Therefore, the school level models were accepted as valid representations of what goes on in Australian secondary schools.

Profile of Secondary Schools as Learning Organizations—Model 1

Table 3 reports the significant estimation loadings of the observed variables for each construct in Model 1. The strength of the loadings indicates which of the manifest variables predominated in the definition of their construct. In these results for the final Model 1, school profile was defined as the size of the school in 1997 and the school area. The gender of the principal was not significant in this model. The strength and positive sign of the loadings indicate that the larger, metropolitan schools predominated. Similarly for teacher profile, the genders of the teachers and the years at their school were dropped from the model because they did not satisfy the criterion for inclusion. The significant characteristics of the teachers in this model are their years of experience and their age. For all the other constructs in the model, the observed variables contributed significantly.

Table 4 reports the nature and strength of the relationships between the 11 latent variables in Model 1. Five variables emerged as direct predictors of OL: School Autonomy (p=0.35)[1], Staff Valued (p=0.32), Leader (p=0.16), Distributed Leadership (p=0.15) and School Profile (p=-0.12). Resources (t=0.65)[2] and Leader (t=0.63) emerged as the two dominant factors in terms of their total effect on Organizational Learning. However, Active Involvement (t=0.44), School Profile (t=0.37), School Autonomy (t=0.35), Distributed Leadership (t=0.34), and Staff Valued (t=0.32) contributed strongly. Community Focus

Table 4. Direct, Total and Indirect Effects and Correlations of Latent Variables Influencing Organizational Learning—Model 1

Variable	Direct Effects p	JknStd Error	Total Effects t	Indirect Effects i	Correlation r
TEACHER PROFILE $R^2 = .33$ $(d = 0.83)$ $Q^2 = .28$					
School Profile	.55	.07	.55	–	.55
RESOURCES $R^2 = .10$ $(d = 0.94)$ $Q^2 = .06$					
School Profile	–.32	.08	–.32	–	–.32
LEADER $R^2 = .53$ $(d = 0.68)$ $Q^2 = .51$					
School Profile	–	–	–.23	–.23	–.25
Resources	.73	.06	.73	–	.73
COMMUNITY FOCUS $R^2 = .61$ $(d = 0.62)$ $Q^2 = 60$					
School Profile	–	–	–.18	–.18	–.11
Resources	–	–	.57	.57	.63
Leader	.78	.03	.78	–	.78
DISTRIBUTED LEADERSHIP $R^2 = .62$ $(d = 0.62)$ $Q^2 = .58$					
School Profile	–.16	.07	–.34	–.18	–.31
Resources	.25	.09	.57	.32	.65
Leader	–	–	.43	.43	.69
Community Focus	.55	.07	.55	–	.73
STAFFING POLICIES $R^2 = .69$ $(d = 0.56)$ $Q^2 = .66$					
School Profile	–	–	–.16	–.16	–.19
Teacher Profile	.12	.06	.12	-	.06
Resources	.31	.09	.71	.40	.71
Leader	.29	.11	.55	.26	.76
Community Focus	.33	.09	.33	–	.75
ACTIVE INVOLVEMENT $R^2 = .87$ $(d = 0.36)$ $Q^2 = .85$					
School Profile	–	–	–.23	–.23	–.29
Teacher Profile	–	–	.03	.03	–.10
Resources	.16	.06	.77	.61	.77
Leader	.60	.07	.73	.13	.90
Community Focus	–	–	.08	.01	.80
Staffing Policies	.24	.06	.24	–	.81
STAFF VALUED $R^2 = .69$ $(d = 0.56)$ $Q^2 = .67$					
School Profile	–	–	–.24	-.24	-.20
Teacher Profile	–	–	.02	.02	-.03
Resources	–	–	.62	.62	.71
Leader	–	–	.55	.55	.75
Community Focus	–	–	.23	.23	.70
Distributed Leadership	.34	.08	.34	–	.73
Staffing Policies	–	–	.13	.13	.74
Active Involvement	.56	.09	.56	–	.80
SCHOOL AUTONOMY $R^2 = .83$ $(d = 0.41)$ $Q^2 = .82$					
School Profile	–	–	–.24	–.24	–.19

(continued)

Table 4. (Continued)

Teacher Profile	–	–	.02	.02	–.09
Resources	–	–	.70	.70	.73
Leader	–	–	.64	.64	.85
Community Focus	–	–	.18	.18	.80
Distributed Leadership	.22	.07	.22	–	.75
Staffing Policies	–	–	.18	.18	.78
Active Involvement	.74	.06	.74	–	.90
ORGANIZATIONAL LEARNING	R^2= .87	(d= 0.36)	Q^2= .86		
School Profile	–.12	.04	–.37	–.25	–.33
Teacher Profile	–	–	.01	.01	–.20
Resources	–	–	.65	.65	.77
Leader	.16	.07	.63	.47	.84
Community Focus	–	–	.22	.22	.75
Distributed Leadership	.15	.06	.34	.19	.80
Staffing Policies	–	–	.11	.11	.74
Active Involvement	–	–	.44	.44	.86
Staff Valued	.32	.06	.32	–	.85
School Autonomy	.35	.09	.35	–	.87

Notes: JknStd refers to the Jackknife Standard Error of the Direct Effects path coefficient.
d is the residual standard error.

(t=0.22) had a moderate and indirect effect whereas Staffing Policies had the smallest, significant total (t = 0.11) and indirect effect on OL. Teacher Profile had no influence on OL.

The hypothesized initial model was tested and resulted in Model 1 (Figure 1). The combined effect of variables in this model explains 87 per cent of the variance of OL, with a Q^2 = 0.86 indicating a very stable outcome measure and stable model. It is acknowledged that the estimates in analyses are inflated because of aggregation bias. However, the parallel individual level model explained 70 percent of the variance of OL which was associated with a high Q^2 = 0.70 indicating stability of the outcome measure and model. These measures indicate that the school level model results can be interpreted with some confidence and Model 1 can be accepted as a well-defined model.

Model 1 illustrates the nature and strength of the significant relationships between the variables in this study. It offers a snapshot of Australian secondary schools conceptualized as learning organizations and presents a profile of secondary schools summarizing the significant characteristics and processes, and their interrelationships, that promote OL.

A closer examination of this profile reveals negative paths associated with the external predictor, School Profile. This indicates that the smaller schools (less than 600 students) rather than the larger schools (above 600 students) are more likely to be identified as achieving OL outcomes. Staff of these smaller secondary schools perceive their schools as having sufficient resources to improve staff

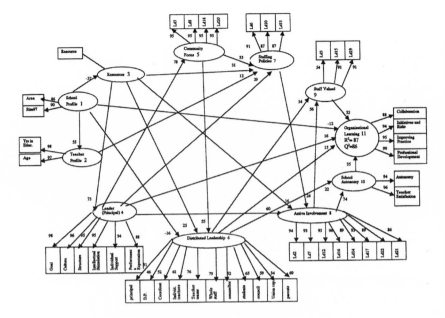

Figure 1. Model of the Relationships Between
Variables Influencing Organizational Learning

effectiveness. This perception is a strong, indirect predictor of OL and operates through its strongest association with the principal's leadership style. These perceptions seem contrary to the reality of resourcing schools since it would be more likely that the larger schools attract more government funding. Perceptions of adequate resourcing are also associated with staffing policies that are consultative and that take account of teachers' competencies.

Principals who practise transformational leadership emerge as strong promoters of OL outcomes. Furthermore, when transformational leaders establish a community focus within their school then these factors (i.e., smaller schools, adequate resources, transformational leadership, and community focus) result in a greater distribution of leadership responsibilities throughout the school community (including students and parents). This distributed leadership promotes OL outcomes directly as well as through helping staff feel valued, having staff perceive the principal as securing a high degree of autonomy for the school and engendering an overall satisfaction with the leadership in the school.

This profile represents a secondary school that is successful at promoting OL. Elements of this profile are referred to in the model which is used to address the research questions in more detail.

ANSWERING THE RESEARCH QUESTIONS

What are the identifying characteristics of secondary schools where OL is promoted and facilitated?

Model 1 clearly indicates the four categories of characteristics that identify Australian secondary schools as learning organizations. These are described in Table 2 as characteristics:

- indicative of a collaborative climate; schools where staff collaboration is the norm;
- that facilitate taking initiatives and risks; schools where staff feel free to experiment;
- that support improving school practices; schools where the staff review programs and performance regularly;
- that encourage professional development; schools where staff engage in professional development activities.

An examination of the estimated loadings of these four factors, provided in Table 3, defining the variable OL, indicates that the four observed variables all loaded strongly on this latent construct. These four categories of characteristics were empirically confirmed as being valid and reliable representations of what is understood by the OL construct in Australian secondary schools.

What conditions inside and outside Australian high schools account for variations in OL? That is, why are some schools seen as learning organizations and others are not?

Model 1 indicates the nature and strength of the relationships between the variables predicting OL. Size of school was a significant characteristic of the school in this model. The principal's gender was not a factor in promoting OL. The larger metropolitan schools, staffed by experienced and ageing teachers, did not provide the environment most conducive for OL. The smaller metropolitan and country schools were more likely to perceive that sufficient resources were available to promote staff effectiveness. This perception of sufficiency was usually associated with a school principal employing transformational practices. Such practices were instrumental in establishing school characteristics that promoted OL.

The principal in this model was visible, accessible, and interested in student progress. This active involvement in the core work of the school helped to generate teacher satisfaction with leadership and a sense of school autonomy, which was strongly associated with OL. The principal's interest and involvement in the school also established a school climate in which staff contributions were valued and OL fostered. The principal often established strong links and a productive working relationship with the community. Responsiveness to the community supported a greater distribution of leadership in the school that influenced OL directly as well as indirectly through valuing staff contributions, influencing teacher satisfaction with leadership, and establishing a high degree of school autonomy.

The evidence from this research has demonstrated clearly that the predominant conditions accounting for variations in OL between Australian secondary schools are perceived availability of resources together with a principal skilled in transformational leadership and actively involved in the core work of the school. Effects of these conditions are mediated and supported in schools where teachers are satisfied with the leadership and experience higher levels of school autonomy. A strong condition explaining the variation in OL between schools was the process of distributing leadership in the school so that a wider range of sources of leadership was identified by teachers, such as whole school staff working together, teacher teams, students, parents and other members of the community.

What proportion of OL is accounted for by school leadership?

The best estimate of the proportion of OL accounted for by school leadership in Model 1 can be calculated by multiplying the path coefficient of the direct effect of leadership on OL by their correlation. The proportion of OL accounted for by the principal (Leader) is 13 percent (0.16 x 0.84). The variable Distributed Leadership represents all other sources of leadership in the school. The proportion of OL accounted for by the whole school staff, teacher teams, community members and students is 12 percent (0.15 x 0.80). The total proportion of OL accounted for by the total sources of school leadership is 25 percent. This provides clear evidence for the strong contribution of school leadership to explaining the variation in OL between schools.

What leadership practices promote OL in schools?

Evidence for the key role of transformational leadership practices in the internal processes of the school has been provided by other studies (Leithwood, Tomlinson, & Genge, 1996; Silins, 1994a). This research has supported six factors as promoting OL. These six factors correspond reasonably closely to the transformational leadership concept developed by Leithwood and his collaborators. These are described in Table 2 as: Vision and Goals; Culture; Structure; Intellectual Stimulation; Individual Support; and Performance Expectation. An examination of the estimation loadings provided in Table 3 of the six factors defining the variable, Leader, indicates that the six observed variables all load strongly on this latent construct. All six factors contributed to defining the kind of leadership practices that promote OL.

CONCLUSION

Peters is right when he says that the core paradox in a world of massive change "is fostering (creating) internal stability in order to encourage the pursuit of constant change" (1987, p. 395). If educational reforms are not to continue to be thwarted by the robust nature of established school practice, then stability for change, moving ahead without losing their roots, becomes the challenge (Mulford, 1998). This challenge may be able to be met in education and elsewhere by focusing on a change strategy where learning comes to be seen as "the single most important resource for organizational renewal in the postmodern age" (Hargreaves, 1995, p. 11). In this strategy, the school is viewed and treated as a learning organization.

The range of factors that contribute to OL, and what it means for an Australian secondary school to provide stability or equilibrium (Leithwood & Louis, 1998) through OL, is now clearer. The results of the LOLSO Project confirm and sharpen the newly evolving research literature on OL in schools and, in particular, the contribution of leadership to OL. We identified four factors that contribute to OL in Australian secondary schools. These four factors are collaborative climate, taking initiatives and risks, improving school practices, and professional development.

First, the collaborative climate factor confirms that the change in paradigm is away from the teacher in his or her own classroom to the development of learning communities which value differences, support critical reflection and encourage members to question, challenge and debate teaching and learning issues (Peters, Dobbins, & Johnson, 1996). Our findings agree with others (eg, Lieberman, 1988; Newmann et al., 1996; Leithwood & Louis, 1998) who have concluded that collective responsibility for student learning, in addition to improved technical teaching practices and curriculum, is fundamental to educational reform. In brief, de-privatization of teacher practice is the key. De-privatization is most likely to occur in a transparent, inclusive, collaborative school climate. A climate where there is a spirit of openness, honesty, and trust. A climate where staff are valued, committed and mutually support one another.

Second, we show that OL involves taking initiatives and risks. It means acting rather than always reacting. Support, including reward and organizational structures, is used to promote inquiry, experimentation, and initiative. We believe that this finding counters a major criticism of the nonschool OL literature in its contention (Gheradi, 1999, p. 103) that the field of OL has been "developed and institutionalized as problem-driven, as the production of instrumental knowledge." Our findings show that OL is not just problem-driven but also involves what Turner (1991) coined as "learning in the face of mystery." Learning in the face of mystery is important because it acts to reinforce the importance of the de-privatization of teacher practice.

Our belief is reinforced by the third of four factors defining OL in secondary schools, improving school practices. Regular and critical monitoring of the environment and examination of current practices, both in the light of achieving school goals and the relevance of those goals ensures the school is continuously learning. It also ensures the school does not feel constrained to look "outside the box"—outside its existing goals, processes and structures (Weick & Westley, 1996).

Fourth, we show that OL means recognizing and acting on the need for staff to be continuously learning. This includes learning how to work, and learn, in teams. Ongoing professional development involving readings and the use of internal and external expertise is of high priority.

A condition of note explaining the variation in OL between secondary schools is the process of distributing leadership in the school so that a wider range of sources of leadership is identified by teachers. These sources of leadership include whole school staff working together, teacher teams, students, parents and other members of the community. We suspect that there are strong implications here for a need in secondary schools to work across the traditional subject department boundaries. Distributive leadership contributed directly to OL and indirectly through its contribution to staff feeling valued and to beliefs that the school had secured a high degree of autonomy.

The direct and indirect contributions of leadership to OL in secondary schools are not only becoming clearer but are shown to be significant. The predominant direct conditions accounting for variations in OL between Australian secondary schools are size of school together with a principal skilled in transformational leadership and actively involved in the core work of the school. Along with Leithwood, Jantzi, and Steinbach (1999), we found that the transformational leadership practices included identifying and articulating a vision, fostering the acceptance of group goals, structuring the school to enhance participation in decisions, providing intellectual stimulation, and conveying high expectations. The principal's leadership embraced the active involvement of others in leadership roles and promoted the commitment of all school leaders to the core work of the school and to being visible and accessible; these elements of leadership proved to be important predictors of OL.

OL offers a way for a school to make sense of paradox, to ride the "see saws" of change (Handy, 1994), and to establish and maintain a sense of connectedness, direction, and continuity. OL offers the potential of stability for change, an opportunity for schools and the societies they serve to move ahead without losing their roots. In other words, it is a change strategy with the potential to address current change agendas. As such, it is a change strategy that continues to be worthy of support, further development, and analysis.[3]

NOTES

1. p = Direct Effects path coefficient, see Table 4.
2. t = Total Effects, see Table 4.
3. At least three areas of analysis identified in this chapter deserve further attention: the sequential and developmental nature of the identifying characteristics of OL; the importance of partnership with bodies external to the school, especially central office; and the relationship between OL and student outcomes. Early data on the last of these areas, student outcomes, can be found in Silins, Zarins, and Mulford (1999).

REFERENCES

Adams, R.J., & Khoo, S.T. (1993). *Quest—The interactive test analysis system*. Hawthorn, Victoria: Australian Council for Educational Research.

Berends, M., Heilbrunn, J., McKelvey, C., & Sullivan, T. (1998). *Monitoring the progress of new American schools: A description of implementing schools in a longitudinal sample*. Draft series paper DRU-1935-NAS for RAND.

Bishop, P., & Mulford, B. (1999). When will they ever learn?: Another failure of centrally-imposed change. *School Leadership and Management, 19*(2), 179-187.

Blase, J. (1993). The micropolitics of effective school-based leadership: Teachers' perspectives. *Educational Administration Quarterly, 29*(2), 142-163.

Bodilly, S. (1998). *Lessons from new American schools' scale-up phase*. Santa Monica, CA: RAND.

Brown, M., Boyle, B., & Boyle, T. (1999*). Commonalities between perception and practice in models of school decision making systems in secondary schools in England and Wales*. Paper presented at the annual meeting of the American Educational Research Association, Montreal.

Chapman, J. (1997).Leading the learning community. *Leading and Managing, 3*(3), 151-170.

Deal, T., & Peterson, K. (1994). *The leadership paradox: Balancing logic and artistry in schools*. San Francisco: Jossey Bass.

Duke, D., & Leithwood, K. (1994). *Defining effective leadership for Connecticut's schools*. A monograph prepared for the Connecticut Administrator Appraisal Project, University of Connecticut, Hartford, Connecticut.

Geijsel, F., Van Den Berg, R., & Sleegers, P. (1999). The innovative capacity of schools in primary education: A qualitative study. *International Journal of Qualitative Studies in Education, 12*(2), 175-191.

Gheradi, S. (1999). Learning as problem-driven or learning in the face of mystery. *Organization Studies, 20*(1), 101-124.

Glennan, T. (1998). *New American schools after six years*. Santa Monica, CA: RAND.

Handy, C. (1994). *The age of paradox*. Boston, MA: Harvard Business School Press.

Hannay, L., & Ross, J. (1999). *Self-renewing secondary schools: The relationship between structural and cultural change*. Paper presented at the annual meeting of the American Educational Research Association, Montreal.

Hargreaves, A. (1995). Paradoxes of change: School renewal in the postmodern age. *Educational Leadership, 52*(7), 14-19.

Jöreskog, J.D., & Sörbom, D. (1989). LISREL VI: Users' reference guide. Chicago: Scientific Software.

Leithwood, K. (1992). The move toward transformational leadership. *Educational Leadership, 49*(5), 8-12.

Leithwood, K. (1993). *Contributions of transformational leadership to school restructuring*. Invited address, annual conference of the University Council for Educational Administration, Houston, Texas.

Leithwood, K. (1994). Leadership for school restructuring. *Educational Administration Quarterly, 30*(4), 498-518.

Leithwood, K., & Duke, D. (1999). A century's quest to understand school leadership. In J. Murphy & K. Louis. (Eds.), *Handbook of research on educational administration*. Washington, DC: American Educational Research Association.

Leithwood, K., & Louis, K.S. (Eds.). (1998). *Organizational learning in schools*. The Netherlands: Swets & Zeitlinger.

Leithwood, K., Jantzi, D., & Steinbach, R. (1998). Leadership and other conditions which foster organizational learning in schools. In K. Leithwood & K.S. Louis (Eds.), *Organizational learning in schools* (pp. 67-90). The Netherlands: Swets & Zeitlinger.

Leithwood, K., Jantzi, D., & Steinbach, R. (1999). *Changing leadership for changing times*. Open University Press.

Leithwood, K., Leonard, L., & Sharratt, L. (1998). Conditions fostering organizational learning in schools. *Educational Administration Quarterly, 34*(2), 243-276.

Leithwood, K., Tomlinson, D., & Genge, M. (1998). Transformational school leadership. In Leithwood, K. (Ed.), *International handbook on educational leadership* (pp. 785-840). Norwell, MA: Kluwer Academic Press.

Lieberman, A. (1988). *Building a professional culture in schools*. New York: Teachers College Press.

Limerick, B., & Nielsen, H. (Eds.). (1995). *School and community relations*. Sydney: Harcourt Brace.

Louden, W., & Wallace, J. (1994). *Too soon to tell: School restructuring and the National Schools Project*. Melbourne: Australian Council for Educational Administration Monograph No. 17.

Louis, K.S. (1994). Beyond "managed change": Rethinking how schools improve. *School Effectiveness and School Improvement, 5*(1), 2-24.

Louis, K.S., & Marks, K. (1998). Does professional community affect the classroom? Teachers work and student experiences in restructuring schools. *American Journal of Education, 106* (August), 532-575.

McLaughlin, M. (1998). Listening and learning from the field: Tales of policy implementation and situated practice. In A. Hargreaves, A. Lieberman, M. Fullan, & D. Hopkins (Eds.), *International handbook of educational change* (pp. 70-84). Dordrecht, Netherlands: Kluwer.

Mulford, B. (1994). *Shaping tomorrow's schools*. Melbourne, Victoria: Australian Council for Educational Administration Monograph No. 15.

Mulford, B. (1998). Learning organisations and change: Educational literature, research, and issues. In A. Hargreaves, A. Lieberman, M. Fullan, & D. Hopkins (Eds.), *International handbook of organizational change* (pp. 616-641). Norwell, MA: Kluwer Academic Publishers.

Mulford, W., & Silins, H. (1998). *School leadership for organizational learning and student outcomes: The LOLSO Project*. Paper presented at the 25th national conference of the Australian Council for Educational Administration, Gold Coast, Australia. September.

Mulford, W., Hogan, D., & Lamb, S. (1997). *Local school management in Tasmania: The views of principals and teachers*. Launceston: University of Tasmania.

Newmann, F., and associates. (1996). *Authentic achievement: Restructuring schools for intellectual quality*. San Francisco: Jossey-Bass.

Peters, J., Dobbins, D., and Johnson, B. (1996). *Restructuring and organizational culture*. National Schools Network Research Paper No. 4. Ryde, NSW: National Schools Network.

Peters, T. (1987). *Thriving on chaos*. London: Harper and Row.

Reitzug, U. (1994). A case study of empowering principal behavior. *American Educational Research Journal 31*(2), 283-307.

Sarason, S. (1998). *Political leadership and educational failure*. San Francisco: Jossey Bass.

Sellin, N., & Keeves, J.P. (1997). Path analysis with latent variables. In J.P. Keeves (Ed.), *Educational research, methodology, and measurement: An international handbook.* (pp. 633-640) (2nd ed.). Oxford: Pergamon Press.

Sheppard, B., & Brown, J. (1999). *Leadership approach, the new work of teachers and successful change.* Paper presented at the annual meeting of the American Educational Research Association, Montreal.

Silins, H.C. (1992). Effective leadership for school reform. *The Alberta Journal of Educational Research, 38*(4), 317-334.

Silins, H.C. (1994a). The relationship between transformational and transactional leadership and school improvement outcomes. *School Effectiveness and School Improvement, 5*(3), 272-298.

Silins, H.C. (1994b). Leadership characteristics and school improvement. *Australian Journal of Education, 38*(3), 266-281.

Silins, H., Zarins, S., & Mulford, W. (1998).*What characteristics and processes define a school as a learning organisation? Is this a useful concept for schools?* Paper presented at the national conference of the Australian Association for Research in Education, Adelaide, Australia. November.

Silins, H., Zarins, S., & Mulford, W. (1999). *Leadership for organizational learning and student outcomes—The LOLSO Project.* Paper presented at the annual meeting of the American Educational Research Association, Montreal, Canada. April.

Smylie, M., Lazarus, V., & Brownlee-Conyers, J. (1996). Instructional outcomes of school-based participative decision making. *Educational Evaluation and Policy Analysis, 18*(3), 181-198.

Turner, B. (1991). *Rethinking organizations: Organizational learning in the nineties.* Paper presented at the EFMD Research Conference, Isida, Palermo.

Van Den Berg, R., & Sleegers, P. (1996). The innovative capacity of secondary schools: A qualitative study. *International Journal of Qualitative Studies in Education, 9*(2), 201-223.

Watkins, K.E., & Marsick, V. (1993). *Sculpting the learning organization.* San Francisco: Jossey-Bass.

Weick, K., & Westley, F. (1996). Oganizational learning: Affirming an oxymoron. In S. Clegg, C. Hardy, & W. Nord (Eds.), *Handbook of organizational studies* (pp. 440-458). Thousand Oaks, CA: Sage Publications.

CHAPTER 13

THE TRANSFORMATION OF SECONDARY SCHOOLS INTO LEARNING ORGANIZATIONS

Bruce Sheppard and Jean Brown

By most accounts, secondary schools are troubled organizations. Unlike their elementary counterparts, they can no longer lay claim to a clear set of widely endorsed purposes such as the development of basic literacy and numeracy skills. Nor are they assumed, as in the case of colleges and universities, to be a source of practical employment skills, professional expertise, or esoteric knowledge. In an era preoccupied with "value addedness," their claims to legitimacy are regularly called into question (e.g., Sarason, 1990; Sergiovanni, 1995). This is especially so in the face of radically new, and exceptionally ambitious expectations for twenty-first-century students. These students, some argue, must be educated to become "the new professionals, the highly trained

Advances in Research and Theories of School
Management and Educational Policy, Volume 4, pages 293-314.
Copyright © 2000 by JAI Press Inc.
All rights of reproduction in any form reserved.
ISBN: 0-7623-0024-8

symbolic analysts or knowledge workers who manage the new high-tech information economy" (Rifkin, 1995, p. 174).

Secondary schools are not known for their ability to respond flexibly and productively to the need for change, whatever its source. Indeed, many view them as intractable (Deal, 1990). This is not a view we share, however. Rather, we believe that earlier approaches to change in secondary schools have been ill conceived, and that the inadequacy of these approaches can be explained in part by a superficial understanding of how they function. From a psychological perspective, earlier efforts to change these institutions have been premised on behavioristic or "empty vessel" conceptions of the collective learning that must take place in any organization for successful change; tell them what they need to know and do and they will do it.

But, to continue with a psychological point of view, what are needed are approaches to change premised on more contemporary understandings of human learning. A constructivist (e.g., Prawat & Peterson, 1999) view of collective learning, for example, would account for an organization's responses to change in terms of such variables as perception, knowledge acquisition, organizational memory, procedural and declarative knowledge structures, and the like (e.g., see Scott, this volume). Using the conceptual tools associated with this view of learning, we can begin to appreciate some of the reasons for differences in elementary and secondary school responses to change. For example, a significant proportion of the knowledge structures stored in the collective memory of secondary school staffs are associated with, or informed by, individual academic disciplines (Siskin, 1991), and the pedagogical content knowledge (Shulman, 1987) required to teach them well. Structures such as these are among some of the most central intellectual tools used by secondary school staffs, individually and collectively, to interpret the challenges they face, and to make sense of the changes advocated by those outside of the organization.

The vast majority of secondary reform efforts of the past 15 years have had little to do with disciplinary conceptions of secondary school teachers' work. Instead, they have been about such matters as school and classroom structures, numbers of course credits, assessment practices, and integrated curriculum. It is not surprising, as a consequence, that these reforms often have been dismissed as trivial, wrong headed, or irrelevant. Before this view is likely to change, there will need to be significant modifications in the intellectual tools used by secondary school staffs to interpret the challenges they face and make sense of others' proposals for reform.

Figuring out how this happens was the main purpose of the study summarized in this chapter. We wanted to know in some detail how secondary school staffs gradually adapt the collective intellectual tools they use to make sense of their work and the changes that need to be made in the nature of that work. We also wanted to know about the role of leadership in this transformation; how important to the collective learning of secondary staffs is school leadership, what are the sources of that leadership, and which forms of leadership are most helpful?

FRAMEWORK

We could find little prior theory sufficiently well developed and tested to provide detailed guidance to our research. So, in spite of our initial preferences for what Miles and Huberman refer to as "tight research designs" (1994), we adopted a quasi-grounded approach to the study (Strauss & Corbin, 1994). The "quasi" part of this otherwise grounded approach included two sets of ideas, one about the role of teachers in developing schools as learning organizations, and one about the types of leadership that would be helpful for that task.

Teachers

Propositions about the role of teachers in transforming schools into learning organizations were borrowed most directly from Fullan (1995) but also were quite similar to Senge's (1990) learning disciplines. In a brief article, Fullan makes a compelling theoretical case for teachers becoming increasingly more expert in six domains of knowledge which he describes as follows:

- *Teaching and learning*: Focused on the technical core of schooling, this domain is about what Senge (1990) would call the discipline of "mental models" as it concerns theories of learning, disciplinary knowledge, how diversity in the student population affects such learning, uses of technology and other matters related to being an effective classroom teacher;
- *Collaboration*: With this domain, closely akin to Senge's (1990) "team learning" discipline, Fullan argues for the importance of teachers building "collaborative work cultures inside and outside the school," and "assuming direct responsibility for changing the norms and practices of the entire school" (p. 233);
- *Context*: Fullan argues that, as part of this domain, teachers need to become experts in relation to parents, their local communities, the businesses and other agencies in those communities, as well as the broader directions being considered by governments. This entails broadening and deepening teachers' mental models;
- *Change processes*: Teachers, Fullan argues, are always in the midst of usually complex change processes. They should know more about these processes, especially how to manage them in ways that are productive for their schools and students;

- *Continuous learning*: This domain, Senge's (1990) "personal mastery" discipline, is about remaining continuously engaged in the learning identified in the other five domains;
- *Moral purpose*: Closely related to Senge's (1990) discipline of "shared vision," this domain calls for teachers to develop and maintain a collective commitment to "making a difference in the lives of students, especially the disadvantaged" (p. 234).

These ideas about teachers' roles in organizational learning informed some of our data collection and analysis.

Leadership

Approaches to leadership that appear to support the development of learning organizations emphasize the need to move away from technical, hierarchical, and rational models of such leadership toward more culturally sensitive, collaborative approaches in which, for example, teachers are viewed as partners (Barksdale, 1998; Blase, 1993; Brown, 1995; Caldwell, 1997; Handy, 1994; Hargreaves & Evans, 1997; Leithwood, 1994; Sheppard, 1996). These forms of leadership are referred to as "transformational" by some. One model of such leadership developed in school contexts by Leithwood and his colleagues (e.g., Leithwood, Jantzi, & Steinbach, 1999) helped guide this study. The eight dimensions or categories of leadership practices which appeared in Leithwood (1995) were used to frame some of our survey questions as well as to guide the analysis of some of our qualitative data. These dimensions included:

- develops a widely shared vision for the school
- builds consensus about school goals and priorities
- holds high performance expectations
- models behavior
- provides individualized support
- provides intellectual stimulation
- strengthens school culture
- builds collaborative cultures

METHOD

Sample Selection

Data were collected in two moderately sized high schools, subsequently referred to by the pseudonyms "Vision Collegiate" and "Town Pride Secondary School," located in two districts in Newfoundland. These schools were selected on the basis of their reputations as innovative schools. Both were provincial and national leaders in many areas of curriculum and school management. Both were particularly well known for their educational uses of technology, possessed leading-edge equipment, and were supported by corporate and community partnerships. The principals of both schools had received provincial and national recognition for their roles. Vision Collegiate had 37 teachers and 618 students; Town Pride Secondary School had 40 teachers and 710 students.

A total of 14 interviews were conducted with teachers and administrators at Town Pride Secondary School, and 20 interviews at Vision Collegiate. Documents reviewed for the study included staff meeting minutes, school improvement committee minutes, school improvement plans, newspaper clippings, daily school announcements, and school academic achievement reports. In addition, a leadership survey measuring practices associated with Leithwood's dimensions of transformational leadership was administered to the entire school staff. Protocols for the interviews and document analysis reflected Fullan's six domains of teacher learning and Leithwood's conception of transformational leadership.

Analysis

The primary procedures for data analysis were those specified by Miles and Huberman (1994) for the development of causal networks. After being condensed, field notes along with interview transcriptions and school documents were content analyzed. Survey data also were summarized and used in the development of the causal networks. Together, the networks and the narratives tell "the story" of change and organizational learning in the two schools, with special attention to roles of teachers and those in formal leadership positions.

To create the causal network for each school, we first organized the raw data for each school by "events" and "states" that provided evidence of either change or contribution to change. An event-state matrix for each school was constructed from these data without explicit attention to the ideas loosely framing the study: this was the most fully grounded portion of our work. Data in this form then were presented to the entire teaching staff of the schools for feedback, correction, and verification. Following this feedback, the causal networks for each school were constructed. Drafts of the networks were shared with the school principals and one teacher at each school, allowing for further correction and verification.

Results

The causal networks for each school which are summarized in Figures 1 and 2 consist of a series of concrete events arranged chronologically and divided into time periods labeled Origins, Iteration 1, Iteration 2, and Iteration 3. In addition to events, states (conditions such as "district dissatisfaction") which cut across the time periods were included in the networks. Leadership influences are evident

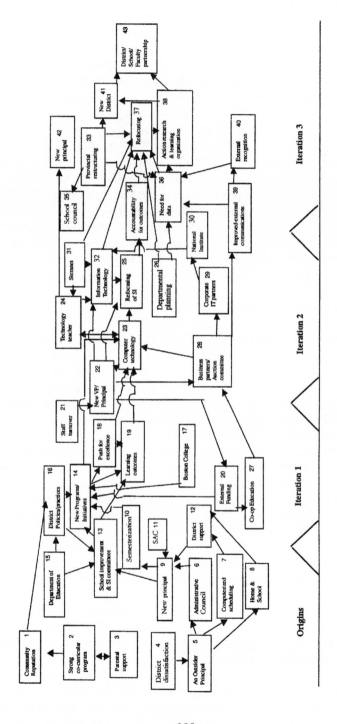

Figure 1. Causal Network for Town Pride High School

throughout both causal networks. Narrative descriptions of the causal networks included below refer to the numerals associated with each variable in the networks.

The Story of Change and Learning at Town Pride High School

Origins

The causal network displayed in Figure 1 reveals that teachers in this school demonstrated knowledge and skills consistent with Fullan's six domains. From the beginning (origins) of the period included in our study, there was evidence of connections with the outside community. For many years prior to 1986, Town Pride High School had established a reputation (1) as a leader in the field of choral performance and in various sports (2). It enjoyed strong parental and community support (3) for these co-curricular components and was viewed by many teachers as an elite school. Teachers aspired to obtaining a teaching position there and all teachers were subject area specialists. At this stage, we were unable to find evidence of any other of Fullan's domain of teachers' knowledge. Academic achievement appeared to be average for the province and was defined narrowly in terms of provincial public examinations. Most staff in the school were content with this standard, so academic achievement received no special attention by either the community or the school.

It was the school board that provided the vision of what the school should become during this stage. On several occasions, the school board expressed concerns (4) that the school was not performing as well academically as one would expect. The school board's desire to make changes in the school was demonstrated by the appointment of a new principal from outside (5) the school district, a move that negatively impacted teacher morale. It appears that, at this point, teachers were very traditional in their teaching strategies and largely operated independently of one another and outside groups. "Groupthink" (Janis, 1982) and perceived public support created a belief on the part of teachers that the school board was unreasonable and that their decision to appoint an outsider as principal was wrong.

In spite of lower morale and a diminished sense of self worth among teachers, the newly appointed principal, Tom, with the help of an administrative council (6) composed of himself, the vice-principal, and six department heads, embarked on two major initiatives: computerized scheduling (7) and a home and school association (8). As a consequence of this change in school administration, the school began to think more systemically. Teachers became more aware of the potential influence of the school board and the new principal developed more formal connections with the community.

Reflecting growth in Fullan's first domain of teacher knowledge, the school began to develop its expertise in technology. The establishment of an administrative council led to more collaboration and distributed leadership. It was this collaboration and the development of technological expertise that influenced the appointment of the new principal when Tom was appointed as assistant superintendent within that school district three years later. The person (9) to replace him came from within the school. He was a department head who had worked closely with Tom on the administrative council (6) and had been heavily involved in the computerized scheduling (7). This appointment was viewed positively by the school staff and became a boost to their morale.

Iteration One

During Iteration One, more evidence of teacher knowledge in Fullan's domains emerged. Teachers developed a broad repertoire of teaching strategies. The school initiated several major initiatives that required collaboration both inside and outside. The principal and a team of teachers began to recognize the need to develop expertise in change and sought to develop such expertise through school improvement committees. Also, the teaching staff began to develop a shared vision of what they wanted their school to become over the next three to five years and made commitments to work toward improving their school and to making a difference in students lives (19). The combined efforts of various school improvement committees challenged the status quo and resulted in a push for excellence (18) in academics as well as in co-curricular activities.

The new principal (9), George, continued to focus on the computerized scheduling which led to the semestering (10) of courses. Recognizing the need for continuous learning, in the spring of his first year as principal, George attended a conference sponsored by the provincial School Administrators' Council (11). The focus of this conference was school improvement. Building on concepts learned at the conference, he worked with department heads and school board administration (12) to initiate a school improvement process (13) at Town Pride. Through this process, several school improvement committees were formed. These committees led to increased levels of collaboration and over the course of the next few years played a major role in several improvement initiatives (14). Some of the efforts were initiated by the committees themselves, some by the school administration, and others by sources outside the school such as the Department of Education (15), the school board (16), or Boston College (17) which introduced advanced placement (AP) courses in the province.

The school became a pilot school for the implementation of two provincial initiatives: a special education program and a computer studies program. Also, it became heavily involved in the implementation of resource-based learning, a policy initiative of the provincial Department of Education (15). District administration (12) supported each of these initiatives, and all six of Fullan's domains of teacher knowledge were in evidence. By this time teachers had developed considerable expertise in bringing about change. An emphasis on resource-based learning produced a direct focus on learning with students at the centre. As part of resource-based learning also was encouragement of the use of a broad repertoire of teaching strategies, a focus on learning outcomes, and teacher collaboration in respect to instructional planning and delivery. The dependence on learning resources also stimulated recognition of a need on the part of teachers to develop computer skills. The school's successful bid to become a pilot school for both computer technology and the special education initiative, along with the introduction of advanced placement courses reveal the commitment to learning and to making a difference in the lives of all students that had developed in the school by this point.

Successful implementation of all these initiatives was largely dependent on the existence of external partnerships. At this stage, partners provided funding that supported team learning and the risk taking needed if the school was to explore options that did not fall within the boundaries of traditional norms or practices. In addition to the internal school teams, partnerships with various federal government agencies (20), that otherwise had no jurisdiction over, or obligation to, the K-12 school system, contributed much to the school's success. Employment Canada provided $20,000 to support implementation of an attendance policy; $60,000 to support program development for resource-based learning; and $215,000 to encourage early leavers to continue their formal education. Initial computer resources provided by the Department of Education and the school board through the pilot program in computer studies (15) were expanded by the Co-operative Agreement for Human Resource Development (20) between the provincial and federal governments. Through this agreement the school received funding for three projects valued at $68,000.

Iteration Two

During this stage, all domains of teacher knowledge became increasingly evident. Staff turnovers (21) both influenced and were influenced by the impact of information technology. In Fall 1990, a new vice-principal (22), Ted, within six months became acting principal as George (9) took educational leave. Bringing with him strong proposal writing skills, Ted was a key player in obtaining external funding (20) for technology (23). In addition, retirements allowed the hiring of Dave (24), a technology education teacher with strong technical skills. When Ted became the principal, Dave became the vice-principal. This new strength in the area of emerging technology led to the refocusing of school improvement (25) to give particular emphasis to this area. As the focus of the instructional program committee shifted toward technology, each department within the school (26) was given increasing responsibility to develop its own improvement plans relative to programs. This move revealed a developing trust in the expertise of teachers in each department to bring about improvements that would enhance student learning. Recognition of this level of trust led to new levels of teacher confidence in their own professional expertise which was further enhanced by increased professional development opportunities resulting from the newly established partnerships. Many teachers were committed to continuous learning and were gaining expertise as systems thinkers as a consequence of collaboration with one another and with outside partners.

Other federal government funds, $400,000 in total, allowed the school to develop and implement two co-operative education programs (27), a career exploratory program and a Family Living, subject-based program. An immediate effect of the new programs in cooperative education was improved communication with (39), and involvement in, the school by those outside the school including business and community leaders, some of whom were also parents. Outside community groups were beginning to feel responsible for student learning. Building on this new relationship, a group of these business community leaders voluntarily organized an auction committee (28) to hold annual community auctions of art works, travel packages, arts and crafts, merchandise, and services to raise money for additional technology (23) resources for the school. Beginning in 1991, these auctions raised approximately $100,000. This allowed the school to increase its number of computers for instructional purposes. Two other federally funded projects, totalling approximately $500,000, were targeted at connecting the school with the community by providing services in areas of communications, literacy, youth and senior outreach and at partnering with the local business community to ease the transition between school and work and youth employment. Additionally, from 1994, the school partnered with two major telecommunications corporations (29) which provided technology hardware, a school-wide computer network and internet access. One of these corporate partners also provided training for a school team of six teachers, administrators, business, and board representatives at a national institute (30) for school-business partnerships.

During Iteration 2 as well, Town Pride was able to avail itself of services provided by Stemnet (31), an educational network supported by the federal and provincial governments. Stemnet provided Internet access to all schools and teachers in the province and provided training to lead teachers in each school. These partnerships significantly advanced the school's capacity to offer leading edge technology programs, to implement computers across the curriculum, and to enhance the use of information technology (32) in the learning process.

Iteration Three

This stage began with provincial restructuring (33). Such restructuring included a new emphasis on accountability and testing with respect to student learning (34), and required the formation of a school council (35) composed of teachers, parents, and community representatives. Within this restructuring context, increased levels of external funding (20), and a growing number of business partners (28), the school administrators began to recognize the need to be more directly accountable to their various stakeholders. Even though they had received external recognition (40), locally, provincially, and nationally, for their successes, for the most part, they did not have data (36), beyond general impressions, to demonstrate the impact of their various initiatives on student learning. While results from standardized tests and attendance records were quite positive, they were aware that many things that they and their stakeholders valued were not assessed. If they were to be accountable, they believed that they needed to enhance the assessment of their improvement efforts.

During fall 1996, these administrators initiated a school-university partnership to help them (37) increase both their accountability and growth through action research and a learning organization framework (38). District office (41) personnel have recognized the progress that the school has made and has recognized the value of the school-university partnership. Recently, Ted has moved to a senior administrative role with the district and Dave has assumed the principalship (42). Since Ted's move, the district has entered into a similar partnership (43) with the university with the expressed intent of enhancing organizational learning in all its schools using Town Pride as a model.

The Story of Learning and Change at Vision Collegiate

Origins

Figure 2 displays the causal network for Vision Collegiate. Like Town Pride, this school had a history of community and parental support (1). Over the 40 year period of the school's existence, teachers and students were proud to be associated with it. The school was viewed as one of the elite schools (2) in the province and only teachers recognized as specialists were hired. Before personal computers were introduced to other schools in the province, the principal at this school had developed a computerized administration program to develop student and teacher schedules. In fact, many schools throughout the province adopted Vision's program between 1985 and 1990. Also, in fall 1990, the school engaged in a major Department of Education (3) pilot project in computer studies.

Because of their perceived success, however, there was little recognition of the need for change or improvement. In a stable climate where parents, the community, students, and the school board (4) were satisfied with the status quo, teachers continued to function within the school largely as if it was a closed system. There was no perceived need to develop or enhance their connections with the outside, and teachers, though strongly collegial, worked independently of one another. Developing partnerships, engaging in school improvement efforts, or developing expertise in the change process were not considerations.

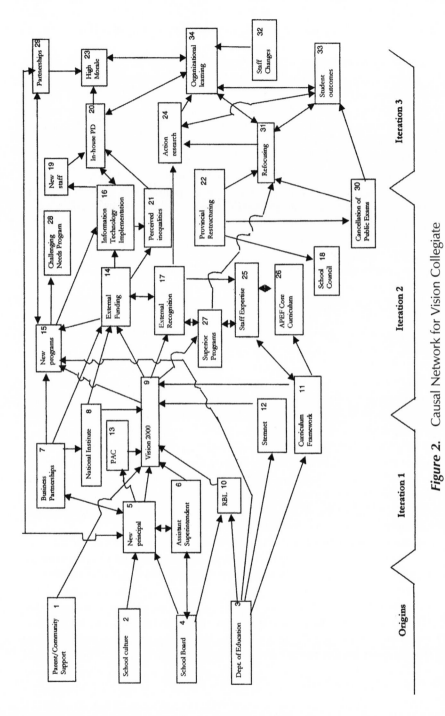

Figure 2. Causal Network for Vision Collegiate

Origins   Iteration 1   Iteration 2   Iteration 3

304

Iteration One

A new vision was created, at this stage, with the arrival of a new principal (5) in September 1991 after the former principal became an assistant superintendent (6) in the same school district (4). The new principal acknowledged the strength of the teaching staff at the school, and the strong collegial relationships that existed among them. He also admired the accomplishments of his predecessor in building such a strong school culture, and therefore maintained a strong relationship with him until he retired in 1996.

However, the new principal was not content with the isolated way that schools typically were run. He wanted to forge much stronger links with the business community (7) as a means of more fully integrating education into the community. In October 1992, he initiated a meeting with a major telecommunications corporation which resulted in a formal partnership extending the school's commitment to technology and acting as a catalyst for change within the school. An immediate consequence of this partnership was an invitation to send a team to a week-long national institute (8) where school, school board personnel, and business sector representatives from across Canada were to meet. The theme of this conference was "Excellence in Education," with workshops, keynote speakers, opportunities to form and maintain networks among participants, and for vision planning. The six representatives from the school were: the local CEO of the telecommunications corporation, the principal, a district assistant superintendent, the school board chair, the district science co-ordinator, and the school's technology teacher/network administrator.

Iteration Two

Other partnerships have followed, including one with the local telephone service provider. In fall 1993, the beginning of Iteration Two, a vision statement, Vision 2000 (9) was formalized, with a focus on creating an electronic school. Indirectly, the provincial Department of Education (3) was influencing the change. Many teachers in the school were committed to the Department's policy of resource-based learning (10); the school was committed to excellence in providing to students the provincial curriculum (11); and the school was working directly with Stemnet (12). As well, a Parent Advisory Committee (PAC)(13), composed of teachers, departments heads, school administrators and parents, was created to facilitate the implementation of Vision 2000.

Based on Vision 2000, the PAC wrote two funding proposals: one to the Communications Technology Co-operative Education Youth Internship Program, and another to Human Resources Development Canada (HRD). In spring 1994, the school was informed that they had HRD approval for Phase 1 of their proposal (14), with a budget estimate of $250,000. Phase One of Vision 2000 was the start of implementing the information technology plan (16), in which the school's library was turned into a Learning Resources Centre with a Local Area Network (LAN) incorporating capacities for data, voice, and video. In addition, each classroom was provided with at least three nodes on the network.

In fall 1994, the Communications Technology Co-operative Education Youth Internship Program (15) began. Teachers cite the tremendous gains afforded by the technology present in the school. One teacher commented that "paperless courses, improved research efforts, higher quality work, and the teacher moving from sage to learner and facilitator are the sorts of sweeping changes that have altered this learning environment."

Resource-based learning (10) is a philosophy that this staff seems to have embraced. This was true prior to their access to information technology, but brought frustration at a time when budgets and professional development opportunities were severely reduced. One teacher said "resource-based teaching is the Department's [provincial department of education] way of saying we don't have money to resource this properly so teachers, you do this for us." Another teacher commented that "currently, it appears that resource-based learning is flourishing." This seems largely due to the current extent of resources (especially its LAN and Internet access) and the speed and ease of access. Web-based resources, in-house websites, and e-mail communication with parents and colleagues were noted as direct changes in teaching and learning at Vision Collegiate.

Innovations such as these were being recognized (17) beyond the local community. In 1994, the principal won the prestigious inaugural Fortis Award for Leadership in Education. In 1995, four teachers won provincial and national awards. In the same year, Vision Collegiate became a pilot school for the establishment of a School Council (18) reaffirming the school's commitment to partnerships and the recognition of the need to connect individuals other than teachers to student learning.

Technological improvements continued with the support of the business partners (7) and additional school board (4) funding. Also, new proposals were written and funded, allowing the extension of the Communications Technology Project and the implementation of phases 2 and 3 of Vision 2000, which included a multimedia lab. The PAC (13) raised $50,000 for equipment purchase for the multimedia lab. To support the implementation, new teachers (19) were carefully chosen to add to the strength of the school. Particularly significant was an addition of a second teacher-librarian in the newly designed Learning Resource Centre. This person was chosen because of his expertise in teacher-librarianship, networks, and information technology. The two teacher-librarians, working with the school's technology teacher, and several other teachers with expertise in this area, were able to provide considerable in-house professional development (20) for information technology—evidence that teachers were committed to continuous learning and to helping each other in that respect.

Iteration Three

By 1996 tension had begun to exist between the school board and the school. Because the school was successful in obtaining funding, resources, and services from its business and community partners, the board saw an increasing gap (21) between the facilities and programs available at Vision Collegiate and those available to other schools in the district. But from the Vision Collegiate teachers' perspective, the board tried to reduce this gap by treating schools unequally. By 1997, further uncertainty was created when, through restructuring (22) of the provincial educational system, the old school board was replaced by a board more than double the size, one serving 85 schools and 35,000 students.

Board personnel had been "streamlined" as a part of this restructuring so that, even though their responsibilities were greater, their numbers were greatly reduced. Additionally, because most of members of the senior management team were new, the staff and partners at Vision Collegiate were uncertain of the amount of support they could expect from them. In fact, there were restrictions on the number of days available to teachers for professional development (20). In spite of this, Vision staff were quite confident that they had developed a collective expertise that would allow them to move forward without school board assistance, should that be necessary. Teacher morale remained extremely high (23). A member of the school's action research team (24) commented that "because of the directions that the school has taken, the school is in a much stronger position to react to whatever changes are introduced."

The level of staff expertise (25) in their subject areas was demonstrated through the large number of Vision Collegiate teachers who served on provincial curriculum committees, creating new provincial curriculum frameworks (11), and a new core curriculum for the Atlantic Provinces (APEF) (26). Their commitment to making a difference to students' lives was reflected in the pride that they displayed in their academic program. Vision staff boasted that their program was superior (27): they offered local and advanced placement courses; piloting of new courses was constant; the arts held a prominent position in the curriculum (an Art Gallery is now online). As one teacher commented, "The number and variety of courses we offer is as good as any school in the province and better than most." As well, teachers were quick to point out that school success, as measured through the standard measures of scholarships and other performance indicators, was clearly documented.

By January 1997, Vision Collegiate was challenged with special needs students (28) as part of their student population. For many schools, such a shift in their student populations becomes a huge hurdle, one that can take many years to adapt to in a productive manner for the students. Vision Collegiate, however, while having to make significant program and instructional changes, did so quickly and without noticeable strain. The staff already had accepted the idea of integration of special needs students into the regular classroom several years prior to their arrival. And the many external partnerships which had been forged, and courses like entrepreneurship, cooperative education, and law provided students with work experience and many speaking and job opportunities. Active participation by 151 external partners (29) in school programs was a clear indication that outside groups had adopted responsibility for student learning.

In the spring of 1997, the Department of Education cancelled the provincial public examinations (30) for senior high school courses. This change in student assessment procedures caused some concern for teachers. For Vision Collegiate, a school that consistently attempted to exceed provincial averages, there was now no intra-provincial measure. Many teachers were uneasy about students having to rely on school-based assessments. It is apparent that teachers at Vision Collegiate, while professionally mature relative to most of Fullan's six domains, had little confidence in their own assessment skills especially in relation to nontraditional learning outcomes.

Staff seemed to be well informed about programs and strategies to support teaching; however, they were not nearly as clear in matters relating to the impact of these programs or strategies. In the evidence we collected, there were statements about the nature of the impact on student learning, student discipline, and levels of motivation, but little reference to specific data. For example, when asked about specific evidence of improved student learning, improved discipline, or improved levels of motivation, no one was able to point to data in support of the claim that improvements had been realized.

Nonetheless, at least the leadership team at Vision Collegiate demonstrated their recognition of the importance of assessing the impact of the school's efforts on student learning; they appear to have accepted the familiar edict that "what gets measured, or assessed, gets valued" (Stoll & Fink, 1996, p. 166). The leadership team, realized that if they did not assess the learning that they believed to be important (however difficult to assess), other agencies would do it for them. The potential of action research (24) began to be explored.

By the end of our study, Vision 2000 was viewed as completed, and the school was in the process of refocusing (31). During iteration 3, significant staff changes (32) had occurred; the school principal took study leave, several key teachers retired, and three teacher-members of the PAC were promoted to other positions outside the school. The vice-principal was acting principal and a teacher on staff had replaced him as vice-principal. While the school continued to thrive, the process of change appeared to have slowed.

At a whole-school professional development session held in 1998, during a discussion of where they have been and where they were headed, staff focused on student outcomes (33). Teachers were aware of being held accountable in a manner unprecedented in their lifetime, and aware that they needed to connect what they were doing with student success. During that session, and with the assistance of their university partners, they concluded that an organizational learning framework (34) would facilitate their future growth. Where Vision Collegiate was to go from that point had not yet been determined, but the commitment to partnerships and to information technology suggests that these innovations had become institutionalized in the culture of the school.

Leadership for Organizational Learning and Change

Evidence concerning the nature and sources of leadership is to be found throughout the causal networks (Figures 1 and 2). In this section we briefly summarize some of that evidence but focus primarily on the survey evidence which is not fully reflected in the causal networks.

Leadership practices

Those in formal leadership roles, especially school principals, were key players throughout the collective learning and change processes captured in Figures 1 and 2. Principals in both schools initiated many of the innovations which served as the focus for staff learning. They also initiated the school improvement process which served as a framework for learning how to respond to the innovations. Additionally, those in principal roles kept staff informed of major new initiatives that were being sponsored by outside agencies, and set up teams that would guide the implementation of any new initiative. They were key players in proposal writing for external funding, active members of all the leadership teams, and instigators of the hiring of teachers with expertise in technology. Principals served as liaisons to outside groups.

One part of the leadership survey asked teachers to identify words that best described leadership in the school. At Town Pride 93 to 95 percent of the staff chose the words visionary, change-oriented, visible, supportive, goal-oriented, and holding high expectations. Other highly rated characteristics were collaborative (86 percent), intellectually stimulating (88 percent), democratic (77 percent), and participatory (76 percent). Inconsistent with these percentages was the extent to which teachers perceived the leadership to be decentralized (51 percent) and inclusive (60 percent); these results, though, are consistent with percentages regarding sources of leadership (noted below) which indicate the significance of those in formal leadership roles (principal and vice-principal). Ratings of teachers at Vision Collegiate were similar to those at Town Pride, with the exception that 93 percent of respondents chose "inclusive" as a word describing leadership in their school.

Another component of the survey assessed the level of agreement among teachers in respect to the existence of leadership practices associated with the dimensions of transformational leadership. Teachers in both schools perceived transformational leadership practices to exist. In fact, there was more than 70 percent agreement on all survey constructs that leaders in both schools exhibited behaviours consistent with transformational leadership.

Sources of Leadership

The interview data summarized in Figures 1 and 2 portray a central, and we suggest, necessary role for those in formal positions of leadership, especially principals. Nonetheless, leadership provided by the committee structure in both schools had a significant impact on the learning changes that took place. For example, while Vision Collegiate had no formal school improvement committee unlike Town Pride, department heads, the parent advisory committee, and the empowerment felt by teachers appeared to foster innovation among staff even more than the formal committees at Town Pride. All teachers that were interviewed at Vision Collegiate clearly articulated the existence of a collaborative work environment within the context of a trusting relationship. While most credited the principal for initiating their major change initiative, it was obvious that they had taken ownership of implementation themselves

Leadership at Town Pride, while collaborative, appears to have been more hierarchical and more involved in directing major initiatives. Several teachers made a clear distinction between administration and teachers. They indicated that the principal and vice-principal were respected for making executive decisions, and moving forward as the active leaders in the school. The "consultative" nature of the administration surfaced repeatedly during the interviews. This was in reference to a clear separation between communication among staff, and communication between staff and administration. While this was in no sense perceived to be adversarial, the staff felt a strong adherence to traditional protocol; the responsibility for direction lay solely with administration. This view appears to have limited the range of influence staff had on learning and change in the school.

Even though the nature and style of leadership appears to be somewhat different in both schools, both were functional and brought successes to their schools. In both schools, the administrators and teachers held a mutual respect for one another. Teachers at both schools attributed their success to the willingness of teachers to work together and to the supportiveness of the administration.

The prominence of formal leadership roles in both schools, evident in the causal networks, was confirmed in the results of the leadership survey. When asked to indicate the extent to which various individuals or groups provided leadership for school improvement, the largest percentage of teachers in both schools placed the principal as the primary source (93 percent at Town Pride and 100 percent at Vision Collegiate). This was followed by the vice-principal with 81 percent at Town Pride and 90 percent at Vision Collegiate.

The level of support for other sources of leadership, however, indicates that teachers also were important sources leadership. Of three sources of leadership that we identified as collaborative (administrative/teacher committees, teacher committees, and whole staff), the number of teachers recognizing them as providing leadership ranged from 53 to 77 percent at Vision Collegiate and from 35 to 58 percent at Town Pride. In both schools, outside sources of leadership (school board, district office personnel, parents, and other community members) were perceived to be sources of leadership by slightly more than a quarter of the staff. This suggests that the approach to leadership at each school was not purely hierarchical; teams of teachers were involved in the process, as were various business and community groups, acting as partners.

DISCUSSION AND CONCLUSION

We began this chapter by noting that secondary schools often respond to changes proposed by outsiders as trivial, wrongheaded, or irrelevant. We also noted that before this is likely to change, there will need to be significant modifications in the intellectual tools used by secondary school staffs to interpret the challenges they face and make sense of others' proposals for reform. Figuring out how this happens, we claimed, was the main purpose of our study. So the questions motivating our inquiry were about how secondary school staffs gradually adapt the collective intellectual tools they use to make sense of their work to the changes that need to be made in the nature of that work. We also wanted to know, in particular about the nature and sources of leadership in this transformation.

The two sets of concepts used to partially frame our otherwise grounded study were of some use in helping answer these questions. One of these sets of concepts was borrowed from Fullan (1995). Our assumption was that, as secondary schools gradually take on the features of learning organizations, growth will be observed in the six "domains" of knowledge Fullan argues are required of teachers for this evolution. Evidence from the study supports this assumption. Teachers in the two case schools established partnerships with outside groups that resulted in significant additional funding and new program initiatives that were viewed by the multiple partners as relevant in the current global context. These teachers and their administrators also took ownership of the change process, and in doing so, formalized collaborative structures for their work as a means of changing traditional norms and practices in their schools.

Staffs in the two schools eventually came to focus directly on teaching and learning, even though that was not their starting point. Resource-based learning and computer technology initiatives were instrumental in creating that focus. Eventually, as well, both school staffs evolved into continuous learning communities, taking responsibility for their own professional development especially in developing information technology expertise. Finally, these staffs adopted programs targeted at the needs of all students ranging from the gifted to the mentally challenged, evidence of what Fullan refers to as a moral commitment to preparing all students for the twenty-first century.

A second set of concepts helping to frame the study were the dimensions of practice associated with Leithwood's (1995) model of transformational leadership. Our assumptions in this case were threefold: first, transformational leadership practices help foster organizational learning; second, such practices are an important contribution whatever the source of leadership; and third, organizational learning will be fostered by multiple, distributed sources of leadership. Both interview and survey data support the importance we assumed for transformational leadership practices. This was especially so for principals and vice principals who were unarguably central to the learning and change that took place in both schools, and between the schools and their partners.

These were leaders with a mission even if, at the outset, it was as vague as "doing school differently." It soon became very specific in both case schools, clearly energizing the administrators, as well as providing a focus for considerable learning on the part of their staffs. Aside from the direction-setting activities of these administrator leaders, the intellectual stimulation they provided staff and the support that came with that stimulation were the most prominent aspects of their practices inside the school. Outside the school, typical transformational images of leadership do not do justice to the work of these school leaders; they were aggressively entrepreneurial and managed very well without depending much on the help or approval of their districts. In this respect, they had much in common with the transformational leaders described in Leithwood, Jantzi, and Steinbach (1999).

Fullan's six domains of teacher knowledge and Leithwood's transformational leadership practices by no means exhaust what our evidence has to say about the transformation of secondary schools into learning organizations, however. By way of conclusion we point to four other results of special importance. First, shared knowledge structures stored in the long term memories of both schools (Senge's mental models), during the period we described as "origins," were huge impediments to any new, nonroutine, collective learning. These knowledge structures, in combination, created a shared self concept of the school not only as "not broken" but too good to be further improved. So occasional challenges to the status quo by the district or members of the community were interpreted as ill-informed or wrongheaded. These are textbook cases of what Argyris (1996) refers to as "organizational defensive routines." The insight from our data is that the roots of such defensive routines are to be found in the knowledge structures stored in the organization's long term memory and are unlikely to change until those knowledge structures change.

A better understanding of just how such change in knowledge structures can be brought about is a second result of some importance, in our view. It did not happen "naturally" in any sense of that word. Left to their own devices, it seems very unlikely, for example, that teachers' prevailing views of their work and the changes that needed to be made in their schools would have changed in other than very slow and incremental ways. But evidence from the cases also makes clear that this is not because teachers are only capable of single loop learning. Given appropriate stimuli and conditions, the teachers in the two schools learned and implemented in their classrooms very significant changes in a relatively short period of time. Our evidence on this matter, we believe, highlights the "daily-ness," spontaneity, and immediacy of teachers' work environments, and the dysfunctional nature of that environment as a place for reflective practice. So intrusions into that environment are necessary as stimulants to reflective practice and double loop learning.

What those stimulants might be is the third lesson from our study worth special mention. The answer evident in our case study data is "good ideas from competent leaders able to find lots of (financial) support for their implementation." This is not an easy answer, certainly not one that will be applauded by those hoping for a "do more with less" quick fix for schools. Indeed, the financial support that the administrators in these case schools were able to find far exceeds what would be accessible to the "average" secondary school, making this lesson of questionable value on a large scale.

While the additional funding these schools were able to find seemed a critical part of the stimulation for organizational learning, it is not possible to separate the effects of competent leadership and good ideas from extra money. There is some evidence from other sources that competent leadership and good ideas alone may be enough to stimulate considerable learning and change (Leithwood, Leonard, & Sharratt, 1998). But it will take more research to clarify what value extra money adds to ideas and leadership: more value to some ideas than others, to be sure.

Finally, the results of our study offer an important lesson not only about the nature and sources of leadership but also about how to maintain the continuity of its focus over time. Remarkable in the case of both schools was the coherent focus on learning and change sustained by a succession of administrative leaders. There is no more certain method of wasting a school's investment in learning and change than to constantly shift the nature and focus of the school, as typically happens when formal leaders change. What was remarkable in our two secondary schools was evidence that it is possible to change the people occupying formal school leadership roles without changing the nature and focus of the schools' learning and improvement efforts. The most important mechanisms for sustaining this continuity appear to have been the formal goal setting and school improvement planning processes adopted by each school. These processes allowed one leader to build systematically on what his/her successor had accomplished and each leader demonstrated a willingness to take on this task rather than embarking on some entirely new set of priorities as is more often the case. Indeed, as the "learning school" of strategy formation (Mintzberg, Ahlstrand, & Lampel, 1998) argues, it may be that such formal planning processes are of greatest value in providing continuity to both the focus for learning, and the framework in which such learning takes place across the apparently inevitable succession of people occupying school administrators' positions.

REFERENCES

Argyris, C. (1996). Skilled incompetence. In K. Starkey (Ed.), *How organizations learn* (pp. 82-91). London: International Thompson Business Press.

Barksdale, J. (1998). Communication technology in dynamic organizational communities. In F. Hesselbein, M. Goldsmith, R. Beckhard, & R. Schubert (Eds.), *The community of the future* (pp. 93-101). San Francisco: Jossey-Bass.

Blase, J. (1993). The micropolitics of effective school-based leadership: Teachers' perspectives. *Educational Administration Quarterly, 29*(2), 142-163.

Brown, J. (1995). *Images of leadership: Searching for common features*. Paper presented at Canadian Society for the Study of Education, Montreal, Quebec. June.

Caldwell, B. (1997). The impact of self-management and self-government on professional cultures of teaching: A strategic analysis for the twenty-first century. In A. Hargreaves & R. Evans (Eds.), *Beyond educational reform: Bringing teachers back in*. Philadelphia: Open University Press.

Deal, T. (1990). Reframing reform. *Educational Leadership, 47*(8), 6-12.

Fullan, M. (1995). The school as a learning organization: Distant dreams. *Theory into Practice, 34*(4), 230-235.

Handy, C. (1994). Introduction: Beginner's Mind. In S. Chawla & J. Renesch (Eds.), *Learning organizations: Developing cultures for tomorrow's workplace* (pp. 45-56). Portland, OR: Productivity Press.

Hargreaves, A., & Evans, R. (1997). Teachers and educational reform. In A. Hargreaves & R. Evans (Eds.), *Beyond educational reform: Bringing teachers back in*. Philidelphia: Open University Press.

Janis, I.L. (1982). *Groupthink*. Boston, MA: Houghton Mifflin.

Leithwood, K. (1994). Leadership for school restructuring. *Educational Administration Quarterly, 30*(4), 498-518.

Leithwood, K. (1995). *The sources and nature of leadership: Staff survey*. Toronto, ON: OISE.

Leithwood, K., Jantzi, D., & Steinbach, R. (1999). *Changing leadership for changing times*. The Netherlands: Swets & Zeitlinger.

Leithwood, K., Leonard, L., & Sharratt, L. (1998). Conditions fostering organizational learning in schools. *Educational Administration Quarterly, 34*(2), 243-276.

Miles, M., & Huberman, A. (1994). *Qualitative data analysis: A sourcebook of new methods*. Beverly Hills, CA: Sage.

Mintzberg, H., Ahlstrand, B., & Lampel, J. (1998). *Strategy safari: A guided tour through the wilds of strategic management*. New York: The Free Press.

Prawat, R.S., & Peterson, P.L. (1999). Social constructivist views of learning. In J. Murphy & K.S. Louis (Eds.), *Handbook of research on educational administration* (2nd ed.) (pp. 203-226). Washington, DC: American Educational Research Association.

Rifkin, J. (1995). *The end of work*. New York: Putnam.

Sarason, S. (1990). *The predictable failure of educational reform*. San Francisco: Jossey-Bass.

Senge, P. (1990). *The fifth discipline*. New York: Doubleday.

Sergiovanni, T. (1995). *The principalship: A reflective practice perspective*. Boston: Allyn & Bacon.

Sheppard, B. (1996). Exploring the transformational nature of instructional leadership. *Alberta Journal of Educational Research, 42*(4), 325-344.

Shulman, L. (1987). Knowledge and teaching: Foundations of the new reform. *Harvard Educational Review, 57*(1), 1-22.

Siskin, L. (1991). Departments as different worlds: Subject subcultures in secondary schools. *Educational Administration Quarterly, 27*, 134-160.

Stoll, L., & Fink, D. (1996). *Changing our schools*. Philadelphia: Open University Press.

Strauss, A., & Corbin, J. (1994). Grounded theory methodology: An overview. In N.K. Denzin & Y.S. Lincoln (Eds.), *Handbook of qualitative research* (pp. 273-285). Thousand Oaks, CA: Sage.

CHAPTER 14

CONCLUSION
WHAT WE HAVE LEARNED ABOUT
SCHOOLS AS INTELLIGENT SYSTEMS

Kenneth Leithwood

As a direct follow up to *Organizational Learning In Schools* (Leithwood & Louis, 1998), the authors of this book have aimed to extend our understanding about sources of individual learning in school contexts. We have aimed to further understand the nature of collective learning in small groups and across whole schools. We have inquired about the conditions which hamper and foster collective learning. As well, we have pursued questions about the contribution of collective professional learning to the quality of classroom pedagogy, student achievement, and student engagement with school. A number of chapters have either explored or advocated strategies for improving the collective learning capacities of schools and some of their individual members. And, as the problem most thoroughly addressed by the book, many chapters aimed to

Advances in Research and Theories of School
Management and Educational Policy, Volume 4, pages 315-330.
Copyright © 2000 by JAI Press Inc.
All rights of reproduction in any form reserved.
ISBN: 0-7623-0024-8

uncover the forms of leadership that are productive in building the intellectual capacities of schools.

This chapter first sums up and comments on the implications of what has been learned through the collective efforts of the authors, in most cases leaving aside evidence about school leadership. Then it focuses on what has been learned about the contributions of leadership to organizational learning, summing up the forms of leadership discovered to be useful for this purpose.

DEVELOPING THE INTELLECTUAL CAPACITIES OF INDIVIDUALS AND TEAMS

Three chapters (2, 3, 4) explicitly addressed the development of individual and team capacities. In chapter 2, Coffin and Leithwood inquired about the sources of principals' on-the-job learning in contexts which allowed principals many alternative sources for such learning. Within these opportunity-rich environments, principals selected the school district and the relationships developed with people in the district as the primary sources of their professional learning. The district far outweighed, for example, the school, professional associations, and universities as a source of professional learning for reasons Coffin and Leithwood trace to the nature of the knowledge most useful for principals in their everyday problem solving. This knowledge, variously described as "procedural" and "conditionalized," is "how to" knowledge, often in tacit form, typically acquired through experience by those (e.g., superintendents) who have lived the principal's role and understand the unique school environment in which the principal works. Most usefully, this knowledge is co-constructed as principal and fellow principal or district colleague deliberate about the solution to a real and often pressing problem in the principal's school. Reinforcing the case for adopting a "distributed" view of cognition, the least frequent sources of learning for principals were those arising from within the principals themselves or, to use Perkins' (1993) term, the "person-solo."

In chapter 3, Chrispeels, Brown, and Castillo examined how school leadership teams developed in a context which provided explicit training for the teams. Results of this study demonstrated growth over the four-year period of the study on the part of the school leadership team along seven dimensions including:

- Role acquisition: from the role of learners in the first year to learners, staff developers, data collectors, conflict mediators, action researchers, and communicators by the fourth year.
- Principal-staff relations: from a laissez-faire role on the part of principals to active participation in the teams.

- Professional relations: from being isolated teams within the schools to teams well connected to the work of other groups within the school, and teams whose many roles were widely accepted by other staff members.
- Relations with parents, community, and students: from no involvement with parents, community or students in the first year, to at least active solicitation of their views as a normal part of decision making by the fourth year.
- Relations with the school district: from initial appreciation for the training provided but resistant to district initiatives, to a strong sense of common purpose with the district after four years.
- Use of data: from no use of systematically collected data for problem solving, to the active collection and use by the team of their own data.
- Attention to teaching and learning: from little direct attention to student learning, at the outset, to systematic monitoring of student progress in key curriculum areas by their fourth year.

This is one of the few studies of how the learning capacities of teams can develop over time, and what conditions foster and inhibit that development. Results of the study demonstrate the gradual acquisition of cognitive resources by the school leadership team allowing it to think more effectively on behalf of the school as a whole. Indeed just the creation of such a team provides an example of a school enhancing its intelligence, as the term was defined in chapter 1, by adding a structure responsible for learning on behalf of the organization as a whole. But these results also demonstrate that once an additional structure for organizational learning has been established, considerable education will typically be required if it is to perform this task competently.

In chapter 4, Scott reported the results of a study of secondary school administrative team learning, and the conditions which influenced it. Evidence from this study showed that all three teams processed large amounts of information which came to their attention in many different forms. Major team tasks served to focus the attention of the teams, and team members were adept at asking questions in order to understand issues. Experience, especially the experience of the more senior principals, was a major source of knowledge for all teams, and, during meetings, the teams addressed the issues facing them with the knowledge at hand. Members of each team distributed information to one another with principals as the main source of such information. Much of this information originated in the district and was disseminated through meetings with other principals and district staff. Exploratory or double loop learning was rare among all the teams.

In relation to several other aspects of the learning process, however, there was considerable variation across the three teams. In particular, one of the three teams engaged in extensive knowledge acquisition from other schools, and held each team member responsible for bringing information to the team meetings. This was information that sometimes required consultation with others prior to the meeting.

But the two other administrative teams had learning processes that were deficient in this key area.

Implications

Two closely related implications for school practice arise from these three chapters that warrant further consideration. One of these issues concerns the district's contribution to the professional learning of school leaders. Clearly it is central to such learning, as both the Coffin/Leithwood and Scott chapters indicated. At least this is the case in the contexts in which these studies were undertaken, contexts which featured large, well-established district offices staffed by experienced and well-trained administrators. But what of contexts absent some or all of these critical features, as in the case of quite small school systems, school systems organized without districts (e.g., New Zealand), many of the very "lean" LEAs in the United Kingdom, and the newly amalgamated and financially downsized districts in Canada (e.g., Ontario). Circumstances such as these offer school leaders little access to the knowledge and problem-solving resources on which chapters 2 and 4 reported they relied so heavily. Such increasingly common circumstances suggest that the continuing, on-the-job professional growth of school leaders will depend on them making far greater use of alternative sources of knowledge and problem-solving support.

Implied in these findings is the need for aspiring school leaders, as well as those in the role, to acquire the habits and dispositions of "intentional learners"—people who approach their role with a continuous growth ethic, and take full responsibility for what Senge (1991) refers to as "personal mastery." This entails, among other things, becoming less dependent on hierarchical and easily accessible sources of professional knowledge, taking personal responsibility for seeking out relevant knowledge, and more actively interpreting and constructing for themselves the applications to their own context of ideas developed in other contexts. It will likely mean, as well, initiating the development of relationships with peers, perhaps university faculty, and others, specifically for the purpose of building up one's problem-solving support systems. Growing access to sophisticated communications technology means that physical proximity is no longer a critical condition for establishing such networks of professional resources.

The second issue in need of further consideration arising especially from chapters 3 and 4 is the nature and use of data for decision making in schools. Perkins (1993) has conceptualized a knowledge acquisition system as consisting of four variables: knowledge, representation of that knowledge, knowledge retrieval, and constructing or assembling existing knowledge into new knowledge structures. As he points out, the productivity of the knowledge acquisition system starts with adequate knowledge. Without such knowledge, the remaining components of the system are largely impotent.

One of the central purposes of structures such as teams is learning on behalf of the school organization. Chapters 2 and 3, in particular, suggest that while many such teams are relatively good at knowledge representation, retrieval, and assembling, they remain impotent in Perkins' terms because of inadequate knowledge. That is, they fail to systematically collect data relevant to the problems they are attempting to solve, and/or they do not access relevant evidence from such sources as published research. This creates the distinct possibility that teams challenged by ill stuctured or nonroutine problems, in particular, will inadequately understand the "current state," the "goal state," as well as the many of the "constraints" in transforming the current state into the goal state, to borrow concepts from the problem-solving literature (e.g., Frederiksen, 1984). Lack of attention to ensuring access to relevant knowledge not possessed by members of the group is a widespread disability in schools. This disability is fed, in some schools, by an outdated norm of self-sufficiency (if not anti-intellectualism among some administrators, in my experience) and a long-standing disregard for the research base supporting educational practice. While there was a time, perhaps 25 years ago, when such disregard was functional, the stock of research-based knowledge about school practice has matured enormously since then. Practitioners aiming to foster the intellectual capacities of their schools ignore it at their peril.

BUILDING THE INTELLECTUAL
CAPACITIES OF SCHOOLS AND DISTRICTS

Six chapters addressed the challenge of capacity building across whole schools, and in the case of one chapter, across districts. In chapter 5, Leithwood, Leonard, and Sharratt synthesized evidence from three comparable studies about district and school conditions giving rise to collective learning. This study provides compelling, if indirect, evidence of the importance of taking into account, in a collective learning context, Vermunt and Verloop's (1999) comprehensive taxonomy of individual learning processes, classified as cognitive, affective, and metacognitive (or regulatory). A clear, meaningful, and well understood mission, for example (a condition found to be important at both school and district levels) likely contributes to such affective processes as motivation. On the other hand, another condition to emerge from the data, collaborative and harmonious cultures, may stimulate cognitive processes, as well, by creating opportunities for collective relating, analyzing, and applying. And the specific conditions associated in this study with school and district strategies potentially provide formal mechanisms for metacognitive processes such as planning and monitoring.

Larson-Knight, framing her study reported in chapter 6 as an exploration in systemic reform, argued that such reform depends on coherence among at least the most powerful variables affecting the reform process. Her nominations for such variables were leadership, school culture, and organizational learning. Results of her case studies in three schools with reputations for successful reform initiatives demonstrated a very high level of coherence among these variables in only one of the schools. In two of the schools at least some features of one or more variables came into conflict with one another. Evidence from this study identified features of each of the three variables accounting for school improvement success and painted a picture of complex interactions among these variables and features. Data from the study also demonstrated the nature of the influence of transformative leadership practices on the content and form of school culture, and the conditions influencing organizational learning. Depending on their form and content, school cultures served largely to enhance or detract from the possibilities for organizational learning.

In chapter 7, Hallinger, Crandall, and Seong described the principles, assumptions and operations behind the computer-based version of a simulation program aimed at building the capacities of its users. Designed as problem-based and interactive, the simulation allows educators to tackle the task of creating an organization that is able to learn and adapt to change. A team learning format is modeled and considerable "cognitive scaffolding" is provided so that users can proceed at their own pace. The development of instructional tools such as this one seems a critically important task as the basis for efforts to increase schools' intellectual capacities on a large scale.

Elliott, in chapter 8, provided a catalogue of interventions districts could use to increase their own and their schools' intellectual capacities. Interventions include the establishment of new policies, introduction of accountability and monitoring systems, and the provision of information and feedback. Also included in Elliott's catalogue are strategic planning, training and recruitment, process facilitation, and the provision of models and other types of information about school improvement. Interventions aimed at changing school structures and changing organizational culture complete the catalogue. Some features of these interventions are shared among several of the nine types of interventions and multiple such interventions are often used simultaneously by districts. Indeed, evidence suggests that using multiple interventions is likely to have the greatest positive effect on the collective capacity of schools.

Although empirical evidence about the nature and effects of each of these interventions is quite limited, the chapter offers an intriguing menu for district leaders in their capacity-building efforts with schools. It also provides a launching pad for subsequent research on district contributions to the collective intellectual resources of schools.

In chapter 9, Cibulka considered what might be done about the policy environment in which schools and districts find themselves that would foster organizational learning, rather than hinder it, as is so often the case. This chapter identified policy-related structures with the potential for contributing to such learning: commissions, legislative committees, program evaluation, and accountability requirements and standards are examples of such structures. But an important condition determining their value for this purpose is the development of a policymaking culture much more attuned to finding "the best solution" for improving education, and less driven by highly conflictual, interest-group bargaining. This chapter provided some challenging but quite practical advice for how this might begin.

In chapter 10, Dibbon claimed that increases in the learning capacities of schools can be captured, for practical purposes, in four stages. Each stage specifies the nature of organizational learning processes characteristic of not only individual school members, but teams, and the school organization as a whole. To assist school leaders in diagnosing the status of their school, this chapter also suggested questions that could be asked of staff that are likely to provide appropriate diagnostic information. The chapter used data collected from secondary school staffs to vividly illustrate the meaning of each stage of organizational learning.

Implications

Arising from these six chapters are four implications for subsequent research worth further discussion. First, in comparison with the comprehensive taxonomy of learning processes outlined by Vermunt and Verloop (1999), for example, results of chapter 5 seem narrowly focused (this conclusion would apply to chapters 11 and 12 also). The implication is that more conceptual and empirical effort should be devoted to understanding the collective affective and metacognitive learning processes used in schools.

Second, and growing out of this first implication, it is time to adopt more sophisticated theoretical tools for understanding organizational learning in schools. Many chapters in this text represent the early, often descriptive, stages of research about capacity development. With several exceptions, they are data rich but theory lean. In the chapter (2) making explicit use of situativity theory, for example, the theory is mostly used for post hoc explanation of results rather than guiding the data collection and analysis. As the many editorial references to it in this and the first chapter imply, one very promising body of theory for explicitly guiding future research on intellectual capacity development in schools is distributed cognition and situativity theory.

From such a theoretical perspective, by way of illustration, a conception of schools as intelligent systems can be traced in part, to understandings of distributed cognition, initially developed in the 1920s and 1930s by Wilhelm Wundt, the "father" of scientific psychology, and the Russian school of cultural-historical psychology described in the writings of Leont'ev, Luria, and Vygotsky (Cole & Engestrom, 1993). Central to the understanding of distributed intelligence is the activity system (Cole & Engestrom, 1993); a person and the knowledge they carry in their heads is part of a large number of activity systems. These systems are the objects to which the individual's knowledge is related and without which it has very little meaning. For example, what the individual teacher knows about the grouping of students for reading instruction depends for its meaning and value on "knowledge" codified in the school's structures for how to organize children into class groupings, and a set of widely shared norms concerning the appropriateness of reading groups, and the curriculum materials that have been developed for use in such groups. So the activity system, which is the learning of reading in groups, depends on knowledge found not just in the teacher's head, but also in the curriculum material, the timetable and the expectations for suitable practice. Changes to any element of this complex system potentially changes the capacity of the system as a whole. At minimum, a change for the better likely requires adjusting other elements of the system to take account of changes in that focal element, what Fuhrman and her colleagues (1993) (and Larson-Knight in chapter 6) refer to as "coherence."

As a third implication, Hallinger, Crandall, and Seong's chapter (7) and the chapter by Elliott (8) both report theoretically promising interventions designed to build the capacities of schools. Nonetheless, many theoretically promising interventions in education have failed to deliver on their promises in real schools, and especially on a large scale. So further research about these interventions, along with careful evaluations of their consequences for organizational learning in schools are important future tasks.

A fourth and final implication for research arises from Larson-Knight's study (chapter 6). This study began the important work of better understanding the complex interactions associated with school organizations in the midst of learning their way to significantly improved practices. While the study selected three obviously important variables for examination, clearly this cannot be considered the whole story; indeed, we don't have any idea just what proportion of the story it is. It remains for future research to tell us more of the story—to identify other important variables, describe how these variables interact, and sort out the consequences of these interactions for developing the intellectual capacity of schools.

ORGANIZATIONAL LEARNING EFFECTS

Results of the study reported by Marks, Louis and Printy in chapter 11 indicate that school capacity for organizational learning exerts a large effect on pedagogical quality, as well as on both the school average level of authentic student achievement and student scores on standardized achievement measures. Similarly the evidence provided by Silins, Mulford, Zarins, and Bishop in chapter 12 confirmed the presence of a significant relationship between organizational learning and student outcomes, in this case student engagement with school. These results also indicated that organizational learning is more evident in smaller metropolitan and county schools. The primary conditions associated with such learning were the availability of adequate resources, a principal skilled in transformational approaches to leadership, and continuity of leadership initiatives over time (discussed more fully below).

The quality of the evidence reported in chapters 11 and 12 goes some distance toward confirming the apparently common sense contribution of organizational learning in schools to important outcomes for students. While systematic empirical inquiry about organizational learning effects on students has just begun, these two studies offer impressive evidence for the claim that the collective learning of staff lies at the core of successful efforts to improve schools.

Finally, in chapter 13, Sheppard and Brown reconstructed the 10-year evolution of two secondary schools and the outcomes of that evolution. Although enjoying solid reputations in their own communities at the beginning of this period, they were relatively self-satisfied organizations with few of the capacities required for productively adaptating to a changing environment. By the end of this period, however, both schools had transformed themselves into "continuous learning communities." Among the main factors accounting for this evolution were the development of partnerships with groups and individuals outside the school, and the gradual assumption of ownership on the part of staff for school improvement. But the key factor was leadership. This is examined more fully in the next section, but suffice to say at this point that evidence from this study suggested that competent leaders with good ideas, and leaders who are able to find the resources to implement those ideas, make a powerful contribution to the development of more intelligent schools.

Implications

Little empirical evidence exists outside the covers of this book to justify the seemingly obvious claim that fostering the intellectual capacity of schools will result in good things happening for students. And "seemingly obvious claims," as we should all be painfully aware by now, have wasted an unconscionable amount of public resources and professional effort in the past. In their examination of the relationship between organizational learning and student outcomes, chapters 11 and 12 model appropriately sophisticated techniques for such quantitative research. Techniques such as these need to be applied in other contexts, and with a wider array of student outcome measures, in order to increase the robustness of claims that can be made about the contribution of organizational learning to school effects, and to further clarify the conditions mediating those effects. Equally important (and stimulated by chapter 13) is the need to further understand how the intellectual capacities of schools develop over the long run. Does it always look the way it was described in the two case schools in chapter 13? Probably not—they were pretty unique organizations to begin with. What is common to such development across schools, and what differences make a difference? Can these developmental processes be managed in such a way so as to increase the certainty of capacity development? There is a very fertile agenda for future research here.

LEADERSHIP FOR DEVELOPING THE INTELLECTUAL CAPACITIES OF SCHOOLS

Six of the 12 main chapters shed light on the forms of leadership that contribute to the intellectual capacity of schools. Of these, four adopted the same conceputal point of departure, a model of "transformational" school leadership developed by Leithwood and his colleagues (e.g., Leithwood, Jantzi, & Steinbach, 1999). Emerging out of writings also concerned with charismatic, visionary, cultural, and empowering concepts of leadership, the focus of this form of leadership is on the commitments and capacities of organizational members. Higher levels of personal commitment to organizational goals and greater capacities for accomplishing those goals are assumed to result in extra effort and greater productivity. Authority and influence are not necessarily allocated to those occupying formal administrative positions, although much of the literature adopts their perspective (Leithwood & Duke, 1999). Rather, power is attributed by organization members to whomever is able to inspire their commitments to collective aspirations, and the desire for personal and collective mastery over the capacities needed to accomplish such aspirations.

A recent review of empirical research on transformational school leadership (Leithwood, Tomlinson & Genge, 1996) offers modest amounts of evidence for the contributions of such leadership to student participation in school, a variety of psychological teacher states mediating student learning (e.g., professional commitment, job satisfaction), as well as organization-level effects such as organizational learning, and the development of a productive school climate. The six chapters explicitly addressing leadership in this book add further evidence concerning the effects of transformational leadership on organizational learning. They help, as well, to pinpoint specific leadership practices responsible for such learning.

Although sharing a consistent focus, the generic meaning of transformational leadership is subject to varying interpretations in educational leadership literature. Kowalski and Oates (1993), for instance, accepted Burns' (1978) original claim that transformational leadership represents the transcendence of self-interest by both leader and led. Dillard (1995, p. 560) preferred Bennis' modified notion of "transformative leadership—the ability of a person to 'reach the souls of others in a fashion which raises human consciousness, builds meanings and inspires human intent that is the source of power'." Leithwood (1994) used another modification of Burns, this one based on Bass' (1985) two-factor theory in which transactional and transformational leadership represent opposite ends of the leadership continuum. Bass maintained that the two actually can be complementary. The model of transformational leadership in schools developed by Leithwood and his colleagues includes eight leadership and four management dimensions. Included among the leadership dimensions are: building school vision; establishing school goals; providing intellectual stimulation; offering individualized support; modeling best practices and important organizational values; demonstrating high performance expectations; creating a productive school culture; and developing structures to foster participation in school decisions. Management dimensions (a sample of the maintenance functions required of school administrators) include staffing, instructional support, monitoring school activities, and building relationships with the community. Each of the total of 12 dimensions is associated with more specific practices. The problem-solving processes used by transformational leaders also has been described (e.g., Leithwood, Steinbach, & Raun, 1993).

Chapters 2 and 11 were framed by conceptions of leadership not explicitly associated with Leithwood's model of transformational leadership. Chapter 2 was about sources of learning for school leaders, not the nature of their leadership. But it did report evidence about the practices of senior leaders that fostered the learning of principals, practices that also seem likely to foster learning on the part of teachers when exercised by school-level leaders. These practices, associated with the transformational dimension "intellectual stimulation," included being demonstrably knowledgeable about professional matters and the district's activities, along with a close knowledge of the principal's school context.

When principals perceived these qualities, they were inclined to confide in district leaders and to seek them out as problem-solving resources, as the need arose. Principals were further persuaded to look to district leaders as a source of learning when they perceived them to be empathetic to their work, a component of the transformational dimension "individualized support." From this study we can conclude, in sum, that a combination of intellectual stimulation and individualized support on the part of leaders may well contribute significantly to individual organizational learning.

The study reported in chapter 11 measured a conception of leadership comprising cognitive, affective, and behavioral elements organized around three components of leadership labelled "intellectual leadership," "supportive leadership," and "facilitative leadership." As evidence from this study indicates, the combination of these leadership dimensions significantly contributes to a school's organizational learning capacity. Intellectual leadership, tapping the extent to which new information reaches the school, closely approximates the transformational dimension "intellectual stimulation." Similarly, supportive leadership, focused on welcoming teachers' ideas and being encouraging of their work, closely parallels the transformational dimension "individualized support." Facilitative leadership, including, for example, power sharing and nonauthoritarian forms of practice, resembles the transformational practices associated with the dimensions "building a collaborative culture" and "creating structures for shared decision making."

The remaining four chapters explicitly addressing relationships between leadership and organizational learning took Leithwood's model of transformational leadership as a point of departure for data collection and analysis. Chapter 5, the study most strongly influenced by this model, found specific practices associated with all eight transformational leadership dimensions to influence organizational learning. The vision provided by some leaders had a powerful influence on the learning of some teachers. During goal setting activities, learning was associated with encouraging teachers to reflect on their previous years' practices. Associated with the dimension "demonstrating high performance expectations," organizational learning was reported to result from encouraging teachers to be creative, to try new instructional strategies, and generally to adopt a norm of continuous professional growth.

Teachers also were encouraged to learn when principals modeled a continuous professional growth norm themselves, and when principals provided moral, as well as more tangible, forms of individualized support for teachers' professional development such as money, books, time, and the like. Organizational learning was stimulated when leaders challenged staffs to re-examine some of the assumptions underlying their practices, provided them with new ideas, explicitly promoted formal professional development experiences, and diagnosed individual teacher professional growth needs as well as assisted in meeting them. These are all practices associated with intellectual stimulation.

Principals were reported to foster learning through culture-building practices which included, for example, demonstrating a strong interest in students and a clear priority for meeting their needs. Treating teachers with respect, hiring staff who share the school's philosophy, and encouraging parental involvement were also practices contributing to organizational learning through their effect on the school's culture. Structuring the school to enhance participation in decisions, also a dimension of transformational leadership, fostered school capacity development when principals encouraged participation on committees, actively engaged themselves in such work, and distributed leadership to teachers by having them give workshops, lead staff meetings, and manage the budget. Collaborative work and learning that resulted from it were also fostered when principals made appropriate adaptations to the physical structure of the school, restructured the timetable, and created teacher leadership roles.

Results reported in chapter 6 provided strong support for the contribution of two dimensions of transformational leadership to organizational learning, individualized support (including the provision of resources) and intellectual stimulation. Intellectual stimulation took the form of encouraging teachers to engage in a broad range of professional development experiences, and bringing teachers into contact with external people and their ideas. Specific practices associated with individualized support included encouragement for such professional development, the provision of time and money required to participate in it, as well as expert consultant assistance in implementing new instructional practices.

Evidence provided in chapter 12 suggested that transformational leadership practices accounted for 13 percent of the variation in organizational learning in the sample of Australian schools included in this study. Indeed, the total variation accounted for by all sources of leadership (students, parents, and so forth) was 25 percent. Most of the dimensions of Leithwood's model of transformational leadership (except modeling) contribute to this outcome. In particular, this chapter indicated that it was important for leaders to be visible, accessible, interested in student progress—generally involved closely in the core work of the school. These "practices" helped to generate teacher satisfaction with leadership and a sense of school autonomy, which was strongly associated with professional learning. Principals' interest and involvement also established a school climate in which staff contributions were valued and staff learning was fostered. Strong links with the community supported greater distribution of leadership which had both direct and indirect influences on organizational learning. As Silins, Mulford, Zarins, and Bishop argue:

> predominant conditions accounting for variation in [organizational learning] are perceived availability of resources and a principal skilled in transformational leadership actively involved in the core work of the school.

Finally, chapter 13 offers evidence to suggest that organizational learning is greatly influenced, over the long run, by leaders' own ideas (intellectual stimulation). This study demonstrated, further, how important it is to the long term improvement of a school for the inevitable succession of formal leaders to be consistent in the ideas and directions they encourage the staff to pursue, to build the capacities of the school in a consistent direction over the long term. But good ideas, as this study also illustrated in a dramatic way, usually need to be accompanied by significant financial resources if they are to be well implemented. These resources provide for not only the "individualized" support of teachers as they struggle to learn the skills for implementing the new ideas, they also provide institutional support above and beyond the needs of individual staff members.

This study suggests that intellectual stimulation needs to be conceptualized broadly enough to encompass consistency of ideas over time across a succession of leaders. Also suggested by this study is the need to extend the "individualized support" dimension of transformational leadership to include something that might be labelled "individual and institutional support."

Implications

Actually more than implications. Results of the six chapters explicitly inquiring about the contributions of school leadership justify four *claims* by way of conclusion:

- School leadership, especially the leadership provided by school principals, is an important (if not the single most important) "condition" fostering the intellectual capacity or organizational learning of schools.
- Specific practices associated with transformational orientations to leadership account for most of these leadership effects.
- While specific practices associated with all dimensions of transformational leadership have been linked to organizational learning, a combination of practices associated with two such dimensions, in particular—individualized support and intellectual stimulation—are the most potent, and likely essential, practices.
- Previous interpretations of these two dimensions need to be extended to account for their potency. Intellectual stimulation needs to be extended to include, in organizational contexts featuring a succession of leaders, the provision of a consistent and coherent set of ideas for change over time. Individualized support needs to be extended to include the acquisition of resources not just for the development of individual staff members but for institutional development, as well (technology and other elements of infrastructure, for example).

While there is still much to learn about the specific leadership practices that foster capacity development in schools, there is not much doubt that most such practices will be consistent with transformational orientations to school leadership.

CONCLUSION

One section of the introduction to *Organizational Learning in Schools* (Leithwood & Louis, 1998) addresses something the authors refer to as "the evidence problem." There we observed, as we have in this text as well, that the case for capacity development or organizational learning in schools is theoretically compelling. But empirical evidence to support the claim that increases in such capacity will improve organizational effectiveness or productivity is embarrassingly slim. As part of the support for this view, for example, we quoted Weick and Westley's claim that "there appear to be more reviews of organizational learning than there is substance to review" (1996, p. 440). A review of empirical research on organizational learning specifically in schools, we added, "would make a very quick read, indeed" (1998, p. 7).

Since writing that introduction (admittedly not too long ago) most of what has changed is represented in this current text. So a capacity development or organizational learning perspective on schools and how they change has not exactly caught on fire empirically yet. It has become very fashionable in education circles over the past half dozen years, however, as in other types of organizations, to adopt the language of the "learning organization," and to extrapolate wildly from evidence collected in very different contexts, as though organizational type mattered little.

If one believes, as I do, in the power of insights available through using capacity-building as a frame to guide research about educational change, there is cause for worrying about faddism in all of this, and, as is typical of ideas suffering this treatment, dismissal of the ideas in favor of the next flavor before they have had time to mature. So this is a plea for better treatment—for more serious and sustained treatment—of this orientation toward educational change and leadership than has been awarded in the past to total quality management, outcomes-based education, and strategic planning, to name just three of many that have been imported from a different context, superficially understood, understudied, often badly implemented, and usually rejected after great expense and anguish. It also is a comment on realistic expectations. Developing the intellectual capacity of schools, if we can figure out how that is done, will not automatically lead to school heaven. It will not, by itself, solve the intractable problems of inequity, lack of consensus about educational purposes, a shrinking educational resource base, or wrongheaded policies from governments. It will only increase the likelihood of developing reasonable solutions within the constraints of the institution itself. I, for one, would be happy to settle for that.

POSTSCRIPT: ALTERNATIVE CONCLUSION FOR THOSE WITH ESPECIALLY WELL-CULTIVATED SENSIBILITIES

Now I'm a country music fan. Yes, its true. And, as I compose the last few sentences of this book (August 1999), drop-dead gorgeous Faith Hill has a song at the top of the country music charts entitled "The Meaning of Life." It's a ballad about two good old boys pondering THE BIG QUESTION as they drink themselves into oblivion at their local watering hole. Far as they can figure, the question has many answers, and a lot of them confict. You know—get up early/go to bed late, drink more/drink less, and so on. So as I'm listening to this song on my truck radio for about the 18th time, I begin to think that, metaphorically, there are some answers here to "The Meaning of Educational Change" (wouldn't that make a great title for a book?). In fact the metaphor works at two levels—stay with me now!

At one level, the meaning of educational change is many things. There is no silver bullet. No one should delude themselves into thinking that building the intellectual capacity of schools is one, even though it offers some pretty powerful insights. So we need to approach this perspective on educational change with realistic expectations. At a second level, the meaning of educational change is whatever you make of it (isn't that a radically constructivist, positively post-positivist thought?). And a school with greater intellectual capacity can make more of it than a school with less.

Works for me. I wonder what Michael will think of it.

REFERENCES

Bass, B.M. (1985). *Leadership and performance beyond expectations*. New York: The Free Press.

Burns, J. (1978). *Leadership*. New York: Harper & Row.

Cole, M., & Engestrom, Y. (1993) A cultural-historical approach to distributed cognition. In G. Salomon (Ed.), *Distributed cognitions: Psychological and educational considerations* (pp. 1-46). Cambridge, UK: Cambridge University Press.

Dillard, C.B. (1995). Leading with her life: An African-American feminist (re)interpretation of leadership for an urban high school principal. *Educational Administration Quarterly, 31*(4), 539-563.

Frederiksen, N. (1984). Implications of cognitive theory for instruction in problem solving. *Review of Educational Research, 54*(3), 363-407.

Fuhrman, S.H. (Ed.) (1993). *Designing coherent education policy*. San Francisco: Jossey-Bass.

Kowalski, J., & Oates, A. (1993). The evolving role of superintendents in school-based management. *Journal of School Leadership, 3*(4), 380-390.

Leithwood, K. (1994). Leadership for school restructuring. *Educational Administration Quarterly, 30*(4), 498-518.

Leithwood, K., & Duke, D. (1999). A century's quest to understand school leadership. In J. Murphy & K.S. Louis (Eds.), *Handbook of research on educational administration* (2nd ed.) (pp. 45-72). San Francisco: Jossey-Bass.

Leithwood, K., & Louis, K.S. (1998). *Organizational learning in schools*. The Netherlands: Swets & Zeitlinger.

Leithwood, K., Jantzi, D., & Steinbach, R. (1999). *Changing leadership for changing times*. Buckingham, UK: Open University Press.

Leithwood, K., Steinbach, R., & Raun, T. (1993). Superintendents' group problem-solving processes. *Educational Administration Quarterly, 29*(3), 364-391.

Leithwood, K., Tomlinson, D., & Genge, M. (1996). Transformational school leadership. In K. Leithwood, J. Chapman, D. Corson, P. Hallinger, & A. Hart (Eds.), *International handbook of educational leadership and administration* (pp. 785-840). The Netherlands: Kluwer Academic Press.

Perkins, D.N. (1993). Person-plus: A distributed view of thinking and learning. In G. Salomon (Ed.), *Distributed cognitions: Psychological and educational considerations* (pp. 88-110). Cambridge, UK: Cambridge University Press.

Senge, P. (1991). The learning organization made plain. *Training and Development, 45*(10), 37-44.

Vermunt, J.D., & Verloop, N. (1999). Congruence and friction between learning and teaching. *Learning and Instruction, 9*(3), 257-280.

Weick, K., & Westley, F. (1996). Organizational learning: Affirming an oxymoron. In S. Clegg, C. Hardy, & W. Nord (Eds.), *Handbook of organizational studies*. Thousand Oaks, CA: Sage Publications.